This book is dedicated to those people who contribute to the greater good of mountain biking by working on advocacy issues and trails, creating festivals, organizing or volunteering at cycling events, and fighting for a shared-use vision of the wilderness.

Rocky
Mountain Books

# Backcountry
# BIKING in the
# Canadian Rockies

## Doug Eastcott

*Cover and title page photos by John Gibson.*

We acknowledge the financial support of the Government of Canada through the
Book Publishing Industry Development Program (BPIDP) for our publishing activities.

*Printed and bound in Canada by*
*Kromar Printing Ltd., Winnipeg*

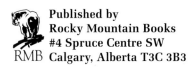

**Published by**
**Rocky Mountain Books**
**#4 Spruce Centre SW**
RMB **Calgary, Alberta T3C 3B3**

**ISBN  0-921102-69-0**


**Canadian Cataloguing in Publication Data**

Eastcott. Doug, 1948-
  Backcountry biking in the Canadian Rockies

  Includes index.
  ISBN 0-921102-69-0

  1. All terrain cycling--Rocky Mountains, Canadian (B.C. and
Alta.)--Guidebooks.* 2. Trails--Rocky Mountains, Canadian (B.C. and
Alta.)--Guidebooks.* 3. Rocky Mountains, Canadian (B.C. and
Alta.)--Guidebooks.*  I. Title.
GV1046.C32R62 1999  796.6'3'09711  C99-910768-2

# CONTENTS

# BIKING AREAS

### Central East Slopes – 22
Banff National Park, Kananaskis Country, Peter Lougheed
& Elk Lake provincial parks

### Southern Rockies – 139
Waterton Lakes National Park, Fernie & Crowsnest Pass
areas, Oldman & Castle River drainages

### Kootenay & Columbia – 205
Yoho & Kootenay national parks, Cranbrook, Kimberley,
Invermere and Golden areas

### Fraser Valley – 250
Mount Robson Provincial Park, McBride & Valemount areas

### Northern East Slopes – 262
Willmore Wilderness, Grande Cache, Jasper National Park,
Cadomin area, Forestry Trunk Road, David Thompson
Highway and Nordegg

# ACKNOWLEDGEMENTS

Many people shared the trails and provided support and encouragement in the production of this edition of Backcountry Biking. It was a big project and one of the best parts was the enthusiastic and generous people met along the way. Special thanks to those of you who have shared your trails and ideas through the years.

Some folks went above and beyond any of my expectations and deserve special recognition for their contributions.

Jeff Shugg for keeping my aging Mantis welded together, she's comin' apart again!

Jim Greenfield for major enthusiasm and always being game for yet another crazed atomic dog ride.

Steve Johnson for enthusiasm, information and generous hospitality at Frontier Lodge.

Lyle Wilson and Scott Brunner for generously sharing information and trails.

For the Northern East Slopes area: Jim Greenfield and Anne Alexander, Dave Moir, Tom Peterson, Brian and Vicki Wallace;

Bikesmith in Hinton and members of Cutline Cruisers;

Frontier Lodge and its staff, especially Steve and Donna Johnson, Doug and Joyce Ritchie, Brad Larson and Trevor Knight.

For the Central East Slopes area: Rob Haag, Brad Hill, Jeff and Gail Shugg, Dave Millard, Greg Achtem, John Evely, Marion Schaffer, Sean Tosh, Steven Murray and Robin McKeever;

Rob Boux at Rebound Cycle in Canmore for enthusiasm and super deals;

Rick Crawford at Spokes and Attire in Calgary for the good deals;

Norm Person at Lifesport in Calgary for the good deals;

Bow Cycle in Calgary for the good deals;

Brian Cooke at Bicycle Café in Canmore for the smokin' deals.

For the Kootenay and Columbia area: Scott Brunner at Columbia Sports in Invermere, Lyle Wilson, Gerry Israelson, Ed Abbott and helpful staff at Kimberley Alpine Resort.

For the Southern Rockies area: Gord Tuck at the Tuck Shop in Coleman, Stu Dalziel, the enthusiastic staff at Fernie Alpine Resort, Darren Yuers, staff at Ski Base in Fernie.

Tony and Gillean Daffern, enthusiastic editors and publishers who always seem to be in touch with the scene. Janice Redlin who edited the text, Marcelle MᵃᶜCallum who processed the photos and Ana Tercero who input the maps.

Gerhardt Lepp who had the vision to make the first edition of this book a reality way back in 1987 and provided words, advice and ideas for the second edition.

Cécile Lafleur who shared the trails and provided so much of the support and understanding required to bring this project to fruition.

Inspired action and scenic photos have been provided by the following talented photographers: John Gibson, Stephen Wilde, Gillean and Tony Daffern and Cécile Lafleur.

I thank you all.

# PREFACE

Mountain biking is an ever changing, evolving and growing sport and recreation. When the first edition of *Backcountry Biking* appeared in 1987, mountain bikers were viewed as crazed folks who belonged to some sort of lunatic fringe. When Gerhardt Lepp wrote edition 1 of this book he was a pioneer, frequently taking his bike to places that had never before seen fat tires.

By the time edition 2 appeared, mountain biking was becoming accepted as a legitimate trail-based recreation and riders were going on long and exotic rides. Skill levels and equipment were on the upswing and difficult trails were being ridden. But we were still in our infancy, as so much lay ahead and still does in the unwritten future where all is possible.

The scene continues to evolve and skill levels have increased to the point where I never say "that can't be ridden," for I know that someday, someone will ride it. Standards have increased dramatically. Trails that were pushed and carried by riders five years ago are now ridden clean on a regular basis. Some riders are so skilled and talented that they are just plain inspirational. Equipment has improved too, from bikes purpose-built specifically for downhilling to basic equipment such as suspension being standard on production bikes. All this has led to rider-built trails with stunts designed to test skill levels and build or bruise egos, and continued into other trends such as lift and helicopter assisted biking.

In locations where trails are few, riders are getting together and building some superb singletracks, rides that are just pure fun. The extreme trend in sports has led, in addition to downhilling, to endurance riding. From the obvious 24 hour races to atomic-dog riders on long wilderness and high mountain trails, mountain bikers are pushing their own limits and the limits of the sport into new areas of the mind and the land.

This very act of pushing hard and having fun, enjoying bikes and going everywhere has been a spontaneous occurrence. It has also raised concerns— some legitimate and some that are nothing more than bicycle phobia, but nevertheless these concerns are making access to riding areas an issue and that means active rider involvement in access issues is essential.

To keep this book current with developments in the sport, I've reviewed and updated the trails from edition 2. Some had to be deleted—hardly anyone wants to ride on gravel roads these days, and new trails have been added from brand new rider-built trails to trails that I previously thought too hard for enjoyable riding but that now are the norm. You'll also find an updated rating system, more endurance rides and an expanded area of coverage including Invermere, Cranbrook, Kimberley and Nordegg. Elevation profiles and new photos round out the coverage.

May all your rides be exciting explorations of your self and the natural world.

Canmore, Alberta
November, 1998

Grande Cache

Yellowhead Hwy · to Edmonton →

16

Edson

NORTHERN

47

Hinton

40

Mt Robson

16

Prov Park

Jasper

Jasper National Park

EAST

FRASER VALLEY

Icefields Parkway

93

Rocky Mountain House

David Thompson Hwy

11

Red Deer

SLOPES

Columbia Icefield

Saskatchewan River Crossing

2

93

Banff National Park

40

Field

Lake Louise

Golden

Yoho National Park

1A

CENTRAL

Calgary

Trans-Canada Hwy

1

Banff

1A

Vancouver

Canmore

1

Revelstoke

Kootenay National Park

93

EAST

KOOTENAY & COLUMBIA

Kananaskis Country

High River

N

Radium

Assiniboine Provincial Park

40

SLOPES

ALTA. / B.C.

AREA MAP

95

SOUTHERN

Pincher Creek

Cranbrook

3

Coleman

6

ROCKIES

CANADA

3

93

Waterton

USA

# INTRODUCTION

The Rocky Mountains stretch along the western edge of the North American continent. In Canada they reach from the International Boundary in the south to the Liard River in the north. The crest of the Rockies forms the Continental Divide and for more than 800 kilometres forms the boundary between the provinces of Alberta and British Columbia. Rocky Mountain streams drain into three oceans. Streams on the west slope flow into the Fraser and Columbia rivers, then west to the Pacific Ocean. Across the Divide the east slope streams flow into the Saskatchewan River, then northeast to Hudson Bay and on to the Atlantic Ocean; farther north the east slope streams flow through the Athabasca River to the Mackenzie River and the Arctic Ocean.

The Rockies are bordered by the Great Plains to the east and by the Columbia Mountains to the west. The Columbias include the Purcell, Selkirk, Monashee and Cariboo mountains and are separated from the Rockies by the Rocky Mountain Trench, a massive valley system created by faults. Most of the Canadian Rockies are of sedimentary origin and limestone and shale are the most common rocks. There are, however, some notable exceptions such as the lava layers and volcanic rocks to the south of Crowsnest Pass.

The Rockies are commonly divided into four distinct zones in an east-west direction. The foothills border the great plains and are a region of sandstone and shale hills and ridges usually covered by grass, Douglas fir and limber pine in the south but forested in the north. There's some good early season cycling to be found in the foothills. West of the foothills the jagged and rugged limestone peaks of the front ranges clearly define the eastern edge of the mountains. This region tends to be hot and dry in summer and many of the creeks are without water by mid-season. The front ranges offer excellent cycling on good trails. Farther west the front ranges grade into the main ranges, a region of high peaks and glaciers along the Continental Divide. The main ranges do not exist in the extreme south, but farther north they provide some fabulous high-elevation summer cycling. The western ranges lie between the main ranges and the Rocky Mountain Trench and are composed largely of metamorphic rocks with a distinct shale-like character. The trails here tend to be steep with lots of elevation gain. The trench is a deep and broad valley occupied by the Fraser, Columbia and Kootenay rivers. In the north it is heavily forested, but farther south grasslands predominate.

The trails in this book (with a few transgressions west of the trench) are restricted to the Rockies. Included are trails from the International Boundary in the south to the vicinity of Grande Cache and McBride in the north. A territory of this size contains hundreds of trails and I managed to test ride well over 300 of them. You will find more than 200 of the best trails described here along with some substantial options.

This book is separated into five cycling areas based on the riding experiences available, the main access routes and the nature of the country. The Southern Rockies lie just north of the International Boundary and include both the east and west slopes in an area of colourful mountains. The region is typified by numerous cyclable passes across the Continental Divide and access on gravel roads of varying quality.

The Central East Slopes provide superb cycling on an extensive network of good trails. The area typically has paved-road access and is complemented by resorts and recreational facilities. The Kootenay and Columbia cycling area lies west of the Divide on the Pacific slope and is a land of deep valleys with grasslands and lush forests. It holds a wide variety of cycling opportunities complemented by warm lakes and numerous resort communities. To the north lies the Fraser Valley, similar to the Columbia in many ways but much wilder and more remote. To the east across the Divide is the Northern East Slopes cycling area characterized by a relatively wild landscape with a northern feel. Here the typical cycling experience is a long ride through remote country. Each of these areas is described further in a separate area-introduction.

The Canadian Rockies is a range of 4000 metre-high peaks and many areas have considerable vertical relief. The lowest trailhead elevation in this book is 730 metres at McBride and the highest rideable trail is on the summit of Canoe Mountain at an elevation of 2654 metres. Elevation gains in the range of 500-1500 metres are common on many of the trails.

Variety is the word best describing Rocky Mountain weather. Warm or cold temperatures can occur at any time of the year so it's best to be prepared. Spring can be warm and some trails on the east slopes and in the valley bottom of the Rocky Mountain Trench may be rideable as early as April, but the riding season really gets underway in May. June tends to be the wettest month. In June, July and August the days are warm enough to ride wearing shorts and a jersey, and the strong summer sunshine makes sunscreen standard equipment. July and August are the warmest months, usually providing excellent cycling at all elevations. Average temperatures are considerably cooler in September and more so in October, but this is a wonderful time of the year for cycling. The days are warm and the autumn colours and new snow add a magical touch to the landscape. Mountain weather can be very unpredictable. No matter how hot and sunny the weather is when you start out in the morning, take a rain jacket and an extra layer of insulation— it can rain or snow when you least expect it. The temperature can drop quickly in the mountain environment and frost is not uncommon at night, even after a warm day. While snow may fall at any time of the year, you can count on it in September and October.

Obtaining drinking water from the streams and lakes along the trails is a special concern for backcountry travellers. Bad water may lead to infection by Giardia lamblia, a protozoan causing diarrhea, nausea, severe stomach cramps and listlessness. The infective strain is most commonly found in dogs, humans and beavers, and sometimes goes by the name "beaver fever." The organism enters waterways through the feces of these animals, and streams in the valley bottoms, along which many of the trails lead, are more likely to be contaminated. This is especially true in the foothills, where most streams are shared with cattle. Always start a backcountry cycling trip with a full supply of water and only collect drinking water from small springs and creeks. Larger streams receive water from a larger watershed and are more likely to be contaminated. I have used water from many of the routes in this guide with no ill effects, but that does not guarantee that the water is safe. The decision, and the risk, is yours.

# Land Managers and their Policies

The land in the Rockies falls under the jurisdiction of a variety of management agencies. Their policies tend to change from time to time, so it is always a good idea to stop by these agencies and check things out. This also serves to remind them that mountain bikers are a part of their constituency and that their policies need to address our needs. Most of these agencies have public consultation processes through which you can make your opinions known, and volunteer programs through which you can contribute to trail improvement and join in other activities beneficial to the sport of mountain biking. Do not hesitate to inquire.

## Parks Canada

This book includes trails in five national parks. Remember that it's a privilege to be able to ride your bike on trails in a national park and act accordingly; your conduct will have a direct impact on the future of mountain biking in the national parks. Preservation and use of the parks are governed by the National Parks Act and Regulations, which do not even mention bikes. Off-road cycling is generally controlled by means of a restricted activity order from the Park Superintendent. If such an order is in place, bikes are legally restricted to the cycling trails designated and you could be charged if you are found cycling on other trails. The list of designated trails changes from time to time so check with the park information centres for information about trails and areas that are currently open for trail bicycling.

## British Columbia Provincial Parks

The trails in this book lead into or through a number of British Columbia provincial parks. Regulations governing the use of this land are similar to those of the national parks but are, perhaps, a bit less restrictive and less rigorously enforced. Check with the authorities at each park to find out their policies toward mountain bikes and which trails are open for your use.

## British Columbia Forest Service

The forest service operates on a mandate of multiple use, but logging is their principal business and this means clearcuts and good gravel access roads. Each forest district has a free map of the roads and trails, and a recreation officer who is in charge of providing opportunities for camping and trail-based recreation. Many of the forest service trails are too steep for enjoyable cycling, but there are some notable exceptions.

## Alberta Provincial Parks

The trails in this book lead into the Peter Lougheed and Willmore Wilderness provincial parks. Regulations governing the use of this land are similar to those of the national parks, but are less restrictive. Some trails in Peter Lougheed Provincial Park have been closed to bicycling. Inquire at the Park Information Centre for up-to-date trail information.

## Alberta Forest Service

The forest service operates on a mandate of multiple use and each forest district provides some camping and recreational opportunities. Most of the trails are old exploration roads and little attempt is made to plan, control or regulate usage.

## Kananaskis Country

Locally known as "K Country," this provincial recreation area is managed jointly by several Alberta government agencies for multiple use. An excellent network of trails and other recreational facilities has been developed with only minor restrictions on bicycles. You can expect to share these trails with everything from hikers to cows. Check with the information centres for up-to-date mountain biking information. Kananaskis Country managers are to be commended for maintaining an even-handed approach to shared use of the trails.

**Private Property**

A few routes described in this book cross private property and you must request permission before riding on this land. I have queried most landowners and they are currently amenable to use by bicyclists. Sentiments can change; please respect the owners' wishes.

# MOUNTAIN BIKING

A mountain bike is a simple yet elegant machine that provides one of the best ways to enjoy the backcountry of the Rockies. With the fresh air and a close-to-nature feel, mountain biking offers a unique experience second to none. For some riders it's an action-packed activity that is an end in itself—the true aficionado's passion for involvement, competition, speed, adrenaline, skill and self-reliance. For others it is a means for getting in step with the natural world around them: the beauty of the mountains, contemplation, catching rays, enjoying the outdoors, fresh air, fun and the camaraderie of the group. Mountain biking creates a tremendous opportunity for personal growth and learning. Experience and skill development takes one from novice to expert, desires range from soft adventure to hard core, and fitness levels enter the equation to alter everything yet again. Enjoyment of healthy exercise and adventure in a natural setting are important factors that we all share in the fun, somewhat crazy spirit of this sport.

Mountain biking is a wonderful sport, but like all activities that take place in the untamed outdoors, it can be hazardous. Bikes routinely travel over rough and technical terrain at high speeds, and long distances are easily covered, often leading participants into remote areas. Under any of these circumstances, accidents can have serious consequences. The author and publisher urge you to learn proper techniques for safe mountain bicycling and wilderness travel before you set out on any of the trails described in this book. Your safety on the trail is your responsibility and yours alone. Let me say it again: mountain biking is a sport that can be dangerous. Common sense is your biggest single asset and if you combine it with knowledge, skill and experience, you'll have everything going for you.

## Ride Safely

- Choose trails that match your physical condition. Mountain biking is very strenuous. Do not decide to get in shape by cycling one of the harder trails in the book.
- Pick trails suited to your skill level. Cycling a trail beyond your abilities will result in extensive pushing or perhaps a crash and serious injuries. It is totally unacceptable to create new, easier trails around the technical bits just because they are too difficult for you. Get off of your bike and walk if the trail is too difficult or seems dangerous.
- Know how to repair your bike and carry adequate tools and parts to do so on the trail. A checklist is included on page 15. I always carry a repair kit

with me, tucked into a pocket of my water pack. Put together your own kit and don't leave home without it.

- Use proper safety gear and protective clothing. The most important single item is a helmet—wear it. Other important items include gloves, eye protection, adequate clothing, matches, a knife and first-aid supplies.

- Know your intended route. Some trails are clearly marked and signed. Others are not. Even with the guidebook and a map, judgement will be required at some trail junctions. Be prepared to backtrack if necessary.

- When travelling in remote country, let someone know where you are going and when you will be back.

- The more rugged and remote the trip, the better prepared you will need to be. Carry food, water and clothing appropriate to the trip you have chosen.

- Be alert for bears, watch for fresh tracks and bear shit, and take appropriate precautions such as making noise. Learn how to behave in a bear encounter situation.

## Free Advice: Take It or Leave It

- Most cyclists choose to carry their food, extra clothes and repair kit in a water pack or fanny pack.

- Learn how to repair and maintain your own bike. This will give you the know-how and skills required to fix your bike should it break down on the trail. Many organizations and cycle shops offer courses.

- Ensure that your bike is "tuned-up" on a regular basis. Doing so decreases the likelihood of having a breakdown in the middle of nowhere (which is usually where it happens).

- Learn proper riding techniques. Courses, books and riding with more accomplished cyclists will help you to improve. Good riding technique improves your safety margin and eases your impact on the land.

- Be prepared for the unexpected. See the day-trip checklist on page 15. Remember, you can cycle a long way in a day, sometimes much farther than you would care to walk.

- Carry adequate maps and other navigational aids and know how to use them. The outline maps in this book are intended only to give you a sense of the route; definitive information on the lay of the land comes from 1:50,000 scale topographic maps. Unfortunately, most topo maps do not accurately show positions of trails and roads.

- Remember, when the going gets too tough you can always get off your bike and walk.

- Trails overgrown by vegetation are usually easier and safer to cycle after leaf fall. Visibility is much improved and trail hazards such as drop-offs and bears are much easier to spot.

- Be spiritual; celebrate the land and the sport whenever you ride.

- Learn about and enjoy the geology, plants, wildlife and history of the Rockies. Use your mountain bike to enhance your enjoyment.

- Use a bell to alert hikers, equestrians and other riders of your approach.

- Fording streams can be anything from trivial to very dangerous. If the water is deep or fast flowing, carry your bike above the water. To cross shallower streams with stepping stones, use your bike as a walking stick, locking up the brakes and leaning on it as you step from stone to stone.

- Pfisterer's Rule: only half of the trip is uphill!

# SOURCES OF INFORMATION

The focus of this book is on places to ride your bike, but I am making some assumptions about your knowledge and experience. Primarily, that you already have a bike and know how to ride it. If this isn't the case, there are lots of good shops that will be happy to help you out and there are a number of guiding and teaching organizations that can provide excellent instruction. Clubs are a great way to get introduced to riding and benefit from the companionship and experience of others. Bike maintenance and repair is a whole specialty area, but if you plan to travel in remote places then you must have the skills to make trailside repairs or else be prepared to walk out of the backcountry. Backcountry travel and trip planning are essential skills for safe wilderness travel. You can learn them in a formal setting or by hanging with experienced travellers.

If you don't have the knowledge and experience discussed above, then I urge you to take some steps to get it. There are lots of courses, books and videos on these subjects, the learning is fun and it makes your trips a whole lot safer and more enjoyable. Here are a few books and organizations.

## Organizations
- Outdoor Program Centre, University of Calgary, 403-220-5038
- Frontier Lodge, Box 1449, Rocky Mountain House, AB T0M 1T0, 403-721-2202
  e-mail: frontldg@telusplanet.net

## Bicycle Maintenance
- Mountain Bike Maintenance, Rob Van der Plas, Bicycle Books, 1989
- Easy Bicycle Maintenance, Bicycling Magazine, Rodale Press, 1985

## Riding Skills
- Mountain Biking, John Olsen, Stackpole Books, 1989
- Mountain Biking Skills, Bicycling Magazine, Rodale Press, 1990
- Mountain Bike!, W. Nealy, Velo News Books, 1992

## Natural History
- Handbook of the Canadian Rockies, Ben Gadd, Corax Press, 1995
- Bear Attacks: Their Causes and Avoidance, Steve Herrero, Nick Lyons, 1985

## Maps
- Gem Trek maps available for a variety of areas, usually very accurate.

## Hiking Guidebooks
- Kananaskis Country Trail Guide, Volumes 1 and 2, 3rd edition, Gillean Daffern, Rocky Mountain Books, 1996 and 1997
- Canadian Rockies Trail Guide, revised edition, Brian Patton, Summerthought, 1999
- The David Thompson Highway: A Hiking Guide, revised edition, Jane Ross and Daniel Kyba, Rocky Mountain Books, 1998
- Hiking the Historic Crowsnest Pass, Jane Ross and William Tracy, Rocky Mountain Books, 1992

## Tourism
- Alberta Tourism, P.O. Box 2500, Edmonton, Alberta T5J 2Z4. Phone (in Alberta) 1-800-222-6501, (outside Alberta) 1-800-661-8888. Publications of interest include: Campgrounds in Alberta, Accommodation Guide, Highways Map and Visitor's Guides for any areas or towns of interest to you.

- Tourism British Columbia, Parliament Buildings, Victoria, British Columbia V8V 1X4. Phone 1-800-663-6000. Publications of interest include: Accommodation Guide, Road Map and Parks Guide, Super Camping Guide and Visitor's Guides for areas and towns of interest.

## Repair kit checklist

- tube
- tire patch kit (check glue, often-opened tubes tend to dry out)
- tire levers
- chain breaker
- Allen keys... all sizes for your bike
- wrenches... all sizes for your bike
- headset wrench to fit your bike
- spoke wrench
- screwdrivers... types required for your bike
- spare nuts, bolts, chain links, wire
- oil in a small container

## Day-trip checklist

- bike with cyclometer and bell, tuned and in good working order
- helmet
- repair kit
- tire pump
- shorts and jersey
- cycling shoes
- gloves
- sunglasses
- jacket and extra clothing as appropriate to weather and trip
- pack (back or fanny)
- water system and water
- food and energy bars
- map
- guidebook
- matches
- knife
- toilet paper
- first-aid kit
- rain gear
- camera

## GOOD FORM

Once viewed as the new kid on the block, mountain biking is now taking its place as a legitimate trail-based recreation. In many areas of the backcountry, mountain bikers form one of the larger user groups. Hikers and equestrians are no longer surprised to meet bikers on the trails; in fact, they now expect to meet them. Mountain biking has come of age as a recreational activity, however, legitimacy brings with it responsibility. Bikers have no need to ride apologetically but, under all circumstances, you must ride as a responsible member of the trail community.

Mountain biking is not a crime, yet some land managers are busy making it into one. Why? Close encounters of the worst kind: horses spooked and their rid-

ers thrown, people surprised and frightened, buzzed or even knocked down. Experiences like these make people angry. Land managers, being on the conservative side of life, tend to overreact to complaints and, rather than stop the perpetrators of these deeds, they take the easy way out by restricting the activity itself. Many people seem to have an ingrained bias against bicycles and will take steps to restrict them whenever they possibly can.

There is no excuse for a rude riding style and self-regulated and sensible behaviour is essential if mountain bikers are to retain access to the many trails described in this book. The actions of each individual mountain biker influence the attitude of the public toward mountain bikers in general. This has a profound affect on the acceptability of the sport, which really means access to trails. Already we have seen many of the trails in the national parks and several other areas closed to mountain bikers. Most of it has been with scant justification; nebulous and poorly documented reasons such as "environmental damage" or "public safety concerns" are given when politics is more likely the underlying reason. Many mountain bikers, being strong individualists, feel that "every law creates an outlaw" and go for it anyway, but becoming a mountain-bike bandit is hardly the answer to trail closures. Renegades only harden perceptions and attitudes, even if they are unreasonable.

## Respect Others

All backcountry users have a common cause in the preservation of the land and their access to it. Respect other trail users—they are your allies and have the same right to be there as you. Land managers have already demonstrated that they will take action when mountain bikers infringe on the rights of others.

Part of the problem is one of perception. You may cruise by a group of hikers and be in full control of your bike so, as far as you are concerned, there is no problem. But they may not see it that way. If they perceive you as a threat to their safety because they think you were going too fast or lacked control, or if they think you were damaging the natural environment, then there is a problem. And, unfortunately, this problem soon becomes a problem for all mountain bikers. Like it or not, there is only one way around this difficulty. You must ride such that, not only are your real impacts on others minimized, but also such that others perceive your impact to be minimal. Any time you are around non-mountain bik-

ers it is imperative that you ride with a distinctly non-aggressive style.

- Be friendly and courteous.
- Avoid excessive speed.
- Warn others of your approach, especially from behind.

## Respect The Land

Mountain biking is a celebration of the land, the machine and you. Without the incredible natural surroundings, what would biking be? Just another roll through the asphalt jungle! Let's be honest here, mountain biking does impact the land and the trails. Just being in the backcountry has an effect on some of the more sensitive species such as grizzly bears and wolves. Riding off of the trail kills plants, and brake-sliding on steep hills causes erosion that destroys trails. And there are renegade riders out there who just plain do not care. If you are not willing to treat the land with respect, then stay home. Learn and practice appropriate skills such as "leave no trace," and "pack-in, pack-out." You demonstrate your respect for the land in the way you ride, so ride in such a way that your impact on the environment is minimal.

- Stay off trails when they are excessively muddy.
- Avoid shortcutting on switchbacks.
- Avoid brake-sliding.
- Avoid riding on trail shoulders.
- Stay on the trails.

IMBA suggests the following Rules of the Trail ©

1. Ride on open trails only.
2. Leave no trace.
3. Control your bicycle!
4. Always yield the trail.
5. Never spook animals.
6. Plan ahead.

## No Bikes Allowed

Just how often do we have to see signs like this before cyclists will have had enough? Get involved soon or these signs will be everywhere and you will have very few satisfying places to ride your bike. Trail closures are becoming commonplace in the Rockies. From the national parks where the unspoken agenda seems to be to eliminate mountain bikes from the backcountry, to Canmore where urban sprawl and wildlife corridors take precedence over all forms of recreation including bikes, trail closures are now a fact of life.

Why are cyclists taking the hit so often when it is clear that golf courses, housing developments, roads, hikers and even equestrians are getting off relatively unscathed? At times it seems that land managers, like most North Americans, are somewhat bike-phobic. Run down on the roads and kicked off the trails is a somewhat pessimistic summary of the situation. The question on everyone's lips ought to be "How should I respond to this kind of arbitrary and unfair treatment?" Cyclists are disorganized and notoriously independent, yet effective lobbying of bureaucrats requires both organization and mutual effort. Most cyclists would rather ride their bikes than sit through often tedious meetings in order to secure their place on the trails. Nevertheless, if you want to have good singletrack trails to ride on in the future, you will have to get involved in ensuring that your rights are respected.

## Get Involved

As a mountain biker you have as much right to access the trails as anyone else does. Insist on your rights, but know that with rights come responsibilities. When you ride, set a good example and enhance the credibility of the sport by respecting the rules of the trail and being friendly and courteous to other trail users.

Join and work for your local advocacy group and IMBA, organizations that can effectively lobby for your interests as a mountain bicyclist.

- Calgary Mountain Bike Alliance, 1111 Memorial Drive N.W., Calgary, AB T2N 3E4 e-mail: cmbikea@cadvision.com
- Alberta Bicycling Association, 11759 Groat Road, Edmonton, AB T5M 3K6 e-mail: aba@compusmart.ab.ca
- International Mountain Bicycling Association, Box 7578, Boulder, CO 80306-7578 U.S.A. e-mail: IMBA @aol.com
- Work on trails. Most land management agencies have a program by which you can participate on trail maintenance projects.
- Friends of Kananaskis Country, (403) 678-5508
- Banff National Park, (403) 762-1470
- Calgary Area Outdoor Council, (403) 270-2262

Use the political process. Write letters to ministers, politicians, superintendents and administrators to ensure that they are aware of how much you value access to the trails described in this book. Ask them to explain the specific rationale behind trail closures, demand fair treatment of all user groups, and a voice in their land access policies and issues.

Most land management agencies utilize public consultations in their planning processes. Participate and let them know what you expect.

## Riding the Backcountry

Mountain biking is a sport that delivers adventure. In writing this guide, I did not want to take away from that spirit of adventure, but I did want to provide you with an adequate safety net of information. Think of this book as a friend telling you about a biking trail. In the sidebar I've included the essential details about the routes. The text adds information about the tricky spots, the country and the fun of it all. There are pictures to help you get enthused and outline maps to help you understand the layout of the trails on the landscape. Putting it all together into a quality riding experience is up to you. The advance preparation and mindset you bring to the ride fully determines the type of riding experience you will have, thus it's possible to totally enjoy a mud thrash just as much as riding a buff singletrack on a perfect day. A guidebook can not hold your hand and I want you to have the opportunity to experience that same sense of excitement and adventure that I found when cycling these trails for the first time. No guidebook can cover every little detail, and a bit of trial and error will be required on some of the trails. Your biggest asset when mountain biking (besides the guidebook and a topo map) is common sense.

The focus of this book is on good quality backcountry rides at a variety of levels of stamina and skill. In order to offer a quality experience, I look for a combination of scenery, adventure, good trail, challenge, excitement, variety and natural world interest. Each rider has personal expectations of a ride and these can be satisfied by carefully choosing the right trail. However, I fully believe that any rider can have a good time on any trail if he or she so chooses.

This book is organized around mountain bike rides and a ride usually involves a combination of several individual trails or trail segments linked together. Each ride has a trailhead to trailhead format. When selecting trails my preference was for loops, with out-and-back rides being the second choice. Some point-to-point rides are unavoidable and offer wonderful experiences, but there are inevitably car shuttle problems. Remember that two cars will be required for any point-to-point ride unless you finish with sufficient energy to either retrace your tracks or cycle on the road back to your starting point. Of course, a part of any trail can be cycled as an out-and-back and this is a good way to go if you are looking for a short trip or if you want to cycle only the initial easier part of a trail. The options described vary from major rides with their own trail description to minor side trails or possibilities for you to enhance your trip.

There are many possible approaches to the rides. You can get to know one area well by travelling its trails extensively and supplementing your riding with hikes, climbs and extra readings. Another possibility is to check out all the cruiser trails in the Rockies, or how about a tour of the many fire lookout trails described in the book? For the endurance riders the choices are obvious, and there are lots of tough and technical singletracks for those who have the skill levels to handle them. Folks who like hiking will find numerous bike 'n' hikes described, with additional possibilities limited only by your imagination.

The Rockies are full of classic mountain bike riding opportunities, but that begs the question of just what is a classic anyway. This is a very subjective matter and my classic just might be your dog! It really depends on preferences. I've referred to a few of the rides as classic and I'm using the word in the sense of enduring favourite. Some of the rides are described as outstanding and I think you will agree, but I'll leave it up to you to prepare your own personal list of the classics. Naturally some rides are better than others because they combine more of the factors that make a ride into a quality experience. But that doesn't mean the rest of the rides are not worth doing, it all comes back to the point about how much fun you have on a ride depending on your attitude and expectations.

## Extended Rides

Ambitious riders can easily put together extended rides using the trails in this book, other trails and the extensive network of gravel roads. Enjoyable overnight travel is really determined by your ability to make creative use of a support vehicle or to cycle with a pack on your back or a trailer behind your bike. Another option is to cycle to a base camp, then take day hikes and rides from your camp. One obvious area with lots of possibilities for extended rides is Kananaskis Country, where you can link trails for days on end and travel either self-sufficient or have a support vehicle drive from camping spot to camping spot while the riders take to the high country. Farther south and west some long mountain tours can be made by utilizing logging roads in the Elk and Bull River valleys to connect the trails. For example, use the maps and your imagination to link Bragg Creek or Canmore with Fernie or Cranbrook. To the north a long wilderness ride in the front ranges is possible by linking the Berland, Wildhay and Snake Indian valleys. Another ambitious possibility is to

ride from Ya-Ha-Tinda Ranch to the Clearwater Valley, over to the Ram, then through to the North Saskatchewan Valley. Rides like this are likely to be major atomic-dog style adventures that will have to be self-supported.

On a more formal note the Trans-Canada Trail Association is currently delineating a shared-use route across the Rockies from Calgary to Wasa Lake. To the south in the United States, a Great Divide cycling route has been identified from the Mexican border to the Canadian border and you can expect a similar initiative in Canada. It's relatively easy to figure out a route as far as Canmore, but farther north it becomes considerably more difficult.

## Trail Talk

**bike 'n' hike** A trip where you ride part way to your destination, then leave your bike and hike the rest of the way.

**doubletrack** Two parallel tracks, usually made by motor vehicles.

**fireroad** A road leading into the backcountry, usually in the national parks, originally built for purposes of fire protection.

**ford** What you use to get to the trailhead. Seriously, it is a place where the trail crosses a stream without the benefit of a bridge. If the water is shallow you may be able to ride across. If it is deep you will have to carry your bike and wade.

**4WD road** A rough road or track of a quality suitable for a four-wheel-drive vehicle, but not necessarily open to use by same.

**loop** A one-way ride that begins and ends at the same point.

**out-and-back** A ride in which you retrace your tracks, returning to the starting point.

**point-to-point** A one-way ride in which you begin at point a and end at point b. Two vehicles will usually be required to make this type of ride any fun at all.

**singletrack** Just one fairly narrow path to ride on.

**technical riding** Riding that requires considerable bike-handling skills to negotiate obstacles found on the trail. Those without good handling skills will find themselves pushing or carrying their bikes through technical sections of trail.

**trail** What you ride your bicycle on, which could be anything from a paved road to a gnarly singletrack.

**2WD road** A paved or gravel road of a quality suitable for a two-wheel-drive vehicle, but not necessarily open to use by same.

## A Note About Trail Conditions

Trail conditions change continuously throughout the season and from year to year. Some years are dry and the riding is pleasant, others are wet and the riding is hard work and muddy. Spring can arrive early (good) or late (bad). Along some trails the bushes grow thicker by the year. The presence of large horse parties or livestock, especially when combined with wet conditions, can virtually destroy what was formerly a good trail. Bridges wash away; new bridges get built; fun-filled doubletracks are "improved" to become high-grade logging roads. Expect the unexpected in your travels and be prepared both mentally and physically to deal effectively with whatever you find.

## ABOUT THE PROFILES

The numbers at the left edge represent hundreds of vertical metres. In this case 1400 m and 1500 m.

The numbers on the bottom are kilometres.

Note that loop trails and out-and-back trails start and finish at the same elevation. Point-to-point trails usually start and finish at different elevations.

# USING THIS BOOK

**xx TRAIL...map xx** Trail number and map number, allows this trail to be identified easily, both elsewhere in the text and on the maps. Map number refers to the line map at the back of the book showing the layout of the trail, local features, related trails and distances.

**Type** A one-phrase description of the layout and type of trail. Layout possibilities are a loop, an out-and-back, a point-to-point or a network. Trail types include 2WD road, 4WD road, and singletrack trail.

**Rating** is shown in the format of physical difficulty/technical difficulty.

**Physical difficulty** refers to how strenuous the ride is by giving an idea of the physical exertion required to travel the route. It is influenced by time required, elevation gain, length, steepness, amount of pushing or carrying, and nature of stream crossings. The ratings are: easy, moderate, difficult and extreme.

**Technical difficulty** describes the level of skill required to comfortably cycle this trail. Factors influencing technical difficulty include rideablity, nature of the obstacles, steepness, exposure, visibility, and the number and length of the technical sections. The ratings, in order of increasing difficulty, are: novice, intermediate, advanced and expert.

**Adverse conditions** such as wet weather, snow, high runoff levels and concentrated use by livestock can increase the difficulty rating beyond the stated level.

**Other users** This category gives you some idea of who you can expect to meet on the trail and with what frequency.

The other users are hikers, equestrian, motorized and livestock modified by degree, 1 = little, 10 = outrageous.

**Distance** In kilometres for the route described. This figure is a return trip distance except for point-to-point rides where it is specified as being one-way. Most travel is on dirt but if there is a substantial distance on-pavement, then this distance is specified in parentheses. See the trip log and route map for partial distances. It is worth noting that every cyclometer seems to measure a little differently and that inaccuracies seem to be inherent in these gizmos. Variations in the range of 10 per cent are common, so you should use the stated distances as an approximate guide.

**Time** An estimate in hours is given for an average cyclist (if there is such a critter) of the skill level stated to complete the trip.

**Map** NTS 1:50,000 topographic map reference. These maps will give you detailed information about the lay of the land, but the trails described in this book may or may not be shown on the maps.

**Season** The season when this trail is usually at its best. In general lower elevation trails will be rideable from May through to the end of October. Trails at higher elevations are usually snow-free from early July until mid-October. Many of the unbridged streams may be uncrossable during periods of high water, usually coinciding with high rainfall or hot weather.

**Land Agency** The land managers who have primary responsibility for this land. See the section on land managers and their policies.

# CENTRAL EAST SLOPES

This riding area includes trails in the country drained by the Bow River and its tributary streams: the Kananaskis, Elbow, Sheep and Highwood. It is a very popular riding area owing to its proximity to the city of Calgary, the presence of several well-known resorts, and a large number of well-constructed trails. Besides Calgary, the major population centres are Banff, Canmore and Bragg Creek, linked by Highways 1, 40 and 22, and a number of secondary roads.

The landscape is typical of the east slopes of the Rockies with grasslands and low foothills in the east, ragged limestone peaks in the front ranges and high mountains along the Continental Divide to the west. This country is rugged yet accessible and many of the areas are hauntingly beautiful, with some still very wild despite their proximity to a large urban area. Protected landscapes include Banff National Park and Peter Lougheed, Mount Assiniboine and Elk Lakes provincial parks. Kananaskis Country is a large provincial recreation area that is managed for multiple use.

This is one of the best mountain-biking areas in the Canadian Rockies and all of the trails described can be cycled on a day-trip basis from Calgary. Mountain-biking trails in the central east slopes include everything from paved bicycle paths and gravel roads to doubletracks and breathtaking singletracks. In the national park you can expect lots of easy cruising on fireroads and a few singletracks of variable quality depending on other users. Kananaskis Country has an exceptional network of trails that make super cross-country rides. With the extensive trail network, rides of all lengths and difficulties are possible, and the ones described here are among my fa-

vourites. These trails are popular, and opportunities for solitude are limited, especially on weekends. You will encounter horses and hikers, but off-road vehicles are generally restricted throughout the area. Some trail closures have occurred for a variety of reasons, but user conflicts seem to be at a manageable level. Use tends to be concentrated on selected popular trails, which sets the stage for conflict, so please do your part to maintain cordial relations with other trail users.

With Calgary to the east, the central east slopes riding area has a population base approaching a million people. As a result, there has been extensive development of recreational facilities and resorts, good road access and trail networks. Every imaginable service associated with modern-day tourism and recreation is available somewhere here. Calgary is home to several cycle clubs and the Calgary Mountain Bike Alliance, a very effective cycling advocacy group.

Banff National Park is one of the most important and busiest national parks in Canada. Mountain biking is legally restricted to designated trails and a brochure describing the cycling trails is available from Park information centres and local bike shops. Remember that it is a privilege to ride your bike on trails in a national park and conduct yourself accordingly. The history of mountain biking in this park has been one of ever-increasing closures until only a handful of good riding opportunities remain. The Bow Valley Mountain Bike Alliance was formed to resist additional closures; join up and help ensure the success of this group. The local cycling scene is quite active and eight rides ranging from paved paths to old roads and challenging singletrack begin at or close to the town of Banff. The townsite is a major tourist and commercial centre and has many attractions—power shopping seems to be one of the biggest. Camping with showers is available at the Tunnel Mountain campground and budget accommodation at the Banff International Hostel and at the YWCA. Bike shops are numerous; you'll find their logos on the park bike brochure.

Also located within Banff National Park, Lake Louise is a visitor centre notable for its tremendous scenery. Four cool mountain bike trails originate here. Local cyclists are a small but active group and Wilson Mountain Sports is the local shop. Camping with showers is available in the village and budget accommodation at the International Hostel.

Canmore is a major population centre located just east of the national park. Notable for its scenery and friendly attitude, Canmore has an active cycling scene with a riding club and regular races. Local shops of note include Rebound Cycle, the Bicycle Café and Altitude Sports. Numerous good rides can be found near town and in the surrounding area. A number of pathways run through the townsite and offer mellow and scenic rides in their own right. The Canmore Nordic Centre has a popular network of trails that includes many rider-built singletracks. Races are often held here, including the prestigious World Cup and 24 Hours of Adrenaline races. Camping with and without showers is available in town and in the surrounding area.

Kananaskis Country is a provincial recreation area located on the east slopes south of the Trans-Canada Highway. This area has a shared-use approach to its trails and other natural resources and offers a tremendous range of mountain-biking opportunities. It has many good trails, although the ever-present cattle often impair their quality. Kananaskis "pre-cows" (until early July) offers trails less chewed up by hooves and without the ubiquitous cow patty. The trails are a very extensive network and there are opportunities to customize rides of all lengths and difficulties. Most of the trails are described here and detailed maps of the trail network are available at information centres. Rides in the Kananaskis Valley are accessed by means of Highway 40. Although not officially off-limits to bikes, I have not included the trails of the Kananaskis Range such as Ribbon Creek, Galatea and Buller Pass because they are so popular with hikers. I urge you to either avoid them entirely or go on a weekday when it is less crowded. Kananaskis Country is also accessed by secondary highways 68, 66 and 546, which lead into the Sibbald, Elbow and Sheep valleys respectively. These too are great riding areas with lots of good trails. Highways 541, 40 and SR 940 provide access to the rides of the Highwood Valley.

# 1 PIPESTONE TRAIL                          map 1

Photo: Gerhardt Lepp.

*Gerhardt Lepp on the smooth singletrack of Pipestone trail.*

**Gentle backcountry ride**

**Type** out-and-back on singletrack
**Rating** moderate/novice
**Other users** hikers-2 equestrian-2
**Distance** 13.4 km
**Time** 1-2 hours
**Map** 82 N/8 Lake Louise
**Season** June to mid-October
**Land agency** Parks Canada

**Access**
In Lake Louise village, the trailhead is located off of Slate Road, on the north side of the Trans-Canada Hwy., west of the Pipestone River.

| | |
|---|---|
| 0.0 | trailhead |
| 0.9 | junction, keep left (Mud Lake trail to right) |
| 1.7 | spur trail to left |
| 6.7 | end of high-grade trail, end of cycle trail |

A highway to nowhere—this trail is the perfect place to spend a couple of hours rolling in the woods. And what more could you ask for than the sound of rushing water and the breeze in your hair; just you and your bike cruising on a good trail.

The route is well constructed to high standards with a compacted gravel and silt tread, much of which is covered with spruce and pine needles. It is well drained and provides acceptable cycling in wet weather as long as you don't mind a little silty spray. Not far from the trailhead a short side trail leads to Mud Lake. Meanwhile, the main trail climbs gently for 2 km, then parallels the Pipestone River. The official cycle route and good tread end at km 6.7. Beyond, the trail is rooty and muddy and, don't ask me why, closed to bikes.

It is an exciting ride back to town. If you choose to ride fast—and who wouldn't on this good trail—watch for hikers, horses and other cyclists.

17

16

15

3          6          9          12      13.4

# 2 LAKE LOUISE TRAMWAY                    map 1

Here is your chance to reach Lake Louise on the same route taken by the genteel Rockies visitor of 1913-30. Back then, an open tram car ascended a gentle grade from Laggan station on the CPR to the Chateau on the shores of Lake Louise. Imagine their eager anticipation of arrival at the lake. Slip back in time and pretend you are on the tram!

Make your way through the village to the log CPR station, then cross the bridge and cycle up the old tramline right-of-way. The riding is easy, the route is smooth and well compacted, visibility is good. Ride past the Louise Creek trail (closed to bikes), cross two busy roads and the next thing you know you are steaming up to the Chateau. I doubt that the old tram had to thread its way through parking lots full of motor homes and Mercedes to reach the lake, but you will! Then you will have to share the once quiet and tranquil shoreline with hundreds of modern day pilgrims.

This lake is one of those few places in the world where nature's sublimity cannot be diminished by crowds of humanity. And once you've paid homage in this temple of nature you, gentle cyclist, can just slip away into the woods, back to the peace and quiet of nature.

**Family fun on historic trail**
**Type** point-to-point on 4WD road
**Rating** easy/novice
**Other users** hikers-3  equestrian-2
**Distance** 5.3 km one way
**Time** 1 hour
**Map** 82 N/8 Lake Louise
**Season** June to mid-October
**Land agency** Parks Canada

**Access**
In Lake Louise village, the trailhead is on the banks of the Bow River near the CPR station.

| | |
|---|---|
| 0.0 | trailhead |
| 0.1 | bridge across Bow River |
| 1.8 | Louise Creek, bridge and trail junction |
| 2.5 | Lake Louise Road crossing |
| 3.3 | Moraine Lake Road crossing |
| 4.5 | Louise Creek trail joins from the right |
| 4.7 | parking lots |
| 5.3 | Lake Louise |

# 3 MORAINE LAKE TRAIL

map 1

This is one of the best rides in the Lake Louise area. Not only is it technically challenging, it leads to a beautiful mountain lake surrounded by the high, glacier-clad peaks of the Bow Range. The route leads through old growth forests of subalpine fir and Engelmann spruce with an understory of rhododendron and heather. In July and August the forest floor is a high mountain flower garden.

Although there are a variety of ways to cycle this trail, my favourite is as an out-and-back from the village in combination with the first part of the Lake Louise Tramway trail (#2) and Moraine Lake Road. Follow the Tramline to the crossing of the Moraine Lake road, turn left and spin along the pavement to the signed beginning of the cycling route. Depending on your time and energy you can cycle the trail as an out-and-back from this point or you can make a loop by continuing to Moraine Lake on the pavement and returning on the trail.

Riding toward Moraine Lake, you'll find the trail rocky and rooty, offering lots of technical work as it climbs well up onto the side of Mount Temple. Once it turns the corner into the Moraine Creek valley the route becomes very scenic with views of The Ten Peaks, Moraine Lake, The Tower of Babel and Consolation Valley. This section of narrow, somewhat exposed, sidehill trail offers delightful cycling for advanced riders. On the return trip from Moraine Lake to the village, you'll encounter a combination of gentle uphill and fast, bumpy, downhill riding. With all of the best views at your back, this direction is much less scenic but provides exciting technical cycling with little elevation gain.

**Classic high mountain ride**

**Type** out-and-back on 2WD road and singletrack

**Rating** moderate/intermediate

**Other users** hikers-2  equestrian-2

**Distance** 30 km

**Time** 3-5 hours

**Map** 82 N/8 Lake Louise

**Season** mid-June to mid-October

**Land agency** Parks Canada

**Access**
In Lake Louise village, the trailhead is on the banks of the Bow River near the CPR station.

| | |
|---|---|
| 0.0 | Tramway trailhead |
| 3.3 | Moraine Lake Road turn left |
| 5.0 | cycle trail leaves road to right (continue on road if you wish to make a loop) |
| 5.6 | junction with Paradise Valley trail, turn right |
| 6.4 | junction, turn left onto Moraine Lake trail |
| 14.8 | trail ends in parking lot beside lodge |
| 15.0 | Moraine Lake |

# 4 ROSS LAKE
map 1

A sweet mountain singletrack winds from Lake Louise across Kicking Horse Pass on the Continental Divide to Ross Lake. The lake is a pretty little tarn set at the foot of Narao Peak in Yoho National Park. The trail was opened in 1997 on a trial basis after extensive lobbying by local riders, the agreement specifies lack of user conflicts and rider maintenance of the trail as conditions.

Keep right at the initial junction and roll along a wide singletrack through a subalpine forest of fir and menziesia. The farther along the trail you go, the narrower and more perfect the singletrack becomes, however a few rocky sections will test your skills and provide entertaining moments. This is a valley bottom ride but several viewpoints look out over the peaks of the Bow Valley and Kicking Horse Pass. The trail crosses two creeks, then descends to a long boardwalk at Ross Lake. This is a perfect place to take a break and enjoy the quiet natural setting. The trail beyond the lake is closed to bikes.

My favourite way to ride this trail is to begin in the village of Lake Louise and cycle up the tramline trail (#2), take a quick peek at Lake Louise, then ride up through the parking lots and ride the singletrack to Ross Lake. Return the same way for a total distance of 26 km.

**Rugged ride to Ross Lake**

**Type** out-and-back

**Rating** moderate/intermediate

**Other** users hikers-1

**Distance** 14.6 km

**Time** 2-3 hours

**Map** 82N/8 Lake Louise

**Season** June through October

**Land agency** Parks Canada

## Access

The trailhead is hidden in the trees just northwest of Hillside Cottage, the highest of the staff residences behind the Chateau Lake Louise. Access is through the staff parking lots.

| | |
|---|---|
| 0.0 | trailhead |
| 0.01 | junction, keep right |
| 6.0 | enter Yoho Park |
| 7.3 | Ross Lake |

# 5 REDEARTH CREEK                                        map 2

The Redearth fireroad is of little interest in its own right, but if you treat this trip as a bike 'n' hike, it provides access to some spectacular country just east of the Great Divide. The trail is always within the trees but there are lots of viewpoints. Pilot Mountain towers to the east of the valley while Copper Mountain lies to the west and the peaks of the Sawback Range can be seen across Bow Valley.

Although the fireroad climbs out of the Bow Valley and into the valley of Redearth Creek, the hills are gentle and the road is smooth making this a relatively painless ride. You'll cross a couple of bridges and pass by a backcountry campground before reaching the Shadow Lake trail (closed to bikes) and the warden cabin. The cabin marks the end of the cycling route. Park your bike and continue on foot to the destination of your choice—there are plenty of possibilities. The return to the highway offers a fast and pleasant finale to a great day.

## Options

Popular hiking destinations include Shadow Lake, Gibbon Pass, Ball Pass and Egypt Lake. The privately-owned Shadow Lake Lodge makes a good destination for the tea-and-cookies crowd while Gibbon Pass is an excellent place to view larches in autumn. If you are feeling truly energetic I recommend a loop hike that includes Shadow Lake, Whistling Valley and Egypt Lake. Get an early start if you plan to do this trip.

**Bike 'n' hike to Shadow Lake**
**Type** out-and-back on 4WD road
**Rating** moderate/novice
**Other users** hikers-3  equestrians-3
**Distance** 25 km
**Time** 3-4 hours
**Map** 82 O/4 Banff
**Season** mid-June to mid-October
**Land agency** Parks Canada

**Access**
The trailhead is on the south side of the Trans-Canada Hwy., 20 km west of Banff and 10 km east of Castle Junction.

| | |
|---|---|
| 0.0 | trailhead |
| 0.5 | join fireroad, turn right |
| 8.7 | bridge across Redearth Creek |
| 12.2 | Shadow Lake trail to right |
| 12.5 | end of road, trail to Egypt Lake |

# 6 STONEY SQUAW SAMPLER

maps 3, 3A

Parks has been notably restrictive in its policy toward mountain bikes. However, it has designated most of the trails in the immediate vicinity of Banff townsite as open for cycling. Thus these exciting little trails, which ordinarily wouldn't be of much interest, have become a focus for mountain biking largely as a result of becoming legal.

Begin this trip by pedalling up Norquay Road to the main ski hill parking lot. From here it is a 2 km side trip to the summit of Stoney Squaw. You'll want your narrow handlebars for this gnarly little trail, a tight, rooty, rocky, twisty passage with some steep sections. On the way you'll pass through a stand of doghair pine as well as some more typical subalpine forest. The summit provides respectable views of the Bow Valley around Banff while the descent is bumpy and way more fun than the trip up leads you to expect.

Back at the parking lot head for the lodge and continue on down the drainage to the sign at the Fortymile Creek trailhead. In the "good ol' days" this was the starting point for one of the best rides in Banff National Park. But I digress…. Your trail is the one called "horse trail to Banff." This rocky, singletrack descent winds around Stoney Squaw Mountain and ends at the highway, leaving you to exit through a gate in the fence and return to town.

**Rugged ride near town**

**Type** loop on 2WD road and singletrack

**Rating** moderate/intermediate

**Other users** hikers-3  equestrian-5

**Distance** 18.3 km

**Time** 2-3 hours

**Map** 82 O/4 Banff

**Season** June through October

**Land agency** Parks Canada

**Access**

In Banff, begin by cycling up the Mount Norquay access road. The distance log begins where you cross Hwy. 1.

| | |
|---|---|
| 0.0 | trailhead |
| 7.0 | parking lot, Stoney Squaw singletrack on right |
| 9.0 | summit, retrace tracks |
| 11.0 | parking lot, turn right |
| 11.3 | Mount Norquay day lodge |
| 12.7 | follow the "trail to Banff" to the right |
| 16.3 | junction, keep right |
| 16.5 | gate in fence exits onto Trans-Canada Hwy. |
| 18.3 | end of ride |

# 7 TUNNEL MOUNTAIN TEASERS

maps 3, 3A

There are several minor trails in the vicinity of Banff townsite that are open for use by mountain bikers, but the number of trails is steadily diminishing as park officials seemingly work toward eliminating mountain biking from the park. The park publishes a mountain bike trail brochure that, in combination with a visit to the Information Centre or one of the local bike shops, can help you find out which trails are currently legal. Remember that Park wardens may charge you under the National Parks Act if you are found on closed trails.

Beginning above Bow Falls, this trail gradually descends eastward to the river and provides exhilarating riding as it winds and climbs below the cliffs of Tunnel Mountain on its way to the Hoodoos viewpoint. This trail is always popular with hikers and cyclists as it is close to town and the campground. The setting is spectacular—alongside the Bow River or on the edge of the escarpment with mountain peaks towering above dry hillsides covered with stands of Douglas fir and juniper. From the hoodoos the trail loops through the forest to the paved Tunnel Mountain Road. At this point you have options: you can return to town by riding on trails behind Tunnel Mountain Campground or return on the road. If you want more riding keep right on the paved road, then turn right on Banff Avenue to Cascade Ponds picnic area and make an out-and-back ride on the Watertower Trail.

**Fun trails close to town**

**Type** loop on 2WD road and singletrack

**Rating** easy/intermediate

**Other users** hikers-6 equestrian-4

**Distance** 12.5 km

**Time** 1 hour

**Map** 82 O/4 Banff

**Season** May through October

**Land agency** Parks Canada

**Access**
In Banff, begin at the Bow Falls viewpoint on Tunnel Mountain Road.

| | |
|---|---|
| 0.0 | trailhead |
| 3.7 | Tunnel Mountain Campground to left |
| 4.4 | Hoodoos viewpoint |
| 4.8 | junction, turn left |
| 5.6 | junction, keep left |
| 5.9 | cross paved road |
| 7.2 | pass under powerline |
| 7.5 | Tunnel Mountain Road, left to town (right to Watertower) |
| 12.5 | end of ride |

# 7A WATER TOWER TRAIL

maps 3, 3A

Ride past the picnickers and the ponds and follow a singletrack to the northeast as it heads into the trees, then climbs up an almost impossible-to-ride-up set of steps. The remainder of the trail to the watertower is a sweet singletrack that snakes along the top of the escarpment above the Trans-Canada Highway (and the former Cascade River) where a hillside garden of Douglas fir and juniper frame the almost endless peaks of the Bow Valley. A gravel road leads from the water tower to Johnson Lake, the local swimming hole and formerly the site of some great rides; alas, all illegal now. Return the way you came.

## Singletrack treats

**Type** out-and-back on 2WD road and singletrack

**Rating** easy/intermediate

**Other users** hikers-3 equestrian-4

**Distance** 8.4 km

**Time** 1 hour

## Access

Begin at Cascade Ponds picnic area off the Lake Minnewanka Road just north of Highway 1.

| | |
|---|---|
| 0.0 | trailhead |
| 3.2 | water tower |
| 4.2 | Johnson Lake, retrace tracks |
| 8.4 | end of ride |

# 8 SPRAY LOOP

maps 3, 3A

Spray Loop is a pleasant ride that features the ramparts of Mount Rundle and the lower Spray Valley. It begins at the historic Banff Springs Hotel and finishes at beautiful Bow Falls. An easy ride, this trail is suitable for families and even tot-trailers will travel in style.

From the Banff Springs Hotel ride south on the Spray River fireroad (#14) until you come to a bridge across the river at km 5.9. This is a good spot for a picnic or a break beside the river. Cross the bridge and ride north passing the campsite and some spectacular lower valley views. At km 10.5 you have an option to take the singletrack that descends to the river, then cross a bridge and climb up to the main fireroad near the hotel. But I suggest you just keep cruising on the fireroad through to the golf course, then take a break beside Bow Falls. This is one of Banff's premier attractions and your start point is just up the hill.

**Gentle ride close to town**
**Type** loop on 4WD road
**Rating** easy/novice
**Other users** hikers-4 equestrian-4
**Distance** 12 km
**Time** 1-2 hours
**Map** 82 O/4 Banff
**Season** May through October
**Land agency** Parks Canada

**Access**
The trail begins at the Banff Springs Hotel in Banff. A gated gravel road at the south side of the upper parking lot is the trail.

| | |
|---|---|
| 0.0 | trailhead |
| 5.9 | junction, turn left and cross bridge |
| 6.3 | campground |
| 10.1 | junction with singletrack, keep right |
| 11.3 | golf course |
| 11.6 | Spray River bridge |
| 12.0 | Bow Falls |

# 9 BOW VALLEY BOMBER

maps 3, 3A

Bow Valley Bomber waltzes you away from the urbanized mountain environment of the Banff area. It is a combination of the Sundance bike path, the Healy Creek fireroad and paved roads. The route is perfect for families but be aware that part of the return route is on the shoulder of the busy Trans-Canada Highway.

Cycle past the Cave and Basin historic site and onto the Sundance trail. This paved bicycle path winds alongside the Bow River and Sundance Creek with a stunning view of Mount Bourgeau and Mount Brett to the west.

Turn right onto the Healy Creek fireroad, a gravel road that leaves the Sundance trail at the 2.9 km point. This smooth, needle-covered doubletrack is part of the original access road to Sunshine Village. There is not much in the way of views from the pine forest but the cycling is still pleasant. Watch for the resident beavers in the pond at the east end of the trail.

At the west end of the trail, cross the bridge over Healy Creek, turn right and follow Sunshine Road to the Trans-Canada Highway.

Return to Banff on Highway 1, but watch for a gate in the fence 1.3 km east of the Bow River bridge. Cutting through this gate will get you off the freeway and onto quiet Vermilion Lakes Drive for the final few kilometres to town.

## Options

Cycle the Sundance pathway as a 7.4 km out-and-back trip. This paved path rolls through the pines to a picnic area at the head of the Sundance Canyon trail, a rugged 2.4 km interpretive hike that winds through the sloping limestone slabs beside the creek.

**Family fun near town**

**Type** loop on 2WD and 4WD roads

**Rating** easy/novice

**Other users** hikers-1 equestrian-2 motorized-4

**Distance** 20.3 km (15.5 on pavement)

**Time** 2-3 hours

**Map** 82 O/4 Banff

**Season** May through October

**Land agency** Parks Canada

**Access**

In Banff, begin this ride at the Bow River bridge on Banff Avenue.

| | |
|---|---|
| 0.0 | Bow River bridge, turn right on Cave Avenue |
| 1.6 | Cave and Basin historic site, Sundance trail beyond |
| 4.2 | Turn right onto Healy Creek trail (Sundance Canyon 0.8 km to left) |
| 7.1 | junction, keep right (Brewster Creek trail to left) |
| 9.1 | Healy Creek bridge, Sunshine Road |
| 9.4 | Trans-Canada Hwy., turn right |
| 13.3 | gate through fence to right |
| 20.3 | Bow River bridge in Banff |

# 10 ALLENBY PASS
maps 3, 5

Allenby Pass is a long, physically and technically difficult ride that is very rewarding for strong and skilled riders. Expect to encounter a bit of everything on this trail, including some rough and rocky riding that will pound both you and your bike. Closure of the Bryant Creek trail has turned this into an out-and-back ride and made the rewards a little less substantial than they used to be. My advice is to go only after a run of dry weather. The trail passes two privately owned lodges that could be a worthwhile part of your trip plan; service is available by prior arrangement. Of course, they might prefer you to ride something with four legs rather than two wheels!

The cycling is easy as the route follows the Sundance trail, the Healy Creek fireroad, then the Brewster Creek fireroad as far as Sundance Lodge. Past the lodge the nature of the trip changes as the trail turns to singletrack and becomes rough and

**Hard-core enduro-ride**

**Type** out-and-back on 4WD roads and singletrack

**Rating** extreme/intermediate

**Other users** hikers-3 equestrian-4

**Distance** 73.6 km

**Time** 6-9 hours

**Map** 82 O/4 Banff

**Season** July to mid-October

**Land agency** Parks Canada

**Access**

1) In Banff, begin at Cave and Basin and cycle west on the paved Sundance trail.

2) From the Sunshine interchange on Hwy. 1, drive south for 0.8 km

sometimes very muddy. This is wild and lonely country with the peaks and hills of the Great Divide to the west and the slabs of the Sundance Range to the east. The trail passes the Sundance warden cabin, then Half-Way Lodge on its journey to the middle of nowhere. Beyond Half-Way the trail climbs to the pass on a series of very rocky switchbacks where the view of the valley below will take your breath away (that is if you have any left!). Allenby Pass is a sweeping alpland well above treeline with vistas and temptations in every direction. Enjoy your stop at this remote and exotic spot, but remember to save some energy for the long and arduous trip back to town.

**Options**

Cycling as far as Sundance Lodge or the bridge at km 18.8 offers a very pleasant moderate/intermediate backcountry trip. The lodge is 29 km return from the Cave and Basin trailhead in Banff.

to the trailhead. Cycle 1.9 km east on Healy Creek trail and join the route log at km 5.5. Using this trailhead reduces the length of the trip by 7.2 km.

| | |
|---|---|
| 0.0 | Cave and Basin trailhead |
| 2.6 | junction with Healy Creek trail, turn right |
| 5.5 | junction with Brewster Creek fireroad, turn left (trailhead #2 is to right) |
| 14.4 | Sundance Lodge |
| 15.9 | Fatigue Pass trail to right |
| 18.8 | bridge |
| 26.6 | Sundance warden cabin |
| 31.5 | Half-Way Lodge |
| 36.8 | Allenby Pass |

*Photo: Gerhardt Lepp.*

# 11 CASCADE FIREROAD

map 3

A mere shadow of its former self—this cycling trip follows the southern end of the old Cascade fireroad. The road once extended for 70 km through the front ranges of Banff Park to Ya-Ha-Tinda Ranch on the Red Deer River, but much of it has now been reclaimed. The Cascade Valley is known for its large grizzly bear population and cycling is allowed only as far as Stoney Creek to reduce the chance of conflict with bears. The route leads up a wide forested valley between Cascade Mountain and the Palliser Range where elk and sheep are often seen. No longer in use, the road has a good gravel surface and is an easy ride suitable for families and tot-trailers.

The route climbs over a low summit to avoid the canyon of the Cascade River, then crosses a bridge to a campground and picnic site in a beautiful setting beside the river. It then climbs gently up the valley to the end of the cycle trail at the Stoney Creek bridge, yet another wild and beautiful spot. Return the way you came.

## Options

Cycling this road can give you a head start for hikes to Dormer Pass, Wigmore Creek or Flint's Park.

**Gentle backcountry ride**

**Type** out-and-back on 2WD road

**Rating** easy/novice

**Other users** hikers-1 equestrian-3

**Distance** 30 km

**Time** 2-4 hours

**Maps** 82 O/4 Banff
82 O/5 Castle Mountain

**Season** May through October

**Land agency** Parks Canada

### Access

From Hwy. 1 at the east Banff interchange, drive north on Lake Minnewanka Road for 3.7 km and turn left into the Upper Bankhead parking lot. The trail begins at the kiosk.

| | |
|---|---|
| 0.0 | trailhead |
| 6.5 | Cascade River bridge |
| 15.0 | Stoney Creek |

# 12 LAKE MINNEWANKA
maps 3, 4

Do you like challenging and technical singletrack cycling? This trail is, without a doubt, the best legal singletrack in Banff National Park. The entire route is a narrow, rolling trail with very little elevation gain. The riding is technical and fun. This trip is relatively straightforward from the trailhead to the warden cabin. However, near the east end of Lake Minnewanka and continuing on to Ghost Lakes it gets very rough and pushes the limits of enjoyment for most cyclists.

Begin by cycling past the locked gate, the boat launch and the picnic area. The trail starts as a wide path leading to the bridge across Stewart Canyon, then climbs what turns out to be the only hill of any significance on the route. A somewhat exposed section of trail on a steep scree slope high above the lake produces an eyeful of views. Mounts Inglismaldie, Girouard and Peechee in the Fairholme Range are the prominent peaks across the lake.

There follows some very delightful cycling as the route rolls and winds its way along grassy sidehills and through open forest above the shore. It offers continual variety: stands of Douglas fir, pleasant pebble beaches scattered with driftwood, pine forest with buffaloberry and rocky outwash fans. Parts of the forest were burned in the spring of 1989 in a prescribed fire set by park wardens. As you approach the east end of Lake Minnewanka the trail becomes considerably more difficult, some sections will challenge even the most hard core of riders. As you round the corner the massive opening of Devil's Gap forms the eastern skyline and rolling foothills are visible beyond. This is a good point to take stock of your energy reserves and think about turning back as you are only half way through the ride. Strong riders can continue on to the ford between the Ghost Lakes before turning back.

**Classic ride along lakeshore**

**Type** out-and-back on singletrack

**Rating** difficult/intermediate

**Other users** hikers-3 equestrians-1

**Distance** up to 54.4 km

**Time** 5-8 hours

**Maps** 82 O/6 Lake Minnewanka
82 O/3 Canmore

**Season** May through October

**Land agency** Parks Canada

**Access**
From Hwy. 1 at the east Banff interchange, drive 6 km north on Lake Minnewanka Road to the parking lot on the north side of Minnewanka Dam. Ride through the picnic and boat launching area to the signed trailhead.

16

15

14

10                    20                    27.2

**Options**

Cycle the trail as described and continue east through the spectacular Devil's Gap (#228) to the end of the Ghost River Road. Follow the road east for 16 km to its junction with SR 940 at the Bar Cee Ranch, then continue southeast on SR 940 for another 26 km to its junction with Highway 1A. This 76 km point-to-point ride will guarantee your status as an atomic dog of remote mountain trails.

| | |
|---|---|
| 0.0 | trailhead |
| 2.0 | Stewart Canyon bridge |
| 8.3 | junction, keep right (Aylmer Pass to left) |
| 16.7 | warden cabin |
| 24.0 | east end of lake |
| 26.7 | junction, turn right (left is high water route) |
| 27.2 | ford, time to turn back (Devil's Gap trail across ford) |

*Sidehill singletrack high above Lake Minnewanka.* Photo: Gerhardt Lepp.

# 13 MOUNT SHARK TO GOAT CREEK     map 5

**Scenic cruise in Spray Lakes valley**

**Type** point-to-point on 2WD and 4WD roads and singletrack

**Rating** difficult/novice

**Other users** hikers-2 equestrian-1

**Distance** 40.3 km one way

**Time** 3-5 hours

**Maps** 82 J/14 Spray Lakes Reservoir
82 O/3 Canmore

**Season** May through October

**Land agency** Kananaskis Country, Parks Canada

## Access

**south** Begin this trip at the Mount Shark trailhead. On SR 742, drive 38.8 km south from Canmore or 28.6 km north from Kananaskis Trail. Turn west and go another 5.4 km to the trailhead.

**north** End this trip at the Goat Creek trailhead located on SR 742, 9 km south of Canmore.

| | |
|---|---|
| 0.0 | trailhead |
| 6.0 | junction, keep right (Spray trail to left) |
| 6.5, 6.7 | junctions, keep right (Bryant Creek trail to left) |
| 7.2 | junction, go left |
| 9.6 | Turbulent Creek bridge, canyon |
| 12.1 | junction with Spray River fireroad, keep right (left leads to Banff) |
| 13.8 | cross Canyon Dam |
| 24.6 | gate, motorized vehicles on road |

Hate hills, like scenery? Try this big ride on for size! The Spray Lake sceni-cruiser follows single-track trail and old roads for the entire length of Spray Lake and continues on up the valley to the Goat Creek trailhead just below Whiteman's Gap. You could take a burley and the kids on the section from Mount Shark to the gate at km 24.6.

From the parking lot ride west on the Watridge Lake trail passing to the north of the lake, then descending a long hill to a bridge over the upper Spray River. This section of trail deeks in and out of Banff National Park as it winds around the end of Spray Lake, crosses Bryant Creek bridge and comes to a major trail junction. Keep to the right and follow the wide trail alongside Spray Lake. The views just keep on coming at you, Turbine Mountain, Kananaskis Range and the Spray Mountains. Check out the canyon and waterfall at Turbulent Creek before continuing on to the junction with the Spray fireroad. Pay attention here and be sure to take the right-hand trail that climbs up the hill. Soon you will cross Canyon Dam, the structure that creates this huge reservoir, and follow along a restricted access road with no cars—yahoo! More of the same old stuff—big lake, views, easy rolling.

Past the gate at km 24.6 you will have to share the road with cars until you leave the road at the Spray Lakes Dam. Cross through the gravel pit and ride along a sometimes marshy doubletrack, it's the one bit of adversity on the trip and soon ends at a good quality former logging road. Roll through the logged forest featuring more views of the Spray Valley, Ha Ling Peak and Whiteman's Gap. Soon you will come to the Goat Creek pumphouse, go downstream to a bridge and cross the creek. From here ride up the meadow to the pond, keep left and climb up to the Goat Creek trail, then head right to the parking lot.

**Options**

Haven't had enough? You could follow Goat Creek trail through to Banff or you could ride on SR 742 through Whiteman's Gap and down to Canmore.

| | |
|---|---|
| 29.1 | pass Spray Lakes Dam, keep left (right leads to SR 742) |
| 30.5 | through gravel pit and onto doubletrack under powerline |
| 32.2 | another dam, keep left on old logging road (right leads to SR 742) |
| 38.4 | Goat Creek and pumphouse, go downstream |
| 38.7 | bridge, ride up through meadow |
| 38.9 | ride across berm to left of pond<br>follow singletrack up hill |
| 39.3 | junction with Goat Creek trail, turn right (left leads to Banff) |
| 40.3 | Goat Creek parking lot |

# 14 SPRAY RIVER FIREROAD                    maps 3, 5

As we go to press this trail is closed to the public through November 1999 to permit undisturbed study of grizzly bears. The closure extends from Goat Creek junction south to the park boundary. Given the precedent of the Bryant Creek closure I don't expect it to ever re-open to bikes, although Parks could easily implement a partial opening based on a quota system. I've left it in just in case they do that.

This is fireroad cruising at its finest. The Spray River fireroad provides easy riding on what was formerly a gravel road from the Banff Springs Hotel to the Spray Lakes Reservoir. No longer used by vehicles, the road is being allowed to revert to trail status. It follows alongside the Spray River in the bottom of a major valley and links with a number of other trails, giving you the chance to customize your ride. Campsites along the route provide the option of an overnight trip.

**Scenic backcountry cruiser**

**Type** point-to-point on 4WD road

**Rating** difficult/novice

**Other users** hikers-1 equestrian-1

**Distance** 51.5 km one way

**Time** 4-7 hours

**Maps** 82 O/4 Banff
82 J/14 Spray Lakes Reservoir
82 O/3 Canmore

**Season** June to mid-October

**Land agency** Parks Canada

**Access**

**north** The trail begins at the Banff Springs Hotel in Banff. A gated gravel road at the south side of the upper parking lot is the trail.

From the north trailhead the road follows the Spray River through mature spruce forest below Mount Rundle. A bridge at km 5.9 is the turn around point for the Spray Loop; at km 10.0 the Goat Creek trail forks to the east. A short distance later the fireroad bends to the west to follow the river through a gap between Sulphur Mountain and the Goat Range.

This upper part of the valley is wild country bounded by the ridges of the Goat Range to the east and the peaks of the Sundance Range to the west. Watch for washed-out bridges and parts of the road as this section gets little maintenance. South of Fortune Camp wide gravel flats along the river provide views south to Mount Shark and Tent Ridge. Several avalanche paths cross the road shortly before it crosses the park boundary and meets the Mount Shark to Goat Creek trail. Option 1 turns left here. (If you are travelling south to north this unmarked junction in the middle of a hill is easy to miss.) The route to the Mount Shark trailhead follows the track to the right. Cycle west along the shore of Spray Lake and turn left at the junction with the Bryant Creek trail. Follow this singletrack for 0.7 km, then turn left again, crossing a bridge over the Spray River. An ever improving gravel trail leads the final 6 km to the trailhead. Although it may sound confusing, this route is well signed and easy to follow.

**Options**

Spray Lakes Campground. Join the route log of the Mount Shark to Goat Creek ride (#13) at km 12.1 and follow it through to the gate and campground at km 24.6.

A long 84.6 km loop trip can be made in conjunction with Mount Shark to Goat Creek (#13) and Goat Creek (#15).

**south**  Begin this trip at the Mount Shark trailhead. On SR 742, drive 38.8 km south from Canmore or 28.6 km north from Kananaskis Trail. Turn west and go another 5.4 km to the trailhead.

| | |
|---|---|
| 0.0 | north trailhead |
| 5.9 | Spray Loop trail joins from left |
| 10.0 | Goat Creek trail to left |
| 39.1 | junction, keep right (Spray Lakes West Road to left [#14]) |
| 44.6 | junction, keep left (Bryant Creek trail to right) |
| 44.8 | junction, keep left (Bryant Creek trail to right) |
| 45.5 | junction, keep left and cross bridge |
| 51.5 | Mount Shark trailhead |

# 15 GOAT CREEK TRAIL
maps 3, 5

The Goat Creek trail is a very pleasant way to travel from Canmore to Banff. It's a perfect outing for families providing a car shuttle can be arranged, and even burleys can travel this trail in comfort. This trail is a good ride in either direction or as an out-and-back from either trailhead. Many riders choose to begin in Canmore and cycle through Whiteman's Gap to the trailhead.

The trail is a smooth, dirt and gravel doubletrack that can be cycled slow and leisurely or, as some riders seem to prefer, a time trial course. Either way, watch out for other users and a couple of tricky corners and bridges.

The trail rolls gently through pine and spruce forest as it follows along Goat Creek between the crags of Mount Rundle and the wooded ridges of the Goat Range. The Goat Creek trail ends with a bridged crossing of the Spray River near the junction with the Spray River fireroad. Turn right and follow the fireroad to Banff. Be prepared for a touch of culture shock when your quiet roll in the woods ends in a very busy hotel parking lot!

## Options

1. Make a loop by returning on the Trans-Canada Highway from Banff to Canmore (58.2 km).

2. Make a 48.4 km loop with the Rundle Riverside trail (#16) and SR 742.

**Family fun on gentle trail**

**Type** point-to-point on 4WD roads

**Rating** moderate/novice

**Other users** hikers-4 equestrian-2

**Distance** 19.2 km one way

**Time** 1-3 hours

**Maps** 82 O/3 Canmore
82 O/4 Banff

**Season** June to mid-October

**Land agency** Kananaskis Country
Parks Canada

**Access**

**east** From the Bow River bridge in Canmore follow SR 742 for 9.0 km to trailhead on the west side of the road, just beyond Whiteman's Gap.

**west** Begin at Banff Springs Hotel.

| | |
|---|---|
| 0.0 | Goat Creek trailhead |
| 1.0 | Park boundary |
| 9.2 | Spray fireroad, turn right |
| 13.3 | junction, go right to golf course or left to Banff Springs Hotel |
| 19.2 | Spray River bridge by golf course or hotel |

2  4  6  8  10  12  14  16  18 19.2

# 16 RUNDLE RIVERSIDE & BANFF TRAILS          maps 3, 3A, 5

The Rundle Riverside trail runs from the Banff Springs Golf Course to the park boundary and is considerably more hard-core than most people expect with lots of roots and rocks and steep little ups and downs. Many folks get sucked in because the Banff Trail, which runs from the park boundary through the Canmore Nordic Centre, is smooth and easy.

Beginning at the Spray River bridge, follow the golf course road, take the fork to the right, then watch carefully for the unsigned trailhead kiosk in the trees on the right. This marks the start of the Rundle Riverside trail. If you like technical singletrack, this trail will leave a smile on your face. It's rough, rocky and rooty throughout, but don't be surprised if you encounter a misguided family or someone on a go-to-market style bike struggling along the trail. Past the national park boundary the trail climbs up a hill and joins the Banff Trail (#17A), an easy gravel road that leads through the Canmore Nordic Centre trail network to the day lodge. From the lodge you can make a fast descent to town on a singletrack known as the Canmore trail (#17I), or you can follow the paved road.

## Options

This trail can be combined with the Goat Creek trail (#15) and SR 742 to make a Mount Rundle loop ride of 48.4 km.

**Rugged ride from Banff to Canmore**

**Type** point-to-point on 2WD roads and singletrack

**Rating** moderate/intermediate

**Other users** hikers-1

**Distance** 18.5 km (4.3 km on pavement) one way

**Time** 1-2 hours

**Map** 82 O/3 Canmore

**Season** June to mid-October

**Land agency** Parks Canada, Kananaskis Country

**Access**

**west** In Banff cycle the road that leads past Bow Falls to the Banff Springs Golf Course.

**east** In Canmore follow the paved road to the Canmore Nordic Centre.

| | |
|---|---|
| 0.0 | Spray River bridge in Banff |
| 2.9 | golf course loop road forks, keep right |
| 4.3 | turn right onto Rundle Riverside trail |
| 12.5 | Park boundary |
| 12.9 | gravel "Banff Trail" begins |
| 18.5 | Canmore Nordic Centre day lodge |

# 17 CANMORE NORDIC CENTRE

map 5

Photo: John Gibson.

Canmore Nordic Centre is a premier cross-country ski area in winter and it is rapidly becoming the best network of mountain bike trails in the Bow Valley. The centre includes parking, day lodge with restaurant, lockers and showers, and nearby Trail Sports offers bicycle rentals. Those who cycle up to the centre will be rewarded by an exciting singletrack descent back to town.

The centre includes numerous cross-country ski trails offering moderately strenuous mountain bike riding suitable for novices and families, even tot-trailers will work on these trails. All of these trails have something to offer, some of the best are described below.

In addition to the ski trails, the Nordic Centre boasts many fine singletrack trails built specifically for mountain bike races. These challenging and exciting trails will leave you pumped and screaming for more! The race trails are not easy and are not suitable for novices. The race courses vary from year to year but the featured courses are perennial favourites that link up most of the singletrack. To date the individual singletrack trail segments are rarely named and are not signed

**Mountain bike playground**
**Other users** hikers-2
**Map** Canmore Nordic Centre Summer Trails brochure
**Season** May through October
**Land agency** Kananaskis Country

**Access**
From Canmore follow SR 742 for 3 km to the Nordic Centre. All trails begin at the day lodge.

making them difficult to locate even with the course maps. Races are held throughout the summer and the courses are marked shortly before race day.

With so many trails in a small area it is easy to get confused. Almost all of the ski trail junctions are numbered and numbers are shown on the trail map available at the day lodge as well as on several large signs on site. Remember that the site is bounded below by the river, above by Mount Rundle, and that the day lodge is located at the east end of the site (to the right as you look down to the river). Once you are able to recognize the Banff Trail, which runs the full length of the site at a mid-elevation, you will be well on your way to unlocking the secrets of this area's trails.

*Skull Mountain (#17F).*
Photo: Gillean Daffern.

# 17A BANFF TRAIL

map 5A

An easy riding gravel road that crosses the Nordic Centre from east to west, the Banff Trail never gets muddy. Banff Trail offers easy access to the lower trails and an easy bailout when you get tired or confused while riding the other trails. Many folks ride to Banff by following this trail to its western extremity where it meets the Rundle Riverside trail (#16) and enters Banff National Park. Note that the Rundle trail is rough and rooty, not easy riding and not suitable for novices.

**Family fun on gentle trail**

**Type** out-and-back on ski trail

**Rating** easy/novice

**Distance** 11 km

**Time** 1-2 hours

0.0     day lodge

2.5     rehabilitated strip mine, great views

5.5     Banff Trail ends, Rundle trail begins, time to retrace your tracks

# 17B GEORGETOWN TRAIL

maps 5A, 5B

Now a ghost town with only a few foundations remaining on site, Georgetown was an active coal mining village during the years 1890-1916. This ride is on a wide doubletrack with lots of interpretive markers to enhance your understanding of the history of the area. Ride west on the Banff Trail, then descend along ski trails to the signed trail. A steep downhill leads to Georgetown with ruins and views to entertain you. Roll east out of town on the old railgrade, then climb up to a bench and roll east to the Canmore trail. Climb up to the day lodge.

**Gentle ride to ghost town**

**Type** loop on 4WD road and ski trail

**Rating** easy/novice

**Distance** 6.3 km

**Time** 1-2 hours

0.0     day lodge, ride out on Banff Trail

1.5     jct. 31, leave Banff Trail and veer right

1.7     jct. 30, turn right down hill

1.8     jct. 29, Georgetown sign, go straight—trail descends steep hill

2.4     ruins, trail junction, turn right and descend

2.5     Georgetown flats, keep right

4.3     junction, go left (right leads 1.7 km to day lodge)

5.0     junction, go right, up hill (left continues 0.5 km to join Three Sisters Drive in Canmore)

5.1     Canmore trail, turn right, up hill

5.5     junction, sign for day lodge, go straight

6.3     day lodge

## 17C  2.5 KM RECREATIONAL TRAIL

Nordic Centre map

Follow the blue arrows and you can't get lost. This trail has lots of steep hills and fast corners to entertain you.

**Aerobic challenge**
**Type** loop on ski trail
**Rating** easy/novice
**Distance** 2.5 km
**Time** 0.5 hour

## 17D  5 KM RECREATIONAL TRAIL

Nordic Centre map

Follow the red arrows. This trail is more fun than the 2.5 with lots of hills and corners as well as some good views of the valley.

**Aerobic challenge**
**Type** loop on ski trail
**Rating** easy/novice
**Distance** 5 km
**Time** 0.5-1 hour

## 17E  10 KM RECREATIONAL TRAIL

Nordic Centre map

Let the yellow arrows guide you around this calorie burner. With lots of fast hills and corners and long enough for a good workout, this trail will put you through your paces.

**Aerobic challenge**
**Type** loop ski trail
**Rating** moderate/novice
**Distance** 10 km
**Time** 1-2 hours

## 17F  CANADA CUP RACE COURSE

map 5C

Canada Cup is a series of seven races held at various locations across the country. The course heads west from the day lodge into the hills above the Banff Trail, then crosses and returns below it. Terminator, Skull and The Gorge are technical highlights of this course.

**Technical delight**
**Type** loop on ski trails and singletrack
**Rating** moderate/advanced
**Distance** 8.8 km
**Time** 0.5-1 hour

## 17G  WORLD CUP RACE COURSE                    map 5D

Developed for the 1998 World Cup Race #6, this course makes a figure eight above and below the day lodge. Featuring Nectar Noodle, the Chute and Devonian Drop, this course challenged the best riders in the world and they responded with times as quick as 28 minutes per lap.

**Technical delight**

**Type** loop on ski trails and singletrack

**Rating** moderate/advanced

**Distance** 8 km

**Time** 0.5-1 hour

## 17H  KILLER B'S RACE COURSE                    map 5E

Killer B's is a local race that climbs steeply above the day lodge before dropping through the Nectar Noodle and Coal Chutes to Georgetown, then climbing back up again.

**Technical delight**

**Type** loop on ski trails and singletrack

**Rating** moderate/advanced

**Distance** 10.4 km

**Time** 0.5-1 hour

## 17I  CANMORE TRAIL                             map 5A

This trail is the fastest way from the Nordic Centre to downtown Canmore. Begin at the Canmore trail sign at junction 1 near the east end of the Biathlon area and follow the signs downhill. Stay on the main track past a dramatic valley viewpoint until you can see the powerhouse below you. At this point core riders can play on the sketchy sidehill, others have a choice of the stairs or contouring around to the end of Three Sisters Drive.

**Short connector trail**

**Type** point-to-point on 4WD road and singletrack

**Rating** easy/intermediate

**Distance** 3.5 km

**Time** 0.5 hour

# 18 CANALSIDE TO QUARRY LAKE    map 5A

Eye-popping views on an easy trail, this is a good ride for the whole family and makes an excellent evening excursion.

Beginning at the gate, follow the dike alongside the TransAlta canal. The trail is flat and the views are amazing in all directions. The East End of Rundle, Egahay Nakoda and the Three Sisters tower overhead and the peaks of the Fairholme Range form the northeastern skyline. After crossing over a small spillway the trail climbs up to the powerline. Turn left and follow the easy downhill doubletrack under the powerline. Where the trail dips into a (usually dry) creekbed turn left and follow the trail down and across a grassy meadow to Quarry Lake. This is the local swimming hole and is the perfect place for a picnic and a swim to wrap up your ride.

**Family fun on gentle trail**

**Type** point-to-point on 4WD roads

**Rating** easy/novice

**Other users** hikers-3

**Distance** 5.2 km

**Time** 1 hour

**Map** 82/3 Canmore

**Season** May through October

**Land agency** Town of Canmore, private

**Access**

Park at Quarry Lake, just off of SR 742, 1.6 km south of Canmore or ride up from town.

| | |
|---|---|
| 0.0 | parking lot, ride up SR742 |
| 0.9 | gate beside canal, turn left |
| 3.1 | junction with powerline trail, turn left (right leads to powerhouse and TransAlta subdivision) |
| 4.4 | keep left into dry creekbed |
| 4.6 | junction, turn left |
| 5.0 | Quarry Lake |
| 5.2 | parking lot, end of ride |

Photo: Cécile Lafleur.

# 19 SOUL BROTHER

Photo: John Gibson.

The benchland trails offer some of Canmore's most scenic riding and the Soul Bro is one of the best. Once in the category of secret trails, the cat is now out of the bag so to speak, and these trails see a lot of use and abuse.

The benchlands are terraces on the side of the Fairholme Range and extend from east of the Alpine Club of Canada Clubhouse through to the Banff Park boundary. There are networks of trails to explore throughout this area, the Soul Bro is just a sampler to get you started. The key words are exploration, courtesy to others and sensitivity to the environment. Notice the little technical bits and tight corners that made this ride one of the best, and notice how they have all been cut off or bypassed by those who are incapable of riding them. If you'd rather have a straight trail with no technical riding—then stay the hell on the highway, you'll find it perfect.

The future of these trails is uncertain, the town has zoned the entire area as conservation land for use as a wildlife corridor; golf courses are allowed but mountain biking and hiking? In addition any of the land not within the conservation zoning is

**Scenic singletrack treats**

**Type** loop on singletrack

**Rating** moderate/intermediate

**Other users** hikers-4 equestrian-1

**Distance** 9.8 km

**Time** 1 hour

**Map** 82/3 Canmore

**Season** May through October

**Land agency** Town of Canmore

**Access**
In Canmore begin at the Cougar Creek trailhead at the top of Elk Run Blvd.

| | |
|---|---|
| 0.0 | trailhead |
| 1.0 | take left fork and climb steep hill |
| 1.2 | junction, stay right and up hill (left = explore) |

subject to development—many a local rider has seen favourite trails disappear under housing tracts and golf courses. I hope the irony of this doesn't escape you—develop the hell out of the place, then tell people to go elsewhere for recreation, the environment is too fragile.

Enough ranting!

Begin by riding alongside Cougar Creek, then veer left to climb and push up onto the actual benches. Once the trail forks left the angle of climb becomes more relaxed and you get an opportunity to appreciate the open forest and scenic qualities of this ride. The high point of the ride features expansive views of the Bow Valley, well worth a bit of your time. The remainder of the trail is flat or downhill—woo hoo!

The trail stays high on the bench and enters the forest before turning sharply and heading for the valley below. There are lots of junctions and side trails to explore, intentionally or otherwise, fun and good riding no matter what. Just remember home is downhill. If you manage to follow the route log successfully you'll come out on the lowest bench just above the Trans-Canada Highway. This section of trail along a grassy ridge graced with Douglas fir and aspen is one of the best, but the finale is a rather sketchy gravel downhill. Once across the Silvertip Road, climb a sidehill singletrack to get above the hoodoos and continue on a good gravel trail that parallels the road back to the start point.

| | |
|---|---|
| 1.2 | junction, turn left |
| 1.5 | junction, keep right (left = explore) |
| 2.8 | top of climb, great views |
| 3.1 | junction, keep right (left = explore) |
| 4.3 | junction, turn left and descend (right = explore) |
| 4.5 | junction, go left (right = explore) |
| 5.0 | junction, go right |
| 6.0 | junction, go right |
| 6.6 | four-way junction, go straight through and up hill onto ridge above Trans-Canada Highway |
| 8.1 | junction, go left, sketchy downhill |
| 8.2 | cross Silvertip Road, take singletrack up and to right |
| 9.4 | cross Benchlands Terrace |
| 9.8 | end of ride |

# 20 POCATERRA-WHISKEYJACK LOOP                    map 10

*Kananaskis Lookout (#21).*

This ride climbs into the hills on the Pocaterra and Whiskeyjack trails and returns on the paved Wheeler and Lodgepole bicycle paths. The route links a variety of trails to provide an opportunity to explore some beautiful country. All junctions are well signed and the creek crossings are bridged. This and other trails in the area are shown on a detailed map available at the visitor centre.

The Pocaterra trail is a splendid ride through meadows and alongside the creek featuring dramatic views of Mount Wintour and the Opal Range to the east. Most of the trail is a smooth old road. The trail skirts a canyon and climbs up rideable grades to its high point.

At km 9.8 turn right onto the Whiskeyjack trail. You'll need good braking skills for this steep and sometimes rough descent that leads to Boulton Campground and on to the parking lot by the trading post.

The return trip is on the paved Wheeler and Lodgepole bicycle paths, which provide enjoyable cycling through pine forest along the valley floor. They are all signed, but can be a tad confusing where they wander through the Boulton and Elkwood campgrounds. Be forewarned, these bicycle paths are popular, even crowded and are frequently used by inexperienced cyclists.

**Rugged backcountry ride**

**Type** loop on 4WD road and paved bike path

**Rating** moderate/intermediate

**Other users** hikers-3

**Distance** 25 km (10.7 on pavement)

**Time** 2-5 hours

**Map** 82 J/11 Kananaskis Lakes

**Season** July to mid-October

**Land agency** Alberta Provincial Parks

### Access

The trailhead is located at Pocaterra Hut near the intersection of SR 742 and Kananaskis Lakes Road. The trail is a doubletrack southeast of the hut.

| | |
|---|---|
| 0.0 | Pocaterra trailhead |
| 1.2 | group camp area |
| 8.3 | junction, keep right (left goes to Hwy. 40) |
| 9.8 | junction with Whiskeyjack trail, keep right (left is Kananaskis Lookout trail) |
| 14.3 | Boulton Campground, turn right onto Wheeler bike path |
| 19.2 | cross highway |
| 23.7 | highway and visitor centre, turn left |
| 25.0 | Pocaterra trailhead |

# 21 KANANASKIS FIRE LOOKOUT                    map 10

If you like identifying peaks then this is the perfect trip for you; the Kananaskis Fire Lookout provides a panoramic view of the mountains and valleys of Peter Lougheed Provincial Park. The cycling is cruiser-style riding with a fair bit of elevation gain and loss. The route follows the Pocaterra trail, climbs to the Kananaskis Fire Lookout, and returns on the Elk Pass, Lakeside, Wheeler and Lodgepole trails.

Cycle up the Pocaterra trail (#20) and just keep right on climbing up the Kananaskis Fire Lookout access road, also known as the Lookout trail. You'll need to push a seriously low gear to get those fat tires to roll up to the lookout. With peaks from the Italian group, the British and French Military groups, and the Royal group, this spot is a peak-namer's dream come true. When you've had enough, it's time to choose between coasting back down the smooth road the way you came up or continuing around the loop.

Continue onward by rolling down the rough track that leads south to Elk Pass and joins the Hydroline trail (see #22), a smooth dirt road under the powerline. It drops into the steep valley of Fox Creek, joins the Elk Pass trail, then climbs out of the valley and provides a smooth descent to the Elk Pass trailhead.

You can return to your starting point on the highway or follow a series of paved bike paths. To get to the bike path cycle west (left) on the pavement of Kananaskis Lakes Road to the Lakeside trail at the Mount Sarrail trailhead. This trail meanders through mature pine forest along Lower Kananaskis Lake, passes through the Lower Lake campground and climbs up to Boulton Campground. Follow Wheeler and Lodgepole bike paths back to Pocaterra Hut.

**Classic ride with lots of vertical and good views**

**Type** loop on 4WD roads, singletrack and paved bike path

**Rating** difficult/intermediate

**Other users** hikers-2

**Distance** 35.4 km (16.5 km on pavement)

**Time** 3-5 hours

**Map** 82 J/11 Kananaskis Lakes

**Season** July to mid-October

**Land agency** Alberta Provincial Parks

**Access**
The trailhead is located at Pocaterra Hut near the intersection of SR 742 and Kananaskis Lakes Road. The trail is a doubletrack southeast of the hut.

| | |
|---|---|
| 0.0 | Pocaterra trailhead |
| 8.3 | junction, keep right |
| 9.8 | junction, keep left (right is Whiskeyjack trail) |
| 12.1 | Kananaskis Fire Lookout |
| 15.5 | junction with Hydroline trail, turn right |
| 16.8 | junction, keep right (left is Elk Pass trail) |
| 18.9 | Kananaskis Lakes Trail (road), turn left to reach bike path |
| 19.7 | turn right onto lakeside bike path |
| 24.7 | cross highway and follow Wheeler bike path to left |
| 29.6 | cross highway |
| 34.1 | highway and visitor centre, turn left |
| 35.4 | Pocaterra trailhead |

# 22 ELK PASS & ELK LAKES PROVINCIAL PARK   map 10

This ride is an outstanding Rockies bike 'n' hike that takes you from the Kananaskis Lakes area over Elk Pass to Elk Lakes Provincial Park in British Columbia and some spectacular hiking. Elk Pass is a low break in the Continental Divide that was considered along with Kicking Horse Pass as a route for the Canadian Pacific Railway. Moose, elk and bears are common here even though they are seldom seen.

Power your way up the smooth dirt road as it climbs through spruce and pine forest. The road passes under the powerline and drops steeply to the bridge over Fox Creek and a trail junction. Hydroline trail to the left offers an easier climb to the pass, while Elk Pass trail to the right provides a more interesting route along Fox Creek, although the upper part of it has a loose surface harder to pedal along. Since the two routes join at the summit of the pass, a good option is to cycle up the smoother Hydroline and return on the more interesting Elk Pass trail.

Cross over the broad summit and race down the powerline road to the large meadow at the end of Elk Lakes Pass Road. It's a short distance to the park trailhead.

## Options

1. Elk Lakes. An 8.4 km hiking trail, closed to cycling, leads past Lower and Upper Elk lakes and along gravel flats to spectacular Petain Falls.

2. Elk Lakes Pass Road. This gravel road can be used to make several extended cycling trips, including loops with Weary Creek Gap and Fording River Pass.

**Bike 'n' hike to Elk Lakes**

**Type** out-and-back on 4WD road

**Rating** difficult/novice

**Other users** hikers-4

**Distance** 19.4 km

**Time** 4-6 hours

**Map** 82 J/11 Kananaskis Lakes

**Season** July to mid-October

**Land agency** Alberta Provincial Parks, BC Forest Service, BC Provincial Parks

**Access**

**north** On Hwy. 40, drive 50.4 km south from Hwy. 1, then go 11.5 km west on Kananaskis Lakes Road.

**south** Drive north on Hwy. 43 from Sparwood to Elkford and continue on the gravel Elk Lakes Pass Road for 87 km to the end of the road at Elk Lakes Provincial Park.

| | |
|---|---|
| 0.0 | trailhead |
| 2.1 | junction, keep left for Hydroline trail (right is Elk Pass trail) |
| 3.4 | junction, keep right (left leads to Kananaskis Lookout) |
| 5.1 | Elk Pass, junction, keep left (Elk Pass trail joins from right) |
| 9.6 | Elk Valley Road, turn right |
| 9.7 | Elk Lakes Provincial Park boundary |

# 23 SKOGAN PASS

map 6

Skogan Pass is a big dog sort of ride that works best in combination with Jewell Pass, but can be done on its own with a car shuttle. It's an exciting ride that links the resort area at Ribbon Creek with the Bow Valley near Canmore. The doubletrack over the pass was built to access the powerline, although very little of it actually follows the powerline right-of-way. Skogan Pass was named by Don Gardner, designer of the Ribbon Creek and Canmore Nordic Centre cross-country ski trails. It is a Norwegian word meaning a magic forest with elves and trolls.

Begin the ride by climbing up the cross-country ski trails on a gravel track that passes below the Nakiska Ski Area. Stay right at the road junction at Marmot Creek. When the trail intersects the powerline you have the option of a side trip to the viewpoint on Hummingbird Plume Hill. The main trail keeps climbing along the powerline with lots of views and wanders through pine forest and cutblocks. The open fir forest carpeted with grouseberries makes the summit area one of the more appealing parts of the ride. Be sure to take the right-hand fork at the pass.

**Rugged ride over high pass**

**Type** point-to point on 4WD roads

**Rating** difficult/intermediate

**Other users** hikers-2

**Distance** 18.6 km one way

**Time** 2-4 hours

**Maps** 82 O/3 Canmore
82 J/14 Spray Lakes Reservoir

**Season** mid-June to mid-October

**Land agency** Kananaskis Country

**Access**

**south**  On Hwy. 40, drive 23 km south from Hwy. 1 to the Ribbon Creek recreation area. The trailhead is 1 km west on the right side of the road.

**north**  From the Deadman Flats interchange on the Trans-Canada Hwy., drive south for 1.5 km to a parking lot near the Alpine Resort Haven. The trail follows a dirt road south to the powerline.

The north side of the pass provides a seemingly endless downhill ride—a fitting reward for all the climbing on the way up. Hillside meadows below the pass present a striking view of the Three Sisters and the peaks of the Bow Valley. The pace is fast and furious as you negotiate tight corners and rocky sections. Watch out for a few rolls in the trail, which, at high speeds, can mean way too much air. Keep an eye out for the short connecting road to the resort at Pigeon Mountain.

## Options

An outstanding loop trip of 50 km can be made by combining this ride with Jewell Pass (#27) and Stoney trail (#29). Put this loop on your "must ride" list.

| | |
|---|---|
| 0.0 | south trailhead, trail is to left, up the hill |
| 0.4 | junction with Skogan Pass trail, turn right |
| 1.7 | cross Ruthie's trail |
| 2.6 | keep right on road |
| 2.7 | junction, turn right |
| 3.0 | junction, keep right (Marmot Basin road to left) |
| 4.3 | powerline, keep left (Stoney trail to right, Hummingbird Plume Lookout straight) |
| 6.5 | junction, keep right |
| 7.0 | powerline |
| 8.0 | four-way junction, go straight (slightly left of powerline) |
| 8.3 | gate |
| 10.3 | junction, keep right |
| 10.3 | Skogan Pass |
| 12.6 | trail to Pigeon Mountain to right |
| 15.0 | trail rejoins powerline |
| 18.3 | four-way junction, turn right |
| 18.6 | north trailhead |

*Spring sunshine on Terrace trail. Mount Kidd in the background.*

# 24 EVAN-THOMAS BIKE PATH & TERRACE TRAIL    map 6

The paved Evan-Thomas bicycle path and the Terrace trail can be combined with a short section of Highway 40 to make a pleasant valley-bottom ride.

The Evan-Thomas bike path (easy/novice) can be very busy and attracts some *extremely* inexperienced cyclists. Expect the unexpected, including kids, pets and trailers. One of the few truly easy rides, the trail is a paved path winding through very scenic meadows and pine forest. It passes Kananaskis Golf Course and the Mount Kidd Recreational Vehicle Park and ends at Wedge Pond, a small lake and popular picnic spot. This is the point where families and inexperienced riders should turn back.

Those with intermediate cycling skills can continue around the loop by riding south on Hwy. 40 to the Galatea trailhead and return on the Terrace trail along the west side of the valley. This moderate/intermediate trail is a generally smooth singletrack of dirt and gravel with lots of tight winding corners that offer exciting riding. Given the limited visibility, you'll need to keep an eye out for hikers and cyclists who frequent this trail and may be difficult to spot.

From the Galatea trailhead, cross the suspension bridge over the Kananaskis River, then turn right at the junction. The trail follows the edge of a terrace on the west side of the river offering a good view of the Kananaskis Valley. You can see duffers on the golf course where the white sand traps, manicured green grass and water traps contrast with the wild tangle of the beaver ponds. The Wedge, Limestone Mountain, Fisher Peak and Mount McDougall create spectacular views to the east while the folded ramparts of Mount Kidd tower overhead. The singletrack trail ends at the Ribbon Creek Alpine Village where a paved cycle path descends to the Ribbon Creek trailhead.

**Family fun and singletrack treats**

**Type** loop on paved bike path and singletrack

**Rating** moderate/intermediate

**Other users** hikers-4
casual cyclists-8

**Distance** 23.3 km (15.6 km on pavement)

**Time** 2-3 hours

**Map** 82 J/14 Spray Lakes Reservoir

**Season** mid-May to mid-October

**Land agency** Kananaskis Country

**Access**

**north** On Hwy. 40, drive 23 km south from Hwy. 1 to the Ribbon Creek recreation area. Drive 1.6 km west to the Ribbon Creek trailhead.

**south** Galatea trailhead is on the west side of Hwy. 40, 33 km south of Hwy. 1.

| | |
|---|---|
| 0.0 | north trailhead |
| 1.1 | bridge |
| 7.8 | cross Hwy. 40 |
| 9.0 | Wedge Pond picnic area for loop, ride south on Hwy. 40 |
| 12.3 | Galatea trailhead |
| 12.8 | junction, turn right |
| 20.0 | paved trail begins, Ribbon Creek Village |
| 20.8 | paved trail crosses village road |
| 23.0 | cross Ribbon Creek, ride upstream |
| 23.3 | end of ride |

# 25 EVAN-THOMAS CREEK                          map 6

**Wilderness explorer**

**Type** out-and-back on 4WD roads
**Rating** difficult/intermediate
**Other users** hikers-2  equestrian-3
**Distance** 30 km
**Time** 4-6 hours
**Map** 82 J/14 Spray Lakes Reservoir
**Season** July to mid-October
**Land agency** Kananaskis Country

**Access**
On Hwy. 40, drive south from Hwy. 1 for 27 km to the Evan-Thomas Creek trailhead.

| | |
|---|---|
| 0.0 | trailhead |
| 9.0 | junction, keep left (Rocky Creek to right) |
| 15.0 | Evan-Thomas Pass |

This trail is an old exploration road that climbs from the Kananaskis Valley to Evan-Thomas Pass. It is a popular horse trail used by the local outfitter for day and overnight rides.

The first 9 km offers good cycling on a doubletrack trail through open country with lots of views. The remainder of the trip to the pass is much more challenging with the road becoming narrow, rough and frequently wet. Willow thickets, washed-out road, a wayward creek and boggy ground alternate with better sections of road.

If you persevere, you'll find the pass to be a pretty place with open subalpine meadows surrounded by limestone peaks.

## Options

Hard-core backcountry explorers can continue on to the Elbow River. The road on the north side of the pass fades out and a steep and rugged trail continues on for 7 km to the Little Elbow River where it joins the Elbow trail (#51) for the final 12 km to Little Elbow Campground.

# 26 BALDY PASS

The Baldy Pass loop is a good hard-core spin. Easy graded old roads and a bit of singletrack take you up to the pass where the real action awaits. The descent is steep and frequently off-camber with lots of rocks and roots, not to mention hikers.

Begin by winding your way through the Field Station and take a right on the Baldy Pass trail. This old doubletrack climbs gently into the basin back of Baldy Mountain. Watch carefully for the junction at km 8.3. The trail gets narrower and passes some decks of rotting logs that date back to the days of World War II when the Field Station was a camp for German prisoners of war. Eventually the trail becomes an action-packed singletrack and climbs onto a windswept ridge above Baldy Pass. The transition of trees across the rocky pass shows their reaction to microclimates; pine and spruce form a typical subalpine forest on the west side, whitebark pine occupies the rocky windswept ridge and subalpine fir grows on the cooler east side of the pass.

This descent is one of the best but if the thought of advanced level singletrack scares you then it is best to turn back now. Let's ride! Drop down the scree to the summit of the pass, then plunge into the valley. Off-camber trail and lots of roots make this trail very tricky in wet weather. It's all rideable and very exciting and, if you stop for a minute, there are some great views too! Low down the trail splits, keep right and race onward until you come to Highway 40. A short roll on pavement takes you past Barrier Lake and back to the trailhead.

## Technical delights

**Type** loop on 4WD roads and singletrack

**Rating** moderate/advanced

**Other users** hikers-5

**Distance** 20.2 km (5.7 km on pavement)

**Time** 2-3 hours

**Maps** 82 O/3 Canmore
82 J/14 Spray Lakes Reservoir

**Season** mid-June to mid-October

**Land agency** Kananaskis Country

## Access

Park at the Colonel's Cabin parking lot at the University of Calgary Field Station on Hwy. 40, 9.1 km south of Hwy. 1.

| | |
|---|---|
| 0.0 | trailhead, follow gravel road to east of building |
| 1.2 | junction, turn right (left is Lusk Creek trail) |
| 4.7 | junction, keep right (left to Lusk Creek) |
| 8.3 | junction, turn right |
| 10.4 | trail crests ridge |
| 10.5 | Baldy Pass |
| 13.8 | junction, keep right |
| 14.5 | Highway 40, turn right |
| 20.0 | turn right into Field Station |
| 20.2 | end of ride |

# 27 JEWELL PASS

This popular cycling route connects the Bow Valley with the Kananaskis Valley at Barrier Lake via the Quaite Valley and Jewell Pass trails. The gentler slopes of the Quaite Valley trail make it more enjoyable to ride this route from north to south. Both trails are popular with hikers, so use extra caution.

From Heart Creek trailhead a rip-rolling singletrack parallels the Trans-Canada Highway for 3 km. At Quaite Creek it joins the Quaite Valley trail, a good gravel doubletrack that passes a backcountry group campsite at a meadow, then turns right for a beautiful climb to the summit of Jewell Pass.

There isn't much of a view from this low pass and the junction on the summit is a bit confusing; the Jewell Pass trail is the smooth singletrack to the right. This trail is showing a lot of wear and tear owing to poor riding habits so remember: ride through the mud holes, not around them; and ride, don't slide down the hills. The lower parts of this trail present some tricky technical riding across bridges and past boulders. Keep an eye out for Jewell Falls on the west side of the valley. Farther down, a sidehill above the creek provides a good view of Barrier Lake and Mount Baldy. The Jewell Pass trail joins the Stoney trail at the powerline near a small secluded bay on Barrier Lake. Turn left and ride through to the trailhead at Barrier Dam.

## Options

1. A 30 km loop can be made to the east with Stoney trail (#29) and the Trans-Canada Highway.

2. A 50 km loop can be made with Stoney trail and Skogan Pass (#23).

3. A local favourite is to continue east on Stoney trail and return on Prairie View trail (#28) for a 25 km ride that is a hard-core technical delight.

## Singletrack treats

**Type** point-to-point on 4WD roads and singletrack

**Rating** moderate/intermediate

**Other users** hikers-6

**Distance** 13.7 km one way

**Time** 1-2 hours

**Map** 82 O/3 Canmore

**Season** mid-June to mid-October

**Land agency** Kananaskis Country

## Access

From the Lac des Arcs interchange on the Trans-Canada Hwy., drive south to the Heart Creek trailhead.

| | |
|---|---|
| 0.0 | trailhead |
| 0.8 | four-way junction, go straight |
| 3.0 | turn right onto the Quaite Valley trail |
| 4.7 | group camp |
| 5.0 | junction, keep right |
| 6.7 | Jewell Pass, four-way junction, keep right |
| 9.6 | powerline |
| 9.7 | Stoney trail, turn left to Barrier Dam and Bow Valley Park (right to Ribbon Creek) |
| 11.1 | junction, turn right (left to Bow Valley Park) |
| 12.3 | junction, turn right |
| 13.7 | Barrier Dam trailhead |

# 28 PRAIRIE VIEW TRAIL

maps 6, 6A

Photo: Greg Achtem.

If you like challenging technical singletrack trails or screaming-fast fireroad descents, then you're sure to enjoy this ride. An old road climbs high on the side of Barrier Mountain to a superb panorama of mountains and prairies. Singletrack trails complete the loop. This is a local favourite with hikers and mountain bikers so be courteous to others and have fun.

The old road provides a sometimes strenuous uphill workout on a well-drained track as it climbs to the old lookout site. For those who do not want to climb over the ridge and ride the singletrack, this is the turn-around point. The trail continues as a singletrack climbing steeply through the cliffs to a high vantage-point overlooking prairies and peaks.

Psych yourself up for some big fun as you carry your bike up the trail. From the top of the cliffs a limestone trials garden leads to a careering downhill singletrack that descends through forest and across sidehills. Watch your bar ends as the trail squeezes and bumps its way through a forest of doghair pine to emerge on the summit of Jewell Pass. Then delight in the challenging technicalities of the Jewell Pass trail (#27) and return to the trailhead on Stoney trail (#29).

## Options

See trails #27 and #30 for other riding combinations with this trail. Great vistas await those who hike to the lookout on the summit of Barrier Mountain.

**Classic ride on rugged trail**

**Type** loop on 4WD roads and singletrack

**Rating** moderate/advanced

**Other users** hikers-6

**Distance** 14.5 km

**Time** 3-4 hours

**Map** 82 O/3 Canmore

**Season** mid-June to mid-October

**Land agency** Kananaskis Country

## Access

Begin at the Barrier Dam picnic area located beside Hwy. 40, 8.7 km south of Hwy. 1.

| | |
|---|---|
| 0.0 | trailhead |
| 1.4 | cross powerline |
| 1.9 | cross Stoney trail |
| 5.2 | site of old lookout |
| 5.6 | high point, trail to summit and Barrier Lookout |
| 7.6 | Jewell Pass, four-way junction, turn left |
| 10.5 | Stoney trail, turn left |
| 11.9 | junction, turn right |
| 13.1 | junction, turn right |
| 14.5 | trailhead |

# 29 STONEY TRAIL

maps 6, 6A

Stoney trail follows the west side of the Kananaskis River and leads from the grasslands on the edge of the mountains into the scenic and forested valley at Ribbon Creek. The trail is a gentle gravel and dirt doubletrack, easy enough for a family out-and-back excursion. Chinook winds tend to keep this route dry and it can often be ridden as early as April and as late as November.

The trail begins as a good gravel road through the Scouts Jamboree Centre and soon passes a site used by local native people for the Ti-jurabichubi ceremony. Chief John Snow describes this as "being thankful for life, the beautiful creation, the rain, the sun, and the changing seasons." Give thanks, then roll past the pumphouse and along a doubletrack beside the Kananaskis River as far as the site of an old log bridge. This was part of the first road into the valley and was built in 1934 during the Great Depression. It ran from Seebe to a camp for the unemployed that was later used as a German prisoner-of-war camp during World War II. Today, it is the University of Calgary Environmental Sciences Centre.

To continue onward, backtrack for about 200 m to a gravel track leading to the south. This track climbs gently and crosses under the powerline before turning south at a major junction. It continues as a smooth dirt and gravel doubletrack through mixed forest and meadows, crossing Prairie View trail (#28), then joining the powerline on the north shore of Barrier Lake.

From Barrier Lake, Stoney trail closely follows the powerline for 12 km to Ribbon Creek. This section is a rolling dirt and gravel doubletrack that features lots of views, beautiful mixed wood forest and grassy meadows.

## Options

A shorter ride can be made by arranging to begin or end the trip at Barrier Dam.

**Family fun on gentle and scenic trail**

**Type** point-to-point on 4WD roads

**Rating** moderate/intermediate

**Other users** hikers-1  equestrian-1

**Distance** 23.1 km one way

**Time** 2-4 hours

**Maps** 82 O/3 Canmore
82 J/14 Spray Lakes Reservoir

**Season** April through November

**Land agency** Kananaskis Country

### Access

**north** From the Bow Valley Park interchange on the Trans-Canada Hwy. drive south for 0.5 km to a T-intersection and parking lot. The gated road continuing straight is the trail.

**mid** From the Barrier Dam picnic area located beside Hwy. 40, 8.7 km south of Hwy. 1.

**south** On Hwy. 40, drive 23 km south from Hwy. 1 to the Ribbon Creek recreation area. The trailhead is 1 km west on the right side of the road.

| | |
|---|---|
| 0.0 | north trailhead |
| 2.2 | pumphouse to left |
| 3.4 | fork, keep right (left leads 0.2 km to old bridge) |
| 6.3 | T-junction, turn left |
| 8.5 | junction, Prairie View trail to right, Barrier Dam to left |
| 9.7 | junction, keep right |
| 11.1 | Jewell Pass trail to right |
| 21.3 | transformer |
| 21.5 | powerline climbs to right (cutoff to Skogan Pass trail) |
| 23.1 | south trailhead |

# 30 GRAND SLAM

maps 6, 6A

The Grand Slam is an endurance ride par excellence. This route is a combination of trails so check out the specific trail descriptions for details.

From Heart Creek trailhead ride up and over Jewell Pass (#27), then follow Stoney trail to Barrier Dam. Ride across the dam, cross Hwy. 40 and enter the U of C Field Station, then ride up to Baldy Pass (#26). Enjoy the technical delights of the descent of Baldy, then follow the highway back to Barrier Dam. Cross the dam and ascend Prairie View trail (#28). Climb through your tiredness, through the cliff band and up to the big prairie view. With a bit of technical wizardry ride the rocks and roll and bump your way down to Jewell Pass, scream on down to the group camp and keep hauling right down to the trail junction just before the highway. Turn left and unwind on the final few kilometres to the end of the ride.

**Hard-core enduro-ride, classic trails**

**Type** loop on 2WD roads, 4WD roads and singletrack

**Rating** extreme/intermediate

**Other users** hikers-5

**Distance** 49.9 km

**Time** 4-6 hours

**Map** 82 O/3 Canmore

**Season** May through October

**Land agency** Kananaskis Country

**Access**

From the Lac des Arcs interchange on Hwy. 1, drive south to the Heart Creek trailhead.

| | |
|---|---|
| 0.0 | trailhead |
| 3.0 | junction, turn right |
| 6.7 | Jewell Pass, turn right |
| 9.7 | Stoney trail, turn left |
| 11.1 | junction, turn right |
| 13.7 | Barrier Dam trailhead, turn right on Hwy. 40 |
| 14.5 | turn left into Field Station |
| 14.8 | Colonel's Cabin parking follow gravel road leading to left out of lot |
| 16.0 | junction, turn right Baldy Pass |
| 23.1 | junction, turn right |
| 25.2 | high point on ridge |
| 25.3 | Baldy Pass |
| 28.6 | junction, turn right |
| 29.3 | Highway 40, turn right |
| 35.2 | turn left to Barrier |
| 35.6 | Barrier trailhead |
| 37.5 | junction, follow Prairie View trail |
| 41.2 | high point, views |
| 43.2 | Jewell Pass, go straight |
| 46.9 | junction, turn left |
| 49.9 | end of ride |

# 31 KANANASKIS EIGHT                                        map 6A

Photo: Stephen Wilde.

**Technical and scenic ride**

**Type** loop on 4WD roads and singletrack

**Rating** moderate/advanced

**Other users** hikers-4 equestrian-4

**Distance** 23 km

**Time** 2-3 hours

**Map** 82 O/3 Canmore

**Season** May through October

**Land agency** Kananaskis Country

**Access**
From the Bow Valley Park interchange on Hwy. 1, drive south for 0.5 km to a T-intersection and parking lot. The gated road continuing straight is the trail.

| | |
|---|---|
| 0.0 | trailhead |
| | pumphouse to left |
| 3.4 | fork, keep right (left leads 0.2 km to old bridge) |
| 6.3 | junction, turn left |
| 8.5 | junction with Prairie View trail, turn right |
| 10.8 | turn right onto singletrack |
| 13.0 | junction with YMCA trails, turn right |
| 14.6 | junction, turn right, up hill |
| 15.4 | junction, keep left |
| 16.0 | turn right onto singletrack |
| 17.4 | junctions, go left or right |
| 19.3 | old bridge picnic spot, go left |
| 23.0 | end of ride |

Kananaskis Eight combines Stoney trail with some challenging singletracks on the east end of Barrier Mountain and alongside the Kananaskis River for a hard-core rider's delight.

Begin by rolling south on easy doubletrack into the Kananaskis Valley, following the Stoney trail (#29) as far as its junction with Prairie View trail. Hang a right here and climb up the switchbacks as far as the ridge, but watch carefully for the single-track that drops to the right. This gnarly, twisty, steep little trail will test your advanced riding skills and get the endorphins pumping. At the bottom keep right at all junctions to skirt the Y Camp and follow a sometimes muddy horse trail over the hill back to the Kananaskis Valley. Watch closely on the right at km 16 for the singletrack that will take you along the escarpment above the river and down to the old bridge site. This narrow little intermediate trail has lots of challenges and exciting bits and you can watch the kayakers playing in the river below. From the old bridge it's a fast doubletrack. Roll out to the trailhead in the meadows at the edge of the mountains.

# 32 LUSK PASS

maps 6, 6A

Lusk Pass isn't much of a ride by itself, but it can be used as an alternate start for Jumpingpound Ridge, Jumpingpound Loop or Cox Hill to give those rides a little extra pizazz. This trail is an essential connector for a ride from Kananaskis to Bragg Creek. Short and mostly doubletrack with a few sections of singletrack, the trail is consistently stony with well-drained soils as it passes through open forests of lodgepole pine and juniper.

Ride across SR 968 and up the embankment. Almost immediately Lusk trail enters its own quiet valley away from the road and climbs gently alongside Lusk Creek. As you progress up the valley a couple of steep hills will make you work to gain the pass.

With the summit at such a low elevation the views are few and far between, but there are some good vistas of the Bow Valley and the Fisher Range. Once over the summit the drop to the east is fast and fun, but also short as the east trailhead is much higher than the west one.

## Options

With a vehicle shuttle this trail can be cycled one-way from east to west, a direction that is considerably more fun.

**Short backcountry trail**

**Type** point-to-point on singletrack

**Rating** easy/intermediate

**Other users** hikers-2 equestrian-4

**Distance** 8.1 km

**Time** 1-2 hours

**Maps** 82 J/15 Bragg Creek
82 O/2 Jumpingpound
82 O/3 Canmore

**Season** mid-May to mid-October

**Land agency** Kananaskis Country

**Access**

**east** The Lusk Pass trail is located on the west side of Powderface Trail, 10 km south of Hwy. 68 and 25 km north of Hwy. 66.

**west** The Lusk Pass trail is located at the Lusk Creek day-use area on the north side of SR 968, 1 km east of Hwy. 40.

0.0    west trailhead

0.3    junction, turn left onto singletrack

3.1    junction, keep left (right leads to Baldy Pass trail)

6.5    Lusk Pass

8.1    east trailhead

# 33 JUMPINGPOUND RIDGE                    map 7

Like singletrack riding? You'll never want to go home! One of the outstanding cycling trips in the Canadian Rockies, the Jumpingpound Ridge trail is a spectacular traverse of a high sandstone ridge and makes for a fine ride in either direction. Travelling south to north provides excellent downhill riding through meadows on the north slope of the ridge.

Beginning at the south trailhead, cycle the doubletrack along Canyon Creek, then begin the steep climb onto Jumpingpound Ridge. Pedal and push up switchbacks through pine forest and small meadows brimming with wildflowers. As it crests the ridge the trail becomes less steep and the views begin. A technical skill-testing section leads to the final climb to the peak.

From the summit the mountain panorama includes Moose Mountain to the east, Cox Hill to the north and Fisher Range and Compression Ridge to the west.

**Classic high mountain ride**
**Type** loop on 2WD road and singletrack
**Rating** moderate/intermediate
**Other users** hikers-5
**Distance** 23 km
**Time** 2-4 hours
**Map** 82 J/15 Bragg Creek
**Season** mid-June to mid-October
**Land agency** Kananaskis Country

**Access**
**south** The trail starts on the east side of Powderface Road, 100 m north of Canyon Creek, 15 km north of Hwy. 66, and 20 km south of Hwy. 68.

*Cox Hill (#34).*

The north slope of the ridge offers some of the most spectacular and exciting ridge riding in the Rockies. You'll be tempted to ride fast to squeeze maximum fun out of this trail and its perfect setting. But take a few breaks or you'll miss some of the best things this trail has to offer, like flower-filled alpine meadows and a sweeping panorama of the front ranges of the Rockies. Just as the trail enters the trees the Cox Hill trail forks to the right. Keep left and continue descending the north end of the ridge on the smooth switchbacking trail, and riding as if there were a hiker around every corner.

## Options

1. Hard-core riders will want to combine Jumpingpound Ridge with Cox Hill (#35).

2. Combine this trail with Lusk Pass trail.

**north** The trail is located on the east side of Powderface Road, 24.3 km north of Hwy. 66 and 10.7 km south of Hwy. 68.

| | |
|---|---|
| 0.0 | south trailhead |
| 0.7 | junction, turn left (right is Canyon Creek trail) |
| 5.8 | junction, keep right |
| 6.3 | summit |
| 9.5 | junction, keep left (Cox Hill trail to right) |
| 13.7 | north trailhead, turn left and cycle up road |
| 23.0 | south trailhead |

# 34 COX HILL
map 7

One of the best rides in the Rockies, this trail is a great ride by itself or in combination with Jumpingpound Ridge. The climb up Cox Hill is hard work but the rewards are big for radical riders searching for adrenaline. The summit is spectacular and the ride down the north side is guaranteed to shorten the life of your brake pads.

Pedal and push up the switchbacks on the north end of the Jumpingpound Ridge trail on a singletrack that just seems to get steeper the higher you go. Turn left at the junction at treeline and enjoy the steep drop to the saddle between Jumpingpound Ridge and Cox Hill. This and more elevation must be regained by riding and pushing your bike up the south side of Cox Hill. The trail is good in the trees, but becomes steeper and more challenging as it climbs into the alpine meadows and along the ridge to the summit. Prepare to be wowed by a dazzling view of Calgary and the prairies, the east ridge of Jumpingpound Mountain, Moose Mountain to the south, and range after range of the Rockies to the northwest.

After a short but exciting roll along the summit ridge, the trail takes the big plunge down the northeast ridge. In 6.7 km the trail drops 700 m in a long, continuously rideable drop that will thrill you, maybe spill you and certainly leave you with an ear to ear grin. You can go very fast on this winding, technical trail, so watch for horseback riders and hikers.

## Options

Hard-core riders will want to combine Jumping-pound Ridge with Cox Hill (#35).

**Classic high mountain ride**

**Type** loop on 2WD road and singletrack

**Rating** difficult/advanced

**Other users** hikers-5

**Distance** 22.3 km

**Time** 2-4 hours

**Maps** 82 J/15 Bragg Creek
82 O/2 Jumpingpound

**Season** mid-June to mid-October

**Land agency** Kananaskis Country

## Access

**south** The trail is located on the east side of Powderface Trail, 24.3 km north of Hwy. 66 and 10.7 km south of Hwy. 68.

**north** Park at the Dawson trailhead on Powderface Trail, 3 km south of Hwy. 68.

| | |
|---|---|
| 0.0 | south trailhead |
| 4.2 | junction on Jumpingpound Ridge, turn left |
| 7.5 | summit |
| 14.2 | junction, turn left |
| 14.6 | Dawson trailhead, turn left |
| 22.3 | end of ride |

# 35 JUMPINGPOUND RIDGE & COX HILL                    map 7

Probably the only legal world-class ride in the Canadian Rockies (the now closed Mount Assiniboine ride was another), Jumpingpound Ridge and Cox Hill has it all. Big climbs, wild descents, major singletrack treats, alpine ridge riding, superb scenery and reasonable access combine for near perfection. The route combines Jumpingpound Ridge (#33) and Cox Hill (#34) into one long ride. To set up the ride you can park at Dawson and ride the road first, park at Canyon Creek and ride the road last or do a car shuttle.

From Canyon Creek trailhead follow Jumpingpound trail as it climbs to the top of the ridge. Hard work and some technical delights are rewarded by big meadows and even bigger views. The spectacular natural setting is part of what makes this ride so special, the other part is the near perfect riding. From the summit the trail stays on the ridge and descends on fun-filled singletrack through flower-filled meadows. Turn right onto Cox Hill trail and drop to a saddle. Now more skill and stamina-testing climbing will push your limits and bring you to the top of Cox Hill. Views, views, views! When you've had enough it's time for one sweet downhill to the trailhead. Ride the ridge, wiggle through some switchbacks, then obey the law of gravity and speed downward. Did I say speed? Phew! Watch out for uphill traffic. Roll out to the parking lot and finish up the ride.

**World-class high mountain ride**

**Type** loop on 2WD road and singletrack

**Rating** difficult/advanced

**Other users** hikers-5 equestrian-1

**Distance** 36.9 km

**Time** 3-5 hours

**Map** 82 J/15 Bragg Creek

**Season** mid-June to mid-October

**Land agency** Kananaskis Country

**Access**

**south** The trail starts on the east side of Powderface Trail, 100 m north of Canyon Creek, 15 km north of Hwy. 66, and 20 km south of Hwy. 68.

**north** Park at the Dawson trailhead on Powderface Trail, 3 km south of Hwy. 68.

| | |
|---|---|
| 0.0 | south trailhead |
| 0.7 | junction, turn left (right is Canyon Creek trail) |
| 5.8 | junction, keep right |
| 6.3 | Jumpingpound summit |
| 9.5 | junction, turn right onto Cox Hill trail |
| 12.8 | Cox Hill summit |
| 19.5 | junction, turn left |
| 19.9 | Dawson (north) trailhead, turn left |
| 36.9 | south trailhead, end of ride |

# 36 SIBBALD FLATS
map 7

**Foothills cruiser**

**Type** loop on 2WD and 4WD roads and singletrack

**Rating** easy/novice

**Other users** hikers-2  equestrian-5 livestock

**Distance** 16.5 km (4.3 on pavement)

**Time** 1-3 hours

**Map** 82 O/2 Jumpingpound

**Season** mid-May through October

**Land agency** Kananaskis Country

## Access

**west**  Begin at the Dawson trailhead on Powderface Trail, 3 km south of Hwy. 68.

**east**  Drive 17.9 km south of the Trans-Canada Hwy. on Hwy. 68. Turn left and follow the Demonstration Forest south loop road for 3.7 km to the Spruce Woods trailhead.

This short trail provides an easy introduction to the exciting world of backcountry biking and is a gentle way to gain some experience in singletrack and doubletrack riding and routefinding. Almost as a bonus it also provides a tour of a beautiful valley with classic foothills vistas including Cox Hill and Moose Mountain. From west to east the trail is a gentle downhill ride as it passes through open meadows, some incredible patches of cow parsnip, and spruce and pine forests. Generally well drained, it's suitable under most weather conditions; all stream crossings are bridged and most of the trail junctions are well marked.

Beginning at the Dawson trailhead the singletrack riding comes first and the riding is easy as you descend along Jumpingpound Creek. Once you reach the flats the trail joins an old doubletrack, which you follow almost to the end of the trip. You can finish by going left on the gas well road if you like, but I prefer to continue on the trail. The final short section to the east trailhead is a singletrack winding through trees and meadows and finishing up with the steepest hill of the whole trip. Return the way you came or ride back on the road.

**Options**

If you crave a little more riding, make an out-and-back excursion on the Tom Snow—North trail or on the Moose Mountain gas well access road.

| | |
|---|---|
| 0.0 | west trailhead |
| 0.4 | junction, turn left |
| 1.4 | Sibbald Flats, trail bends to right |
| 2.2 | cross a logging road |
| 2.5 | cross another logging road |
| 3.6 | junction with minor road, keep left |
| 5.5 | junction, keep left |
| 5.6 | junction, turn right and cross bridge over Coxhill Creek |
| 6.1 | trail turns left off of gas well road |
| 6.5 | four-way junction, turn left (right and straight is Tom Snow—North trail) |
| 6.8 | junction, keep left |
| 7.2 | junction, turn left and cross bridge |
| 7.3 | east trailhead |
| 9.2 | Hwy. 68, turn left |
| 13.5 | junction of Hwy. 68 and Powderface Trail (road), turn left |
| 16.5 | west trailhead |

# 37 JUMPINGPOUND MOUNTAIN LOOP         map 7

**Rugged high mountain ride**

**Type** loop on 4WD roads and singletrack

**Rating** difficult/advanced

**Other users** hikers-5 equestrian-2

**Distance** 35.6 km

**Time** 3-5 hours

**Maps** 82 J/15 Bragg Creek
82 O/2 Jumpingpound

**Season** mid-June to mid-October

**Land agency** Kananaskis Country

**Access**
Park at Dawson trailhead on Powderface Trail, 3 km south of Hwy. 68.

| | |
|---|---|
| 0.0 | trailhead |
| 0.4 | junction, turn left (right is Cox Hill) |
| 1.9 | keep right |
| 2.5 | keep left |
| 5.5 | gas well access road, turn right and ride up road |
| 12.9 | junction, go left up hill |
| 16.9 | gas well |
| 18.4 | leave road and hike-a-bike to right up to top of east ridge ride and push westward along East Ridge trail |
| 21.9 | Jumpingpound Mountain summit |
| 22.3 | join Jumpingpound Ridge trail and ride north |
| 25.2 | junction, turn right onto Cox Hill trail (left is Jumpingpound trail) |
| 28.5 | Cox Hill summit |
| 35.2 | junction, turn left |
| 35.6 | Dawson trailhead |

More fun for serious riders. This variant of the Jumpingpound Ridge and Cox Hill ride is almost as sweet as the original.

The ride warms up on a singletrack snaking through the aspen woods and cow parsnip meadows of the Sibbald Flats trail (#36). Then comes the gas well access road. Most of the elevation is gained on this moderately-angled track where you can punish yourself and your friends to your heart's content. Once you depart the road it is a combination of ride and hike-a-bike to the summit of Jumpingpound Mountain. From the summit the trail is the same as for Jumpingpound Ridge, taking the option over Cox Hill (#34) with its ultra-fun descent back to the trailhead.

# 38 EAGLE HILL & DEER RIDGE    map 7

This ride is a beautiful foothills tour with extensive aspen forests, views of the front ranges and lots of ups and downs. Unfortunately, the trail can get severely messed up by grazing cattle during midsummer, more so if the weather has been wet.

Begin by riding south on the gravel access road to the trailhead. The trail begins with a feast of meadows, ponds and foothill views as it winds through groves of aspens and up a gentle valley. Note the junction with the Deer Ridge trail at km 3 for your return trip. Roll on over hill and dale until the trail climbs up onto windswept Eagle Hill. This scenic hotspot overlooks the front ranges of the Rockies as well as Morley Flats and Moose Mountain.

The return trail is a fast and exciting run through the aspen woodland. Turn right for Deer Ridge and endure the big grind up the cutline to the ridge. There follows a sweet section of trail that winds through pine forest along the ridge with views to the highway below. The descent is fast and action packed, but all too soon you come to the pond in the meadow and it's all over.

**Rugged foothills tour**

**Type** loop on singletrack
**Rating** moderate/intermediate
**Other users** hikers-2  livestock
**Distance** 15.8 km
**Time** 2-3 hours
**Map** 82 O/2 Jumpingpound
**Season** mid-May to mid-October
**Land agency** Kananaskis Country

**Access**
On Hwy. 68, drive 21.9 km south of Hwy. 1 to the Sibbald Lake recreation area and park in the day-use parking lot. The trail begins 0.1 km before the parking lot.

0.0    trailhead
0.3    junction, keep right
1.6    junction, go straight
3.0    junction with Deer Ridge trail, go straight
7.4    Eagle Hill summit, retrace tracks
11.8   turn right on Deer Ridge trail
13.2   Deer Ridge summit
14.8   junction, keep left
15.5   junction, turn right
15.8   end of ride

# 39 TOM SNOW TRAIL—NORTH                                   map 7

Are you looking for a good but almost unknown foothills ride? With Moose Mountain forming a scenic backdrop to the west, this trail winds its way to the headwaters of Bragg Creek, then descends along Moose Creek to the Sibbald Flats area. Along the way it passes through typical foothills country with an attractive vegetation mosaic of willow meadows, grasslands, aspen groves and forests of lodgepole pine and spruce. There is active logging continuing in this area, so you can expect to find a few less trees, some better vistas, and trails altered or even replaced with logging roads.

One of the real pluses of this trail is that it comes into condition early in the season. Coincidentally, this is also the best time to see wildlife and tracks. When I cycled the trail I saw tracks of elk, moose, deer, coyote, wolf and bear. Later in the season one might expect to find tracks of the elusive tire clan: mud dawg, ground control, smoke and megabite, not to mention cows, hikers and horses.

The Bragg Creek section of the trail consists of old roads and wide singletrack. Generally well drained, hard packed and bumpy with a few short boggy sections, it provides riding that is fast and fun, but watch for numerous trees across the trail. The junction at the summit is obvious if you are riding north but travelling south it is less so—you want to take the grassy track that makes a hard left off of Moose Creek trail. The Moose Creek section is a well-maintained doubletrack on soils that could be soft or muddy during wet weather.

**Rugged and scenic backcountry ride**

**Type** point-to-point on singletrack

**Rating** moderate/novice

**Other users** hikers-2  equestrian-6 livestock

**Distance** 16.6 km one way

**Time** 2-3 hours

**Maps** 82 J/15 Bragg Creek
82 O/2 Jumpingpound Creek

**Season** May through October

**Land agency** Kananaskis Country

**Access**
**south** In Bragg Creek, cross the bridge over the Elbow River and drive 10 km west to the West Bragg picnic area. The trail is the gated road continuing to the west.

**north** Drive 6 km west of Kananaskis Country boundary on Hwy. 68, turn left and follow the Forest Management loop road to the Spruce Woods trailhead.

0.0    south trailhead

1.7    junction, keep right

2.7    junction, keep left (right is Telephone trail)

3.2    junction, keep right up hill

5.0    leave road and take singletrack to right (road veers left and crosses creek)

10.0    summit

10.1    junction, keep right (East Ridge trail to left) this junction not obvious when travelling north to south

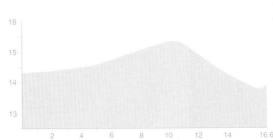

Photo: Stephen Wilde.

10.2  cutblock, 1992 vintage

14.2  junction, keep left on bypass trail (trail to right is rocky and muddy)

15.3  trail joins road, keep right

15.5  trail leaves logging road, keep right

15.8  four-way junction, go straight (left is Sibbald Flats trail)

16.1  junction, turn left

16.5  junction, turn left and cross bridge

16.6  north trailhead

# 40 TELEPHONE TRAIL                                    map 7

Telephone Trail is a fun combination of old exploration roads and singletrack but beware, this trail can get severely muddy—go in dry weather only. The trail winds through mixed-wood foothills forest and part of it follows the route of a forestry telephone line that once connected the Elbow and Jumpingpound ranger stations. Located in an area of low rolling foothills, there are no major peaks or landmarks, and although the trail is marked with ski trail signs, it has several junctions with seismic roads where you could easily get lost. To make matters worse, active logging is altering the north end of this trail. So don't be surprised if you find 'dozers, big mud and a severely messed up trail. Call the Forest Service and let them know your opinion.

The trail loops to the north around a low foothill and the first 6 km is a solid and well-drained singletrack covered with pine needles. Recent logging activity has turned the north end of the loop into a muddy road. I suggest you cut left at km 6.7, thereby avoiding most of the logging before rejoining the main trail at the S-bend (a place where many people lose track of the route and cycle down the wrong seismic line). The western section of the route is not as well drained and has some boggy and muddy sections. After crossing a low pass the trail joins a good exploration road for the last few kilometres through the meadows along Bragg Creek.

**Rugged foothills ride**

**Type** loop on 4WD road and singletrack

**Rating** moderate/intermediate

**Other users** hikers-2  equestrian-5 livestock

**Distance** 14.8 km

**Time** 2-3 hours

**Maps** 82 J/15 Bragg Creek
82 O/2 Jumpingpound Creek

**Season** June through October

**Land agency** Kananaskis Country

**Access**
In Bragg Creek, cross the bridge over the Elbow River and drive 10 km west to the West Bragg picnic area. A map and sign on the north side of the parking lot mark the trailhead. Ride north up the hill.

| | |
|---|---|
| 0.0 | trailhead |
| 0.5 | four-way junction, go straight |
| 6.7 | junction, keep left (right is main trail, it rejoins at km 8.8) |
| 7.5 | junction, keep left amidst logging debris |
| 8.5 | junction, keep right |
| 8.8 | S-bend junction, keep left (main trail joins from right) |
| 9.5 | cross logging road |
| 10.2 | summit |
| 12.1 | junction, keep left (right is Tom Snow—North trail) |
| 13.1 | junction, keep left (right is Tom Snow—South and Packer's trails) |
| 14.8 | trailhead |

# 41 IRON CREEK-TOM SNOW LOOP    map 7

This is a short ride that, like the other two rides beginning at the Station Flats trailhead (#42, #44), makes a great "after-work" excursion. The route follows the wide Iron Creek trail from the Elbow River to West Bragg and returns on the singletrack of the Tom Snow trail. It is a good early season trip but best done in dry weather.

From its beginning at Allen Bill Pond, the Iron Creek trail is a rough and bumpy old exploration road that passes meadows and wetlands as it climbs and rolls among some low foothills. In winter it is a ski trail. The best thing about this trail is that it allows you to make a loop with the Tom Snow trail. After a few fast downhills you reach the West Bragg trailhead.

Beyond the trailhead gate, follow the old gravel road west along Bragg Creek as it climbs into the hills below Moose Mountain. Watch carefully for the junction at km 14.1 and take the Tom Snow trail departing to the south. It begins as an unpromising, rough doubletrack in an old cutblock, but soon becomes a classic stretch of wide, well-drained singletrack snaking its way through pine and mixed-wood forests. This trail offers fast and fun riding along a smooth, often needle-covered trail where you swoop and glide through the trees. The short steep uphill after the creek will give you a run for your money, then it's all over.

## Options

Either arm of this loop can be combined with the roads leading to and from the village of Bragg Creek to create an easy "espresso loop" complete with a coffee and pie stop.

**Singletrack treats in the foothills**

**Type** loop on 4WD roads and singletrack

**Rating** moderate/intermediate

**Other users** hikers-3  equestrian-5

**Distance** 20.7 km (1.6 km on pavement)

**Time** 2-4 hours

**Map** 82 J/15 Bragg Creek

**Season** mid-April through October

**Land agency** Kananaskis Country

**Access**
Park at Station Flats day-use area on Hwy. 66, 14.5 km west of Bragg Creek.

| | |
|---|---|
| 0.0 | trailhead, cycle east on Hwy. 66 |
| 1.4 | right to Allen Bill Pond parking |
| 1.6 | trailhead at Allen Bill Pond |
| 2.4 | junction, keep left |
| 2.6 | junction, turn right (Fullerton Loop to left) |
| 6.1 | spur trail forks to left |
| 6.4 | trail joins from left, gate |
| 7.4 | T-junction, turn left |
| 8.8 | junction, keep right |
| 8.9 | junction, keep left |
| 9.1 | West Bragg parking, follow road west through gate |
| 10.8 | junction, keep left (Tom Snow—North to right) |
| 14.1 | junction, turn left onto Tom Snow—South trail (Packer's trail to right) |
| 18.2 | Ranger Creek ford |
| 19.8 | junction with Diamond T trail, turn left |
| 20.7 | Station Flats trailhead |

# 42 SULPHUR SPRINGS TRAIL                     map 7

**Singletrack treats**

**Type** loop on singletrack

**Rating** moderate/intermediate

**Other users** hikers-3  equestrian-2

**Distance** 12.6 km

**Time** 1-2 hours

**Map** 82 J/15 Bragg Creek

**Season** mid-April through October

**Land agency** Kananaskis Country

**Access**
Park at Station Flats day-use area on Hwy. 66, 14.5 km west of Bragg Creek.

| | |
|---|---|
| 0.0 | trailhead |
| 0.1 | junction, keep left (right is Diamond T and Tom Snow trail) |
| 0.6 | junction, keep left |
| 1.4 | four-way junction, loop begins here, turn right |
| 5.3 | cross Moose Mountain Road |
| 5.7 | viewpoint |
| 6.7 | four-way junction, turn left (straight is access to Hwy. 66) |
| 7.5 | cross Moose Mountain Road |
| 11.2 | four-way junction, go straight |
| 12.6 | trailhead |

This trail provides classic singletrack cycling as it climbs, swoops and winds through a beautiful foothills setting. Grassy hillsides provide vistas of the Elbow Valley and the peaks beyond while, elsewhere, the trail rolls through aspen and pine forest. It is the site of Ridley's Summer Solstice Mountain Bike Race and it's easy to see why—gruelling uphills combine with long sections of big-ring hammering to produce raging endorphins and a feeling of incredible satisfaction. Given the race course feeling that pervades this ride, I should point out hikers also use this trail. Be careful.

From the trailhead, keep left at the initial trail junction and blast through a meadow and over some hills on the Elbow Valley trail. The signed trail junction at km 1.4 marks the beginning of the loop, which you can ride in either direction. Keeping to the right, the trail climbs, steeply in places, along Sulphur Springs Creek to Moose Mountain Road. Cross the road and climb a bit more to a hilltop vantage point. The meadows here offer a view of Prairie, Powderface, Forgetmenot and Nihahi ridges rolling off to the west. A winding downhill singletrack drops back to the Elbow Valley trail where you turn left to close the loop. This section of trail is rolling with a couple of steep climbs and a seemingly endless downhill section as you return to Station Flats.

# 43 MOOSE MOUNTAIN SUMMIT                                map 7

Ride high, ride wild; Moose Mountain rewards those who reach its summit with fantastic views and an unparalleled mountain descent. You do not have to take your bike all the way to the summit to enjoy this ride and an optional shorter ride is possible.

From the trailhead ride west on the good gravel trail as it climbs into the hills below Moose Mountain. Pass junctions for the Tom Snow trail and keep climbing, but keep an eye open for cyclists speeding down hill as you climb. After km 6.1 you will be climbing up the sweet switchbacks of the Packer's trail, then join the main trail to Moose Mountain. Why this route instead of driving up the road? Well, you came here to ride, didn't you? Besides the rewards are all on the way back down. Enjoy the old road as it climbs at a moderate angle through flower-filled meadows and subalpine forest. As you cross the treeline the nature of the trail changes, the climb gets steeper and the rocks get looser. Time to decide if you want to ride off the summit, or not—it's not easy riding and you have to do a lot of pushing to get there. If not, hide your bike and continue on foot. Hard-core riders will go for the ride off of the summit—it's too much of a plum to even think of skipping it.

Say hi to the towerperson, sign the book, enjoy the view, entertain the hikers, then take the plunge. Yee haw! Steep, loose and sweet; gravity bound for the forest below. It's very fast and very exciting riding as you retrace your tracks back to the trailhead. Watch for others—and never stop grinning!

## Options

For a shorter trip to the summit drive up the Moose Mountain road off of Highway 66 west of Bragg Creek. From the trailhead ride for 1.3 km and join the route log at km 8.9.

**Classic high mountain ride**

**Type** out-and-back on 4WD road and singletrack

**Rating** difficult/advanced

**Other users** hikers-6

**Distance** 30.4 km

**Time** 4-6 hours

**Map** 82 J/15 Bragg Creek

**Season** June through October

**Land agency** Kananaskis Country

**Access**
In Bragg Creek, cross the bridge over the Elbow River and drive 10 km west to the West Bragg ski parking lot. The trail continues past the gate on the road.

0.0   trailhead, ride west
1.7   junction, keep left
5.0   junction, keep right up hill
6.1   wellsite, singletrack begins
8.9   junction with Moose Mountain trail, turn right
14.5  steep singletrack begins
15.2  summit, retrace tracks

# 44 MOOSE-PACKER'S TRAIL!                          map 7

A core rider's delight, Moose-Packer's trail! takes you uphill on a gravel road and brings you back down on a singletrack with all the fun you can handle. Your legs will get a good work-out as you climb more than 500 vertical metres up the view-filled road. Then the trail plunges into the forest for some serious, skill-testing singletrack riding. It's fast, fun and exciting, and one of my favourite trails. Short enough for an evening, it can be extended to a day trip by riding to the mountain summit. One July evening as I was slipping down the switchbacks I came face to face with a cougar. It was unafraid and the wildness and freedom in its jet black eyes mirrored my own love for the freedom of mountain biking in these hills.

Begin this ride with a warm-up on Sulphur Springs trail (#42). When you reach Moose Mountain Road turn right and head for the top; it's gravel, never overly steep, and has tremendous views to keep your mind off of your burning quads. A short roll on the Moose Mountain trail takes you straight into the action of Packer's.

Packer's is one of those once all-but-forgotten trails from a bygone era and it turns out to be tailor-made for today's serious backcountry biker. A smooth and pleasant singletrack, it is part of the original horse packer's trail that provided access to the Moose Mountain Fire Lookout. Roll on, keeping right at the junction with a seismic line and slaloming down the mountain on a series of exhilarating singletrack switchbacks (try saying that quickly three times!). The singletrack joins an old exploration road and rolls east. Watch carefully midway through a long screaming downhill where you want to make an acute right-hand turn onto the Tom Snow trail. Tom begins as a doubletrack in a cutblock, but almost instantly becomes a wide, needle-covered singletrack winding and rolling beside Ranger Creek. Ride fast but watch for horses and hikers. The trail joins the Diamond T trail for a gravel finish.

**Classic singletrack treats**

**Type** loop on 4WD road and singletrack

**Rating** difficult/advanced

**Other users** hikers-1

**Distance** 22 km

**Time** 2-4 hours

**Map** 82 J/15 Bragg Creek

**Season** mid-May to mid-October

**Land agency** Kananaskis Country

**Access**
Park at Station Flats day-use area on Hwy. 66, 14.5 km west of Bragg Creek.

| | |
|---|---|
| 0.0 | trailhead, ride west on Elbow Valley (Sulphur Springs) trail |
| 1.4 | four-way junction, turn right |
| 5.3 | Moose Mountain Road, turn right |
| 10.2 | turn right onto Moose Mountain trail |
| 11.5 | turn right onto Packer's (left is Moose Mountain trail) |
| 12.6 | junction, keep right on singletrack and descend 10 switchbacks |
| 14.3 | wellsite, road begins |
| 15.4 | junction (midway through a long screaming downhill) with Tom Snow trail, turn right (left leads 4 km to West Bragg parking) |
| 15.9 | doubletrack turns to singletrack |
| 19.7 | ford creek |
| 21.1 | junction with Diamond T trail, turn left |
| 22.0 | trailhead |

# 45 AROUND MOOSE MOUNTAIN                                          map 7

This is a ride for the atomic dogs of the mountain bike world. It links up a number of trails to allow you to circum-cycle Moose Mountain. Doug's advice: it isn't easy but endurance riders will love it. Be well prepared for this epic undertaking, you're never far from a road but you are always a long way from your car.

Ride west on the easy old road of the Iron Creek-Tom Snow loop (#41) as it climbs into the hills below Moose Mountain, then turn south and follow the swoopy lines of the Tom Snow trail to Station Flats. Head west on one of the arms of the Sulphur Springs loop (#42), cross the Moose Mountain Road and continue west to ford Canyon Creek and join the Canyon Creek Road. Ride up the road into an ever-narrowing canyon. Eventually there is nothing to do but get your feet wet as the rudimentary trail crosses and re-crosses the creek a seemingly infinite number of times. At last the trail re-forms on the north side of the creek and leads you around the base of Jumpingpound Ridge. I hope you're not tired yet because the next step is to ride Jumpingpound Ridge and Cox Hill trails (#35). The wow factor is high on this section of trail, but by the time you descend Cox Hill trail tiredness will begin to seep into your bones.

**Hard-core enduro-ride**

**Type** loop on 2WD and 4WD roads and singletrack

**Rating** extreme/advanced

**Other users** hikers-5 equestrian-2

**Distance** 75.6 km

**Time** 6-9 hours

**Maps** 82 J/15 Bragg Creek
82 O/2 Jumpingpound

**Season** June through October

**Land agency** Kananaskis Country

**Access**
In Bragg Creek, cross the bridge over the Elbow River and drive 10 km west to the West Bragg picnic area. The gate on the road marks the trailhead.

Photo: Cécile Lafleur.

| | |
|---|---|
| 0.0 | trailhead, ride west |
| 1.7 | junction, keep left |
| 5.0 | junction, turn left onto Tom Snow trail |
| 10.7 | junction, turn left |
| 11.6 | Station Flats, keep right |
| 13.0 | junction, keep right (left is an option) |
| 16.9 | cross Moose Mountain Road |
| 18.3 | junction, turn right (option joins from left) |
| 19.8 | Canyon Creek Road, turn right |
| 26.0 | trail begins numerous fords |
| 34.5 | junction, turn right and begin ascent of Jumpingpound Ridge |
| 40.1 | Jumpingpound summit |
| 43.3 | junction, turn right for Cox Hill |
| 46.6 | Cox Hill summit |
| 53.3 | junction, keep right (Dawson trailhead to left) |
| 59.8 | junction, turn right on Tom Snow trail |
| 65.5 | junction, take grassy trail to left |
| 72.9 | Telephone trail joins from left |
| 73.9 | junction, turn left through gate |
| 75.6 | West Bragg parking, end of ride |

Enough of that tired-talk, keep right at the junction at the bottom of Cox Hill and follow the Sibbald Flats trail (#36) through lush gardens of cow parsnip—ain't she beautiful? Keep rolling east until you reach the gas well access road, cross the creek and pick up the southbound Tom Snow trail (#39). When we reached this point we totalled our energy resources—one Gu and one Power Bar between three guys! The trail climbs gently up to Moose Pass but watch carefully near the summit, your trail is overgrown with grass and doubles back to the left—making a mistake here could be a killer. The trail descends through aspen forest and meadows alongside Bragg Creek. The meadows and woods are beautiful, but your glazed eyes may not register the scenery. Eventually you join with the Telephone trail, finally turning left onto the road you travelled in the morning and glide back to your car.

# 46 ACROSS MOOSE MOUNTAIN

map 7

Photo: Stephen Wilde.

This trip is candy for the hard-core backcountry rider. It features a bit of everything—big climbs, kick-ass descents, perfect singletrack, fast doubletrack, and a hike-a-bike up an exposed mountain ridge. This is a major backcountry adventure with considerable hazards including 17 km of travel at or above timberline on exposed mountain ridges. Make thorough preparations.

From the U of C Field Station follow the Lusk Pass trail (#32) through to Powderface Trail. This is your warm up for the task ahead. Cross the road and follow the Jumpingpound Ridge trail (#33) as it switchbacks up through the forest, then follows a beautiful alpine ridge to the summit of Jumpingpound Mountain. Now the great adventure begins as you strike out along the east ridge toward Moose Mountain. Stay on the ridge, the trail is rudimentary and you will have to push some sections. Eventually you will drop down to a gas well drilling site. The summit doesn't look far off, but it will take about an hour of pushing and carrying to get there. Ham it up for the inevitable gaggle of hikers peering down as you crazed mountain bikers struggle up to the summit.

**Hard-core enduro-ride**

**Type** point-to-point on 4WD road and singletrack

**Rating** extreme/expert

**Other users** hikers-7 equestrian-2

**Distance** 39.3 km one way

**Time** 6-8 hours

**Map** 82 J/15 Bragg Creek

**Season** July through October

**Land agency** Kananaskis Country

**Access**
Park at the University of Calgary Kananaskis Field Station located on Highway 40.

Summit time—say hi to the towerperson, sign the book and push off. The route now follows the Moose Mountain Summit trail (#43), a narrow, steep and exposed singletrack that drops off of the summit and lands you in the treeline meadows below. From here it is fast doubletrack descending, but watch carefully for the left-hand turn that will take you onto Packer's trail (#44). The descent of the Packer's switchbacks is legendary, once down stay on the old road through to the West Bragg parking lot.

**Options**

You can make it shorter by starting at the Jumpingpound trailhead or make it epic by starting at Canmore. Whatever!

| | |
|---|---|
| 0.0 | trailhead |
| 1.2 | junction, go straight (Baldy Pass trail to right) |
| 1.4 | turn right onto singletrack |
| 7.6 | Lusk Pass summit |
| 9.2 | Powderface Trail, turn right |
| 9.3 | turn left onto Jumpingpound trail |
| 13.5 | junction, go straight (Cox Hill to left) |
| 16.7 | junction, go left on summit trail |
| 17.1 | summit of Jumpingpound Mountain ride and push eastward along East Ridge |
| 20.6 | join exploration road |
| 21.6 | drilling platform hike and scramble up summit ridge |
| 24.1 | Moose Mountain summit, fire lookout singletrack begins |
| 24.7 | doubletrack begins |
| 30.4 | junction, turn left onto Packer's trail (right leads to Moose Mountain Road) |
| 34.3 | junction, go straight (right is Tom Snow trail) |
| 37.6 | gate, pass through and continue |
| 39.3 | West Bragg parking, end of ride |

*Powderface Ridge (#49).*

# 47 POWDERFACE CREEK AND PRAIRIE CREEK TRAILS map 7

This is a very cool ride featuring lots of quality singletrack, great scenery, a big climb, and options for longer and shorter rides.

Powderface trail climbs out from the parking lot, but soon becomes a gentle trail with a couple of opportunities for splashing in the creek. Keep left at the junction at km 3.1 unless you want the short option. Gentle grades lure you on but soon you get to test your mettle on a big-ass climb up doubletrack and singletrack to Powderface Pass. Banded Mountain and Nihahi Ridge are the prominent peaks to the west. If you have time and energy to spare, take the optional excursion to the alpine meadows and summit of Powderface Ridge. Descending from the pass is a joy with a few technical spots and switchbacks to keep things interesting. This is a popular hiking trail; be sure to yield the trail.

Turn right and follow the gravel road for 2.7 km to Prairie Creek. The trailhead is located in a very wild and beautiful subalpine meadow. Listen to the birds, smell the flowers, watch for bears; let's ride! Prairie Creek trail is a wide singletrack that parallels the creek from here to the end of the ride. This is cow and horse country so the trail can be pretty chewed up if the weather is wet. Pass some beaver dams and roll through the mixed wood forest to the junction where the short loop rejoins the trail. The trail winds eastward through some valley bottom meadows and then everything changes. Climb up onto a limestone bluff and notice the narrow valley ahead, then ride the oh-so-sweet singletrack through the lower valley. Be prepared for tight trail on sidehill, twist through the groves of aspen, then drop down a rocky hill. It's fast, it's fun. You'll have one of those big biker grins by the time you roll up to the finish line.

## Options

Prairie Link trail offers a shorter ride by climbing over a low saddle on a good singletrack and features the best of lower Prairie Creek trail. Total distance 12.1 km.

Make a side trip from the pass to the summit of Powderface Ridge (#49).

**Classic ride with singletrack treats**

**Type** loop on 2WD roads and singletrack

**Rating** moderate/intermediate

**Other users** hikers-3 equestrian-3 livestock

**Distance** 21.2 km

**Time** 2-4 hours

**Map** 82 J/15 Bragg Creek

**Season** mid-June to mid-October

**Land agency** Kananaskis Country

## Access

Park at the Powderface trailhead on Hwy. 66 west of Elbow Falls. (This loop trip can also be accessed by driving north on Powderface Trail to where Prairie Creek or Powderface Creek trails meet the road.)

| | |
|---|---|
| 0.0 | trailhead, ride up hill on old exploration road |
| 3.1 | junction, keep left (right is Prairie Link trail, see option 1) |
| 6.1 | Powderface Pass; junction, keep right (left is Powderface Ridge trail, option 2) |
| 8.8 | Powderface Trail, turn right |
| 11.5 | Prairie Creek trailhead, turn right |
| 15.2 | junction, keep left (option 1 joins from right) |
| 20.5 | bridge |
| 21.0 | Highway 66, turn right |
| 21.2 | end of ride |

# 48 CANYON CREEK
map 7

Canyon Creek flows in a pretty foothills valley that deepens rapidly as you travel up-valley and eventually becomes a narrow limestone canyon along the south side of Moose Mountain. This ride takes you up a gravel road into the canyon, continues as a rugged no-track ride, and finishes as a doubletrack leading to Powderface Road.

Ride up the easy gravel road into the narrow valley, passing a gas compressor plant and a gated side road posted with ominous poison gas warnings. The road swings west and ends, but a doubletrack continues into the spectacular limestone canyon. The ice cave entrances can be seen high on the cliff to the north. Canyon Creek and wet feet—it sort of rhymes, doesn't it? Negotiating the canyon beyond this point is an arduous ride along the rocky creekbed with little trail to be found, only reasonable at low water levels. Eventually you emerge into the valley west of the canyon where a doubletrack continues through to the Powderface Trail (road).

**Options**

1. Combine this trail with the trail down Prairie Creek (#47) by riding south for 5.3 km on Powderface Road and joining the route log at km 11.5.

2. There is speculation that K Country may close the 6 km of gravel road to vehicles. This would make the trip to the end of the road below the ice caves a very pleasant out-and-back ride for the whole family.

**Rugged backcountry ride**

**Type** point-to-point on 2WD road, singletrack and no-track

**Rating** moderate/intermediate

**Other users** hikers-2 equestrian-2

**Distance** 15.7 km one way

**Time** 1-2 hours

**Map** 82 J/15 Bragg Creek

**Season** May to October

**Land agency** Kananaskis Country

**Access**

From Bragg Creek, drive 19.6 km west on Hwy. 66 to Canyon Creek. Park here and cycle up Canyon Creek Road.

0.0   Hwy. 66 at Canyon Creek Road

6.0   parking lot at end of Canyon Creek Road, follow doubletrack along creek

6.5   track disappears in creekbed

14.0   trail on north side of creek

15.0   Jumpingpound Ridge trail to right

15.7   Powderface Road

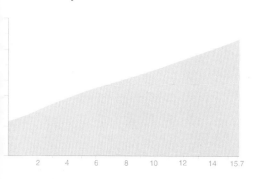

# 49 POWDERFACE RIDGE                          map 7

Welcome to the world of hard-core mountain biking. Some folks may think it's insane to take a bike on this trip, but I'd say they just don't get it! This trip involves a big climb up to the alpine meadows on Powderface Ridge and a long, steep descent back to Powderface Road. The alpine meadows on the ridge provide an excellent view of Calgary and the foothills, as well as Nihahi Ridge and the peaks to the west.

Begin by cycling north on the smooth gravel surface of Powderface Road to the Powderface Creek trailhead. Push and pedal your bike up the steep singletrack to Powderface Pass and the start of the Powderface Ridge trail. More hard work will get your fat tires into the alpine meadows and up to the top of the ridge. Parts of the trail up on the ridge will test your trials skills, it's thrilling—technical riding on top of the world. The trail drops onto the forested east side of the ridge and sidehills across to a grassy spur.

The steep downhill section of the ride begins high above the Elbow Valley and winds through pine forest before taking the plunge. If you enjoy skiing through the trees, you'll enjoy this some-times bumpy downhill drop of 300 m in just 3 km. Just like skiing, remember to keep your eyes on the spaces, not on the trees, and watch for hikers.

**Classic high mountain ride**

**Type** loop on 2WD road and singletrack

**Rating** difficult/advanced

**Other users** hikers-5

**Distance** 16.8 km

**Time** 2-4 hours

**Map** 82 J/15 Bragg Creek

**Season** July to mid-October

**Land agency** Kananaskis Country

**Access**
Drive west on Hwy. 66 to the junction with Powderface Trail (road). The ride proceeds north up Powderface Trail.

| | |
|---|---|
| 0.0 | trailhead |
| 7.1 | Powderface Creek trail, turn right |
| 9.8 | Powderface Pass; junction, turn right (left is Powderface Creek trail) |
| 11.5 | Powderface Ridge summit |
| 16.8 | trailhead |

# 50 QUIRK CREEK & WILDHORSE TRAILS    map 8

**Classic backcountry ride**
**Type** loop on 4WD road and singletrack
**Rating** moderate/intermediate
**Other users** hikers-1 equestrian-1 livestock
**Distance** 28.9 km
**Time** 3-4 hours
**Map** 82 J/15 Mount Rae
**Season** June through October
**Land agency** Kananaskis Country

**Access**
Drive west on Hwy. 66 to the Cobble Flats picnic area located 2 km east of Little Elbow Campground.

| | |
|---|---|
| 0.0 | trailhead |
| 0.3 | ford river and follow gravel road to left |
| 2.5 | junction, keep right |
| 8.7 | T-junction, turn left (right is shortcut to Wildhorse trail) |
| 9.6 | bridge |
| 9.7 | junction, turn right |
| 10.1 | road downgraded |
| 11.3 | unsigned junction, keep left (Wildhorse trail to right) |
| 12.0 | Wildhorse campsite to right |
| 13.6 | Threepoint Canyon, retrace your tracks |
| 15.9 | turn left onto Wildhorse trail |
| 16.5 | keep left past trail sign in meadow |
| 27.6 | junction, turn right (left leads to Little Elbow) |
| 28.6 | ford river |
| 28.9 | end of ride |

With its gradual uphill climb on an old road and sweet singletrack return, this is a trail you'll want to ride again and again. Bonus are the expansive meadows and the deep canyon on Threepoint Creek.

From the trailhead strike out across the gravel flats to the river, pick a good spot and wade across. This ford is usually easy by midsummer. Once across, cycle the old road as it leads downstream, then turns into the broad valley of Quirk Creek. It's a good gravel road that offers easy rolling as it skirts expansive shrub and grass meadows along the creek. The occasional motorbike may be encountered as the road is part of McLean Creek Off-Highway Vehicle Zone.

At km 9.6 you'll cross a bridge over Quirk Creek, then turn right and cycle south on a dirt road that leads to Threepoint Canyon. En route note the unsigned junction with the Wildhorse trail, which you will take on your return. Continue on to the edge of the abyss, the black shale canyon of Threepoint Creek reaches a depth of 140 m and its walls are etched with the trails of bighorn sheep.

Return on the Wildhorse trail, a beautiful rolling singletrack that climbs, winds and drops through meadows and pine forest below Forgetmenot Mountain. This is one of the best rides, but it tends to be very muddy in wet weather. Watch for horses on this trail. The last section is a bit eroded as the trail drops steeply back to the Elbow River. Roll out onto the flats, find your way across the river and it's all over.

2    4    6    8    10    12    14    16    18    20    22    24    26    28.9

# 51 ELBOW LOOP                                          map 9

Elbow Loop is an outstanding mountain bike trip along former four-wheel-drive roads through spectacular high mountain country. Now closed to motor vehicles, the roads have reverted to trail status and the whole area is now part of the Elbow-Sheep Wildland Provincial Park. Although this popular route provides enjoyable cycling in either direction, I prefer counter-clockwise, which leads up the Little Elbow trail over Little Elbow Pass to the forks and returns via the Big Elbow trail.

The dirt and gravel road along the Little Elbow River offers easy cycling in a scenic valley. At the Mount Romulus backcountry campsite the work begins as the road takes you up a beautiful climb to Little Elbow Pass. Rest stops are rewarded with striking views of Mount Romulus to the north and the Opal Range to the west. A trail 1 km north of the pass offers an optional trip to Tombstone Lakes. At the summit of the pass the limestone peaks of the Opal Range tower above the larches and meadows while the Misty and Highwood ranges form the southern skyline. The descent from the pass is an exciting roll on somewhat loose gravel. Watch for the big sign indicating the Big Elbow trail to the left before the bottom of the hill (lots of cyclists have raced past this junction), but don't rush away—make an excursion at least to the Elbow bridge. This area of subalpine meadows, surrounded by rugged limestone peaks, is one of the most scenic and beautiful places in the Rockies.

The Big Elbow trail offers slightly more challenging cycling on several sections of singletrack built to bypass the rampaging river and on some steep, rocky downhills. Gravity is your friend on this part of the trail and the speeds are exhilarating. The trail descends into the broad Elbow Valley for a delightful roll on gravel "tripletrack" with occasional washed-out sections where creeks cross the road. Pine and poplar forest and meadows highlight the peaks that surround this beautiful valley. A suspension bridge crosses the Little Elbow River and returns you to the trailhead.

**Classic high mountain ride**

**Type** loop on 4WD roads and singletrack

**Rating** difficult/intermediate

**Other users** hikers-3  equestrian-4

**Distance** 43 km

**Time** 3-6 hours

**Maps** 82 J/10 Mount Rae
82 J/15 Bragg Creek

**Season** July to mid-October

**Land agency** Kananaskis Country

**Access**
From Bragg Creek drive 32 km west on Hwy. 66 to Little Elbow recreation area. Parking is provided near the campground entrance as well as at the suspension bridge where the trip log begins. The route leads west along the campground road.

| 0.0 | trailhead |
| 1.0 | gate |
| 11.6 | Mount Romulus camp to right |
| 18.8 | Little Elbow Pass |
| 22.0 | junction, turn left (Tombstone Camp, Elbow headwaters to right) |
| 38.0 | Threepoint Mountain trail to right |
| 42.9 | suspension bridge |
| 43.0 | end of ride |

23
22
21
20
19
18
17
16

10        20        30        43

# 52 ELBOW & SHEEP
map 9

This ride is a combination of half of the Elbow Loop (#51) (your choice as to which half) plus the Sheep trail (#58). It is a classic trip, but few riders do it as a single ride because of the long car shuttle required.

The trail is an old road that follows alongside the Little Elbow River, then climbs up rideable grades to cross Little Elbow Pass. From the pass incredible mountain vistas unfold in every direction. A fast and exciting descent drops you off the pass, past Tombstone Campground, and on to the Elbow bridge—a perfect spot. From the bridge, climb past the junction with the Elbow Lake trail and up to Sheep Pass just below treeline. The old road races down into the Sheep Valley, then you enter the world of wet feet with innumerable creek crossings ahead. Pass the old range riders' cabin and ride through historic Burns meadows below the overhanging north wall of Gibraltar Mountain before rolling eastward down the valley to the trailhead.

**Classic high mountain ride**
**Type** point-to-point
**Rating** difficult/intermediate
**Other users** hikers-3 equestrian-5
**Distance** 45 km one way
**Time** 4-6 hours
**Maps** 82 J/10 Mount Rae
82 J/15 Bragg Creek
**Season** July through October
**Land agency** Kananaskis Country

**Access**
**north** From Bragg Creek drive 32 km west on Hwy. 66 to Little Elbow recreation area. Parking is provided near the campground entrance as well as at the suspension bridge where the trip log begins. The route leads west along the campground road.

**south** From Turner Valley drive 38 km west on SR 546 to the Junction Creek picnic area at the end of the road. The trail is the gated road at the west end of the picnic area.

| | |
|---|---|
| 0.0 | north trailhead |
| 11.6 | Mount Romulus Campground to right |
| 18.8 | Little Elbow Pass |
| 22.0 | junction with Big Elbow trail, keep right |
| 23.0 | junction with Elbow headwaters trail, keep left |
| 25.8 | Sheep Pass |
| 31.5 | junction with Burns Lake trail, keep left |
| 32.7 | cabin |
| 35.0 | Burns meadows |
| 45.0 | end of ride |

# 53 HEADWATERS OF THE ELBOW                    map 9

With the towering limestone peaks of the Opal Range to the north and those of the Misty Range to the south, this is a spectacular piece of country. The headwaters of the Elbow River contain six subalpine lakes—Elbow Lake, Tombstone Lakes, Rae Lake and Sheep Lakes—any of which can be reached on a bike 'n' hike day trip.

The trail is an old dirt and gravel road that climbs steeply and you may have to push a bit to reach Elbow Lake, one of the most popular day hikes in the area. There's a backcountry campground in the trees on the south side of the lake. The road crosses the scree slopes along the north shore and rolls through meadows east of the lake—an area alive with wildflowers in June and July. This is a wild and beautiful valley left unusually open by a fire that swept through the area many years ago. Follow the road, a Rocky Mountain roubaix of cobblestone-like bumps (don't be surprised if your arms and shoulders complain), down the upper Elbow Valley to the junction with the Elbow and Sheep trails. The Tombstone backcountry campground is located 1 km north of the junction and could make an excellent base camp for exploratory rides and hikes.

## Options

Tombstone Lakes are nestled into a cirque on Tombstone Mountain and are reached by a side trail off of the Little Elbow trail to the north of the campground.

To get to Sheep Lakes, take the smooth gravel road leading south to the pass at the head of the Sheep River. The lakes can be reached by hiking north from the pass through wide, rolling meadows and clumps of larch. Rae Lake, to the southwest, is best reached from a point 1 km north of the pass.

**Scenic and rugged ride**

**Type** out-and-back on 4WD road and singletrack

**Rating** moderate/intermediate

**Other users** hikers-4  equestrian-1

**Distance** 14.6 km

**Time** 2-5 hours

**Maps** 82 J/10 Mount Rae
82 J/11 Kananaskis Lakes

**Season** July to mid-October

**Land agency** Alberta Provincial Parks, Kananaskis Country

## Access

The trail starts at the Elbow Pass trailhead on the east side of Highway 40, 62.7 km south of Hwy. 1 and 5 km north of Highwood Pass.

| 0.0 | trailhead |
| 1.3 | Elbow Lake |
| 6.3 | junction with Elbow-Sheep Road, turn left (Sheep trail to right) |
| 7.3 | Tombstone Campground (Little Elbow trail to left, Big Elbow trail to right) |

# 54 FORGETMENOT MOUNTAIN ROUNDER                    map 8

This long ride in the front range mountains and foothills is ideal for those with a sense of adventure. It combines five trails and has its share of challenges—from fording the Elbow River, to exciting singletrack cycling in some fairly remote country.

Cross the suspension bridge and ride south on the Big Elbow trail for 5 km to the start of the Threepoint Mountain trail, which is a bit tricky to locate. If you come to the point where the river is beside the road, you have gone a bit too far, the signed junction and ford will be about 0.5 km downstream. Cross the shallow, braided channels, then pedal and push up a pine-covered ridge at the base of Forgetmenot Mountain to the divide between the Elbow and Threepoint valleys. Mount Cornwall lies to the west at the head of a deeply glaciated valley.

South of the divide the singletrack briefly joins an exploration road through meadows along Threepoint Creek, then continues south. This trail tends to be severely messed up by livestock, especially if the weather is wet. Below Threepoint Mountain and Mount Rose the trail passes

**Hard-core enduro-ride**

**Type** loop on 2WD and 4WD roads and singletrack

**Rating** difficult/advanced

**Other users** hikers-2  equestrian-3 livestock

**Distance** 45.7 km

**Time** 4-6 hours

**Maps** 82 J/10 Mount Rae
82 J/15 Bragg Creek

**Season** July to mid-October

**Land agency** Kananaskis Country

**Access**
From Bragg Creek drive west on Hwy. 66 for 32 km to Little Elbow recreation area. Parking is provided near the campground entrance and at the suspension bridge.

10        20        30        40    45.7

*Burns meadows (#52, #58, #59, #60).*

through more meadows and patches of subalpine forest before reaching its junction with the Volcano Creek and Gorge Creek trails.

Continuing the rounder, hang a left and ride the rolling singletrack through meadows along Volcano Creek. At the junction with the Volcano Ridge trail (Find all of these names a bit confusing? Me too.), turn left and follow this old exploration road as it winds alongside Volcano Creek. The trail crosses Threepoint Creek and follows along the edge of the impressive black shale Threepoint canyon all the way to the trail junction on the west side of Hogs Back Ridge.

From this point the route turns north (left), leaves the canyon and cuts across a gentle, meadow-covered divide to connect with the Wildhorse trail (#50). (Finishing on the Quirk Creek trail is easier but quite a bit less satisfying.) Keep left on Wildhorse, a hearty singletrack that rocks and rolls along the lower slopes of Forgetmenot Mountain all the way to the Elbow River. Turn left on the Elbow Valley trail and pedal your weary bones the final 5 km back to the trailhead. If you are lucky, the ford of the Big Elbow will be dry.

| | |
|---|---|
| 0.0 | trailhead, cross suspension bridge |
| 5.0 | hidden junction, turn left onto Threepoint Mountain trail and ford Elbow River |
| 14.4 | junction, turn left onto Volcano Creek trail (right is Gorge Creek trail) |
| 15.4 | junction, keep left |
| 19.0 | junction, turn left onto Volcano Ridge trail |
| 27.5 | junction, turn left (Threepoint Creek and Hogs Back trails to right) |
| 29.8 | unsigned junction, keep left on singletrack of Wildhorse trail (optional Quirk Creek trail keeps right) |
| 40.8 | junction with Elbow Valley trail, turn left |
| 43.9 | ford Big Elbow River (often dry) |
| 45.7 | end of ride |

*Sheep Pass (#52, #58, #59, #60).*

# 55 GORGE CREEK LOOP

map 8

This is one of the best rides in the Sheep River valley. Well signed, it is a combination of challenging singletrack and easy doubletrack in a remote foothills setting with the highlight being an exciting descent into Gorge Creek canyon.

Ride west on the Gorge Creek trail keeping right at the first junction and following alongside the creek in the meadow. The trail climbs steeply through open lodgepole pine forest onto Volcano Ridge. At the top of the ridge there is a good view of Bluerock Mountain to the west. As you leave the summit take the fork to the right—it's a good downhill ride on an old exploration road featuring numerous diagonal drainage ditches that are nicely rounded and, if taken at speed, will provide you with the opportunity to fly for part of the trip.

At km 7.1 turn left and follow a narrow singletrack trail through the willows and meadows along Volcano Creek. This basic trail offers scenic cycling with Bluerock Mountain looming above the west end of the valley. Keep left at two trail junctions and join the Gorge Creek trail.

Gorge Creek is well named. At one instant the trail crowds the edge of the canyon, yielding views of Bluerock Mountain and Mount Rose, and at the next it's time to slide, glide, slip and roll your way to the bottom of the canyon. It is as much a test of your nerve as it is of your bike-handling skills. Meeting horses on this narrow singletrack can be unnerving for both parties, please dismount and get off the trail to let them pass. Beyond the ford the trail is muddy, rooty and rutted making for some difficult travel, but don't be discouraged. After the Bluerock trail junction you get to race along some excellent downhill singletrack through meadows and along sidehill trails above Gorge Creek. Finish up with a short climb up to the trailhead.

**Rugged backcountry ride with spectacular canyon**

**Type** loop on singletrack

**Rating** difficult/advanced

**Other users** hikers-2 equestrian-3 livestock

**Distance** 23 km

**Time** 3-5 hours

**Map** 82 J/10 Mount Rae

**Season** June to mid-October

**Land agency** Kananaskis Country

**Access**
From Turner Valley drive west on SR 546 for 30.5 km to the Gorge Creek Truck Trail. Drive north on this narrow gravel road for 4 km to Gorge Creek trailhead.

| | |
|---|---|
| 0.0 | trailhead |
| 1.3 | junction, turn right |
| 2.5 | junction, turn left (right is Gorge Link trail) |
| 4.8 | junction, keep left (Link Creek trail to right) |
| 5.0 | high point on Volcano Ridge, trail turns right |
| 7.1 | junction, keep left on Volcano Creek trail (right is Volcano Ridge trail) |
| 10.7 | junction, keep left |
| 11.7 | junction, turn left onto Gorge Creek trail (right is Threepoint Mountain trail) |
| 14.8 | junction, keep left (right is Bluerock trail) |
| 17.7 | junction, keep left (right is Indian Oils trail) |
| 21.7 | junction, turn right |
| 23.0 | end of ride |

# 56 VOLCANO RIDGE LOOP                    map 8

This ride makes a loop around Volcano Ridge and Allsmoke Mountain. These foothill ridges are not about to erupt any time soon—it's all sedimentary! This is a long trip that takes you across Volcano Ridge and down Volcano and Threepoint creeks, and brings you back on the Gorge Creek Truck Trail (gravel road).

Begin on the Gorge Creek trail, then follow the Volcano Ridge trail as it climbs steeply up to the ridge, one of the scenic high points of the trip. The trail continues north, passing the junction with the Volcano Creek trail, dipping into two small creek valleys, and descending through pine forest to Threepoint Creek. Prepare to be wowed by the spectacular Threepoint Creek canyon with its black shale walls streaked with sheep trails. The trail winds along the north side of this gorge to the junction of the Threepoint Creek and Wildhorse trails.

Ride east from the junction on either the smooth Threepoint Creek trail, a downgraded road that parallels the canyon, or on Hogs Back trail. Hogs Back is a narrow and exposed but very exciting singletrack that's way more fun and offers spectacular views. If you take this trail, be alert for horses and yield the trail.

**Rugged backcountry ride**

**Type** loop on 2WD and 4WD roads and singletrack

**Rating** difficult/intermediate

**Other users** hikers-2  equestrian-3  motorized-2  livestock

**Distance** 40.3 km

**Time** 5-7 hours

**Maps** 82 J/10 Mount Rae
82 J/15 Bragg Creek

**Season** June to mid-October

**Land agency** Kananaskis Country

**Access**
From Turner Valley drive west on SR 546 for 30.5 km to the Gorge Creek Truck Trail. Drive north on this narrow gravel road for 4 km to the Gorge Creek trailhead.

| | |
|---|---|
| 0.0 | trailhead |
| 1.3 | junction, keep right |
| 2.5 | junction, turn left (right is Gorge Link trail) |
| 4.8 | junction, keep left (right is Link Creek trail) |

*Gorge Creek (#55).*

Photo: Gerhardt Lepp.

Soon you cross the creek and turn right onto North Fork trail, the least enjoyable part of the trip. Tree roots and trail eroded by cattle and horses make for 5 km of brutally rough cycling but, if it's any consolation, the views of the front ranges to the west are excellent.

Those of you with true grit can cycle back on the Link Creek trail, but the rest of us will stick to the Gorge Creek Truck Trail. This winding gravel road follows the meadows along Link Creek and Ware Creek back to the Gorge Creek trailhead. You can expect to eat a little dust on this road, especially on weekends.

| | |
|---|---|
| 5.0 | high point on Volcano Ridge, trail veers right |
| 7.1 | junction, keep right (left is Volcano Creek trail) |
| 15.6 | junction, keep right and follow Threepoint Creek trail (left is Quirk-Wildhorse trail) |
| 20.9 | Hogs Back trail joins from right |
| 23.2 | ford Threepoint Creek |
| 24.0 | junction, keep right onto North Fork trail |
| 28.6 | Gorge Creek Truck Trail (road), turn right and follow road |
| 36.5 | Link Creek trail to right, keep left |
| 40.3 | end of ride |

# 57 BLUEROCK AND INDIAN OILS TRAILS     map 8

This is a trip for tough, strong-willed riders. Bluerock trail, in particular, is steep and frequently used by horses and cattle. It can be rough and muddy, not worth doing unless the weather has been dry for some time. Indian Oils trail is considerably better and when you include the beautiful foothill scenery, this rugged trip is quite worthwhile.

The Bluerock trail begins as an old logging road, but soon turns to singletrack with steep switchbacks winding down to the footbridge across Bluerock Creek. After the bridge, the trail climbs steeply and quite a bit of pushing will be required to get you up onto the shoulder of Bluerock Mountain. This alpine ridge with its expansive vistas is the high point of the ride. Drop off the ridge on a steep downhill trail, negotiate a few muddy sections and roll out to the meadows along Gorge Creek. Gorge Creek trail offers pleasant cycling, pretty meadows and three creek crossings.

The Indian Oils trail is marked by a sign, but it's still easy to miss. It crosses the creek and then leads up through the meadow into the trees. This enjoyable trail takes you up some steep climbs to an excellent vantage point on a ridge overlooking the Sheep Valley. It then switchbacks down from the ridge across open, dry hillsides and finishes with a short rolling section of trail leading back to Sheep River Road.

**Rugged backcountry ride**

**Type** loop on 2WD road and singletrack

**Rating** difficult/advanced

**Other users** hikers-2  equestrian-7

**Distance** 24.2 km

**Time** 4 hours

**Map** 82 J/10 Mount Rae

**Season** June to mid-October

**Land agency** Kananaskis Country

**Access**
From Turner Valley drive 37 km west on SR 546 to the Bluerock Equestrian Staging Area on the north side of the road.

| | |
|---|---|
| 0.0 | Bluerock trailhead |
| 7.0 | summit of ridge |
| 11.1 | junction, turn right (left is Gorge Creek trail) |
| 14.0 | junction, turn right onto Indian Oils trail (left is Gorge Creek trail) |
| 16.7 | junction, keep right |
| 19.0 | summit of ridge |
| 21.4 | junction, turn right |
| 21.8 | Hwy. 546, turn right |
| 24.2 | end of ride |

# 58 SHEEP RIVER

map 9

Photo: Gerhardt Lepp.

The trip through the Sheep Valley provides an outstanding mountain biking opportunity. A good doubletrack leads below the spectacular limestone cliffs of Gibraltar Mountain and into a beautiful front ranges valley. The only drawback, if you can call it that, is that you will get your feet wet in the numerous stream crossings. Strong riders can cycle to the pass at the head of the valley and back as a day trip.

The Sheep trail is an old gravel road with some rough spots and, while an old bridge over the Sheep River at the 3 km point makes for an easy crossing, the next crossing is unbridged and can be difficult at high water levels. Most of the remaining crossings are unbridged but shallow.

The initial part of the trip is dominated by views of Gibraltar Mountain, whose overhanging north face was the site of the first extended aid climb in the Canadian Rockies. The climbers were on the face for 8-1/2 days and many pitches were overhanging for their entire length.

**Scenic cruise in front range valley**
**Type** out-and-back on 4WD road
**Rating** difficult/intermediate
**Other users** hikers-2  equestrian-5
**Distance** 39.4 km
**Time** 4-6 hours
**Map** 82 J/10 Mount Rae
**Season** July to mid-October
**Land agency** Kananaskis Country

20

18

16

5    10    15    20    25    30    35    39.4

Burns meadows is located on private property at the junction with the Mist Creek trail (#60). Here you'll discover remnants of development by the Pat Burns Coal Mines Company. This grassy meadow, with Gibraltar Mountain towering to the east and the ramparts of Rickert's Pass overhead, is one of the most beautiful places in the front ranges of the Canadian Rockies. Not far from the meadow the trail passes an old range riders' cabin, then begins a gradual climb to the pass at the head of the valley.

The pass between the Sheep and Elbow rivers presents an austere but hauntingly beautiful landscape composed of burned-over larch and fir forest. Views include the peaks of the Opal and Misty ranges.

**Options**

1. Burns Creek trail branches to the west at km 13.5 and follows the north shore of Burns Creek for 5.5 km, almost to the base of a 400 m-high waterfall. A steep hike leads above the falls to Burns Lake. This is a good destination for a cycling trip up the Sheep River. Some of the uphill trip will require pushing. but it is all rideable on the way back.

2. Hard-core riders will be interested in the extended Mount Burns Loop (#54).

**Access**

From Turner Valley drive 38 km west on SR 546 to the Junction Creek picnic area at the end of the road. The trail is the gated road at the west end of the picnic area.

| | |
|---|---|
| 0.0 | trailhead |
| 3.0 | bridge |
| 10.0 | Burns meadows; Rickert's Pass trail to left |
| 12.7 | cabin to left |
| 13.5 | junction, keep right (Burns Creek to left) |
| 19.7 | Sheep Pass |

# 59 MOUNT BURNS LOOP
maps 8, 9

A ride you will not soon forget, this extended cycling trip is not for the faint-of-heart or the weak-of-leg. You might call it the "Ironman" route of backcountry biking in the Canadian Rockies. It is a very long and difficult ride suitable for strong, well-prepared cyclists. You must get an early start and have dry weather. The route is a combination of five different trails that enable you to circle around a group of front range peaks including Mount Burns, Bluerock Mountain and Mount Rose.

Begin by cycling the Sheep trail (#58) over to the Elbow River, then descending along the Big Elbow trail (#51) to its junction with the Threepoint Mountain trail (#54). Ford the Elbow and cycle south on this trail, continuing south on the Gorge Creek trail (#55). You have a choice of finishing on the more rigourous but shorter Bluerock trail (#57), or the Indian Oils trail (#57), which is easier but 5.4 km longer.

Refer to individual trail descriptions for details.

**Hard-core enduro-ride**

**Type** loop on 4WD roads and singletrack

**Rating** extreme/advanced

**Other users** hikers-1 equestrians-4

**Distance** 65.4 km

**Time** 6-8 hours

**Map** 82 J/10 Mount Rae

**Season** Mid-June to mid-October

**Land agency** Kananaskis Country

**Access**
From Turner Valley drive 38 km west on SR 546 to the Junction Creek picnic area at the end of the road. The trail is the gated road at the west end of the picnic area.

| | |
|---|---|
| 0.0 | trailhead, follow Sheep trail |
| 10.0 | junction, keep right (Mist Creek trail to left) |
| 13.5 | junction, keep right (Burns Creek trail to left) |
| 19.7 | Sheep Pass |
| 22.8 | junction, Elbow Lake trail to left |
| 23.9 | junction, turn right onto Big Elbow trail (Little Elbow trail to left) |
| 39.9 | junction, turn right onto Threepoint Mountain trail and ford Elbow River |
| 49.3 | junction, keep right on Gorge Creek trail (Volcano Creek trail to left) |
| 50.1 | junction, keep right |
| 53.2 | junction, turn right onto Bluerock trail (Gorge Creek and Indian Oils trails to left) |
| 64.4 | Bluerock trailhead |
| 64.9 | SR 546, turn right |
| 65.4 | end of ride |

Rickert's Pass.

# 60 AROUND THE MISTY RANGE
map 9

This perfect mountain bike trip is big on challenges and rewards. The ride takes you over Elbow Pass and Sheep Pass, then down the Sheep Valley, up and over Rickert's Pass and down Mist Creek trail to the south trailhead. The route circum-cycles the Misty Range, a range of 3000 m peaks deeply carved by glacial cirques, and is a feast for the eyes and the imagination. This trip is long and arduous and not to be taken lightly.

Cycle up the trail to Elbow Lake and enjoy the stunning beauty of this open valley as you bump your way along to the junction with the Sheep trail. The trail over Sheep Pass offers easy riding on an old gravel road through open, burned-over larch and fir forest. The trail drops into the Sheep Valley and leads through numerous stream crossings to Burns meadows. The north face of Gibraltar Mountain towering above the meadow is a sight not soon forgotten.

This marks the beginning of your singletrack adventures. The most difficult part of this trip is the steep push or carry up the Mist Creek trail to Rickert's Pass (545 m in 2.5 km). The track winds uphill from the meadow to an excavation in the hillside and continues along a steep trail through pine and fir forest to alpine meadows where switchbacks lead to the pass. Your hard work on the way up is rewarded with yet another striking view of the Misty Range and the prospect of a long downhill ride.

On the west side of the pass the singletrack quickly drops into a forest of technical delights to test your skills. The last kilometre of the trail follows along an old road with more than a few opportunities for air. Mist Creek trailhead marks the end of the ride, but if you don't have a second vehicle you can complete the trip by cycling on Hwy. 40 for 22.5 km back to your start point.

**Classic high mountain ride**

**Type** point-to-point on 4WD roads and singletrack

**Rating** difficult/advanced

**Other users** hikers-4 equestrian-3 livestock

**Distance** 31.1 km

**Time** 4-6 hours

**Maps** 82 J/10 Mount Rae
82 J/11 Kananaskis Lakes

**Season** July to mid-October

**Land agency** Kananaskis Country

**Access**
**north** The trail starts at the Elbow Pass trailhead on the east side of Highway 40, 62.7 km south of the Trans-Canada Highway and 5 km north of Highwood Pass.

**south** The Mist Creek trailhead is located 17.5 km south of Highwood Pass on Hwy. 40.

| | |
|---|---|
| 0.0 | north trailhead |
| 1.3 | Elbow Lake |
| 6.3 | junction, turn right onto Sheep trail (Elbow loop to left) |
| 9.4 | Sheep Pass |
| 15.6 | junction, keep left (Burns Creek to right) |
| 19.1 | junction, turn right onto Mist Creek trail (Sheep trail to left) |
| 21.6 | Rickert's Pass |
| 31.1 | south trailhead |

# 61 JUNCTION MOUNTAIN FIRE LOOKOUT     map 11

This challenging and rewarding ride leads to a fire lookout perched on the northeast ridge of Junction Mountain. Some sections of the road are steep and rocky and unless you have legs of steel you can expect to push for at least part of the way up.

The trail crosses the Sheep River on a bridge above Tiger Jaw Falls, then climbs over a hill to Dyson Creek. Dyson Falls is a short distance downstream from the shallow ford. Stay right at the fork where the Green Mountain trail meets the Junction Mountain trail and begin the strenuous climb toward the lookout. The trail climbs through a pine and fir forest, then emerges onto the ridge of Junction Mountain where your efforts are rewarded by alpine flowers and a spectacular view. Push and pedal along this alpine ridge while marmots whistle at your passing and the world unfolds below you.

From the lookout you can see Calgary on a clear day. Blue Ridge lies to the east, Bluerock Mountain to the northwest, Mount Rae pokes its head above the Highwood Range and the grey wall of Junction Mountain stands to the southwest.

The return ride is a steep and bumpy thriller.

**Options**

Hard-core riders can make a long singletrack loop by continuing south along the Junction Mountain trail as it makes a steep, switchbacking descent into the valley of Coal Creek. Follow the dirt trail down the valley through eight fords of the creek, then follow the Phone Line and Green Mountain trails to complete the loop. It is 23 km from the summit to the trailhead by this route. The downside is that much of the trail is hidden in the bush and you miss out on the scream down Junction Mountain Road.

**Major vertical and great views**

**Type** out-and-back on 4WD road

**Rating** difficult/intermediate

**Other users** hikers-2  equestrian-3 livestock

**Distance** 26 km

**Time** 4-6 hours

**Elevation** start (low) 1550 m high 2230 m

**Map** 82 J/10 Mount Rae

**Season** mid-June to mid-October

**Land agency** Kananaskis Country

**Access**

Park at Indian Oils trailhead on the south side of SR 546, 35 km west of Turner Valley.

| | |
|---|---|
| 0.0 | trailhead |
| 0.4 | bridge across Sheep River |
| 3.9 | junction, keep right |
| 4.3 | turn right and ford Dyson Creek |
| 4.4 | junction, turn right (Green Mountain trail to left) |
| 13.0 | fire lookout |

# 62 WOLF CREEK-COAL CREEK LOOP    map 11

This ride makes a loop in the hills south of the Sheep River by linking Wolf Creek, Phone Line, Mount McNabb and Price Camp trails. It's a fun roll on dirt trails and exploration roads, but don't even think of coming here in wet weather when the trail gets severely messed up by cattle. This is lower foothills country with no major elevation gain, but there are lots of small hills as the trail cuts across the drainages; there are few landmarks but the trail is well marked with signs.

Start by fording the Sheep River, which may prove difficult before midsummer. The Wolf Creek trail is a smooth dirt road that rises gently through mixed forest to the meadows along the creek, then grows faint as it climbs through pine forest between Mount Dyson and Blue Ridge. The pass between Wolf Creek and Coal Creek is definitely the highlight of the trip, with the gentle terrain giving no forewarning of the spectacular black shale canyon of Coal Creek and the meadow at the pass allowing a clear view of Blue Ridge to the south and Junction Lookout to the west. The trail makes a bumpy descent through meadows to the Wolf Creek backcountry campground and crosses Coal Creek three times.

The Phone Line trail is a smooth, winding singletrack through pine forest. Mostly dry and needle covered, it has a few wet and rooty sections to add challenge. The trail follows the route of an old single wire forestry phone line, part of the old Alberta Forest Service telephone line built in the 1920s from Coleman to Nordegg. The wire was strung on insulators hung from trees. It's all history now, replaced by radios and cellular communications.

**Rugged backcountry ride**

**Type** loop on 4WD roads

**Rating** difficult/intermediate

**Other users** hikers-1  equestrian-3 livestock

**Distance** 27.7 km

**Time** 4-6 hours

**Map** 82 J/10 Mount Rae

**Season** July to mid-October

**Land agency** Kananaskis Country

**Access**

Begin at Sandy McNabb recreation area, 21 km west of Turner Valley on SR 546. Pick up the trail where it crosses the Sheep River by driving to the picnic area at the bottom of the hill and look for the red diamonds on trees that mark the trail.

Photo: Gerhardt Lepp.

The Mount McNabb trail follows a dirt road along the north side of North Coal Creek through some of the prettiest meadows and aspen groves in the area, but you'll get your feet wet in the numerous creek crossings. The trail veers north and follows a cool singletrack through a meadow and over a low pass. Dropping down the north side of the pass is the sweetest part of the entire ride as the singletrack squeezes through the aspens and demands a display of your riding finesse.

The only redeeming feature of the Price Camp trail is that it is short. It is heavily travelled by cattle and laced with poplar roots. The trail is named after a Turner Valley resident who operated a sawmill here in the early 1900s. One more splash across the Sheep River and it's all over.

| | |
|---|---|
| 0.0 | trailhead, ford Sheep River |
| 0.1 | junction, keep left on Wolf Creek trail (Price Camp trail to right) |
| 9.1 | summit |
| 11.1 | junction, turn right onto Phone Line trail (Junction Mountain trail to left) |
| 18.1 | junction, turn right onto Mount McNabb trail (Green Mountain trail to left) |
| 24.6 | junction with Price Camp trail, turn right |
| 27.6 | junction, turn left and ford river |
| 27.7 | trailhead |

# 63 FLAT CREEK                                              map 11

The Flat Creek valley is one of those mountain treasures one hopes will remain undiscovered by development-minded people. The country is classic front ranges—from the meadows to the grassy, wind-blasted hillsides replete with limber pines; from the craggy sandstone outcrops to the towering limestone peaks of Mount Head and the Dogtooth Mountains; not to mention the sparkling streams. The scenery is at its best as you ride west into the mountains. For some entertaining stories about early exploration in this area read *The Buffalo Head* by R. M. Patterson.

The first section of this trail is on private land, please respect the landowners' wishes. Begin by cruising up the restricted access road to the Kananaskis Country boundary, and continue on an easy-riding doubletrack. Go past trail junctions for Wileman Creek and High Rock Ridge. The track fords the creek twice, although this can be avoided by taking a much more exciting singletrack bypass to the right. Soon you reach the Spruce Bluff range riders' cabin and the junction with the trail to Sullivan Pass. The Flat Creek Road continues for another 2 km.

With most of the views behind you and a steady downhill gradient ahead, the return trip is fast and easy.

## Options

1. Turn this into an outstanding loop by riding Grass Pass & Wileman Creek (#65) and returning on SR 541. This results in a ride of 40.2 km, of which 17 km are on pavement.

2. Add Sullivan Pass & High Rock Ridge (#64) for a total of 47.7 km, all on dirt.

**East slopes scenic cruiser**

**Type** out-and-back on 2WD and 4WD roads

**Rating** moderate/novice

**Other users** hikers-1  equestrian-4 livestock

**Distance** 38 km

**Time** 4-6 hours

**Maps** 82 J/7 Mount Head
82 J/8 Stimson Creek

**Season** June through October

**Land agency** private, Kananaskis Country

## Access

Drive 21 km west of Longview on SR 541. Begin at the locked gate east of the Flat Creek bridge.

| | |
|---|---|
| 0.0 | trailhead |
| 8.3 | Kananaskis Country boundary |
| 12.9 | junction, keep right (Wileman Creek trail to left) |
| 13.5 | junction, keep left (High Rock Ridge trail to right) |
| 14.7 | singletrack bypass trail to right |
| 14.8 | first ford; Head Creek trail to left |
| 16.3 | second ford, bypass trail joins from right |
| 17.0 | Spruce Bluff cabin; junction, keep left (Sullivan Pass and High Rock trail to right) |
| 19.0 | road ends |

# 64 SULLIVAN PASS & HIGH ROCK RIDGE    map 11

Sullivan Pass & High Rock Ridge is an exciting trip for the determined and adventurous back-country cyclist. What makes it exciting is the remote country, the beauty of the route along High Rock Ridge, and the exhilarating descent back into Flat Creek valley. It can be combined with the ride up Flat Creek for an enjoyable day trip. Be forewarned, some sections of this route are arduous and a fair bit of pushing is required.

Begin by riding and pushing up an old track to Sullivan Pass. Watch for elk. There follows a steep, cascading descent into the Sullivan Creek valley and onto the good gravel of the Sullivan Creek exploration road. This road could be followed east for about 23 km to SR 541, but the riding in that direction is generally unexciting. Instead, turn right and ride to a wellsite at the end of the road. From the wellsite a cutline leads you upward and wanders about the north side of High Rock Ridge. Just when you are wondering why you are wasting your time on this bush-bash, the trail breaks out to a high point where all the best views and a wild careering downhill section await. A short hike to the top of the ridge provides a worthwhile diversion at this point.

Ride on across open hillsides and meadows with excellent views. The trail remains on the ridge top for 1.5 km, then plunges 485 m over 3.5 km. The downhill riding is a blast, but you really wouldn't want to ascend this route. Rejoin the Flat Creek trail at km 13.5.

**Wilderness explorer**

**Type** loop on 4WD roads and singletrack

**Rating** difficult/intermediate

**Other users** equestrian-2 livestock

**Distance** 17.2 km

**Time** 3-4 hours

**Maps** 82 J/7 Mount Head 82 J/10 Mount Rae

**Season** mid-June to mid-October

**Land agency** Kananaskis Country

**Access**
This loop begins at the Spruce Bluff cabin, km 17 of the Flat Creek trail. Take the trail leading northeast to Sullivan Pass.

| | |
|---|---|
| 0.0 | trailhead at Spruce Bluff cabin (km 17.0 of Flat Creek trail) |
| 2.8 | Sullivan Pass |
| 5.2 | junction with Sullivan Creek Road, turn right |
| 6.2 | gas wellsite, trail is along cutline above |
| 9.2 | junction, turn right |
| 10.5 | high point of trail |
| 17.2 | junction and end of trail (km 13.5 of Flat Creek trail) |

# 65 GRASS PASS & WILEMAN CREEK                    map 11

Photo: Gerhardt Lepp.

This is an exciting singletrack trail that leads along the eastern edge of the Highwood Range. I prefer to ride it as part of an outstanding loop with the Flat Creek trail (#63). By riding up Flat Creek first, and then up Wileman Creek you get the advantage of the best views along Flat Creek and the descent of the Grass Pass trail, which is quite steep.

Leave Flat Creek Road at km 12.9 and shortly thereafter ford Flat Creek (usually easy). The cycling up Wileman Creek is easy and pleasant, but the trail can get severely messed up by horses and cows. Mount Head and Holy Cross Mountain form a dramatic backdrop to a series of meadows. Cross Wileman Creek three to five times during the ascent.

Grass Pass is aptly named. A short 1 km single-track leads southeast to a spectacular vantage point overlooking the Highwood Valley and the peaks of the Continental Divide. R. M. Patterson, adventurer and former owner of the Buffalo Head Ranch, called this place Fir Creek Point and his 'boundary pine' is still alive today. "From the Boundary Pine the nearer summits of the Continental Divide came into view; they were only nine miles away in an air line. Those distant mountains had a way of beckoning to you, and it was so easy just to saddle a couple of horses and hit the trail...." More than 60 years later our

**Rugged backcountry ride**

**Type** point-to-point on singletrack

**Rating** difficult/intermediate

**Other users** hikers-3  equestrian-4  livestock

**Distance** 10.3 km one way

**Time** 2-3 hours

**Map** 82 J/7 Mount Head

**Season** June through October

**Land agency** Kananaskis Country

**Access**

**south** From the Sentinel day-use area on SR 541, 38.4 km west of Longview.

**north** From km 12.9 of Flat Creek trail.

| | |
|---|---|
| 0.0 | north trailhead (km 12.9 of Flat Creek trail) |
| 0.2 | ford Flat Creek |
| 0.8 | junction, keep right |
| 7.3 | Grass Pass; junction, keep right (Fir Creek Point is 1.0 km to left) |
| 10.3 | Hwy. 541 |

mounts may be a little different but the spirit is still the same.

You didn't really think 20 km of up-hill, even if it was gentle, would be without its rewards, did you? The break-neck descent from Grass Pass to SR 541 is guaranteed to shorten the life of your brake pads. Control your speed and keep an eye out for horses and hikers. As you descend you may notice the transition from bunchgrass and limber pines at the summit to Douglas fir, lodgepole pine and aspen in the valley bottom.

## Options

Some folks may wish to do this ride as an out-and-back from the south trailhead. The trail up Pack Trail Coulee to Grass Pass requires pushing a good deal of the way, but Wileman Creek provides easy riding in both directions.

# 66 SHEEP TO HIGHWOOD
map 11

Photo: Gillean Daffern.

**Hard-core enduro-ride**

**Type** point-to-point on 4WD roads and singletrack

**Rating** extreme/intermediate

**Other users** hikers-2 equestrian-4 livestock

**Distance** 46.7 km one way

**Time** 6-8 hours

**Maps** 82 J/7 Mount Head
82 J/8 Stimson Creek
82 J/10 Mount Rae

**Season** mid-June to mid-October

**Land agency** Kananaskis Country

**Access**
**north** Park at Indian Oils trailhead on the south side of SR 546, 35 km west of Turner Valley.

**south** From the Sentinel day-use area on SR 541, 38.4 km west of Longview.

| | |
|---|---|
| 0.0 | north trailhead |
| 0.4 | bridge across Sheep River |
| 3.9 | junction, keep right |
| 4.3 | turn right and ford Dyson Creek |
| 4.4 | junction, keep left on Green Mountain trail (Junction Mountain trail to right) |
| 7.9 | junction, turn right onto Phone Line trail (left is Mount McNabb trail) |

There is something very satisfying about a long-distance cycling trip along the edge of the mountains. Not quite so satisfying is the need for a long car shuttle to make the trip possible. This extended cross-country cycle trip climbs over a number of ridges and passes as it makes its way from the Sheep River to the Highwood River. The route links five previously described rides; check the individual trail descriptions for additional details. In wet years this route can be very muddy and rough owing to heavy use by cattle and horses. This ride works well in either direction, but north to south has you riding down the steepest of the hills.

Begin from the Sheep Valley, cycling along the road to Junction Mountain (#61). Turn onto the Green Mountain trail, a good dirt road, then follow the Phone Line trail (#62) to its junction with the Wolf Creek trail. Turn right and follow this trail upstream for 1.1 km, watching for a track to the left, an old exploration road that provides rather basic travelling for 2.8 km until it intersects Sullivan Creek Road. (If you are travelling south to north this obscure junction is marked by a red paint blaze on a pine tree.) Turn right and, with considerable relief, hammer along the good gravel of the road. As an option, you might cross over Sullivan Pass to Flat Creek. However, the High Rock Ridge trail (#64) is a much more exciting, but arduous, route. Drop off the ridge and head down Flat Creek trail for a short distance. Turn right and ride the Grass Pass & Wileman Creek trails (#65). The ride ends with a kamikaze downhill run off Grass Pass to the pavement of Highway 541. Following the Flat Creek trail (#63) to the highway is an alternative finish.

| | |
|---|---|
| 14.9 | junction, turn right onto Junction Mountain trail along Coal Creek (left is Wolf Creek trail) |
| 15.5 | junction, keep right |
| 16.0 | junction, turn left onto old exploration road |
| 18.8 | junction with Sullivan Creek Road, turn right |
| 23.8 | junction, keep left (Sullivan Pass trail to right) |
| 24.8 | gas wellsite, trail is along cutline above |
| 27.8 | trail joins from left |
| 35.8 | junction with Flat Creek trail, turn left |
| 36.4 | junction, turn right onto Wileman Creek trail |
| 43.7 | Grass Pass |
| 46.7 | south trailhead at SR 541 |

Photo: Gillean Daffern.

Photo: Gillean Daffern.

Photo: Gillean Daffern.

# 67 ODLUM POND                                    map 12

Odlum Creek trail is a very easy and pleasant mountain bike ride. Aside from a major ford of the Highwood River, it is a real cruiser's special on a smooth old road that ends near Odlum Pond, a small lake in a cirque.

A short distance into the ride the Highwood River must be forded—it's knee-deep, 10 m wide and slow flowing in midsummer, but much more difficult to cross early in the season. Shortly thereafter, cross shallow Loomis Creek, keep right at the fork in the trail and ride along a bench above the Highwood River where grouseberries carpet the pine forest and strawberries line the edges of the road. The track parallels Odlum Creek as it climbs steadily but gently into the low mountains west of the Highwood River.

The upper Odlum Valley is covered by spruce and fir forest that bears the scars of logging and fire. The road crosses two sawmill sites and eventually comes to an old log bridge across Odlum Creek. Don't cross the bridge, instead find the rough logging road on the south side of the creek that leads to two beaver ponds surrounded by drowned trees. A game trail continues to Odlum Pond. It's a shallow lake in a meadow dwarfed by a waterfall and the towering limestone walls of the Elk Range.

**Gentle backcountry ride**

**Type** out-and-back on 4WD road

**Rating** easy/novice

**Other users** hikers-1  equestrian-2

**Distance** 26 km

**Time** 2-4 hours

**Map** 82 J/7 Mount Head

**Season** late July to mid-October

**Land agency** Kananaskis Country

**Access**
Park at the Lineham Creek picnic area on Hwy. 40, 93.4 km south of Hwy. 1 and 12 km north of the Highwood Junction. Cycle 200 m north to the gated trailhead on the west side of the highway. Trip distances begin here.

| 0.0 | trailhead |
| 1.6 | ford Highwood River |
| 3.0 | ford Loomis Creek |
| 3.1 | junction, keep right (left is Loomis Creek cut off) |
| 3.9 | junction, keep right (left is Loomis Creek trail) |
| 11.7 | junction, turn left before bridge |
| 13.0 | end of cycling |
| 13.7 | Odlum Pond |

# 68 LOOMIS CREEK
map 12

Photo: Gillean Daffern.

This trail follows an old logging road into the valley of Loomis Creek in the southern end of the Elk Range. Loomis Lake is a steep 1 km hike from the end of the road.

Follow the Odlum Creek trail from the Lineham Creek picnic area, ford the Highwood River, then cross Loomis Creek. Cycle 800 m farther on Odlum Creek Road to the junction with the Loomis Creek logging road.

The trail is a good dirt road that climbs gently through a gap in the range of low mountains west of the Highwood River. After four successive stream crossings you'll pass the old road that leads up Bishop Creek. The valley now opens up and provides pleasant cycling through open mixed forest and meadows. Beyond the sawmill site the road gradually deteriorates and becomes more vegetated. Avoid the lower roads that drop to the creek.

To continue to Loomis Lake, leave your bike at the end of the road and bushwhack up the north side of the creek. It is a short but steep climb up meadows and benches to the lake. Nestled in a cirque below an unnamed peak, the lake is dammed by a wall of terminal moraine.

## Options

A bike 'n' hike up the steep Bishop Creek logging road takes you above treeline to a col below Mount Bishop.

**Bike 'n' hike to Loomis Lake**
**Type** out-and-back on 4WD road
**Rating** moderate/novice
**Other users** hikers-2  equestrian-4
**Distance** 26 km
**Time** 2-4 hours return
**Map** 82 J/7 Mount Head
**Season** late July to mid-October
**Land agency** Kananaskis Country

### Access
Park at Lineham Creek picnic area on Hwy. 40, 93.4 km south of Hwy. 1 and 12 km north of Highwood Junction. Cycle 200 m north to the gated trailhead on the west side of the highway. Trip distances begin here.

| | |
|---|---|
| 0.0 | trailhead |
| 1.6 | ford Highwood River |
| 3.0 | ford Loomis Creek |
| 3.1 | junction, keep right (left is Loomis cut off) |
| 3.9 | junction, turn left (right is Odlum trail) |
| 6.0 | junction, keep right (left is Bishop Creek trail) |
| 10.9 | sawmill site |
| 13.0 | end of road |

# 69 MCPHAIL CREEK

map 13

High foothills, big rock walls, an alpine tarn and a pass on the Great Divide are all highlights of this trip. A pleasant cycle on an old dirt logging road takes you to trails leading to Lake of the Horns, Weary Creek Gap and the Hill of the Flowers.

From the trailhead roll northward through scenic meadows that highlight the peaks of the High Rock Range towering to the west. Soon you come to the ford of the Highwood River, which, by late July, is still knee deep and 15 m wide, but the current is slow.

Beyond the river, take the fork on the right and ride along a bench high above McPhail Creek. Watch for a natural mineral lick to the right of the road. It's a large muddy depression with numerous game trails radiating out into the meadows and open pine forest. This area was burned over in 1936 by a huge fire that swept over the pass from the Elk River valley. R. M. Patterson, in his book *The Buffalo Head*, tells some fascinating tales of his adventures in this valley.

There are several forks in the road, but they all return to the fairly obvious main route in the valley bottom. The road skirts the Hill of the Flowers and rolls on below the ramparts of the High Rock Range before fading out at the head of the valley.

## Options

1. Lake of the Horns. This hike begins on the north side of the road between two small creeks. The trail climbs steeply through several cliff bands on the lower slopes of Mount McPhail, but the lake is well worth the effort and provides a cool dip on a hot day.

2. Elk Trail Pass. The headwall below Weary Creek Gap looks intimidating, but you can hike up a game trail that switchbacks up through the cliff bands. This is the Elk Trail Pass of Indian legends. See #70 for the trail that continues to Elk River valley in B.C.

3. The Hill of the Flowers stands apart from the main range providing vistas in all directions. To gain the summit wander up the south ridge of this pyramid-shaped hill.

**Bike 'n' hike to Lake of the Horns**

**Type** out-and-back on 4WD roads

**Rating** moderate/novice

**Other users** hikers-3  equestrian-5 livestock

**Distance** 24 km

**Time** 4-6 hours

**Map** 82 J/7 Mount Head

**Season** late July to mid-October

**Land agency** Kananaskis Country

**Access**
Park at Cat Creek day-use area on the west side of Hwy. 40, 99.8 km south of Hwy. 1 and 5.6 km north of Highwood Junction. The trail starts at a gated road on the north side of the picnic area.

| | |
|---|---|
| 0.0 | trailhead |
| 2.3 | ford Highwood River |
| 2.6 | junction, turn right (Carnarvon trail to left) |
| 9.7 | Hill of the Flowers to right |
| 10.5 | trail to Lake of the Horns to right |
| 12.0 | end of road, trail to Weary Creek Gap on north side of creek |

2    4    6    8    10    12    14    16    18    20    22    24

# 70 WEARY CREEK & FORDING RIVER PASS LOOP    map 13

Are you an aerobic monster? This ride could be the test. It's a long and challenging trip through remote country where you'll need to be well prepared, but for those riders with the atomic dog mindset the rewards are plenty.

Begin on the McPhail Creek trail (#69) and work your way to the end of the doubletrack below Weary Creek Gap, a pass on the Great Divide. A singletrack leads across the creek and up through the cliffs to the pass. Riding through the summit meadows surrounded by high peaks and snowfields is enough to blow your mind. Follow an old track south until you reach the seismic trail, then turn right and prepare to descend into the Elk Valley. After losing a lot of vertical and negotiating a few exciting drops, you pop out onto the Elk Valley powerline road. Welcome to beautiful British Columbia!

Ride south to the Aldridge Creek trail, which is difficult to identify owing to a massive washout on the lower section. From here to Fording River Pass is where the aerobic monster bit comes into play. Much of the trail ascends at an angle that is just a bit too steep for sustained riding. So push, ride, whatever; it's an 11 km slug to the pass. Fording Pass is high in the alpine meadows with spectacular vistas and peaks in all directions. I have to admit that by the time we got to the pass, our eye for beauty was becoming a bit glazed! The descent is a welcome relief but watch those steep downhills. If you are still feeling a bit of zing the singletrack of the Great Divide trail provides a challenging option and rejoins the cat track farther down the valley. Once across Baril Creek bridge watch closely for the obscure junction where you turn left, then race down to the end of the trail at SR 940. It is 9 km back to your car. Hey, you atomic dog, time to celebrate!

## Options

Use a vehicle shuttle to do a ride across either Weary Creek Gap or Fording River Pass.

**Hard-core enduro-ride**

**Type** loop on 2WD roads, 4WD roads and singletrack

**Rating** extreme/advanced

**Other users** hikers-3 equestrian-3

**Distance** 62.8 km

**Time** 7-10 hours

**Map** 82 J/7 Mount Head

**Season** July through October

**Land agency** Kananaskis Country, British Columbia Forest Service

### Access

Park at Cat Creek day-use area on the west side of Hwy. 40, 99.8 km south of Hwy. 1 and 5.6 km north of Highwood Junction. The trail starts as a gated road on the north side of the picnic area.

| | |
|---|---|
| 0.0 | trailhead |
| | ford Highwood River |
| 2.6 | junction, keep right |
| 12.0 | doubletrack ends |
| 16.7 | Weary Creek Gap |
| 22.0 | Elk Valley powerline road, turn left |
| 28.6 | Aldridge Creek trail, turn left |
| 39.5 | Fording River Pass |
| 47.1 | junction, keep right |
| 47.5 | obscure junction, turn left |
| 53.8 | Hwy. 940, turn left |
| 62.8 | end of ride |

24

22

20

18

16

10    20    30    40    50    60 62.8

# 71 CARNARVON LAKE (ALMOST)     map 13

The trail up Carnarvon Creek offers good cycling and excellent scenery as it climbs into the foothills below the High Rock Range. The trail is best in midsummer when the ford on the Highwood River is easier and the weather is warm enough to make a swim in Carnarvon Lake bearable.

Ride north through scenic meadows, then ford the Highwood River. Stay left at the major trail junction past the ford and cross McPhail Creek. The trail is an old logging road that rolls along the north side of Carnarvon Creek. Stay right at the junction with the Strawberry Hills trail (#72). The many forks in the road can be confusing, but it's a case of taking the road more travelled with pointers and cairns left by others to lead the way.

The impressive walls of the High Rock Range tower above the end of the road. Don't follow the road all the way to the scree slope below the headwall, instead, look for a trail to the north that traverses the scree slope to a waterfall. A short but exposed, moderately difficult scramble over rock bands beside the waterfall leads to the colourful little lake surrounded by meadows and rock walls.

The ride back down the road is most enjoyable. In fact, the trip is over altogether too soon for my liking.

**Bike 'n' hike to Carnarvon Lake**

**Type** out-and-back on 4WD roads

**Rating** moderate/novice

**Other users** hikers-4  equestrian-4 livestock

**Distance** 17.2 km

**Time** 4-6 hours

**Map** 82 J/7 Mount Head

**Season** late July to mid-October

**Land agency** Kananaskis Country

**Access**
Park at Cat Creek picnic area on the west side of Hwy. 40, 99.8 km south of Hwy. 1 and 5.6 km north of the Highwood Junction. The trail starts at gated road on north side.

| | |
|---|---|
| 0.0 | trailhead |
| 2.3 | ford Highwood River |
| 2.6 | junction, keep left (McPhail Creek trail to right) |
| 2.7 | ford |
| 5.6 | junction, keep right (Strawberry Hills to left) |
| 8.6 | Carnarvon Lake trail to right |

Photo: Gerhard Lepp.

# 72 STRAWBERRY HILLS map 13

The Strawberry Hills are part of a rolling esplanade lying just east of the High Rock Range. This forested upland, with its maze of old logging roads, is a great place to explore by bicycle. The trail climbs through open country that has been logged and burnt and has regrown in pine and aspen. There are good views of the pyramid-shaped peak of Mount Strachan and the massive wall of Mount Armstrong, both on the Continental Divide. The riding is easy doubletrack cruising along an old logging road that links the Carnarvon Creek and Fitzsimmons Creek trails. It makes a pleasant loop ride with a return on Hwy. 40. Unfortunately, the dirt road is usually roughened by the hooves of numerous elk and cattle and makes for bumpy cycling, and several fords, including two of the Highwood River, guarantee wet feet. Avoid this trail in wet weather.

The north end of Strawberry Hills trail is reached by cycling up the Carnarvon Creek trail. Turn left and cross the creek near some old log-loading ramps. As you climb into the hills several logging roads branch off causing some confusion in routefinding. Stay right at the first two junctions and generally left thereafter—if in doubt choose the more travelled and obvious fork in the road. A bit of trial and error may be required. After crossing the north fork of Fitzsimmons Creek, turn left at the T-junction and descend Fitzsimmons Creek trail to the Highwood River.

## Options

Follow the Fitzsimmons trail over to Baril Creek, then descend to Highway 40 and return to your starting point.

**Backcountry explorer**

**Type** loop on 2WD and 4WD roads
**Rating** moderate/novice
**Other users** hikers-1 equestrian-2
**Distance** 20.2 km
**Time** 3-4 hours
**Map** 82 J/7 Mount Head
**Season** late July to mid-October
**Land agency** Kananaskis Country

**Access**
**north** Via Carnarvon Creek trail (#71) at 5.6 km point.

**south** Via Fitzsimmons Creek trail (#73) at 5.2 km point.

| | |
|---|---|
| 0.0 | north trailhead |
| 2.3 | ford Highwood River |
| 2.6 | junction, keep left (McPhail Creek trail to right) |
| 5.6 | junction, turn left (Carnarvon trail to right) |
| 5.9 | ford Carnarvon Creek |
| 6.3 | keep right |
| 6.8 | keep right |
| 6.9 | keep left |
| 8.5 | summit |
| 10.9 | four-way junction, turn right |
| 11.0 | ford Fitzsimmons Creek |
| 11.8 | junction with Fitzsimmons trail, turn left |
| 12.5 | ford Fitzsimmons Creek |
| 16.7 | ford Highwood River |
| 17.0 | Hwy. 40, turn left |
| 19.8 | Cat Creek day-use area, turn left |
| 20.2 | trailhead |

# 73 FITZSIMMONS CREEK                                    map 13

This ride begins in the meadows of the broad Highwood Valley and climbs into the hills below the rugged wall of the High Rock Range. It is a good cruiser trip on old roads. The loop includes the Fitzsimmons Creek trail and the Baril Creek trail (#74) with a return on Hwy. 40. These trails are muddy in wet weather.

Leave the trailhead and ford the Highwood River, usually easy by mid-July. Follow the doubletrack across the meadows, then climb steadily along the north side of Fitzsimmons Creek through open lodgepole pine and trembling aspen forest. The massive wall of Mount Armstrong dominates the view to the west and Holy Cross Mountain and Mount Head in the Highwood Range come into view to the east. Ride past the junction with the Strawberry Hills trail (#72) and climb to the summit. Signs of past logging are more obvious near the top of the pass where several old roads branch off the main route. Mount Baril rises across the Baril Creek valley.

Keep left at the trail junction at the top of the pass and enjoy a fast and fun-filled doubletrack ride down to the Baril Creek trail. Cross the double-log bridge over Baril Creek and climb gently to the junction with the Baril Connector. It's easy to miss the trail here because the better road to the right is actually the Baril Connector. You want to take the somewhat poorer looking left-hand fork; if you find yourself climbing way up the mountainside, you have gone too far. The Baril Creek trail is a fast and exhilarating downhill doubletrack that winds along the south side of the creek and ends at Highway 940. Turn left and ride the road back to the Fitzsimmons Creek picnic area.

**Backcountry explorer**

**Type** loop on 2WD and 4WD roads

**Rating** moderate/novice

**Other users** hikers-1 equestrian-2 livestock

**Distance** 22.5 km

**Time** 3-5 hours

**Map** 82 J/7 Mount Head

**Season** late July to mid-October

**Land agency** Kananaskis Country

**Access**
The trail starts at Fitzsimmons Creek picnic area on the west side of Hwy. 40, 2.8 km north of the Highwood Junction.

| | |
|---|---|
| 0.0 | trailhead |
| 0.3 | ford Highwood River |
| 4.5 | ford Fitzsimmons Creek |
| 5.2 | junction, keep left (Strawberry Hills to right) |
| 8.0 | summit; junction, keep left (right also descends to Baril Creek) |
| 9.4 | junction with Baril Creek trail, turn left and cross bridge |
| 9.8 | obscure junction, turn left (right is Baril Connector) |
| 16.1 | trailhead on SR 940, turn left |
| 19.7 | junction with Hwys. 40, 541, turn left |
| 22.5 | trailhead |

Photo: Gillean Daffern.

# 74 BARIL CREEK TO FORDING RIVER PASS    map 13

A good doubletrack trail leads up the valley of Baril Creek toward Fording River Pass. The riding is fun and it paves the way, so to speak, to a beautiful pass on the Great Divide. The extensive alpine meadows of Fording River Pass are an invitation to hike below the spectacular peaks and snowfields of Mount Cornwell and Mount Bolton. Save this trip for dry weather—the lower part of the road can be quite muddy.

The trail is an old dirt logging road that climbs steadily through pine and spruce forest. Note where it joins with the Baril Connector (actually the better road), as this junction can be difficult to locate on the return trip. The trail crosses a log bridge over Baril Creek, then passes the junction with the Fitzsimmons Creek trail. Farther west you'll pass an old sawmill site, then the single-track of the Great Divide trail will begin to parallel the road. The up-trip is easier on the road but the singletrack makes a challenging and exciting return ride. The old road crosses the north fork of Baril Creek and climbs sharply, becoming so steep you may want to hide your bike and hike the rest of the way to the pass.

The ride out is fast and very enjoyable. Watch for the somewhat tricky junction east of the log bridge.

## Options

From the pass, the doubletrack continues down Aldridge Creek to the Elk Valley (see #70).

**Bike 'n' hike to alpine meadows**

**Type** out-and-back on 4WD roads

**Rating** difficult/intermediate

**Other users** hikers-3  equestrian-3 livestock

**Distance** 28.6 km

**Time** 6-7 hours

**Map** 82 J/7 Mount Head

**Season** July to mid-October

**Land agency** Kananaskis Country

**Access**
The trail is on the west side of SR 940, 0.5 km south of Baril Creek and 3.6 km south of the Highwood Junction.

| | |
|---|---|
| 0.0 | trailhead |
| 6.3 | junction, keep right (left is Baril Connector) |
| 6.6 | bridge |
| 6.7 | junction, keep left (right is Fitzsimmons trail) |
| 7.7 | sawmill site |
| 12.0 | steep uphill begins |
| 14.3 | Fording River Pass |

# 75 RYE RIDGE
map 13

Do you like to bike through wild country with superb mountain vistas? This deluxe ride delivers on both counts. The logging roads in the Cataract and Etherington creek valleys offer easy cycling, while the singletrack trail joining them over Rye Ridge is more challenging.

Ride south on the logging road as it turns and rolls up scenic Cataract Creek valley. At km 5.4, where the gravel road turns south and crosses Cataract Creek, stay right on a much rougher grassy doubletrack. Continue up the valley, passing an old range riders' cabin and, as the track climbs steeply on a cutline, watch for a good track to the left. This is soon joined by the singletrack of the Great Divide trail, marked with red blazes. Turn right at the first four-way junction, left at the second and climb to Rye Ridge on a good singletrack.

**Classic high mountain ride**

**Type** loop on 2WD and 4WD roads and singletrack

**Rating** difficult/intermediate

**Other users** hikers-2  equestrian-3  motorized-2  livestock

**Distance** 31.4 km

**Time** 4-6 hours

**Map** 82 J/7 Mount Head

**Season** mid-June to mid-October

**Land agency** Kananaskis Country

**Access**
The trailhead is at the junction of SR 940 and the gated Cataract Creek Road, 11.6 km south of Highwood Junction. From the gate follow the road that descends to the left.

The trail breaks out of the pine forest onto the open windswept meadows of the ridge where there are magnificent views of Mount Etherington and Baril Peak in the High Rock Range, the Highwood Range to the north and peaks as far away as Tornado Mountain to the south. Enjoy the ridge-riding and vistas, then rejoin the trail for a fast slaloming run through the trees as it drops into the valley of Etherington Creek on a wide track covered with wood chips. In the valley the trail is less pleasing as it follows a wet old logging road to the right until it joins with the road along Etherington Creek.

The relatively smooth, fast riding on the dirt surface of Etherington Creek Road is a blast. The upper part of the road is sometimes roughened by cattle and elk, but it gets smoother later in the summer. The lower part of the road is gravel and there are several shallow creek crossings where you can play splash. Watch for horses. Return to the trailhead on SR 940.

**Options**

When I'm on a ride as pleasant and satisfying as this one, I find myself wishing that it would never end. The Baril Connector can help you delay the inevitable. This old logging road crosses a low pass from Etherington Valley to Baril Creek valley and allows you to complete your ride on the Baril Creek trail.

| | |
|---|---|
| 0.0 | trailhead |
| 4.7 | millsite, Raspberry Pass trail to right |
| 5.4 | junction, turn right onto rough track (left is Lost Creek trail) |
| 10.0 | cabin |
| 10.7 | junction, turn left |
| 10.9 | Great Divide trail joins from left |
| 11.3 | four-way junction, turn right |
| 11.6 | four-way junction, turn left |
| 13.7 | trail along open summit ridge |
| 18.6 | junction with road along Etherington Creek, turn right |
| 21.7 | junction, go straight through (Baril Connector to left, Raspberry Pass trail to right) |
| 24.0 | Etherington Campground |
| 25.5 | SR 940, turn right |
| 31.4 | end of ride |

# 76 WILLOW CREEK WANDERER                    map 14

Photo: Gillean Daffern.

An outstanding cruiser-style ride, this trip from Salter Creek to Willow Creek is highly recommended. Beginning in the front ranges, it crosses a pass through the Livingstone Range and descends through two foothills valleys. The cycling is generally easygoing on doubletrack and the east slopes scenery is at its best. Take along some water as the creeks may be dry by midsummer. Completing this ride requires a vehicle shuttle or a long ride back on the road.

The trail climbs along Salter Creek and passes through a long meadow nestled between Mount Burke and Plateau Mountain. From the top of Salter Pass there are impressive views of Sentinel Peak and Sentinel Pass. The track is steep and heavily eroded as it drops off the east side of the pass, then offers exciting cycling as it rolls through a typical foothills landscape of meadows, and poplar and pine forest along Pekisko Creek.

**Classic ride from mountains to foothills**

**Type** point-to-point on 4WD roads

**Rating** difficult/intermediate

**Other users** hikers-1  equestrian-2 livestock

**Distance** 27 km one way

**Time** 3-6 hours

**Maps** 82 J/7 Mount Head
82 J/8 Stimson Creek
82 J/1 Langford Creek
82 J/2 Fording River

**Season** June to mid-October

**Land agency** Kananaskis Country

The rather vague four-way junction with the Willow Creek trail can be a little confusing—follow the snowmobile signs to the right. This grassy road offers smooth and easy riding as it climbs gently and crosses a low divide into the Willow Creek drainage. Don't be led astray near km 19 by an enticing singletrack to the left where the road turns to the right, crosses the creek and climbs through a meadow. The hoof-roughened road continues through pasture land with lots of gates to open and close and cattle to entertain as you roll south to SR 532.

## Options

1. Return to Cataract Creek by road, a 31.7 km ride on good gravel for a round-trip distance of 58.7 km. SR 532 provides a scenic and sometimes windy trip over the pass below Hailstone Butte; dusty SR 940 will make you climb but offers a good downhill ride from Wilkinson Summit back to Cataract Creek.

2. Combine this ride with the trail in Timber Creek (#77).

3. Pekisko Creek to Hwy. 22. If you can arrange a car shuttle, it is possible to turn left at the four-way junction. From here it is easy cycling to the Kananaskis Country boundary and then, on steadily improving roads, across the Cartwright Ranch and on past the historic Bar U Ranch to the highway, a distance of approximately 25 km.

## Access

**north** From Highwood Junction, drive 13.6 km south on SR 940 to Cataract Creek recreation area. The campground entrance road crosses Salter Creek. Begin on the south side of the creek.

**south** From SR 532, 3.8 km west of the Kananaskis Country boundary. The trail finishes just east of the Willow Creek bridge.

| | |
|---|---|
| 0.0 | north trailhead |
| 1.5 | trail keeps left up Salter Creek |
| 2.3 | Mount Burke trail to left |
| 7.0 | Salter Pass |
| 15.0 | four-way junction, turn right (left is Pekisko Creek trail) |
| 18.5 | trail turns right, fords creek and climbs up through meadow |
| 27.0 | SR 532 |

# 77 TIMBER CREEK                                              map 14

This ride has a bit of everything. The lower part is an easy doubletrack winding through a gentle valley and the upper section is a steep, rocky track that climbs through a pass in the Livingstone Range. Timber Creek is a classic foothills valley with aspen forests and meadows highlighted by the hills. Windy Peak, a high grassy ridge in the Livingstone Range, forms its western headwaters. West of the pass the country is typical of the high mountains—subalpine forest and meadows in the valleys surrounded by limestone peaks.

From the east the trail begins as a rutted dirt doubletrack that deteriorates as you proceed up the valley. This trail can be muddy in wet weather and while it may be roughened by livestock, the rutted and chewed-up surface belies the ease with which a cyclist can pass over it. Ride downstream along Willow Creek, keeping right at km 2.6 and making an easy ford. Always following the better track, proceed through several gates and pass a range riders' cabin, keeping right at all major trail junctions beyond. Ford Timber Creek four times—refreshing if the day is hot—and proceed

**Rugged backcountry ride from foothills to mountains**

**Type** point-to-point on 4WD road and singletrack

**Rating** difficult/intermediate

**Other users** motorized-2  livestock

**Distance** 18 km one way

**Time** 2-4 hours

**Map** 82 J/1 Langford Creek

**Season** June through October

**Land agency** Kananaskis Country

Photo: Gillean Daffern.

up the valley as the trail becomes more stony and well drained. Push and ride up the steep, rocky hill to the upper traverse, which leads to the pass. The upper section of trail provides vistas of the Timber Creek valley and the plains to the east. The aptly-named Windy Peak stands to the south; hang on as the west wind buffets and whirls you about, seemingly trying to make you hit rocks or even ride over the edge. The pass is a brief affair where you not only cross the Livingstone Range but also cross from the foothills into the mountains. It is a short hilly ride to the west trailhead.

## Options

1. Make a loop by riding on SR 532. It is 11 km from trailhead to trailhead.

2. Combine this trail with Willow Creek Wanderer (#76) to make a challenging enduro ride.

## Access

**east** From SR 532, 3.6 km west of the Kananaskis Country boundary, turn south (this is the second road east from the Willow Creek bridge).

**west** From SR 532, 2.6 km east of SR 940 and 1.5 km west of the summit.

| | |
|---|---|
| 0.0 | east trailhead |
| 2.6 | junction, keep right and ford Willow Creek |
| 3.3 | junction, keep left |
| 4.4 | gate |
| 6.9 | first ford of Timber Creek |
| 7.1 | junction, keep right |
| 16.0 | summit |
| 18.0 | west trailhead |

2    4    6    8    10    12    14    16    18

# 78 PLATEAU MOUNTAIN                                     map 14

A big part of the excitement of mountain biking is cycling in spectacular high mountain environments. The cycling on Plateau Mountain is not particularly challenging but the esthetics are incredible—you can pedal your fat tires for many kilometres across the alpine tundra at elevations in excess of 2400 m. To the west the peaks of the High Rock Range rise above the meadows like a row of pyramids stamped out of the same glacial mould; to the east the great plains stretch flat and hazy to the horizon while the oil towers of Calgary stand diminutively in the distance. Not quite so pleasing is the presence of two gas wells with compressors chugging away, but they are the reason for the existence of the road.

This mountain is unique in that it was a nunatak, or non-glaciated peak during the last glaciation. Ten thousand years ago, when the surrounding valleys and peaks were covered in ice, the flat top of Plateau Mountain remained ice free. This allowed the development of patterned ground, a periglacial feature consisting of polygons of rock. Freeze thaw action tends to separate

**Gentle ride in alpine meadows**

**Type** out-and-back on 2WD and 4WD roads

**Rating** moderate/novice

**Other users** hikers-2

**Distance** 12+ km

**Time** 3-5 hours

**Map** 82 J/2 Fording River

**Season** July to mid-October

**Land agency** Kananaskis Country

Photo: Gerhardt Lepp.

*The summit of Plateau Mountain is frequently cold and windy—dress accordingly.*

Photo: Gillean Daffern.

rocks from the smaller particles of soil. Thousands of years of this action, uninterrupted by the scouring of glaciers, has resulted in a honeycomb pattern of rocks over the surface of the ground. The plateau also provided a rare, ice-free habitat for plants and animals during glaciation.

In this high and open landscape you will be exposed to the full force of the weather, go prepared for adverse conditions. It is best to pick a calm day to cycle this peak. Bring water.

Cycle up the gravel road as it rises in huge switchbacks across the alpine meadow. At km 4.5 the road forks. The right fork leads to the summit and a radio tower, great views and sometimes glimpses of bighorn sheep. The left fork, which tends to be covered with loose gravel, drops gently for 4.2 km across the plateau to an abandoned drilling platform. There are excellent examples of patterned ground along the way with buttercups, alpine forgetmenots and moss campion growing among the lichen-covered rocks.

**Access**

From Highwood Junction, drive 26.1 km south on SR 940 to Wilkinson Summit. Turn left on Plateau Mountain Road and drive a further 3.9 km to a locked gate near treeline.

| | |
|---|---|
| 0.0 | trailhead |
| 4.5 | junction, turn right (left descends across the plateau) |
| 5.6 | junction, keep right |
| 6.0 | summit |

**Options**

See Twin Summits Odyssey (#79).

# 79 TWIN SUMMIT ODYSSEY                          map 14

This route delivers! Imagine cycling to two summits, across considerable expanses of high alpine plateau, a few steep climbs, a long fast downhill, then throw in some exciting routefinding. A rough, cross-country track linking Plateau Mountain with Hailstone Butte makes it all possible.

Begin by cycling to the summit of Plateau Mountain. On the summit, about 200 m north of the radio tower, a narrow road leads to an old drill site at the southeast edge of the plateau. Follow a faint line of rocks, possibly the route of a pipeline, as it descends southwest to a col. This is one of the most exciting and dramatic places that I have ever travelled with a bicycle: rolling alpine meadows drop away into rocky canyons. Continue along the line of rocks as it drops across the slope to the northeast and dips below treeline to a gas well in a glacial cirque. A smooth gravel road connects with Hailstone Butte Road. After cycling to the top of Hailstone Butte, let your bike coast your tired body back to the Forestry Trunk Road. A short, sometimes dusty ride returns you to the trailhead.

**Rugged high mountain ride**

**Type** loop on 2WD and 4WD roads and singletrack

**Rating** difficult/advanced

**Other users** hikers-1  livestock

**Distance** 38.6 km

**Time** 5-6 hours

**Maps** 82 J/1 Langford Creek
82 J/2 Fording River

**Season** July to mid-October

**Land agency** Kananaskis Country

**Access**
As for Plateau Mountain (#78), but park at the gate by SR 940 and cycle up the road.

| | |
|---|---|
| 0.0 | trailhead |
| 3.9 | locked gate |
| 8.4 | junction, keep right |
| 9.5 | junction, turn left |
| 10.6 | wellsite, follow vague track that descends to col, then veers left across sidehill |
| 13.6 | join gas well access road, turn right |
| 15.7 | junction, turn left (right to SR 940) |
| 17.0 | junction, turn right onto rough road (left goes to more wells) |
| 22.0 | Hailstone Butte Lookout, descend the way you came |
| 27.0 | junction, keep left |
| 28.3 | junction, keep left |
| 32.1 | junction with SR 940, turn right |
| 38.6 | end of trip |

# 80 HAILSTONE BUTTE FIRE LOOKOUT    map 14

Do you like mountaintop vistas? This ride climbs up a gas well-access road and a steep lookout access road to a panoramic view of the southern Rockies and plains.

The ride begins on a well-travelled gas well access road with meadows, pipelines and grazing cattle. Stay right at the first two forks. The route to the fire lookout is a rocky, seldom-travelled road marked by a broken-down green and white gate. It is steep but rideable as it climbs up a valley with cliffs rising above. After a gentle ride past a wet meadow the road begins rising again through huge rolling alpine meadows on the east side of Hailstone Butte. The view keeps getting better and soon the distinctive shape of Saddle Peak rises above the meadow. Push and pedal up the steep switchbacks and along a rocky ridge to the fire tower.

Windy Peak and Saddle Peak, part of the Livingstone Range, can be seen to the south while Beehive Mountain, Gould Dome and The Elevators rise from the High Rock Range to the west. The bustling metropolis of Calgary lies to the north-northwest beyond the rolling foothills. Nearer at hand the steep and colourful Skene Canyon drops away to the east and Plateau Mountain presents its flat top to the immediate west.

**Major vertical and great views**

**Type** out-and-back on 4WD roads

**Rating** difficult/intermediate

**Other users** hikers-1  motorized-1 livestock

**Distance** 20.2 km

**Time** 4 hours

**Map** 82 J/1 Langford Creek

**Season** July to mid-October

**Land agency** Kananaskis Country

**Access**
From Highwood Junction, drive 32.6 km south on SR 940 to the junction with SR 532. The road to Hailstone Butte is a gated road 50 m north of SR 532.

| | |
|---|---|
| 0.0 | trailhead |
| 3.8 | junction, keep right (left goes to gas wells) |
| 5.1 | junction, keep right onto rough road (left goes to more gas wells) |
| 10.1 | Hailstone Butte Lookout |

2    4    6    8    10    12    14    16    18    20.2

# 81 CATARACT CREEK & LOST CREEK                   map 13

Photo: John Gibson.

**Family fun on gentle backcountry ride**

**Type** out-and-back on 4WD roads
**Rating** easy/novice
**Other users** hikers-1 livestock
**Distance** 30 km
**Time** 3-5 hours
**Maps** 82 J/7 Mount Head
82 J/2 Fording River
**Season** mid-June to mid-October
**Land agency** Kananaskis Country

Do you like spectacular mountain scenery and easy cruising on old roads? If so, this route is for you. A logging road follows Cataract Creek and Lost Creek past the Boy Scout bridge to cutblocks in the upper Lost Creek Valley. Most of the creek crossings are bridged, but expect the unexpected. The ride is easy with little elevation gain and provides access for two longer mountain bike trips.

Ride south from the trailhead on a good gravel road as it passes through scenic valley-bottom meadows alongside Cataract Creek. The creek and numerous beaver ponds are popular fishing holes. To the west the ramparts of Mount Scrimger and Mount Etherington define the Continental Divide.

The road crosses a bridge over Cataract Creek and follows Lost Creek to an important junction at km 11.3. Keeping left here leads to the old Boy Scout bridge. Tied together in 1980 by the 153rd Scout Troop, a more substantial road bridge has since been built beside it. The rough logging roads to the south of the bridge access two longer rides—Oyster Excursion and the Great Divide trail. If you are not going on either of these rides keep right at the junction at km 11.3, and continue on the gravel road along the north bank of Lost Creek to cutblocks below Cataract Plateau and Mount Farquhar.

## Options

1. Great Divide trail (#82).
2. Oyster Excursion (#84).

**Access**
The trailhead is at the junction of SR 940 and the gated Cataract Creek Road, 11.6 km south of Highwood Junction. From the gate follow the road that descends to the left.

| | |
|---|---|
| 0.0 | trailhead |
| 4.7 | millsite |
| 5.4 | junction, keep left and cross bridge (right is Rye loop) |
| 11.3 | junction, keep right (to left are Boy Scout bridge, Great Divide trail and Oyster Excursion) |
| 15.0 | road ends in cutblocks |

# 82 GREAT DIVIDE TRAIL

map 13

What an incredible ride! Long, challenging single-track cycling trails are rare in the Rockies and this section of the Great Divide trail is one of the best.

The route follows the Cataract Creek and Lost Creek ride (#81) as far as the Boy Scout bridge. Next comes the difficult and rewarding part of the trip—17 km of challenging, technical singletrack on a ridge along the Divide between Lost Creek and the Oldman River, then through alpine meadows below the Continental Divide. The trip finishes on the Headwaters of the Oldman trail (#83). This is a long ride requiring careful planning and good backcountry travel skills. A long (76 km) car shuttle is required to set it up.

This is a remote stretch of trail where it is possible to imagine you are deep in the wilderness, but there are reminders. From the occasional glimpses of wayward cutblocks, to the sounds of blasting emanating from the Fording River coal mines just across the Great Divide—the heavy hand of humanity lies all about you.

Begin by cycling the smooth gravel road up Cataract Creek and Lost Creek. At km 11.3 follow a dirt road that forks left to the Boy Scout bridge. Keep right at two minor junctions, then about 0.7

**Remote high mountain ride**

**Type** point-to-point on singletrack

**Rating** extreme/advanced

**Other users** hikers-1  equestrian-2

**Distance** 36.2 km

**Time** 6-8 hours

**Maps** 82 J/7 Mount Head
82 J/2 Fording River

**Season** July to mid-October

**Land agency** Kananaskis Country,  Alberta Forest Service

**Access**

**north** The trailhead is at the junction of SR 940 and the gated Cataract Creek Road, 11.6 km south of Highwood Junction. From the gate follow the road that descends to the left.

**south** From Highwood Junction drive 48 km south on SR 940 to Oldman River Road. Turn right and drive 28 km to the end of the road.

| | |
|---|---|
| 0.0 | north trailhead |
| 5.4 | junction, keep left and cross bridge |
| 11.3 | junction, keep left (upper Lost Creek to right) |
| 11.5 | crossing at Boy Scout bridge; junction, keep right |
| 11.6 | junction, keep right |
| 12.2 | junction, turn right (left is Oyster Excursion) |
| 12.5 | turn left onto Great Divide trail |

km beyond the Boy Scout bridge turn right onto a rough logging road. About 300 m west on the logging road look carefully for red blazes marking a singletrack leading to the left into mature spruce forest. Remarkably stupid logging practices have left 20 m of timber on each side of the trail and much of it has blown down across the trail.

The hard part of this trip is now upon you. Push and carry your fat tires for 2 km and 365 vertical metres to the top of the ridge on an often muddy trail.

Once atop the ridge you can resume riding, and what a wild ride it is! Most of the trail from here to the Galena Miracle Mine is a rideable alpine roller coaster with hills to test your climbing and descending skills and some sections of exposed sidehill trail where both your nerve and your skill will be tested.

The trail climbs over and traverses around four minor summits along this ridge, all are at or near treeline. Alpine meadows, larches and wind-blown pines frame views of peaks and valleys extending in every direction. Best of all is the massive wall of the Continental Divide looming above the meadows ahead. The trail winds its way off the ridge and into flower-filled meadows that cling below the cliffs of the High Rock Range. It makes a couple of excursions into the forest, then wanders past an alpine tarn and crosses a steep stream gully as it approaches the abandoned Galena Miracle Mine. Mine timbers and the remains of a cog railway are strewn down a scree slope below the mine shaft. Turn the corner and you're on a wind-blasted ridge high above the Oldman Valley.

Next thing you know it's all over. A steep but rideable trail bypasses the switchbacks of the old mine access road and crosses a meadow to the seismic line near Memory Lake. From the lake a sometimes muddy dirt road leads to the end of Oldman River Road.

| | |
|---|---|
| 14.5 | first summit |
| 27.2 | road to Galena Miracle Mine, turn left |
| 29.2 | four-way junction at Memory Lake, turn left |
| 33.7 | follow rough road to right |
| 36.2 | Oldman River Road |

**Options**

This trip can be cycled without a car shuttle by making a loop from the south trailhead in combination with Oyster Excursion (#84).

# SOUTHERN ROCKIES

The Southern Rockies riding area straddles the Continental Divide and includes a variety of trails accessed from Highway 3. This area is notable for its (count 'em) 10 cyclable passes across the Great Divide. Many of the more remote wilderness rides are on old exploration roads and quad tracks, but a handful of singletracks are notable for the good rides they provide. Trips of all lengths and difficulties can be found here and many of them begin right in the towns. Close to the towns you'll frequently find rider-built trails that will challenge the best of cyclists. You will encounter off-road vehicles and horses on many of the trails in keeping with the multiple use approach to land management that prevails in this area.

East of the Divide the high plains grasslands push right up to the mountains at Waterton and reach almost to the Divide at Crowsnest Pass. Rainfall and wind are the major factors determining the intertwining of grassland and forest in this area. The lower elevations and southern exposures feature the classic foothills mosaic of aspen, Douglas fir, pine and grasses. Higher in the mountains spruce and fir predominate. West of the Divide the climate is moderated by Pacific influences and overall higher rainfall leads to lush forests of fir and cedar. Larches are common in the mountain forests and put on a spectral autumn display.

In the Crowsnest area, the main ranges of the Rockies are absent and classic front range limestone peaks and foothills dominate the scenery right up to the Divide. Farther south in the Castle, Waterton and Flathead valleys the mountains are high and colourful, towering above deep glaciated valleys. In addition to the Rockies standard of limestone and shale, the geology here includes a lot of volcanic rocks. The steel blues, reds and greens associated

with the Purcell lava flow add a lot of colour to the mountains. West of the Divide, much of the country is dominated by the broad and deep valley of the Elk River with its high peaks and massive coal deposits.

Although common throughout the Rockies, coal is synonymous with the story of Fernie and the Crowsnest Pass, a lively, often tragic, history of towns and villages struggling for survival and prosperity. Coal mining is still a mainstay of the economy of the Elk Valley but, throughout the area, forestry and natural gas are also major industries and tourism is increasing in importance. In many ways the tourism potential of this area is undiscovered and I daresay the locals like it that way. There are many things to do besides ride bikes: hiking and scrambling, exploring the historical sites, and checking out the heritage buildings are but a few. The local information centres will be happy to help you find other activities.

Crowsnest Pass is a collection of five small communities located along the Crowsnest River east of the Divide. They share a common history and geographic setting and comprise one of the best centres in Alberta for mountain biking. Nine rides begin and/or end right in town, and the surrounding area holds another dirty dozen rides within a 50 kilometre drive. Many of the trails are old exploration roads now downgraded to doubletracks, others are used by quads in summer and snowmobiles in winter and receive a high degree of volunteer maintenance that includes bridges across the streams. There are a few singletracks dating from historical times and some good rider-built single track. The local riding community is small but active with occasional races. The Tuck Shop in Coleman is a good place for your cycling needs and to tune in to the local cycling scene. There's camping in Bellevue and Blairmore and showers are available at the Mohawk in Coleman. Local attractions include the Coleman Museum and the Frank Slide Interpretive Centre. These sleepy little towns with their turn-of-the-century cottages and buildings and relaxed approach to life provide a delightful and refreshing contrast to the hustle-bustle of Banff and Canmore.

An informal cycling route links the five communities and provides a scenic and historic tour in its own right. It runs from the Star Creek trailhead at 54 Street in west Coleman through town on the streets to 88 Street. Continue east to Blairmore on a doubletrack along the south side of the railway tracks that ends at 105 Street. Cross the tracks and follow 20 Ave. until it crosses the bridge, then follow the river pathway east through Blairmore. The path continues east from 20 Ave. along the river, passes under Highway 3, then joins the highway just as you enter Frank. Turn right into the industrial park, then left on 152 Street to follow a gravel backroad through the Frank Slide and on to the paved road that connects Bellevue and Hillcrest.

Waterton Lakes National Park sits in the very southwestern corner of Alberta in an area where prairie grasslands push right up against towering mountain peaks. The usual restriction of off-road cycling to designated trails applies in the park. The village of Waterton Lakes is a small summer resort that offers most services during the summer season including camping with showers. Waterton is a pleasant base for a variety of mountain-bike trips in the park and surrounding area. Immediately north of the park, five trails lead from prairie grasslands to timberline while, farther west, the wild and beautiful country drained by the Castle River offers spectacular riding on old roads and singletracks.

Deep in the Elk Valley lies Fernie, a small city with a priceless collection of heritage buildings. Once a quiet little town, Fernie is experiencing a revival with resort development proceeding apace both in town and at the ski hill. The combination of great scenery, low-key atmosphere and a wide variety of trails makes Fernie a perfect base for mountain bike adventures. The riding scene here is one of the most dynamic in the Rockies with lots of active riders, frequent races and lots of rider-built trails. The locals are quite generous in sharing their trails and publish a free local trail guide and map—'The Secret of Singletrack'. Just west of town, Fernie Alpine Resort is actively encouraging mountain biking on the hill with lift assisted biking and trails that appeal to riders of every skill level. I've described a variety of rides for this area, but the good folks at Ski Base will be happy to help you customize your rides. Camping is available at nearby Mount Fernie Provincial Park, and showers and budget accommodation can be had at the Raging Elk Hostel.

Elkford is a small coal mine town located in a remote and wild part of the Elk Valley. The town offers most services including a good campground with showers. You'll find the locals to be friendly and happy to share their uncrowded valley and good trails. Three excellent rides begin right in town. Considering its proximity to major population centres, this country is surprisingly wild and offers exciting backcountry riding opportunities on old exploration roads. Highway 43 is the major access route leading north from Sparwood to Elkford and the gravel Elk Lakes Pass road continues up the Elk Valley. A number of rides begin from this road and lead into valleys and passes on the Great Divide to the east and into some beautiful mountains to the west.

# 83 HEADWATERS OF THE OLDMAN RIVER     map 13

This route follows a doubletrack up the Oldman River to Memory Lake near the Continental Divide. The Great Divide trail can be followed from the lake up to the abandoned Galena Miracle Mine on the slopes of Mount Gass.

Cycle up the rough dirt road past the beaver ponds and meadows along the creek. Stay left where the Oyster Excursion departs to the north and ford Oyster Creek. Near the 2 km point, several hundred metres of the original road have been downgraded by the Forest Service to discourage vehicle access. Follow a steep trail up to a sometimes boggy doubletrack seismic line and ride west along the seismic line to Memory Lake. The lake is located in subalpine forest below a break in the High Rock Range. The remains of the abandoned Galena Miracle Mine can be seen high on the slope to the north.

## Options

Great Divide trail (#82), which is marked by red paint blazes, crosses the seismic road 200 m east of the lake and leads north along and across the mine roads for 2.5 km to timberline on Mount Gass.

**Backcountry explorer**

**Type** out-and-back on 4WD roads

**Rating** moderate/novice

**Other users** hikers-1  equestrian-2 motorized-3

**Distance** 14.4 km

**Time** 3 hours

**Map** 82 J/2 Fording River

**Season** mid-June to mid-October

**Land agency** Alberta Forest Service

**Access**
From SR 940 turn west on Oldman River Road and drive 28 km to the end of the road.

| | |
|---|---|
| 0.0 | end of Oldman Road |
| 1.0 | junction, keep left (Oyster Excursion to right) |
| 2.5 | join seismic line and turn left |
| 7.0 | four-way junction, go straight (Galena Miracle Mine and Great Divide trail to right) |
| 7.2 | Memory Lake |

2     4     6     8     10     12     14.4

# 84 OYSTER EXCURSION                                    map 13

Oyster Excursion is a less than totally exciting ride that follows seismic and logging roads from the Oldman River to Cataract Creek. The route is used as a snowmobile trail in the winter and is marked with orange squares.

Ride west on the rapidly deteriorating Oldman River Road and turn north on a seismic line that climbs up onto a grassy terrace. This doubletrack makes at least seven shallow crossings of Oyster Creek and there are some boggy areas to hike around. The valley bottom is a meadow of grasses and willow that turns golden brown in late summer, and Beehive Mountain shows its distinct profile to the south. When I cycled this trail I followed fresh grizzly tracks for more than 10 km. The bear was heading south and I north. We must have passed like two ships in the night.

The route follows a straight seismic line over a low divide between Oyster and Lost creeks. Alberta Forest Service has scraped the road down to mineral soil in an effort to improve it as a snowmobile trail. Unfortunately, this did not improve its quality as a cycling trail and it can be rather muddy when wet. The route eventually leaves the seismic line and heads west on a rough logging road that leads to the Boy Scout bridge. The trip finishes up with an easy and pleasant roll out to the north trailhead on the smooth gravel of Lost Creek and Cataract Creek (#81) roads.

**Backcountry explorer**
**Type** point-to-point on 4WD roads
**Rating** difficult/intermediate
**Other users** motorized-1 livestock
**Distance** 26.2 km one way
**Time** 4-5 hours
**Maps** 82 J/2 Fording River
82 J/7 Mount Head
**Season** July to mid-October
**Land agency** Alberta Forest Service

**Access**
**south** From SR 940 turn west on Oldman River Road and drive 28 km to the end of the road.

**north** The trailhead is at the junction of SR 940 and the gated Cataract Creek Road, 11.6 km south of Highwood Junction.

| | |
|---|---|
| 0.0 | south trailhead |
| 1.0 | junction, turn right (left leads to Memory Lake) |
| 4.0 | junction with seismic line, go straight (left leads to Memory Lake) |
| 10.1 | summit |
| 14.0 | turn right |
| 14.7 | Boy Scout bridge |
| 14.9 | junction with Lost Creek Road, turn right |
| 26.2 | north trailhead |

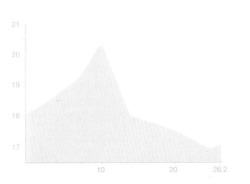

# 85 SHALE CREEK TO CABIN RIDGE                    map 15

Here is your chance to work up a sweat. This route follows a steep dirt bike trail onto Cabin Ridge. The trip up is largely pushing, but the trip back is a challenging downhill ride on a narrow trail. This south-facing route dries out early in the spring.

The trail starts in an open lodgepole pine forest, drops sharply into a branch of Shale Creek, then works its way up the valley through meadows. From the pass at the head of Shale Creek you can hike either north or south to gain the top of the ridge where you can see Tornado and Beehive mountains to the west, the Sugarloaf Fire Lookout to the southwest and the Livingstone Range to the east.

**Major vertical with great views**

**Type** out-and-back on singletrack

**Rating** difficult/advanced

**Other users** hikers-1 motorized-3

**Distance** 9 km

**Time** 3-4 hours

**Maps** 82 G/16 Maycroft
82 J/1 Langford Creek

**Season** mid-June to mid-October

**Land agency** Alberta Forest Service

**Access**

From SR 940, drive 8.2 km up Oldman River Road. Look for a narrow unmarked trail on the east side of the road about 300 m north of the ford at the start of the Hidden Creek trail (#86).

| | |
|---|---|
| 0.0 | trailhead |
| 1.5 | ford Shale Creek |
| 4.5 | summit |

Photo: Gerhardt Lepp.

# 86 HIDDEN CREEK                          map 15

This ride is part of an excellent bike 'n' hike trip. Doubletrack trails lead up Hidden Creek and South Hidden Creek to the base of Tornado Mountain. From the end of the doubletrack the Great Divide trail climbs to the magnificent north notch of Tornado Mountain.

The trip starts with a ford of the Oldman River, usually not possible until midsummer. Shortly after the ford the road splits. The left fork has been partially reclaimed and provides a rough ride, while the right fork is a dirt doubletrack that climbs over a hill before the two routes rejoin. The road continues west, providing an interesting up-and-down ride on smooth but rutted dirt, and the views up the valley to Tornado Mountain and Gould Dome keep getting better. Just as your feet start to dry out the road swings south to cross Hidden Creek and a tributary in three successive crossings. Beyond the third crossing the track turns left and climbs into the valley of South Hidden Creek. The trail climbs steadily passing a large clearcut and rough logging road joining from the south (this road connects to Atlas Haul Road), then ends at the creek.

Watch for the Great Divide trail, a singletrack that climbs up to the right shortly before the end of the road. Advanced riders will want to take their bikes as far as timberline, you'll have to push quite a bit of the way up, but it's almost all rideable on the way down. There isn't much of a trail from timberline to the ridge, but it is a spectacular hike through alpine meadows to the ridge or up the steep scree slope to the notch immediately south of Tornado Mountain.

**Bike 'n' hike to ridge below Tornado Mountain**

**Type** out-and-back on 4WD roads

**Rating** moderate/intermediate

**Other users** hikers-1  equestrian-2  motorized-3

**Distance** 30 km

**Time** 4-5 hours

**Maps** 82 G/15 Tornado Mountain 82 G/16 Maycroft

**Season** mid-July to mid-October

**Land agency** Alberta Forest Service

**Access**
From SR 940, 60.9 km south of the Highwood Junction and 45.1 km north of Coleman, turn west on Oldman River Road and drive 7.9 km to the confluence of the Oldman River and Hidden Creek. Look for an obvious ford on the west side of Oldman River Road where Hidden Creek Road starts.

| | |
|---|---|
| 0.0 | trailhead, ford Oldman River |
| 0.2 | trail forks, go left or right |
| 1.5 | trails rejoin |
| 7.9 | junction, turn left up Hidden Creek |
| 9.5 | junction, keep right (logging road to Dutch Creek to left) |
| 12.7 | right on Great Divide trail |
| 15.0 | timberline, hike begins |
| 17.0 | ridge |

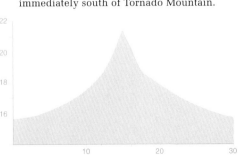

# 87  LIVINGSTONE FIRE LOOKOUT                   map 15

Photo: Tony Daffern.

**Major vertical and great views**
**Type** out-and-back on 4WD roads
**Rating** difficult/intermediate
**Other users** motorized-1
**Distance** 20.6 km
**Time** 4-5 hours
**Map** 82 G/16 Maycroft
**Season** mid-June to mid-October
**Land agency** Alberta Forest Service

**Access**
The trailhead is on the east side of SR 940, 60.9 km south of the Highwood Junction and 45.1 km north of Coleman. The trail is the gravel road directly opposite Oldman River Road. Trip measurements begin at SR 940.

| | |
|---|---|
| 0.0 | trailhead |
| 0.5 | junction, keep right |
| 2.0 | ford Livingstone River |
| 4.2 | junction, turn left |
| 6.1 | gate |
| 10.3 | summit, fire lookout |

The ride to Livingstone Lookout will test your stamina and hill-climbing abilities on the way up and reward you with a great downhill run on the return. The summit ridge and peak offer views of Tornado Mountain and Gould Dome to the west and Whaleback Ridge and the foothills to the east.

The trail begins as a good gravel road. After 0.5 km keep right and cycle the rutted doubletrack to the Livingstone River ford, which is usually easy by midsummer. Continue south for 2 km to a large grassy meadow and watch for the obvious road to the east that disappears into the trees. Where the main track veers left, follow the grassy track ahead.

The uphill is hard work and some pushing is required, especially where the rocky road climbs up a canyon toward the crest of the Livingstone Range. The road improves to a fine shale surface as it climbs through spruce and fir forest to the lookout.

Say hello to the towerperson, sign the guest book, admire the view, then it's time to strut your high speed handling skills on the downhill run.

## 88 BEAVER CREEK LOOP

map 16

Photo: Tony Daffern.

**Family fun on gentle trail**
**Type** loop on 4WD roads
**Rating** easy/novice
**Other users** motorized-3  livestock
**Distance** 9.3 km
**Time** 1-2 hours
**Map** 82 J/1 Langford Creek
**Season** mid-June to mid-October
**Land agency** Alberta Forest Service

**Access**
Begin at the Livingstone Falls
Campground on SR 940, 42.3 km
south of the Highwood Junction
and 63.7 km north of Coleman.

| | |
|---|---|
| 0.0 | Livingstone Falls Campground, cycle north on SR 940 |
| 1.9 | turn right onto 4WD road |
| 3.7 | junction, turn right (left is trail to Westrup Creek) |
| 5.3 | pass |
| 8.5 | junction with SR 940, turn right |
| 9.3 | Livingstone Falls Campground |

This short cycle trip on the lower slopes of Mount Livingstone makes a good evening ride from the Livingstone Falls Campground. Apart from some rocky road on the south end of the loop, most of the trip is on smooth, gravel road.

Roll north on SR 940, then turn right onto a rutted road through mature spruce forest. The road improves steadily as it climbs through a cutblock and passes through an old burn to a fork at km 3.7. The trail to Westrup Creek goes left up the canyon, you want to turn right and follow the south fork across the cutblock to a low pass. Take time to enjoy the view north to Plateau Mountain and west to the peaks of the High Rock Range, then roll onward.

The smooth gravel road on the south side of the small pass provides a good downhill ride that becomes rocky and rough where it enters the pine and poplar forest. Be sure to close any cattle gates and keep an eye open for raspberries and strawberries. Return to the campground on SR 940.

20
18
16
2    4    6    8    9.3

# 89 BEAVER CREEK TO WESTRUP CREEK       map 16

Here is a chance to ride your fat-tires from the mountains to the foothills on a trail that crosses a low pass in the Livingstone Range. The trail climbs up Beaver Creek, then descends along Westrup Creek to the east trailhead.

Cycle up Beaver Creek Road for 1.8 km to the junction below the canyon at the south end of Mount Livingstone. Keeping left, pedal and push through the rough, rocky canyon to a gate and beaver pond. A good, nearly level dirt road continues through meadows and open forest and climbs to the pass.

It soon drops on a smooth, shale surface down the east side of the Livingstone Range; passing a dry grassy ridge where twisted weather-beaten pines, silhouetted against the skyline, are reminiscent of a scene from a Japanese painting. The deep Westrup Creek valley never does give an open view to the east. None of the roads marked on the topo maps are evident, but the obvious route stays close to Westrup Creek, crossing it numerous times. The upper creek flows in a deep shale canyon and where part of the road has collapsed you must follow a narrow footpath. Farther down the road, a large meadow covered in daisies gives a view of the steep eastern side of the Livingstone Range. The remaining rough dirt road is well travelled by cattle and very muddy in wet weather. Be sure to close the gates behind you.

**Rugged ride from mountains to foothills**

**Type** point-to-point on 4WD roads

**Rating** moderate/intermediate

**Other users** motorized-3 livestock

**Distance** 12.3 km one way

**Time** 2-3 hours

**Map** 82 J/1 Langford Creek

**Season** mid-June to mid-October

**Land agency** Alberta Forest Service

**Access**

**west** The trailhead is a rutted dirt road on the east side of SR 940, 1.9 km north of the Livingstone Falls Campground. The trailhead is 40 km south of the Highwood Junction and 65 km north of Coleman.

**east** On Hwy. 22, drive south from Chain Lakes Provincial Park for 10.5 km to Chimney Rock Road. Drive west for 3.5 km and take the right fork for 7.7 km to the gate at the end of the gravel road.

| | |
|---|---|
| 0.0 | west trailhead |
| 1.8 | junction, keep left (right is Beaver Loop) |
| 4.2 | summit |
| 4.6 | high point on ridge |
| 10.4 | Forest Reserve boundary |
| 12.3 | Chimney Rock Road |

# 90 WHITE CREEK                              map 16

The White Creek trail is a doubletrack that climbs to a pass in the Livingstone Range where there are excellent views of Whaleback Ridge and the Porcupine Hills. There is no denying it folks—this is a wet feet trip. I counted 32 shallow creek crossings on the way to the top! In wet weather this route is a mud bath.

The trail starts by dropping into the canyon of the Livingstone River and the first stream crossing—about calf deep in midsummer. Climb up the rutted, dirt road onto a bench above the river, then follow the edge of a deep canyon along the lower part of White Creek. After 2 km of dodging potholes in the pine forest, you emerge into a meadow and cross White Creek. Most of the rest of the trail follows meadows along the valley bottom.

The trail branches to the left at km 6.7 and follows along the creek. The track is rough and you'll have to dodge souvenirs left by cattle. Be sure to close the gates. At km 8.4 there is an outcrop of conglomerate rock embedded with igneous pebbles. At km 13.3 keep to the right and push up a steep hill to the top of the range. A short walk up the hill to the south gives an excellent view of the Porcupine Hills and the sinuous Whaleback Ridge.

**Rugged backcountry ride**

**Type** out-and-back on 4WD roads

**Rating** moderate/intermediate

**Other users** motorized-2  livestock

**Distance** 27.2 km

**Time** 4 hours

**Maps** 82 G/16 Maycroft
82 J/1 Langford Creek

**Season** July to mid-October

**Land agency** Alberta Forest Service

**Access**
The trailhead is located on the east side of SR 940, 14.8 km south of the Livingstone Falls Campground and 4 km north of Oldman River Road. The trail is a dirt road that crosses a meadow for about 300 m to the Livingstone River.

| | |
|---|---|
| 0.0 | trailhead |
| 0.3 | ford Livingstone River |
| 0.5 | junction, turn left |
| 6.7 | junction, keep left and ford creek (right leads to a pond) |
| 9.5 | junction, keep left |
| 9.9 | junction, keep right |
| 11.0 | trail becomes faint in a meadow |
| 13.3 | keep right up hill |
| 13.6 | summit |

# 91 RACEHORSE ROUNDABOUT                    map 18

Photo: Gerhardt Lepp.

**Scenic cruiser**
**Type** loop on 2WD and 4WD roads
**Rating** easy/novice
**Other users** motorized-4
**Distance** 23.9 km
**Time** 2-4 hours
**Maps** 82 G/15 Tornado Mountain
82 G/16 Maycroft
**Season** mid-June to mid-October
**Land agency** Alberta Forest Service

**Access**
Begin at the bridge in the
Racehorse Creek Campground on
the west side of SR 940, 76.3 km
south of the Highwood Junction
and 29.7 km north of Coleman.

| | |
|---|---|
| 0.0 | trailhead |
| 4.0 | left on gravel road |
| 16.1 | junction with SR 940, turn left |
| 23.9 | Racehorse Creek Campground |

This ride provides a pleasant tour of the hills
above Racehorse Creek. The route leads along a
rehabilitated road upstream from the Racehorse
Creek Campground, joins an exploration road
that climbs to the south over a low divide and
returns to the campground on the gravel SR 940.

The trail begins with a ford of Racehorse Creek
just below the bridge on the west side of the
campground, then follows the creek through
open pine and poplar forest and meadows. There
are three fords, the last is by a shallow sandstone
canyon. Not far past the last ford you'll join a good
gravel road that rolls up the valley and crosses the
creek before it climbs up switchbacks and follows
the contours back to the Forestry Trunk Road.
Turn left and return to the campground on SR 940.

2    4    6    8    10    12    14    16    18    20    22    23.9

# 92 DAISY CREEK TO BLAIRMORE     maps 18, 18A

This long backcountry ride takes you along the
western side of the Livingstone Range on a
doubletrack that climbs beside Daisy Creek, then
joins the Blairmore Creek Road for the roll down
to Blairmore. Access across private property may
become an issue on this trail so inquire locally
before setting out.

The track along Daisy Creek starts as a rutted
four-wheel-drive road that rolls up and down
through the hills and later levels out in meadows
alongside the creek. This is classic high foothills
country with open pine and poplar forest and
pleasant meadows. The trail makes two shallow
crossings of Daisy Creek. At km 11.5 take the left
fork and continue up Daisy Creek, turning right
on the Blairmore Creek Road.

Climb up the rough road as it crosses over a low
pass and descends into the valley of Gold Creek.
The road fords Gold Creek and improves in quality as you travel south, but may be subject to
restricted access where it crosses private property. Ride past a mine access road, then on to the
four-way junction where the road to the right
climbs to a mine site on Grassy Mountain. To the
left is the old rail grade that leads to Lille, now
closed where it crosses private property.

Ride straight through the junction and head for
town on Blairmore Creek Road. This used to be a
sleepy little road, but development of private
property is bringing changes. The road is built on
an old railway bed and surfaced with black tailings from the abandoned coal mine on Grassy
Mountain. En route, watch for mining artifacts
that used to include a coal tipple, rusted signs,
abandoned wooden coal cars and part of the
original railway grade. The riding is fast and easy
offering a good view west to Crowsnest Mountain.
As you approach Blairmore the road passes the
Greenhill Mine, a provincial historic site, with
many old buildings.

**Rugged and remote east slopes ride**

**Type**  point-to-point on 4WD roads

**Rating**  difficult/intermediate

**Other users**  motorized-3

**Distance**  32.8 km one way

**Time**  4 hours

**Maps**  82 G/9 Blairmore
82 G/16 Maycroft

**Season**  mid-June to mid-October

**Land agency**  Alberta Forest
Service, private

**Access**
**south**  Blairmore Creek Road
begins on the north side of Hwy. 3
at the centre access to Blairmore
(24th Ave. and 129th St.).

**north**  SR 940 crosses Daisy Creek
31 km north of Coleman and 75
km south of the Highwood
Junction. The trailhead is the four-
wheel-drive road 200 m north of
the Daisy Creek bridge.

| | |
|---|---|
| 0.0 | north trailhead |
| 3.0 | junction, keep right |
| 11.5 | junction, keep left |
| 14.8 | right on Blairmore Creek Road |
| 19.8 | mine road joins from right |
| 23.8 | four-way junction, go straight |
| 32.8 | Highway 3 |

# 93 LILLE

map 18

Perfect for history buffs, the short ride to the ghost town of Lille offers you a chance to cycle into the past; not that you will have to exchange your high-tech mountain machine for a Penny Farthing, although that might be fun. Lille is a designated provincial historic site and both the Frank Slide Interpretive Centre and the Coleman Museum feature artifacts and exhibits of the 1901-1913 life of this little town. Private land-owners have closed the trail between Lille and Blairmore Creek Road so the former loop ride is no longer possible.

Roll up the paved road keeping left on the gravel road at the switchback. Private land development is proceeding in this valley so some parts of the route may change. The route turns left at km 1.4 and follows a doubletrack past some corrals, then generally climbs and keeps left until it joins another gravel road. (A longer and less pleasing option is to stay on the gravel roads instead of taking this doubletrack.) Go left and where the road starts to climb stay left on doubletrack, cross

**Gentle ride to ghost town**

**Type** out-and-back on 2WD and 4WD roads

**Rating** easy/novice

**Other users** motorized-3

**Distance** 15 km

**Time** 2-4 hours

**Map** 82 G/9 Blairmore

**Season** June through October

**Land agency** Alberta Forest Service

under the powerline and come to the first crossing of Gold Creek. There's a bridge upstream (courtesy of the local snowmobile club) and an interesting ruin. Follow the doubletrack over a hill to a junction and cross another bridge. The trail now winds through mixed forest before crossing a small creek and entering the meadow at Lille. Grassy Mountain is the prominent mine-scarred hill at the head of the valley.

The trail enters Lille on what was once called Grassy Mountain Avenue. Above the trail are the foundations and cellars of miners' cottages and stores. Downhill, the prominent stone ruin on the edge of the escarpment was the hotel. On the flat below the hotel you'll find the interesting shapes of the coke ovens and the old railway grade. Two of the mines were located on the hillside east of town.

The town of Lille experienced a boom and bust common to many one company resource towns. In 1901, coal was discovered and West Canadian Collieries was organized using French capital, and a railway was built. Lille grew rapidly to become a town of more than 300 people supported by the mine. By 1913 there was little demand for coke, the mine closed and the fledging town perished.

Once you have explored Lille, it's time to retrace your tracks.

## Access
The ride begins where the paved road to the Frank Slide Interpretive Centre leaves Hwy. 3 in the village of Frank.

0.0   trailhead
1.2   junction at switchback, keep left
1.4   turn left on doubletrack
3.2   left on gravel road
4.2   left on doubletrack
5.3   bridge
6.4   right, cross bridge
7.5   Lille

# 94 HASTINGS RIDGE RIDER
map 18

This is one of the finest cycling trips in the Crowsnest. The uphill is steady but gentle, the upper section is almost level with marvellous vistas, and the downhill is steep and fast. It's one of those wonderful rides you will wish could go on forever.

The trip to Hastings Ridge begins with a short roll on pavement and continues on the good gravel of Adanac Road. At km 7.4 turn right onto a stony doubletrack, then, shortly after the start of a meadow, hang another right. The doubletrack soon turns to a pleasing singletrack that climbs at a steady but easy grade across open slopes and through forested glades before emerging onto the summit of a pass between Hastings Ridge and Hillcrest Mountain. For the next 5.5 km enjoy the challenge of the ride and the perfection of the setting as the trail winds along and about the crest of the ridge. Fortunately, there are lots of places to stop and relax while admiring the view. The big peaks of the Flathead Range occupy the western skyline while to the north lies the Crowsnest Valley. In July this is a ridge of wildflowers. All too soon you realize the ridge ride is coming to an

**Classic high mountain ride**

**Type** loop on 4WD roads and singletrack

**Rating** difficult/intermediate

**Other users** equestrian-1 motorized-2

**Distance** 22.5 km

**Time** 3-5 hours

**Map** 82 G/9 Blairmore

**Season** mid-June to mid-October

**Land agency** Alberta Forest Service

**Access**
Begin this trip in the village of Hillcrest Mines. The route follows the main road leading east from town.

2    4    6    8    10    12    14    16    18    20    22.5

end. Ignore the tracks dropping off to the left and, instead, stay on the ridge and follow a prominent singletrack as it descends obliquely to the right to join the good doubletrack that links Drum Creek with Lyons Creek Road. The optional finish turns left at this point.

Turn right and descend the trail through the Drum Creek valley to Hillcrest. After an initial drop-off, rock and roll along a stony doubletrack set in a classic foothills valley. Expect to get your feet wet in the numerous but shallow creek crossings along the way. On the hillside above the village, the trail passes through the ruins of the Hillcrest Mine. Here, in 1914, 189 men died in Canada's worst mining disaster. Roll on down to the sleepy village of Hillcrest.

**Options**

With a bit of routefinding prowess you can follow a singletrack down to Blairmore and return to Hillcrest on the road. Turn left at km 17.5 and climb to the summit on the doubletrack, then bike in hand, strike off uphill through the open forest and meadows. Keep trending right until you can look across the sidehill. Your goal is to reach the pass where Hastings Ridge joins Turtle Mountain. With a bit of luck you'll find a riders' trail that crosses the sidehill and switchbacks down to the pass. An old singletrack trail crosses the pass and leads almost to Blairmore. You'll be smiling as you roll down this fast and fun trail, then join the Lynx Creek Road for the last short bit, reaching town at km 23.2.

| | |
|---|---|
| 0.0 | Hillcrest, ride east on paved road |
| 2.0 | junction with Adanac Road, turn right |
| 7.4 | turn right just before road crosses creek |
| 12.0 | pass |
| 15.0 | junction, stay on ridge |
| 16.5 | junction, stay on ridge |
| 17.5 | junction, turn right (left climbs over pass and descends to Blairmore) |
| 22.0 | mine ruins |
| 22.5 | Hillcrest |

# 95 WILLOUGHBY RIDGE WANDERER

maps 18, 18A

Photo: Stephen Wilde.

The Wanderer explores the high headwaters country east of the Flathead Range. From valley bottom to timberline, and from pavement to cutline, variety is the keyword on this trip.

Begin by climbing into the hills south of Coleman on York Creek Road. At km 5 stay on the main road, cross the bridge and climb up four switchbacks before turning right onto the trail. This rough 4WD track leads you past the trail to the Dakota crash site and past the gated road to the Ironstone Lookout. Continuing onward, the trail climbs to a low pass (the trail to the left here is a shortcut, ignore it unless you are in a hurry) and uphill to the right, leading you to the best part of the trip as you traverse the ridge below Mount Coulthard. The trail climbs steadily into a lush subalpine zone where hellebore and rhododendron abound. This high country is fantastic. Take

**Backcountry explorer**

**Type** loop on 2WD and 4WD roads and singletrack

**Rating** difficult/intermediate

**Other users** hikers-1  equestrian-1 motorized-3  livestock

**Distance** 36 km

**Time** 4-6 hours

**Maps** 82 G/9 Blairmore 82 G/10 Crowsnest

**Season** July to mid-October

**Land agency** Alberta Forest Service

10            20            30      36

the third turn to the left and climb steeply on an old cutline. Have faith! At times it may seem like you are being led astray, but there are rewards for those who persevere. Enjoy the riding and the country as the trail rolls across this high, larch-covered subalpine ridge. Check your brakes and descend the steep cutline trail into the headwaters of Lynx Creek, watching closely for a road joining from the left. Follow this road down a washed-out section and roll eastward on steadily improving ground. Cool your heels in the creek a couple of times, pass the other end of the shortcut trail, and climb gently to Lyons Creek-Lynx Creek Road. It is a short climb to the summit on this good gravel road and most of the next 10 km is a long screaming downhill back to Blairmore.

It's an exhilarating feeling to roll into town after this ride. Time to hit the local espresso joint for a well-deserved coffee before returning to Coleman.

**Options**

Including either Ironstone Lookout (#97) or the York Creek Dakota Crash Site (#96) will add interest and lengthen your trip.

**Access**

Begin in the village of Coleman at the railway crossing on 81 Street.

| | |
|---|---|
| 0.0 | trailhead, ride south on 83 St., cross the Crowsnest River bridge, turn right on 13 Ave., then follow York Creek Road |
| 5.0 | cross bridge over York Creek and climb four switchbacks |
| 6.2 | junction, keep right on poor road |
| 7.5 | junction, keep left |
| 8.1 | junction, keep left (Dakota crash site trail [#96] to right) |
| 8.9 | junction, keep right (Ironstone Lookout [#97] to left) |
| 9.9 | junction, keep left |
| 10.8 | junction, turn right (left is shortcut route) |
| 10.9 | keep right |
| 11.1 | keep right |
| 12.0 | junction, turn left onto cutline (right leads to basin below Mount Coulthard) |
| 13.5 | turn left onto washed-out road |
| 14.0 | junction, turn left |
| 17.0 | junction, keep right (left is end of shortcut) |
| 19.4 | junction with Lyons Creek-Lynx Creek Road, turn left |
| 30.2 | Blairmore |
| 36.0 | Coleman |

*Dakota crash (#96).*

# 96 DAKOTA CRASH SITE          map 18

It was winter 1946 and the *RCAF* Dakota aircraft was making a flight across the mountains west of Blairmore. Somewhere near Andy Good Peak the unthinkable happened. The plane hit the mountainside, exploded and tumbled down the steep snow-covered slopes. There were no survivors. Winter avalanches and souvenir hunters have worked their ways on the wreckage, but the tail section, a wing, a motor and parts of the landing gear can still be found.

The valley of North York Creek has its own charms, not the least of which is the open subalpine country at the head of the valley. Summer wildflowers on the slidepaths and sweeping ridges and basins above beckon you to explore. Truly hard-core riders have been known to pack their bikes across the Flathead Range and link up with the Ptolemy Creek trail (#104).

This ride begins the same as the Willoughby Ridge Wanderer (#95). At km 8.1 take the fork to the right, crossing the bridge over York Creek and climbing over a low ridge on a doubletrack pitted with a score of sometimes full potholes. Soon the trail crosses North York Creek on another bridge (courtesy of the local snowmobile club). Just beyond the bridge turn left and follow a singletrack along a section of reclaimed road that soon becomes "unreclaimed." It climbs up a steep hill, then rises up generally rideable grades into the upper valley. No routefinding problems here—the track leads right to the wreckage.

Other than a few tense moments descending the steep gravel hill, the return trip is easy and fun.

## Options

1. Combine this excursion with Willoughby Ridge Wanderer.
2. Make a York Creek special by climbing to the Ironstone Lookout, then returning to Coleman.

**Rugged ride to crashed airplane**
**Type** out-and-back on 4WD roads
**Rating** difficult/intermediate
**Other users** hikers-1  equestrian-3 motorized-3  livestock
**Distance** 28.4 km
**Time** 3-5 hours
**Maps** 82 G/9 Blairmore
82 G/10 Crowsnest
**Season** July to mid-October
**Land agency** Alberta Forest Service

**Access**
Begin in the village of Coleman at the railway crossing on 81 Street.

0.0   trailhead, ride south on 83 St., cross the Crowsnest River bridge, turn right on 13 Ave., then follow York Creek Road
5.0   cross bridge over York Creek and climb four switchbacks
6.2   junction, keep right on poor road
7.5   junction, keep left
8.1   junction, turn right onto trail leading to North York Creek
11.1  cross bridge over North York Creek; junction, turn left onto reclaimed road
14.2  plane wreckage

## 97  IRONSTONE LOOKOUT                map 18

As fire lookout trails go, Ironstone is a relatively short and easy one. It is almost all rideable and the view from the top is easily worth twice the effort expended to get there. This is the best single viewpoint in the Crowsnest area with its 360 degree mountain panorama encompassing the Crowsnest Valley to the north and the Castle Valley to the south.

Begin by climbing into the hills south of Coleman on York Creek Road. At km 5 stay on the main road, cross the bridge and climb up four switchbacks before turning right onto the trail. This rough 4WD track leads you past the trail to the Dakota crash site and on to the gated lookout road. The road is rough and rocky and climbs steeply, but if you have strong legs and choose a good line you will be able to ride up most of it.

Willoughby Ridge is composed of volcanic rocks originating from lava flows during the Cretaceous period of earth history. Notice how different these rocks look compared to the limestone so common in the Rockies. Feel the difference under your tires!

After the inspiring beauty of the summit a kamikaze descent would seem in order. To some extent the rough road acts as a speed-limiting factor, but it takes only a fraction of the ascent time to return to the gate and roll back to town.

**Major vertical and great views**
**Type** out-and-back on 4WD roads
**Rating** difficult/intermediate
**Other users** hikers-1  motorized-3
**Distance** 26.2 km
**Time** 3-4 hours
**Maps** 82 G/9 Blairmore
82 G/10 Crowsnest
**Season** July to mid-October
**Land agency** Alberta Forest Service

**Access**
Begin in the village of Coleman at the railway crossing on 81 Street.

0.0   trailhead, ride south on 83 St., cross the Crowsnest River bridge, turn right on 13 Ave., then follow York Creek Road
5.0   cross bridge over York Creek and climb four switchbacks
6.2   junction, keep right on poor road
7.5   junction, keep left
8.1   junction, keep left (Dakota crash site trail to right)
8.9   junction, turn left onto gated road
12.2  trail on upper ridge
13.1  Ironstone Lookout

# 98 STAR CREEK TO YORK CREEK map 18

**Rugged ride in east slope setting**

**Type** loop on 2WD roads, 4WD roads and singletrack

**Rating** moderate/intermediate

**Other users** hikers-1 motorized-5

**Distance** 28.6 km

**Time** 3-5 hours

**Maps** 82 G/9 Blairmore
82 G/10 Crowsnest

**Season** June through October

**Land agency** Alberta Forest Service

**Access**

In Coleman follow 17 Ave. to the west end of town, cross the railway and follow 16 Ave. west for 1.7 km to 54 Street, where the trail leads south.

This ride uses a singletrack to link doubletracks along Star Creek and York Creek into a loop trip from Coleman. A side trip to the crashed Dakota aircraft near timberline in York Creek is a must.

Ride west out of Coleman and head south on 54 Street as it climbs into the hills. Keep right on a gravel doubletrack, then follow the quad track to the left as it loops close to Star Creek where a short side trail leads to the falls. This part of the route passes through an open forest of aspen, pine and fir with classic mountain vistas. Continue on, keeping left at the junctions, pass through a gate high above the creek, then turn left and ford the creek. Keep left at the junction at km 4.3 where the ruins of a log cabin molder in a meadow, cross a small creek and climb up to the Divide. It's a short drop to the good doubletrack of North York Creek. Ride up the valley passing a bridge, then test your stamina against some sketchy gravel hills until you come to the end of the road at the plane wreckage. The tail section, a wing and a motor are strewn about the slope. This plane crashed in winter, 1946, with no survivors; an interpretive sign on site gives details. Above, a small creek cascades over three waterfalls and alpine basins invite exploration.

Descend the hills back to the bridge. You can go either way here. I prefer to cross the bridge and ride the upper trail back to the main York Creek trail and down to town.

| | |
|---|---|
| 0.0 | 16 Ave. and 54 Street |
| 0.5 | keep right, up hill |
| 0.9 | left on quad track |
| 1.0 | Star Creek Falls to left |
| 2.4 | ford creek |
| 2.5 | left |
| 3.3 | right |
| 4.3 | left, cross creek |
| 6.1 | summit |
| 6.5 | right on doubletrack |
| 8.3 | junction and bridge, keep right |
| 11.4 | Dakota wreckage, retrace tracks |
| 14.5 | junction, cross bridge and go left |
| 17.5 | junction, turn left |
| 18.1 | keep right |
| 19.4 | keep left |
| 20.6 | York Creek bridge |
| 25.6 | Coleman, turn left through town |
| 28.6 | end of ride |

10    20    28.6

# 99  NEZ PERCE TO MCGILLIVRAY RIDGE REPEATER  maps 18, 18A

Some people dream of owning the perfect object d'art, others yearn to ski the perfect powder run. If your idea of perfection is a long, fast, steep downhill ride, then this trip is made for you. The ride up to the McGillivray repeater requires a major gear-grinding grunt. You might think of it as a form of gravity storage. The summit is well above timberline and sports the usual excellent views of peaks and valleys. The alpine tundra stretches away over the summit providing opportunities for exploration. As for the merits of the trip down, I'll let you be the judge.

From Coleman, ride through an old mine site along Nez Perce Road, an old road that gets little traffic. Beyond the mine it parallels rushing Nez Perce Creek and, after 5 km of easy rolling, commences a steady and relentless pursuit of the high country. Those with strong legs will excel; others will have to persevere. At about km 8.6 the road climbs to a forested ridge where there are views east to Highway 40 and the Livingstone Range. Shortly after, the trail emerges from the trees and begins a final push for the summit. Don't even think of leaving your bike behind at this point. The effort of the uphill struggle will be amply rewarded later.

The summit offers a perfect view of the surrounding landscape and is a great place to catch a few rays. Crowsnest Mountain and the Seven Sisters are the prominent peaks to the west while the Livingstone Range lies to the east. I highly recommend the hike across the tundra to the main summit.

The trip back down the mountain can be a slow and easy delight if you wish. On the other hand, if the trip up involved gravity storage, then the trip down is a perfect example of gravity release. I found the downhill to be one of the fastest and finest rides anywhere.

**Major vertical and great views**

**Type** out-and-back on 2WD and 4WD roads

**Rating** difficult/intermediate

**Other users** motorized-2

**Distance** 20.6 km

**Time** 3-5 hours

**Maps** 82 G/9 Blairmore
82 G/10 Crowsnest

**Season** mid-June to mid-October

**Land agency** Alberta Forest Service

**Access**
The route leaves Hwy. 3 at a point 0.7 km west of the centre Coleman access and 0.7 km east of the west Coleman access. It is a minor gravel road leading uphill on the north side of the highway.

| | |
|---|---|
| 0.0 | junction of Hwy. 3 and Coleman centre access, cycle west on highway |
| 0.7 | turn right onto rough track leading uphill |
| 1.5 | trail to right leads to Coleman |
| 2.6 | Forest Reserve boundary |
| 3.8 | four-way junction, go straight (link to McGillivray Creek trail is to left) |
| 6.0 | fork, keep left |
| 7.0 | junction, keep right |
| 10.3 | summit, communications facility |

# 100 MCGILLIVRAY CREEK

maps 18, 18A

McGillivray Creek trail leads into a valley below Crowsnest Mountain with an option to climb to the ridge below the Seven Sisters. This pleasant ride along a needle-covered dirt road fords the creek many times. The easiest way to deal with this is to plan to have wet feet. Unless you're a mud puppy, don't even think about coming here in wet weather.

From the historic mining town of Coleman, the route makes a view-filled climb out of the Crowsnest Valley, then follows along a pastoral lane below Crowsnest Mountain to the McGillivray Creek Youth Camp. Continuing up the valley the routefinding is straightforward—at each trail junction take the fork that parallels the creek. The trail is a doubletrack on an old road bed that rolls through mixed-wood forest and sunny glades and passes a tumbledown log building before fading away at the upper end of the valley.

## Options

From the end of the road a singletrack climbs uphill to the ridge below the Seven Sisters. This trail requires an uphill push, but those with advanced downhill skills will enjoy the descent.

**Rugged backcountry ride**

**Type** out-and-back on 2WD and 4WD roads

**Rating** moderate/intermediate

**Other users** motorized-2

**Distance** 23 km

**Time** 3-5 hours

**Map** 82 G/10 Crowsnest

**Season** June to mid-October

**Land agency** Alberta Forest Service

### Access

In Coleman, begin at the junction of McGillivray Creek Road and Hwy. 3, 0.5 km west of the west Coleman access road.

| | |
|---|---|
| 0.0 | trailhead, cycle up McGillivray Creek Road |
| 4.8 | junction, keep right (youth camp to left) |
| 9.0 | log building in ruins |
| 11.5 | old road fades away |

2    4    6    8    10    12    14    16    18    20    22  23

Photo: Gerhardt Lepp.

# 101 DEADMAN PASS–PHILLIPPS PASS COMBO   map 17

This long circle ride crosses two low passes on the Continental Divide as it loops around Mount Tecumseh and Phillipps Peak in the High Rock Range. The many road access points make several options possible.

Cycle up Allison Creek Road to Chinook Lake, a pretty little foothills lake that reflects the crags of Crowsnest Mountain to the east. Continue along the wide shoreline singletrack, then follow a bumpy narrow trail along a wet valley bottom before joining the smooth doubletrack from the Atlas snowmobile area. The track rises gently through open pine and poplar forest to the broad summit of Deadman Pass. Ignore the numerous seismic lines that branch off on both sides of the main trail.

At Deadman Pass take the fork to the left as it plunges into a tunnel of alders and skirts a beaver pond. The route returns to dry pine forest and drops along a cutline into the valley of Alexander Creek where Erickson Ridge rises to the west. Turn left and roll along Alexander Creek Road, a four-wheel-drive road that contours around the mountainside, then descends to join Highway 3 at the weigh scale. You can end your backcountry ride here or elect to continue on over Phillipps Pass back to the start point.

To ride over Phillipps Pass cycle 1 km east on the pavement and turn left into Crowsnest Provincial Park. From the north end of the park follow an obvious gravel pipeline road as it climbs steeply up to the pass. On top the wind invariably howls through the powerlines and cables of the gondola that provides access to the microwave tower on Crowsnest Ridge. Beyond lies Phillipps Lake, which, with no visible outlet, straddles the Great Divide. The trail follows the route of the original road from British Columbia to Alberta as the current route through Crowsnest Pass was impassable owing to lakes and cliffs. Race down the gravel road on the east side of the pass as it drops steeply to meadows and a residential area at the east end of Crowsnest Lake and joins Highway 3.

**Scenic backcountry tour**

**Type** loop on 2WD and 4WD roads

**Rating** difficult/intermediate

**Other users** equestrian-3 motorized-3

**Distance** 37.5 km (7.5 km on pavement)

**Time** 4-6 hours

**Map** 82 G/10 Crowsnest

**Season** mid-June to mid-October

**Land agency** Alberta Forest Service, BC Forest Service

**Access**
Begin at the junction of Hwy. 3 and Allison Creek Road, 5 km west of Coleman.

| | |
|---|---|
| 0.0 | trailhead, ride up Allison Creek Road |
| 2.5 | junction, turn left (right is Atlas Haul Road) |
| 6.0 | Chinook Lake, follow trail along shore |
| 8.5 | junction with 4WD trail, turn left |
| 12.5 | Deadman Pass; junction, keep left |
| 16.0 | junction with Alexander Creek Road, turn left |
| 24.5 | junction with Hwy. 3 near weigh scale, turn left |
| 25.5 | Crowsnest Provincial Park, turn left and follow doubletrack up pipeline right-of-way |
| 28.5 | Phillipps Pass |
| 33.5 | junction with Hwy. 3, turn left |
| 37.5 | beer time |

# 102 RADICAL RACEHORSE

map 17

This is a long, remote ride for strong, well-pre-pared cyclists who enjoy a backcountry chal-lenge. The route climbs to Racehorse Pass, an attractive subalpine pass on the Continental Di-vide and continues westward. Descending into the deep valley of Alexander Creek in British Columbia, it then climbs back into Alberta on the Deadman Pass trail.

The trail to Racehorse Pass is almost too good to be true. It's easy cycling on an old road all the way to the summit, although steep snow slopes may cover the upper part of the road until early July. While the summit is just below timberline, the combination of a severe fire in the 1930s and the work of frequent winter avalanches has cre-ated an open subalpine meadowland. There are numerous opportunities for exploration in the basins to the south of the pass and along the ridge to the north.

Continuing west, a basic doubletrack drops off the pass providing a generally easy ride. At km 20 there is a major fork with the left branch being the quickest and steepest way to reach Alexander Creek, which must be forded to reach Alexander Creek Road. I slid down this route once in early

**Hard-core enduro-ride**

**Type** loop on 2WD and 4WD roads

**Rating** difficult/intermediate

**Other users** equestrian-3 motorized-3 livestock

**Distance** 38.9 km

**Time** 5-8 hours

**Maps** 82 G/10 Crowsnest 82 G/15 Tornado Mountain

**Season** mid-July to mid-October

**Land agency** Alberta Forest Service

**Access**
From Hwy. 3 drive up Allison Creek Road and Atlas Haul Road for 6.5 km to the Atlas snowmobile area. The ride continues up Atlas Haul Road.

| | |
|---|---|
| 0.0 | trailhead |
| 11.0 | junction, turn left |
| 15.7 | Racehorse Pass |

July and you can imagine my dismay when I found the creek in full flood. A part of me said "go for it," but common sense intoned that this could mean losing my bike or... something worse. There was nothing else to do but scramble back up the steep trail and cycle back over the pass. The right branch at km 20 is better travelled, but quickly becomes confusing as it turns north when you want to go south, then dallies along the ridge for some distance before descending into the valley. As with the left branch, once you get to the valley bottom a ford of Alexander Creek is required.

Alexander Creek Road offers easy cycling on a dirt surface with plenty of mud holes and cow patties to dodge around as you roll toward the turn-off for Deadman Pass. Hang a left and climb along the cutline and doubletrack over the forested pass and out to Atlas Haul Road.

| | |
|---|---|
| 20.0 | junction, turn left (trail to right eventually rejoins route) |
| 22.3 | ford Alexander Creek |
| 22.7 | junction with Alexander Creek Road, turn left |
| 22.9 | junction, keep left |
| 28.9 | bridge across Alexander Creek |
| 29.9 | junction, turn left (Alexander Creek Road continues to right for 9 km to Hwy. 3) |
| 33.4 | Deadman Pass |
| 37.4 | junction, keep left (right is trail to Chinook Lake) |
| 38.9 | end of ride |

## Options

Make a moderate/intermediate, 9.4 km, out-and-back cycling trip to the summit of Racehorse Pass by driving to km 11 of the route log. Spend the day exploring this beautiful area.

# 103 PTOLEMY & TENT MOUNTAIN PASSES        map 17

Calling all cruisers! How about a fine mountain bike adventure on a good doubletrack leading across two low passes on the Continental Divide? Although much of the country is more hilly than mountainous, you can expect to find good views, clear, rushing brooks and lush vegetation. The route passes close to two open pit coal mines and through the dying embers of a ghost town.

The ride begins on the access road to the now inactive Tent Mountain Mine. Just before the mine gate, hang a left onto a little-travelled, rocky doubletrack. This old road is all rideable as it climbs up to Ptolemy Pass. Located in the trees, the view from the pass is nonexistent but, a short distance later, the trail breaks out of the woods to a panoramic view of the Flathead Range. There follows a quick descent to the valley of Andy Good Creek. While descending you are sure to notice the funny-looking, terraced mountain in the distance. A fact of life in coal country, this is Corbin Mine. Once you're in the valley, follow alongside Andy Good Creek, turning right at the

**Classic mountain tour**

**Type** loop on 2WD and 4WD roads

**Rating** difficult/intermediate

**Other users** hikers-1  equestrian-1  motorized-3

**Distance** 34 km

**Time** 3-5 hours

**Map** 82 G/10 Crowsnest

**Season** mid-June to mid-October

**Land agency** Alberta Forest Service

**Access**
Begin on Hwy. 3 at the turn-off to the Island Lake Campground. Follow the Tent Mountain Mine access road that leads south from the highway.

junction—a place marked by acres of tailings, a railway and some excellent views of the Flathead peaks—and onto Michel Creek Road.

Follow this good gravel road for 5.8 km and turn right onto Tent Mountain logging road. Almost immediately the road bends to the left, but your route continues straight up a good doubletrack. The trail climbs through and about a wide clearing with lots of terrific scenery until it tops out in a flower-filled cutblock well above the summit of Tent Mountain Pass. Views include Crowsnest Mountain to the east and the mine to the south. The route winds and climbs a bit before descending toward the mine gate.

You could return to the mine access road but I suggest that, instead, you turn left and follow Island Creek Road, a logging road that descends to the ghost town of Crowsnest where only a few buildings and the railway remain. The Inn on the Border, the town's only business establishment, offers food and cold beer for thirsty riders. To return to your start point, cross Hwy. 3 and follow the old road on the north side of Island Lake, crossing the railway and exiting through the campground.

| | |
|---|---|
| 0.0 | trailhead |
| 3.3 | junction, keep right (Ptolemy Creek trail to left) |
| 4.5 | junction, turn left shortly before mine gate |
| 10.0 | Ptolemy Pass; junction, keep left |
| 14.5 | junction with track along Andy Good Creek, turn right |
| 14.8 | junction, keep right |
| 15.2 | junction with Michel Creek Road, turn right |
| 21.0 | turn right onto Tent Mountain Road |
| 21.5 | keep right on doubletrack |
| 23.2 | Tent Mountain Pass |
| 27.8 | junction with Island Creek Road, turn left (right leads back to mine gate) |
| 32.3 | Crowsnest Pass |
| 32.5 | Hwy. 3, cross and follow old highway |
| 34.0 | end of ride |

# 104 PTOLEMY CREEK                                map 17

The Ptolemy Creek trail is a short but interesting ride into a high mountain valley. Located in the Flathead Range, it is part of the access route to the caves of the Andy Good plateau. Most of your fellow travellers on this route are likely to be cavers heading for the subterranean life zone.

The trail is a good, rocky doubletrack that crosses the creek at least seven times. Ptolemy Creek is a crystal clear and beautiful stream, and it is icy cold. Some of the crossings are bridged, but at others you'll have to cool your heels.

The upper valley is a very serene and spectacular place. A spur to the left leads to a good viewpoint and camping spot while the main doubletrack trail offers its own scenic rewards before ending at a steep hiking trail leading to the caves. The ride back to the trailhead is so much fun you'll want to ride pedals-to-the-metal but, when it's all over, you'll wonder why you went so fast!

**Rugged mountain ride**

**Type** out-and-back on 4WD roads

**Rating** moderate/intermediate

**Other users** hikers-2  motorized-2

**Distance** 11.4 km

**Time** 2-4 hours

**Map** 82 G/10 Crowsnest

**Season** July to mid-October

**Land agency** Alberta Forest Service

**Access**
From Hwy. 3 at the turn-off to the Island Lake Campground, follow the Tent Mountain Mine access road south to a fork to the left at km 3.3.

0.0   trailhead

1.6   first of many fords of Ptolemy Creek

4.7   junction, keep right (left leads to good view)

5.7   end of doubletrack

Photo: Stephen Wilde.

# 105 GOAT CREEK–LOST CREEK CIRCLE     map 19

**Scenic cruiser in front ranges**
**Type** loop on 2WD and 4WD roads
**Rating** moderate/novice
**Other users** equestrian-1 motorized-4
**Distance** 31.8 km
**Time** 4-6 hours
**Maps** 82 G/7 Flathead Ridge
82 G/8 Beaver Mines
82 G/10 Crowsnest
**Season** June to mid-October
**Land agency** Alberta Forest Service

**Access**
**north** The Goat Creek trail begins from Lynx Creek Road, 9.7 km north of its junction with Hillcrest to Castle Road.

**south** Follow Carbondale River Road west from its junction with Hillcrest to Castle Road for 2.4 km to a fork to the right, which is Lost Creek Road. Park here or, if you wish, drive 4 km farther on this rough road.

Do you like easy riding on foothills roads with big limestone mountains for a backdrop? If so, these are the trails for you. They provide pleasant cruising on old logging roads in the hills and valleys below the Flathead Range. It's a good place to take the family or to go as a group.

The riding is on old roads, mostly good gravel but with the occasional mud hole. Many of the creek crossings have been bridged courtesy of the Crow Snowriders snowmobile club and, although much of it has been logged, the surrounding forest is rapidly regenerating and covering the hillsides with an attractive mosaic of vegetation, particularly colourful in autumn. Keep an eye open for wildlife, especially bears.

| | |
|---|---|
| 0.0 | north trailhead |
| 5.1 | bridge four-way junction, go straight |
| 5.7 | junction, keep left |
| 7.0 | "Goat" Pass |
| 9.5 | junction with North Lost Road, turn left (right is option 2) |
| 11.2 | junction, keep right |
| 13.0 | junction, keep right |
| 13.3 | junction, keep left (right is option 1) |
| 14.2 | bridge over Lost Creek (end of rough 2WD road) |

Begin by cycling up Goat Creek Road into the hills. After crossing a low but scenic pass the route descends to a junction where North Lost Creek trail (Option 2) branches to the right. To continue the loop, turn left and enjoy a fast 3.8 km roll to a major trail junction where South Lost Creek trail (Option 1) branches to the right. Continue down the valley of Lost Creek until the road meets Carbondale River Road. Close the loop by returning to your starting point on Carbondale River Road, Hillcrest Road and Lynx Creek Road.

| | |
|---|---|
| 18.2 | south trailhead at Carbondale River Road |
| 20.6 | junction with Hillcrest to Castle Road, turn left |
| 22.1 | junction with Lynx Creek-Lyons Creek Road, turn left |
| 31.8 | end of ride |

## Options

You might prefer to cycle this route as a point-to-point with a car shuttle to avoid the dusty gravel road section.

The Lost Creek trails can be cycled as side trips, however, they also make good out-and-back cycling trips in their own right. For a Lost Creek-only trip I suggest you begin at the south trailhead.

## 1. South Lost Creek

From the junction take the south fork and follow a track that climbs gradually alongside the creek. The trail continues climbing into an ever-narrowing valley below the ramparts of the Continental Divide. The road makes its finale where the cutblocks end and huge avalanche paths take over. A rough path continues onward to the pass between Lost Creek and the headwaters of the Carbondale River near North Kootenay Pass.

| | |
|---|---|
| 0.0 | junction at km 13.3 of route log |
| 1.0 | junction, keep right (left leads to Carbondale River) |
| 3.4 | junction, keep right |
| 3.8 | ford creek |
| 8.6 | road ends |

## 2. North Lost Creek

The North Lost trail continues west into the upper reaches of the valley below some impressive ramparts. A spur to the right climbs into a series of cutblocks below Mount Darrah where you can explore to your heart's content.

| | |
|---|---|
| 0.0 | junction at km 9.5 of route log |
| 1.0 | junction, keep left (right leads into valley below Mount Darrah) |
| 2.2 | singletrack begins |
| 6.0 | trail ends |

# 106 MACDONALD CREEK & NORTH KOOTENAY PASSES    map 19

Do you like to take on challenges? Offering everything from carry to cruise, this extraordinary trip requires a bit of that type of mindset if it is to be truly enjoyed. It's a case of pure adventure and the rewards don't come easy. The route climbs over two passes on the Continental Divide where it will sometimes be easier to carry your bike than to push or ride it. This loop caters to strong, skilled and well-prepared cyclists.

Begin by fording the Carbondale River and cycling west on the good gravel road. At km 3 take the left-hand fork that leads up to MacDonald Creek Pass. This is a good dirt track that climbs through a few cutblocks to a subalpine basin, then up a final steep section to the summit. Located just below timberline, the pass is a narrow, winding defile through the mountains with lots of possibilities for on-foot exploration.

The trail exits the pass on a steep 0.5 km downhill slider. The trail that follows is a sometimes good and sometimes rough challenge leading to Corbin Road. Note that parts of the trail are severely washed out and are impassable at high water. Turn right (north) and follow the good gravel of Corbin Road for 7.2 km to a junction. Turn right and begin the ascent of North Kootenay Pass.

**Rugged high mountain ride**

**Type** loop on 2WD and 4WD roads and singletrack

**Rating** extreme/advanced

**Other users** equestrian-2 motorized-2

**Distance** 37.2 km (subtract 6 km if starting on BC side)

**Time** 5-7 hours

**Map** 82 G/7 Flathead Ridge

**Season** July to mid-October

**Land agency** Alberta and British Columbia forest services

## Access

**Alberta** Drive west on Carbondale River Road for 6.1 km to a point where the road turns left and fords the river. Park here.

**BC** Drive north on Corbin Road for 19.3 km from its junction with Flathead Road. Park where the road makes a prominent hairpin turn to the left.

The pass is visible directly above, and the "trail" is visible on a prominent point in front of the pass. Carefully noting the lay of the land now will help you with a couple of routefinding decisions later on. Cycle up the good gravel road to a wellsite, beyond which the road deteriorates and soon ends. Here is where knowing the lay of the land will help you in choosing your direction of travel. A faint trail leads up and to the left from the end of the road. Cross the creek to your left and aim uphill until you join the old cat track that ascends very steeply to the viewpoint that you took note of from the valley below. From here ride and push onward to the desolate summit of North Kootenay Pass.

I find it hard to believe that the first white men over this pass were searching for a route for a railway; it's hard enough to get a mountain bike over it, never mind a train! Now it's time for a downhill boogie back to the trailhead. Be mindful of the challenges ahead, once you get into the timber the old road has been reclaimed and its surface becomes a gnarly sidehill singletrack around boulders and through gullies. Turn onto a trail descending to the right and leading to your second dip in the Carbondale River. A short distance later the trail joins a good road that takes you past the turn-off to Mac Pass and on to your third and final splash before the trailhead.

| | |
|---|---|
| 0.0 | Alberta trailhead, ford Carbondale River |
| 3.0 | junction, turn left onto MacDonald trail |
| 4.8 | junction, keep right |
| 6.7 | "MacDonald Creek" Pass |
| 8.0 | trail eroded by creek |
| 13.3 | turn right and ford creek junction with Corbin Road, turn right |
| 20.5 | junction, turn right observe pass above |
| 24.1 | wellsite |
| 25.3 | road ends, follow track across creek and up hill |
| 27.3 | cat track at viewpoint |
| 28.3 | North Kootenay Pass |
| 31.9 | ford Carbondale River |
| 32.1 | road begins |
| 34.2 | junction with Mac trail, keep left |
| 37.2 | final ford and end of ride |

## Options

MacDonald Creek Pass is a good difficult/intermediate day trip from the Alberta side while North Kootenay Pass is an equally fun difficult/advanced ride. There are plenty of opportunities for foot exploration of the peaks and ridges and the riding is challenging and fun.

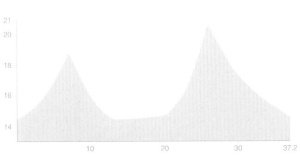

## 107 CARBONDALE HILL LOOKOUT                    map 19

If you like a ride with a view, then this is your kind of trip. The southern Rockies form a horseshoe-shaped front of mountains around the valleys of the Carbondale and Castle rivers. Carbondale Lookout sits atop a high foothill in the middle of this imaginary horseshoe with views in every direction. Take some maps if you like identifying peaks.

The gravel road leading up to the lookout is in good condition and it climbs at reasonable, rideable grades. From its beginning in a valley-bottom meadow beside the Castle River, the road climbs through meadows, groves of aspen, and forests of spruce and pine. As you climb, the forest thins out and the views become astounding, but the summit view is the best. I won't bore you with all the visual details, suffice it to say that all the classical elements of a southern Rockies landscape are well represented.

The roll out is fun and fast. This is a perfect ride for a short day or, perhaps, a sunset excursion.

**Gentle backcountry ride with great views**

**Type** out-and-back on 4WD roads
**Rating** moderate/intermediate
**Other users** motorized-3
**Distance** 9 km
**Time** 1-3 hours
**Map** 82 G/8 Beaver Mines
**Season** mid-May to mid-October
**Land agency** Alberta Forest Service

**Access**
From SR 774 follow Hillcrest to Castle Road north along the Castle River to a junction at km 1.8. Keep right and continue for another 1.2 km to a dirt track on the left.

| | |
|---|---|
| 0.0 | trailhead |
| 1.3 | gate |
| 4.5 | summit, fire lookout |

## 108 MIDDLE KOOTENAY PASS–SUNKIST RIDGE     map 20

This fine ride features two passes, two provinces and classic adventure in a perfect setting. It has its share of steep hills, pushing and requisite bush-bashing along with lots of fast and exciting riding amongst the peaks of the Continental Divide. This long and challenging loop is suitable for skillful, strong and well-prepared riders and should appear on every hard-core's "must ride" list.

The trail up Commerce Creek begins as a good logging road, but beyond the fork at km 4.3 the road deteriorates rapidly. Soon it is just an old exploration trail hemmed in by dense thickets of alder. Thus it continues for the next 6 km, crossing avalanche slopes and climbing through forests of subalpine fir. Any bears in here? Quite likely.

At about km 11 the trail enters an open basin. An upward glance delivers the shocking news that the trail is about to make a very steep head-long push for the top of Sunkist Ridge. It's a short hike-a-bike; take your time and enjoy the view. The summit is a very narrow ridge with some interesting walking along the crest.

The descent begins with a very pleasing traverse of a high alpine basin, but soon the angle of descent becomes very steep and the riding is sketchy at best with lots of washed-out sections and loose gravel. After 1 km of wicked descending, the trail again becomes reasonable and rolls along into some cutblocks where it joins the West Castle route. This is just an old 4WD trail but, after what you've come through, it seems like a high-way. Turn right, cross a creek and ride pedals-to-the-metal (or however else you please) down the valley. It is 10.3 km of easy valley-bottom cruising to the junction with the trail to Middle Kootenay Pass (Alberta trailhead).

**Hard-core enduro-ride**

**Type** loop on 2WD and 4WD roads and singletrack

**Rating** extreme/advanced

**Other users** equestrian-1 motorized-4

**Distance** 46.9 km

**Time** 6-7 hours

**Maps** 82 G/1 Sage Creek 82 G/8 Beaver Mines

**Season** July to mid-October

**Land agency** Alberta Forest Service

**Access**
**BC** From Flathead Road, 61 km southeast of Hwy. 3 at Morrissey, follow Kishinena Road to the left (east) across the Flathead River bridge for 1 km to Commerce Creek Road. Turn left and drive 4.7 km to a fork in the road. Park here and ride up the road to the right.

**Alberta** Follow SR 774 to the West Castle resort. Just before the gate at the resort, a road branches off to the left. Follow this road for 3.1 km to a fork. The Middle Kootenay Pass trail is the right-hand branch.

| | |
|---|---|
| 0.0 | BC trailhead |
| 4.3 | turn right onto rough road |
| 11.1 | trail makes hairpin to left and climbs steeply |

22

20

18

16

14

10     20     30     40     46.9

The trail to Middle Kootenay Pass begins as a good road but, thank the God of mountain biking, it soon deteriorates to an exciting doubletrack with some steep sections. Variously ride and push your fat tires past waterfalls and meadows to the summit of the pass.

Like horses rushing for the barn after a long ride, there'll be no holding you back once you begin the descent along Middlepass Creek. The initial sections below the pass have been extensively ditched to deter vehicular traffic, and that means air time, but use caution; after all this is the middle of nowhere. The trail is a bush-lined, dirt doubletrack where the main traffic seems to be dirt bikes and bears. The forest hereabouts burned in the 1930s and regeneration has been so slow that, even now, it is largely deciduous. Soon you reach a wellsite where the trail becomes a good gravel road descending steadily through forests and across some huge avalanche slopes. With gravity as your ally, this road is a blast, but watch out for the occasional ditch and pile of stones that prevent vehicular access and require a bit of caution. Eight kilometres below the pass the road joins a well-travelled gravel road for the final 8.9 km back to your starting point on Commerce Creek Road.

| | |
|---|---|
| 11.4 | Sunkist Ridge |
| 14.9 | junction with West Castle route, turn right |
| 15.0 | ford creek |
| 25.2 | junction with Middle Kootenay Pass trail, turn left |
| 28.1 | road downgraded, keep right up hill |
| 29.9 | Middle Kootenay Pass |
| 32.6 | wellsite, good road begins |
| 38.0 | junction with good gravel road, turn left |
| 39.4 | bridge across Middlepass Creek |
| 46.9 | end of ride |

## Options

1. Middle Kootenay Pass can be reached as part of a moderate/intermediate out-and-back day trip from either the BC or Alberta side. From the BC trailhead drive an additional 8.9 km and join the trail at km 38 of the route log. The Alberta trailhead is at km 25.2 of the route log. In both cases the trails are clear and easily followed. The summit area, with its lush carpet of rhododendrons, beargrass and glacier lilies, is very scenic, and judging by the tracks on the hillside it appears a few berserk pistonheads think so too.

2. Sunkist Ridge is best reached on an out-and-back basis from the BC side. The ridge offers considerable potential for exploration and excitement. Drive to km 4.3 of the route log. From there it is a difficult/intermediate out-and-back of 14.2 km.

## 109 WEST CASTLE RIVER                       map 20

A valley-bottom ride with plenty of views, the old logging road up the West Castle Valley provides some classic mountain cruising. Much of this country has been logged but, if it's any consolation, the scenery is as good as ever. All in all, this is a great place for the intermediate rider to enjoy the thrills of mountain biking.

The trail is good gravel and clay with a few ruts, mud holes and rotting bridges as befits any respectable 4WD road. It climbs and winds about the valley, but never does find any major hills. Some fording is necessary, so don't try this ride at times of high water.

The mountains here are among the most colourful in the Canadian Rockies—warm reds, greens and steel blues colour the rocks, reflecting the influence of the Purcell lava flow. This type of geology is typical of the country from here south into Waterton.

### Options

An obscure track at km 10.3 leads left from a landing, through the cutblocks, then climbs steeply to Sunkist Ridge (see #108). Drop your bike where the angle of climb becomes excessive and continue to the ridge on foot.

**Gentle backcountry ride**

**Type** out-and-back on 4WD roads

**Rating** moderate/intermediate

**Other users** motorized-5

**Distance** 24.2 km

**Time** 3-4 hours

**Maps** 82 G/1 Sage Creek
82 G/8 Beaver Mines

**Season** mid-June to mid-October

**Land agency** Alberta Forest Service

### Access

Follow SR 774 to the West Castle resort. Just before the gate at the resort, a road branches off to the left. Follow this road for 3.1 km to a fork. West Castle road is the left-hand branch.

| | |
|---|---|
| 0.0 | trailhead |
| 4.7 | bridge |
| 7.4 | junction, keep left |
| 8.7 | junction, keep right |
| 10.2 | ford creek |
| 10.3 | junction, keep right (left is track to Sunkist Ridge) |
| 12.1 | end of road |

18

16

14

10          20      24.2

# 110 SOUTH CASTLE RIVER

maps 20, 21

This cycling route follows an old logging road to the headwaters of the beautiful and remote Castle River valley. It ends below the Castle River Divide, which marks the northern boundary of Waterton Lakes National Park. The route follows a good dirt and gravel road, but erosion at most of the stream crossings has created some challenging riding.

About 13 km into the ride keep left where the road forks. The tracks rejoin after 1.4 km, but the left fork avoids four fords of the Castle River. At km 17 Font Creek Road branches to the right and crosses the river.

Beyond Font Creek the distinctive red shale slopes of Avion Ridge come into view and the subalpine valley becomes more open as you cycle through several recent cutblocks. The rideable road ends in a spruce and fir forest at the base of a 500 m vertical wall of limestone—a good place to look for mountain goats.

## Options

1. A singletrack trail to the south climbs 2 km to the Castle River Divide and boundary of Waterton Lakes National Park. The pass is in the trees with little in the way of views. From the summit a trail to the east climbs up onto Avion Ridge where there are spectacular views in all directions. An option requiring a serious commitment to adventure involves crossing over the Castle River Divide to the Snowshoe trail (#116). Since biking is not permitted between the park boundary and the end of the Snowshow trail, you will have to carry or push your bike over this section. Once in the valley you can scream down the Snowshoe trail and pound the pavement to Waterton or some other suitable pick-up point.

**Gentle backcountry ride**

**Type** out-and-back on 4WD roads

**Rating** difficult/intermediate

**Other users** equestrian-1 motorized-4

**Distance** 48.8 km

**Time** 5-7 hours

**Map** 82 G/1 Sage Creek

**Season** mid-June to mid-October

**Land agency** Alberta Forest Service

**Access**

From the hamlet of Beaver Mines drive west for 14.1 km on SR 774 to the turn-off to Beaver Mines Lake. Follow this road for 3.7 km to the old logging road that leads south up the Castle River. This rough road can be driven for most of its length. However, I suggest that you begin cycling at about km 6.4. This will give you max mountain bike fun and your car will get less abuse.

Photo: Gerhardt Lepp.

2. The Font Creek trail provides an 8 km out-and-back side trip. The junction of Font Creek Road at km 17 of Castle River Road is reasonably obvious. You will have to ford the Castle River before grinding your gears up the rough, moderately steep old road on the east bank of Font Creek. After two shallow fords, the road climbs to the base of a high limestone face along the Continental Divide and eventually deteriorates to the point where you'll find walking preferable to cycling. It is a short hike along the creek through subalpine forest to the col on the south end of Sage Mountain, which overlooks the Castle Valley.

| | |
|---|---|
| 0.0 | trailhead |
| 12.4 | keep left on singletrack (doubletrack to right rejoins later) |
| 13.8 | doubletrack rejoins from right |
| 17.0 | junction, keep left (Font Creek option to right) |
| 19.0 | singletrack from South Drywood joins from left |
| 24.4 | end of road |

# 111 GRIZZLY CREEK                                   map 20

Grizzly Creek—the name alone conjures up exciting images. From a major ford of the South Castle River to one of the finest singletrack rides anywhere, this trip delivers adventure.

An old exploration road leads up the valley to Ruby and Grizzly lakes. Much of the road has been reclaimed providing 8 km of fabulous singletrack including 3 km in subalpine meadows. The trail takes you from the valley bottom to timberline in an area with a real wild country feel about it.

After a short roll from the trailhead you must ford the South Castle. This is difficult at higher water levels making late summer the best time for this trip. The initial 5 km is a fairly wide dirt and gravel track with some alder hedging. Beyond km 5 the road has been "put to bed," as they say. A singletrack trail continues onward, leading almost to timberline before descending to Grizzly Lake. Expect to be challenged by rocks, roots, steep sections and the occasional mud hole along the trail. The trail crosses several slide paths, and larch trees and beargrass are common in the upper sections. I didn't see any sign of bears but this sure looks like the right kind of place.

The ride down is excellent. More so if you reach that Zen-like stage when you, your bike and the trail merge into one. Live for the moment—it's all that exists as you follow this perfect trail through a perfect setting.

**Classic high mountain ride**

**Type** out-and-back on 4WD roads and singletrack

**Rating** difficult/intermediate

**Other users** hikers-1  equestrian-3  motorized-3

**Distance** 27.2 km

**Time** 3-5 hours

**Maps** 82 G/1 Sage Creek
82 G/8 Beaver Mines

**Season** late July to mid-October

**Land agency** Alberta Forest Service

**Access**
From the hamlet of Beaver Mines drive southwest for 14.1 km on SR 774 to the turn-off to Beaver Mines Lake. Follow this road southeast for 3.7 km to the gravel road, which leads south up the Castle River. Follow this rough road for 6.4 km to the trail—a 4WD road on your right.

| | |
|---|---|
| 0.0 | trailhead |
| 1.3 | ford Castle River |
| 5.1 | ford creek, singletrack begins |
| 11.6 | junction, turn right |
| 13.6 | Grizzly Lake |

10          20          27.2

# 112 PRAIRIE BLUFF                           map 21

"Ride low, ride high" might be an appropriate motto for this trip. It's what lies in between that causes all the fuss. The gas well access road that leads almost to the top of Prairie Bluff was the cause of considerable controversy when it was under construction because this is prime wildlife habitat. Accordingly, the road is gated in two strategic places and it's a job just to get your bike through these gates. The road leads to two high-elevation gas wells and I suspect it will be reclaimed when the gas supply is exhausted. So cycle it while you still can!

Great views begin almost instantly on the upward climb. Besides looking over the plains, the summit ridges provide vistas of peaks on and near the Continental Divide from Tornado Mountain in the north to Chief Mountain in the south. Here, you are but one lonely mountain biker rolling along sweeping shale ridges amidst a sea of peaks, high above the hills and plains. From the macro scale of mountain ranges to the micro scale of alpine flowers, this is a very special place to ride.

The steep road will challenge your legs until km 3, when the grades ease somewhat as the road tops a ridge crest. Keep left at the junction and follow the road to its end at a fenced wellsite beyond which a rudimentary track continues upward to the summit. This track provides an incredibly pleasing ridge ride for the determined cyclist.

The descent of the road down to the trailhead is a brake-burning affair. Don't forget the gates!

**Major vertical and great views**

**Type** out-and-back on 4WD roads
**Rating** difficult/intermediate
**Other users** hikers-2
**Distance** 12.8 km
**Time** 4 hours
**Map** 82 G/8 Beaver Mines
**Season** mid-June to mid-October
**Land agency** Alberta Forest Service

**Access**
From Hwy. 6, north of Waterton, take the road that leads to the Shell Waterton complex. Follow this road west for 14.5 km to the Shell field office and continue straight past the field office for another 2 km to a prominent gated road on your right. This is the Prairie Bluff access road.

| | |
|---|---|
| 0.0 | trailhead gate |
| 1.0 | gate |
| 4.3 | junction, turn left |
| 5.2 | gas well |
| 6.4 | summit |

Photo: Cécile Lafleur.

# 113 SOUTH DRYWOOD CREEK                maps 21, 20

The trip up South Drywood Creek begins on the high plains grasslands of the Rocky Mountain front and climbs up a narrow valley to a pretty blue lake at timberline. The ride continues on to an exposed alpine ridge high above the South Castle River.

Along the way you'll be treated to the usual outstanding scenery and wild colours of the Waterton country. The forests of the upper valley were extensively burned in the 1930s and regeneration has been slow. Alpine flowers are abundant in the meadows. Dirt bikes and the occasional 4x4 use this road so timing can be everything. Pick a day when the other users are elsewhere and you will find peace and solitude.

Ride up the rough and rocky doubletrack as it climbs across dry, open hillsides with good views of the valley. Keep right at the fork at km 4.6 and roll along to the shores of Boivin Lake. Known as Blue Lake to the locals, this tarn is set in a steep-walled basin surrounded by alpine ridges.

When you're ready for more adventure return to the fork and ride through an unburned remnant of the original forest. A few good-sized fir trees grow here and best of all is the extensive and

**High mountain ride to lake and alpine ridge**

**Type** out-and-back on 4WD roads

**Rating** moderate/intermediate

**Other users** motorized-5  livestock

**Distance** 14.6 km

**Time** 3-4 hours

**Maps** 82 G/1 Sage Creek
82 G/8 Beaver Mines

**Season** July to mid-October

**Land agency** Alberta Forest Service

**Access**
Drive west from Hwy. 6 on Spreadeagle Road for 8.2 km to a T-junction. Turn right and drive 8.4 km to South Drywood Road on your left. Turn left and follow this road for 5.1 km. The doubletrack on the right is the trail.

2      4      6      8      10      12    13.4

luxuriant larch forest that includes a few ancient trees. With tall, straight-trunked beauties, this grove is incredible in its autumn colours. The trail crests the ridge and follows it to a high point above the lake with views westward over the broad and deep Castle Valley. Extensive ridge walks are possible here, but this can be a windy and inhospitable place. Return the way you came.

| | |
|---|---|
| 0.0 | trailhead |
| 4.6 | junction, keep right |
| 5.2 | Boivin Lake, retrace tracks |
| 5.8 | junction, turn right |
| 7.3 | trail on ridge (option descends to west) |

## Options

Drywood to South Castle. A 3.3 km singletrack drops from the ridge crest to join the old road along the South Castle River (#110) at a point 19 km from the trailhead. Riding this trail, then continuing down the Castle Valley to a prearranged pick-up point is a difficult/advanced option that offers quite a bit of excitement for hardcore backcountry bikers. The descent is a rideable downhill slider on a trail that is rough, rocky, steep and overgrown by alders in a few places.

# 114 SPIONKOP CREEK

map 21

This is a short canyon ride in the front range of mountains. It can be lengthened by 4.7 km each way by cycling the gas well access road.

Spionkop is a pretty mountain-front valley with lots of red and green rocks typical of the Waterton region. The trail is dry and rocky with the occasional easy ford. It climbs into the upper valley and ends in a subalpine forest. Trails leading from here to the upper basins provide the opportunity for additional exploration.

**Scenic backcountry ride**

**Type** out-and-back on 4WD roads

**Rating** moderate/intermediate

**Other users** motorized-2 livestock

**Distance** 8.2 km

**Time** 1-2 hours

**Map** 82 G/1 Sage Creek

**Season** mid-June to mid-October

**Land agency** Alberta Forest Service

### Access

Drive west from Hwy. 6 on Spreadeagle Road for 8.2 km to a T-junction. Turn right and drive 4.3 km to Spionkop Road on your left. Turn left and follow this road for 4.7 km to its end. The doubletrack continuing onward is the trail.

0.0     trailhead

4.1     end of road

# 115 YARROW CANYON                    map 21

Yarrow Canyon—it's an exciting name that con-jures up images of hidden treasures and secret places. From an inauspicious beginning on a gravel road leading to a gas compressor station, to its terminus at the foot of an alpine waterfall, Yarrow Canyon is full of beautiful places. The scenery is typical of the southern Rockies; the flat-lying strata are very colourful with the steel blue basalts of the Purcell lava flow surrounded by red and green argillites. In addition many of the cliffs are covered by lush plant growth induced by high rainfall. Unfortunately, you will have to share it with the rude sounds of the gas compressor and with a bunch of rambunctious cows.

The gate at the start of the trip brings good news: motorized traffic is restricted beyond this point. A short stretch of gravel road leads past the gate to the gas wells and compressor station. Beyond the wells the trail is doubletrack and singletrack rid-ing all the way to the head of the valley. There are no fords—that's right folks, it's a dry-feet trip and the trail surface is gravel and rock, unlikely to become muddy in any weather. The trail climbs steadily but, with only a few steep sections, push-ing is minimal. It then wanders along the timberline, passes a small lake, and ends at a camping spot beside a beautiful waterfall.

The ride out is a fast-paced, sometimes bumpy, downhill course.

## Options

A cool singletrack climbs to the shale ridge north of Mount Newman. You'll have to push your bike up, but it's a great ride down.

**Rugged and scenic high mountain ride**

**Type** out-and-back on 4WD roads and singletrack

**Rating** difficult/intermediate

**Other users** hikers-1  equestrian-2 livestock

**Distance** 20.4 km

**Time** 4-5 hours

**Maps** 82 G/1 Sage Creek
82 H/4 Waterton Lakes

**Season** mid-June to mid-October

**Land agency** Alberta Forest Service

## Access

Drive west from Hwy. 6 on Spreadeagle Road for 8.2 km to a T-junction. Turn left and drive 4 km to a locked gate across the road. Park here and cycle up the road beyond the gate.

| | |
|---|---|
| 0.0 | trailhead and park boundary |
| 1.1 | park boundary |
| 1.7 | gas compressor |
| 2.0 | junction, keep right |
| 2.1 | junction, keep left |
| 4.0 | doubletrack begins |
| 10.0 | singletrack to ridge climbs uphill to right |
| 10.2 | doubletrack ends at lake |

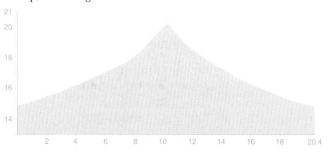

# 116 SNOWSHOE TRAIL
map 21

This old fire road to the Snowshoe Warden Cabin provides easy bicycle access to several good hiking trails. The trip is suitable for families and tot-trailers.

The old road rolls along the north side of Bauerman Creek and through several shallow and sometimes rocky stream crossings on its way to the end of legal cycling at the warden cabin. Anderson Peak rises to the south and the red shale slopes of Avion Ridge can be seen to the north.

**Hiking Options**

1. A hiking trail climbs to the Castle River Divide and up onto Avion Ridge. Hard-core riders can push or carry their bikes to the pass, then ride the South Castle River trail (#110) to a prearranged pick-up point.

2. The Goat Lake trail branches to the north 4 km from Red Rock Canyon. It is a steep 2.5 km hike to this alpine lake where mountain goats are often seen.

3. From Snowshoe Cabin good trails lead to Twin Lakes and Lost Lake.

**Family fun on gentle backcountry trail**

**Type** out-and-back on 4WD roads

**Rating** moderate/novice

**Other users** hikers-3  equestrian-2

**Distance** 16.4 km

**Time** 2-3 hours

**Map** 82 G/1 Sage Creek

**Season** July to mid-October

**Land agency** Parks Canada

**Access**

From Hwy. 5, drive up Red Rock Canyon Road to its terminus at Red Rock Canyon. The trail starts at the bridge on the west side of the parking lot.

| | |
|---|---|
| 0.0 | trailhead |
| 4.0 | trail to Goat Lake to right |
| 8.2 | Snowshoe Cabin |

2    4    6    8    10    12    14    16.4

*Yarrow Canyon (#115).*

# 117 CRANDELL MOUNTAIN CIRCUIT                    map 21

This mellow cycling trip provides a tour of the central region of Waterton Lakes National Park. The ride begins in town and takes you out of the mountains onto the high plains grasslands where, in June and July, you'll find a wildflower paradise. The route re-enters the mountains on a paved road along Blakiston Brook, climbs over a low pass on the popular Crandell Lake trail, then descends the paved Akamina Parkway back to the townsite. This ride makes an ideal family outing except for one factor—the roads in this park are so narrow they are downright dangerous to cycle.

Ride east out of town on Hwy. 5 and up the Red Rock Canyon Road. Turn left into the Crandell Mountain Campground and follow the main access road to the Crandell Lake trailhead on your left. Ride up the wide trail as it climbs to Crandell Lake, a pretty sink-lake surrounded by mountain peaks, and a good spot for a picnic or a refreshing dip on a hot day. The trail climbs above the lake to the pass and the junction with the Cameron Creek trail. Keep right and descend to the highway. It is a fast downhill roll from here to town.

## Options

Experienced riders can combine this trail with Cameron Creek trail (#118).

**Gentle mountain ride**

**Type** loop on 2WD roads and singletrack

**Rating** moderate/novice

**Other users** hikers-6  equestrian-2

**Distance** 23 km (18.7 on pavement)

**Time** 2-4 hours

**Map** 82 H/4 Waterton Lakes

**Season** mid-June to mid-October

**Land agency** Parks Canada

**Access**
Begin in the Waterton Lakes townsite and follow Highway 5 out of town.

| | |
|---|---|
| 0.0 | trailhead |
| 3.2 | junction with Red Rock Canyon Road, turn left |
| 10.2 | junction, turn left on the Crandell Campground road |
| 11.9 | campground trailhead, turn left |
| 12.2 | Church camp trailhead, keep left |
| 13.6 | junction, Crandell Lake to left |
| 14.6 | junction, keep right (Cameron Creek trail to left) |
| 16.2 | Akamina Parkway, turn left |
| 23.0 | Waterton townsite |

# 118 CAMERON CREEK TRAIL                     map 21

The Cameron Creek trail is a challenging skilltester that is pure pleasure for strong inter-mediate riders, but no place for novices. It is a narrow, rocky, twisting singletrack that parallels the parkway as it leads you down the valley to the townsite. With visibility limited in many places, this trail demands all of your attention. Keep a close watch for wildlife (especially bears) and for other trail users. After a breathtaking descent the trail joins the parkway for the final roll into town. Because this trail traverses areas that are impor-tant bear habitat, you should avoid travelling here in spring.

**Technical delights**

**Type** point-to-point on singletrack

**Rating** moderate/intermediate

**Other users** hikers-1

**Distance** 6.6 km one way

**Time** 1 hour

**Map** 82 H/4 Waterton Lakes

**Season** mid-June to mid-October

**Land agency** Parks Canada

**Access**
This trail leaves the Crandell Lake trail at a point 1.6 km north of the Akamina Parkway.

| | |
|---|---|
| 0.0 | trailhead at km 14.6 of Crandell Mountain circuit |
| 6.0 | Akamina Parkway, turn left |
| 6.6 | Waterton townsite |

# 119  Y CAMP TRAIL

map 21

This scenic trail leads across the high plains grasslands to the edge of the mountains on the east side of Waterton Lake. With the mountain front rising to the south and west, the scenery along this trail is simply outstanding. Ditto for the wildflowers in June and July. Watch for wildlife; this area is prime elk habitat and, in springtime, an important area for bears.

Variously known as the Y Camp trail, the Wishbone trail or the Crypt Landing trail, the route begins as an old road, then turns to singletrack. The first section of the trail is a delightful ride, although the cycling becomes more difficult as the grass grows taller during the summer. Vimy Ridge branches to the left at km 7 and the cycling trail continues to the right. Not far past this fork the trail becomes badly overgrown with a luxuriant crop of cow parsnip, nettles and shrubs. This jungle gets thicker as the growing season progresses, but improves again after leaf fall. Most folks do this ride for the spectacular grassland section and turn back when the bush gets too thick for enjoyable cycling. If you manage to get through the jungle, the trail improves as it winds along the shore of Middle Waterton Lake to the end of legal cycling at the campsite.

**Rugged high plains ride**

**Type** out-and-back on 4WD roads and singletrack

**Rating** moderate/novice

**Other users** hikers-2  equestrian-2

**Distance** 22 km

**Time** 2-3 hours

**Map** 82 H/4 Waterton Lakes

**Season** May through October

**Land agency** Parks Canada

**Access**
The trailhead is located on Hwy. 6, 0.5 km south of its junction with Hwy. 5.

| | |
|---|---|
| 0.0 | trailhead |
| 5.4 | ford |
| 7.0 | junction, keep right (left is trail to Vimy Ridge) |
| 11.0 | Wishbone campsite |

# 120 AKAMINA PASS AND KISHINENA CREEK     maps 21, 20

This ride begins in Waterton Lakes National Park, climbs over Akamina Pass and descends along Akamina and Kishinena creeks to the Flathead Valley, just north of the international boundary. The ride finishes at a remote location and you must make prior arrangements for a pick-up. Formerly it was possible to cross into the U.S.A. and make a long loop with Logan Pass, but the customs post at Flathead is currently closed. The alpine and subalpine areas at the head of the valley form the Akamina-Kishinena Provincial Park and Wall Lake is a popular day-cycling destination.

Cruise up the wide, smooth trail to Akamina Pass and enter the province of British Columbia. Soon you'll ride past the B.C. Parks ranger station, the trail to Forum Lake, then the trail to Wall Lake (see options).

Continuing down the valley the route passes a vehicle barricade, then the road gradually improves as it winds through cutblocks and passes several well sites. The road enters the wide, deep Kishinena Valley surrounded by the peaks of the border ranges. Cross the bridge at the four-way junction and continue down the valley. The 114 km sign begins the countdown to km 74 at Flathead bridge and km 0 at Morrissey on Highway 3. The smooth gravel road enters the broad Flathead Valley and turns north, rolling up and down across the drainages of Elder Creek, Nettie Creek and Sage Creek. It passes through several large stands of western larch en route to the Flathead bridge and the end of the ride.

## Options

Wall Lake. This pretty tarn makes an excellent day trip destination. Keep left at the junction at km 3.8 and follow the singletrack trail for 1.8 km to the lake and campsite.

**Remote scenic cruiser**

**Type** point-to-point on 4WD and 2WD roads

**Rating** difficult/intermediate

**Other users** hikers-2  equestrian-2 motorized-2

**Distance** 53.4 km one way

**Time** 4-6 hours

**Maps** 82 G/1 Sage Creek 82 G/2 Inverted Ridge

**Season** July to mid-October

**Land agency** Parks Canada, British Columbia Provincial Parks, British Columbia Forest Service

**Access**

**east**  From Waterton Lakes townsite follow the Akamina Parkway for 13 km to the signed trailhead.

**west**  From Hwy. 3 at Morrissey, 13 km west of Fernie, follow the good gravel of Morrissey, Lodgepole, Harvey Creek and Flathead roads for 61 km to Kishinena Road on the left.

| | |
|---|---|
| 0.0 | east trailhead |
| 1.6 | Akamina Pass |
| 2.6 | ranger station |
| 3.8 | Wall Lake to left |
| 14.4 | four-way junction, turn left and cross bridge |
| 22.9 | Kishinena bridge |
| 45.9 | junction with Sage Road, go straight |
| 52.4 | Commerce Road |
| 52.9 | Flathead bridge |
| 53.4 | Flathead Road |

# 121 SAGE CREEK                                    map 20

*Josephine Falls (#122).*

**Remote scenic cruiser**

**Type** out-and-back on 2WD roads
**Rating** moderate/novice
**Other users** motorized-4
**Distance** 41 km
**Time** 3-4 hours
**Map** 82 G/1 Sage Creek
**Season** mid-June to mid-October
**Land agency** British Columbia Forest Service

**Access**
From Flathead Road, 61 km southeast of Hwy. 3 at Morrissey, follow Kishinena Road to the left (east) across the Flathead River bridge. Sage Creek Road is 7.5 km from the junction. Turn left, drive for 9 km and park.

| | |
|---|---|
| 0.0 | begin riding |
| 19.9 | spur to left below Sage Pass |
| 20.5 | end of road |

A good logging road leads up the valley of Sage Creek and ends below the Continental Divide. Begin cycling wherever you please; I suggest starting about 9 km from Kishinena Road, which still leaves some 20 km of mountain bike cruising. The cycling is continuously easy with a moderate uphill grade.

The valley of Sage Creek is typical of the western slope of the southern Rockies. The creekbed is a sparkling artist's palette of red and green argillites and black lava rocks. At lower elevations the forest is a mix of Douglas fir, pine, larch and aspen. As you move up the valley the effects of a long-past and major fire-storm are evident; much of the forest is deciduous aspen and alder with a few snags standing sentinel. The vegetation is luxuriant and very colourful in the autumn with larches ever present, both near the treeline and in the Flathead Valley. Much of the valley has been logged, especially at the upper end.

The return trip is a long, gentle downhill cruiser with a few steeper sections and the occasional uphill for variety.

# 122 FOREST, FALLS & LAKES                    map 22

One very cool exploration of the hills east of Elkford, this trail offers exciting riding and some very scenic attractions. A couple of access roads were pushed into the area in 1998 and some logging activity may be expected.

Roll out of town on pavement, cross the bridge, then take to the singletrack. The trail climbs for the next 2 km offering a good aerobic workout before topping out at Lost Lake. Along the shore a series of planks provide opportunities for stunts. Roll over the roots, cross a road, keep left at a junction in a meadow and climb up to pretty Lily Lake. Past the lake the trail climbs and dives, crosses another road and reaches the falls trailhead. Some folks choose to ride the pavement up hill to this point, but that means they lose half of the singletrack fun.

Take the falls trail as it dipsy-doodles about and drags you across the roots of all evil. There is little warning of the canyon and the falls until you roll up to the guardrail and look down—Josephine Falls spills over a ledge far below. The singletrack winds along the canyon's edge for more than a kilometre. With the void on your left and the sound of rushing water in your ears, there are views galore but keep your eyes on the trail. Roll on through the woods to the junction in the meadow, across the road and back to Lost Lake. Now the big reward—drop down the twisty, exciting singletrack to town.

**Options**

Combine this ride with River and Mountain trails for a 40 km mostly singletrack tour of the Elk Valley.

**Singletrack treats lead to canyon and waterfall**

**Type** loop on singletrack

**Rating** moderate/intermediate

**Other users** hikers-4

**Distance** 15.2 km

**Time** 1-3 hours

**Map** 82 J/2 Fording River

**Season** May through October

**Land agency** British Columbia Forest Service

**Access**
In Elkford, begin at the junction of Highway 43 and Fording River Road. Ride east on Fording Road.

| | |
|---|---|
| 0.0 | trailhead |
| 0.4 | right on singletrack |
| 3.0 | Lost Lake, keep right |
| 3.4 | cross road |
| 3.6 | junction, go left |
| 4.4 | Lily Lake, junction, go straight |
| 6.8 | cross road |
| 7.4 | north trailhead, go right on Falls trail |
| 9.6 | Josephine Falls |
| 9.8 | junction, keep left |
| 11.6 | junction, keep left |
| 11.8 | cross road |
| 12.2 | Lost Lake |
| 14.8 | left on pavement |
| 15.2 | end of ride |

# 123 RIVER & MOUNTAIN TRAILS         map 22

Cool singletracks in a valley bottom setting, these trails have been used for the Grizzly Grind mountain bike race. These are shared use trails, please yield to others.

To find River trail ride east from the four-way stop on the Fording River Road. Just across the bridge turn left and follow the forest service road to the 2.5 km point where a singletrack drops to the left off the road. Prepare to be entertained by the gyrations of this little trail as it climbs and twists along the banks of the Elk River. When you reach the doubletrack at km 7.5 you want to take the trail to the left that follows along the curve of the river to a rustic bridge. Up and over (gently please) and up to the Elk Lakes Pass road.

Go left on the road and turn right on one of the following: a somewhat overgrown singletrack signed as Mountain trail, or a little farther down the road, an unsigned doubletrack that is the Crossing Creek trail. These two trails meet after a kilometre and Mountain trail (signed) goes off to the left. The town dump is nearby so keep an eye out for bears on this part of the trail. From here to the ski hill the trail is a sweet singletrack snaking its way through the trees and along the edge of river terraces with valley views. It eventually leads you to the Elkford ski hill and the road. Roll down to town with a happy smile on your face.

**Singletrack treats**

**Type** loop on 2WD road and singletrack

**Rating** moderate/intermediate

**Other users** hikers-2

**Distance** 18.7 km

**Time** 1-3 hours

**Map** 82 J/2 Fording River

**Season** May through October

**Land agency** British Columbia Forest Service, private

**Access**
In Elkford, begin at the junction of Highway 43 and Fording River Road. Ride east on Fording Road.

| | |
|---|---|
| 0.0 | trailhead |
| 0.3 | turn left just after crossing bridge |
| 2.8 | turn left onto River trail |
| 7.5 | doubletrack begins |
| 8.2 | bridge |
| 8.5 | turn left on Elk Lakes Pass road |
| 8.6 | turn right on Mountain trail |
| 9.5 | trail crosses Crossing Creek doubletrack |
| 12.5 | cross road |
| 16.2 | ski hill |
| 18.7 | end of ride |

# 124 CROSSING CREEK TRAIL                    map 22

This trail, known locally as Koko Claims, is a doubletrack that climbs up to a pass at timberline, then descends to the Bull River. It's too washed out for most vehicles, but it is used by quads and dirt bikes so you may wish to avoid busy weekends.

Initially the riding is easy on a good trail in the bottom of a deep valley, but at km 6 everything changes as the trail turns northward and begins a steep climb up to the pass. For most of the next 3 km the going is tough, loose rocks and a steep grade necessitate pushing, even descending this section is tricky. Perseverance pays though, once up the hill the trail rolls along at timberline through alpine meadows and groves of small trees with rugged peaks above. Continue a short distance beyond the summit for views into the Bull River valley.

## Options

If you've made shuttle arrangements it is possible to continue westward and descend to the Bull River Road.

**Rugged backcountry ride to high pass**

**Type** out-and-back on 4WD road

**Rating** difficult/intermediate

**Other users** hikers-1 motorized-4

**Distance** 19 km

**Time** 3-5 hours

**Maps** 82 J/2 Fording River
82 J/3 Mount Peck

**Season** July through October

**Land agency** British Columbia Forest Service

## Access

From the four-way stop on Hwy. 43 in Elkford, drive 5.6 km north on the Elk Lakes Pass road. The trail is an unsigned doubletrack on your left.

| | |
|---|---|
| 0.0 | trailhead |
| 1.0 | junction with Mountain trail to left |
| 9.5 | summit |

2    4    6    8    10    12    14    16    18  19

# 125 BOIVIN CREEK TRAIL                    map 22

This is a super ride for novices and families. Strong kids will cycle all of it and strong dads will be able to tow tot trailers up the hill. The riding is easy on an old logging road that climbs at a gentle grade up the valley of Boivin Creek.

Begin at the gate and ride along the gravel surface of the water plant access road. Keep right at km 1.2 on the grassy doubletrack of the old logging road. Watch the bridge at km 1.8, it's a few logs short at each end. This is a pretty valley with towering peaks above and the rushing waters of Boivin Creek below. The grades are never steep but the road is always climbing. The road is used as a ski trail in winter, hence the short grass. At km 6.8 you'll reach the local ski club warming hut, please leave it in good condition. This is a good spot for novices and families to turn back. Stronger riders can continue on to the end of the road at an old sawmill site at km 9.5.

Well, all that gentle uphill is about to give you a lesson in the law of gravity. It's a fast and fabulously fun downhill roll back to the trailhead. You may need to use the brakes a bit and don't forget that tricky bridge. You'll be smiling all the way to the trailhead.

**Family fun on gentle backcountry trail**

**Type** out-and-back on 4WD road

**Rating** moderate/novice

**Other users** hikers-2

**Distance** 19 km

**Time** 2-4 hours

**Maps** 82 J/2 Fording River
82 G/15 Tornado Mountain
82 G/14 Quinn Creek

**Season** July through October

**Land agency** British Columbia Forest Service

**Access**

In Elkford, drive up Natal St. to the switchback and signed trailhead on the left. The trail is the road that continues beyond the gate.

| | |
|---|---|
| 0.0 | trailhead |
| 1.2 | keep right |
| 1.8 | tricky bridge |
| 3.2 | junction, keep left |
| 6.8 | cabin |
| 7.1 | junction, go right |
| 9.5 | end of road |

# 126 ISLAND LAKE

The ride from Fernie to Island Lake Lodge makes a delightful day trip with lots of entertaining options. The road is paved as far as the Mount Fernie Provincial Park campground and continues as a rough gravel road with a few muddy spots. As it climbs up the valley the road passes through a beautiful old growth cedar forest. Here, on the east side of the Lizard Range, high precipitation creates ideal conditions for these ancient and majestic trees. It also provides the main raison d'etre for the lodge at Island Lake—great quantities of snow. The lodge is a beautiful, handcrafted log building set next to Island Lake, a pretty little gem resting below the spectacular ramparts and basins of the Lizard Range. Cyclists are welcome, be it for a coffee break or for a few days of R & R, and there are some good cycling options in the vicinity. The return trip is a fast cruise, but watch for cars.

## Options

Iron Pass. Beyond the lodge the road is much rougher and steeper. The 2.8 km ride up to Iron Pass, elevation 1600 m, provides a good perspective of the upper part of the valley. There are views south to the Elk Valley and north into Iron Creek. The Howling Coyote trail climbs around the peak in the centre of the pass, then descends back to the lake.

For the hard-core backcountry bicyclist, a rough 4WD trail descends from the pass following a powerline along Iron Creek to the Bull River. You will have to either ford the river or make a circuitous powerline excursion to get to Bull River Road. Arrange a car shuttle and/or ride down to the Bull River Inn in the Kootenay Valley.

Inquire locally about singletrack treats for the expert rider.

**Scenic cruiser with options**

**Type** out-and-back on 2WD and 4WD roads

**Rating** moderate/novice

**Other users** motorized-5

**Distance** 23.6 km (7 km on pavement)

**Time** 4-6 hours

**Maps** 82 G/6 Elko
82 G/11 Fernie

**Season** June through October

**Land agency** private, British Columbia Forest Service

## Access

Begin in Fernie. Distances are measured from the highway bridge on the west side of town. Cycle west on Hwy. 3.

| | |
|---|---|
| 0.0 | west bridge |
| 2.3 | turn right onto Cedar Valley Road |
| 3.2 | Mount Fernie Provincial Park |
| 11.7 | junction, Island Lake Lodge to left (Iron Pass to right) |
| 11.8 | Island Lake Lodge |

2    4    6    8    10    12    14    16    18    20    22    23.6

## 127 FERNIE ALPINE RESORT                    maps 23, 23A

Fernie Alpine Resort offers some of the finest lift-assisted biking available in western Canada. Whether you choose to use the lift (possibly lifts in future) or ride up the hill, you will find a wide variety of downhill drops and cross-country trails awaiting your pleasure. Ask for a trail map at Guest Services and, if you are a hard-core, high-skill rider, ask about the expert singletracks.

The easy descents are on the ski hill access roads like Deer Trail, Cedar and Larch. In addition there are quite a few rider-built singletracks that will test expert skills and leave either carnage or adrenaline-induced smiles. New trails are continuously being constructed and the lower area is being developed so you can expect changes to the layout of the trails. Races are often held at the hill and both the downhill and cross-country courses offer good rides.

**Lift assisted biking for riders of all skill levels**

**Type** loops on 4WD roads and singletrack

**Rating** novice to expert

**Other users** hikers-2 equestrian-2

**Distance** your choice

**Time** varies

**Maps**  82 G/6 Elko
F.A.R. Bike & Hike Trail Map

**Season** June through October

**Land agency** private, British Columbia Forest Service

**Access**

Begin at the Fernie Alpine Resort located 1 km off Hwy. 3, west of Fernie. These trails can also be accessed from Mount Fernie Provincial Park.

# 127A CROSS-COUNTRY RACE COURSE      map 23A

This trail includes lots of exciting singletrack as it leads north from the resort, snakes its way through Sherwoody Forest, climbs up onto the ski hill, then descends on a combination of access roads and singletrack. Variations of this course have been used for many races and it offers an excellent recreational ride. Bonus is the old cedar forest and the deciduous new-growth in the cutblocks. I had to dice with a cow moose and her two calves for right-of-way on the trail.

Ride up the rise past El Quad and deal with a slightly uncertain route through the new subdivision where the trail jogs left as it crosses the road, then you're free. The trail junctions ahead are unsigned so follow the route log, there may be flagging at some of them. Roll through the cutblocks, then turn left on Happy Gilmar. This little gem climbs into the cedar forest, winds about, then drops down a fast hill into Sherwoody Forest. There are lots of trails here, none signed, so pay attention to the route. Go left on Sherwoody and keep left, you'll know you're on the correct trail when you drop into a gully and cross a small creek. At Gorby trail turn left and follow the old cat track as it climbs through a forest of big cedars. You'll come to the bottom of Gorby Bowl ski run. Keep climbing all the way to the signed Cedar trail. Speed across the hill on Cedar, then drop left on a funky little singletrack and follow Larch across to El Quad. Finish up by dropping the tight turns under the lift until you come to the day lodge and Griz Inn.

**Singletrack treats**

**Type** loop on 4WD road and singletrack

**Rating** moderate/advanced

**Other users** hikers-1 equestrian-2

**Distance** 12 km

**Time** 1-2 hours

**Access**
Begin this ride at the Griz Inn at the Fernie Alpine Resort.

| | |
|---|---|
| 0.0 | trailhead |
| 0.4 | cross road |
| 0.8 | right |
| 1.2 | left |
| 1.4 | left on Galloway |
| 2.6 | Black Forest joins from left |
| 2.7 | left on Happy Gilmar |
| 4.4 | left on Sherwoody |
| 4.7 | left (right leads to Mount Fernie Provincial Park) |
| 5.6 | left on Gorby |
| 6.6 | Old Goat to left |
| 7.6 | Gorby Bowl, head up hill |
| 8.7 | follow Cedar |
| 10.3 | left on singletrack |
| 10.5 | right on Larch |
| 10.7 | left |
| 10.8 | left |
| 11.0 | right under lifts |
| 12.0 | Griz Inn |

# 128 HARTLEY PASS

maps 23, 23A

This is the great cruiser ride of the Fernie area. The route is scenic with some moderate uphills and fast downhills as it climbs its way out of the Elk Valley to a subalpine pass. You'll be in the company of the legendary Ghost Rider as you ride below Hosmer Peak on your way to the pass. Ghost Rider can be seen from town in the late afternoons of early autumn.

Hartley Lake Road is dirt and gravel with a few bumps, rain ruts and muddy sections, especially in wet weather. Give our greetings to a couple of aggressive dogs near the beginning, then ride past a few homesteads on a rolling upland above the valley. The road ascends more steeply as it climbs to tiny Hartley Lake, pretty but ringed by logs from past logging activities. The pass lies in the timber just above the lake and features the usual great views.

The downhill part of the trip is akin to a slalom course as the road winds its way down the mountainside. Watch for cars. The remainder of the distance to town is just plain fun.

## Options

Cycle off of the north side of the pass for a 2.5 km downhill roll, then turn left onto a doubletrack that leads for another 2.5 km into the valley below the Three Sisters. This is easy riding, but don't forget you have to climb back up the pass to return to town.

It is possible to cycle down to Bull River Road, but a car shuttle will be required to complete this trip.

**Classic mountain cruiser**

**Type** out-and-back on 2WD roads

**Rating** difficult/novice

**Other users** motorized-4

**Distance** 27.6 km (10 km on pavement)

**Time** 3-4 hours

**Map** 82 G/11 Fernie

**Season** mid-June through October

**Land agency** British Columbia Forest Service

## Access

Begin in Fernie. Distances are measured from the highway bridge on the east side of town. Ride east on Hwy. 3.

| | |
|---|---|
| 0.0 | east bridge |
| 0.9 | turn left onto Dicken Road |
| 5.0 | turn left onto Hartley Lake Road |
| 13.2 | Hartley Lake to left |
| 13.8 | Hartley Pass |

# 129 FERNIE TRAILS

maps 23, 23A

The Fernie singletracks are a series of rider-built trails designed to take advantage of this beautiful setting and to test your stamina and riding skills. New trails are added every year, so local knowledge is a big factor in understanding what trails are available and how to find them. These folks deserve a big hand—not all riders are this willing to share their hard-built trails. A local trail map called The Secret of Singletrack is available from Ski Base and is the best way to understand how the trails interconnect.

The trails continuously change with new trails being constructed, development and logging impinging on others, and with wear and tear from ever-increasing numbers of users. Many of the trails have deliberately designed difficulties built in to test your riding skill. Be a sport, if you can't ride them then just walk past and be on your way. Under no circumstances should you destroy the stunts or create new trails around them.

Popular combinations include linking Roots and Ridgemont, and linking Dem Bones with Sherwoody and Fernie Alpine Resort.

**Deluxe rider-built trails close to town**

**Maps** The Secret of Singletrack
82 G/6 Elko
82 G/11 Fernie

**Season** May through October

**Land agency** British Columbia Forest Service, private, City of Fernie, British Columbia Parks

# 129A ROOTS                                          map 23A

This trail is almost all singletrack and offers a good physical and technical challenge for advanced riders as it climbs up onto the slopes of Morrissey Ridge south of Coal Creek. The ride begins on the Educational Forest trails, then cuts up to the original Roots trail. Roots extension continues the fun and Roots hyperextension adds a vertical out-and-back dimension for your riding pleasure. This area is close to the landfill so be on the lookout for bears.

Begin by rolling off of Coal Creek Road, across the bridge and onto the singletrack of the Educational Forest. This is a network of trails but we are just passing through, working our way westward to the powerline. Follow the powerline doubletrack, then climb up to River Road. Soon the Roots singletrack branches to the left and the serious climbing begins. The big challenge is to clean "the root" (not easy) at km 4.3, although some weenies have recently made a bypass route around it. If you can't ride the stunts on these trails, then go find an easier trail. Don't bring the trail down to your level. Soon the trail tops out and you'll race headlong down the rooty and exciting descent to a trail junction. Go left to the road if you've had enough, otherwise keep right on Roots extension. Once again the climbing gets serious and you'll want all the traction you can find. Roots hyperextension joins from the right. This is a must-do for all you aerobic monsters as it climbs steeply and traverses to a high viewpoint. Retrace your tracks displaying finesse and courage as you drop steeply (did I really ride up all of this?) back to the main trail. Keep right and climb a bit more, then enjoy the wild ride back to River Road. Keep right if you want to link to the Ridgemont trails, otherwise go left and drop into the Educational Forest and back to the trailhead.

**Technical delights**

**Type** loop on 2WD road and singletrack

**Rating** difficult/advanced

**Other users** hikers-1

**Distance** 12.7 km

**Time** 1-2 hours

**Access**
In Fernie ride up Coal Creek Road for 0.7 km to a right-hand junction and bridge. The signed trailhead is just across the bridge on the left.

| | |
|---|---|
| 0.0 | trailhead |
| 0.16 | right |
| 0.62 | right |
| 1.16 | keep right |
| 1.24 | left under powerline |
| 2.16 | left on doubletrack |
| 2.6 | right on River Road |
| 3.36 | left on Roots |
| 5.9 | junction, right on Roots extension |
| 6.7 | right on Roots hyperextension |
| 8.3 | viewpoint, retrace tracks |
| 9.9 | right on Roots extension |
| 11.2 | left on River Road (or right 0.4 km to Ridgemont) |
| 11.6 | right into Educational Forest |
| 12.7 | trailhead |

# 129B RIDGEMONT

map 23A

These trails are rider-built singletracks accessed by means of the Ridgemont forest road. The trails can be ridden individually, but also form a network on the lower slopes of Fernie Ridge to the north of Coal Creek. This area is close to the landfill so be on the lookout for bears. It's also scheduled for logging so you can expect to find changes in future. The access described works well if you are continuing on from Roots.

Ride up Ridgemont Road noting the various singletracks as you go along. This is a great place to play and explore, I'll leave the side trip options up to you. Eric's is a great descent and some folks take delight in riding up it too. Sidewinder is easily followed and drops steeply back to town. Trails such as Bear Chutes and other treats are accessed by keeping right at the junction at km 2.4. Deadfall keeps left at km 2.4, then makes a quick right onto singletrack and snakes its way along the ridge before dropping sharply to the powerline west of town. Drop off the powerline, cross the tracks and ride along the dike back of the golf course as you return to town.

## Technical delights

**Type** loop on 4WD road and singletrack

**Rating** moderate/advanced

**Other users** hikers-1

**Distance** 11 km

**Time** 1-2 hours

## Access

In Fernie ride up Coal Creek Road for 2 km to the signed Ridgemont Road on the left. The trail is up Ridgemont Road.

| | |
|---|---|
| 0.0 | trailhead |
| 0.45 | gate |
| 0.7 | bottom of Eric's to right |
| 2.24 | Eric's to right |
| 2.34 | Sidewinder to left |
| 2.37 | left then right on Deadfall (Bear Chutes to right) |
| 4.7 | left on powerline |
| 5.0 | right on singletrack |
| 5.4 | cross railway |
| 6.4 | gate, go left |
| 7.4 | Fairway Dr. & 15 St. |

1    2    3    4    5    6    7  7.4

# 129C  DEM BONES                                    map 23A

*Roots (#129A).*

## Singletrack treats

**Type** loop on 2WD roads, 4WD roads and singletrack

**Rating** moderate/intermediate

**Other users** hikers-2 equestrian-1

**Distance** 9.9 km

**Time** 1 hour

### Access

Begin in Fernie at the west bridge on Hwy. 3.

| | |
|---|---|
| 0.0 | trailhead |
| 0.1 | first right then left on Beach |
| 1.1 | left on doubletrack |
| 1.9 | left up powerline |
| 2.6 | right on singletrack |
| 3.4 | top, keep left |
| 6.8 | maintenance building, go right |
| 7.0 | Mount Fernie park sign |
| 7.2 | turn left |
| 8.3 | turn right |
| 8.8 | left on Hwy. 3 |
| 9.9 | bridge |

Dem Bones is a fabulous trail that I like to ride as an out-and-back from Mount Fernie Provincial Park. Others prefer a loop from town so take your pick. The descent is a fast and exciting shred with lots of tight corners and logs.

To ride it from Mount Fernie, just find the trail back of the campground maintenance building and head up. To ride it as a loop from town, follow the route log by going up Beach Road, then left onto a washed-out doubletrack that climbs up to the powerline. Go left on the powerline doubletrack and strut your stuff on a monster climb, then keep right from the high point and find the singletrack of Dem Bones on the right. The trail gains elevation to a high point where a couple of spurs lead even higher on the mountain and into bear country. Keep left, enjoy the valley view, then roll down, crossing the powerline and on into the bones meadow. Take time to give thanks for this good trail, your bike and the skills to put it all together into such a great ride. Roll on down to the finish by the maintenance building in Mount Fernie Provincial Park.

# 129D SHERWOODY FOREST

map 23A

This area is crisscrossed by a network of single-tracks that offer some challenging riding. The trails are always within the forest and you can expect the usual assortment of logs, roots, tight corners, steeps and drops to test your skills. The junctions are unsigned and new trails are continually being built, making reliable directions and mapping difficult. I suggest using this as an area for exploration. It works well in conjunction with the Fernie Alpine Resort trails and/or with Dem Bones. The trail as far as the valley viewpoint and sometimes beyond is frequented by hikers and families. Please be careful.

**Technical delights**

**Type** loops on singletrack

**Rating** moderate/advanced

**Other users** hikers-3

**Distance** varies

**Time** 1-2 hours

**Access**

Begin at the picnic area in Mount Fernie Provincial Park. The trail descends to the creek and crosses the bridge.

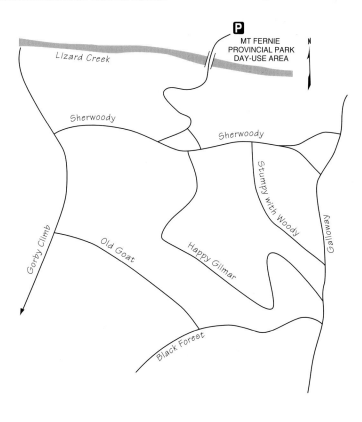

# 130  MORRISSEY RIDGE

maps 23, 23A

Imagine a perfect view of the southern Rockies. This excellent cycling trip leads you from Fernie to the summit of Morrissey Ridge, where that view can be found. At your feet the city of Fernie nestles in the valley below the peaks of the Three Sisters. Away to the east, the mountains of the Continental Divide form a rugged and often snow-covered skyline; to the south stretch the ridges and peaks of the border ranges; to the west, above the Elk Valley, the Lizard Range rises and beyond it lies the Rocky Mountain Trench. It's Fernie's best viewpoint and an excellent spot to spend time catching rays and admiring the view.

Roll out of town on the fine black gravel of Coal Creek Road, passing a few mining relics and the ghost town of Coal Creek along the way. At an old aluminum building at km 9.7 turn right onto a road that is a bit rougher but still easily rideable as it climbs through forests of cedar and fir. Watch for some interesting waterfalls in the valley off to the right. The road continues its steep climb to the summit and ends at two communications installations.

The initial cascading descent delivers as much action, speed and airtime as you and your bike can handle. The remainder of the ride is a fast down-hill cruise. It's a fitting end to a wonderful trip.

**Major vertical and great views**

**Type** out-and-back on 2WD and 4WD roads

**Rating** difficult/intermediate

**Other users** motorized-2

**Distance** 38.2 km

**Time** 3-5 hours

**Maps** 82 G/6 Elko
82 G/7 Flathead Ridge
82 G/11 Fernie

**Season** mid-June to mid-October

**Land agency** BC Forest Service

**Access**
Begin in Fernie at the intersection of Pine Avenue and Coal Creek Road.

| | |
|---|---|
| 0.0 | trailhead, ride up Coal Creek Road |
| 0.7 | educational forest trails to right |
| 2.0 | Ridgemont Road to left |
| 9.7 | junction, turn right |
| **19.1** | **summit** |

# KOOTENAY AND COLUMBIA VALLEYS

The Kootenay and Columbia cycling area, a region of deep valleys and high peaks, lies on the Pacific slope of the Rockies and includes the headwaters of the Columbia and Kootenay rivers. These two rivers flow along the Rocky Mountain Trench, a major valley that marks the western edge of the Rockies and the eastern edge of the Purcell Mountains and Selkirk Mountains. Highway 93/95 is the main north-south transportation route linking the various communities in the valley and, along with gravel forest service roads, provides access to the rides.

This area includes some good technical riding and long wilderness explorations as well as some mellow and very pleasing valley rides. Several almost forgotten old mining trails offer tremendous cycling experiences. Given the el-evation changes and steep nature of the terrain, many of the trails have lots of climbing and descending. This cycling area includes a vast network of forest service roads that are shown on maps available from the British Columbia Forest Service. Too boring and dusty for anything except endurance cycling, they provide access to almost all areas of the Rockies, Selkirks and Purcells. Only selected roads have been included in this book and generally only those seldom travelled by private vehicle.

The climate shows a strong Pacific influence and is noticeably more moderate than that of areas to the east across the Divide. Forests of cedar, spruce and fir are common in the higher-rainfall areas of the mountains. The main valley is drier than the surrounding mountains and, as a result, is graced with grass-

lands and forests of ponderosa pine and Douglas fir. As you move north, the ponderosas fade away and Douglas fir tends to predominate. Larches are common in the mountain forests from Wasa Lake south and put on a colourful display in October.

The main Kootenay and Columbia valleys are settled with Cranbrook, Kimberley, Invermere and Golden being the major communities. Some subsistence agriculture is practised, but logging and mining are the mainstays of the local economy. Tourism is an important industry here and there are several major resort areas and ski hills.

Cranbrook is the major population centre of the Kootenay Valley, but good riding close to town is limited. Kootenay Freewheelers is the local club and they have put together two good rides that begin near the college. There are other trails in the community forest and a rail trail known as Isadore Canyon. Gerick Sports is the local bike shop. Camping with showers is available at several locations. There are two delightful rides south of town on Highway 93 at Elko and others to the north at Wasa and beyond.

Kimberley is a mining and resort town located northwest of Cranbrook on the edge of the Purcell Mountains. The best riding here is in the "nature park," a network of trails on the mountainside just above town. I've described three trail combinations for you to sample, but exploring is also lots of fun. The cross-country ski trails begin near the ski hill and offer lots of mellow riding with the option to join the nature park trails. Kimberley Alpine Resort will take you and your bike up the chairlift, but there is little in the way of attractive riding on the hill at this writing. Bavarian Sports will be happy to update you on the local riding scene.

Attractively located on the shores of Lake Windermere, Invermere offers most services and a lake and beach scene. There are many cycling opportunities in the area with a variety that caters to families and hard-core riders alike. Some of the rides begin in town, but others are remote mountain adventures suitable for hard-core backcountry bikers. Drop in to Columbia Sports and tune in to the local cycling scene. Camping with showers is not available in Invermere but is available south along Lake Windermere and north at Radium.

Farther to the north is Golden, a large town with all services, including camping with showers. Stop by Summit Cycle for the latest in local information. Most of the rides described for Golden begin right in town or in the nearby Blaeberry and Beaverfoot valleys.

Kootenay and Yoho national parks feature spectacular landscapes and limited mountain bicycling opportunities, remember that cycling is permitted only on designated trails within the parks. Several old fireroads provide mellow cycling opportunities in each park. The Ottertail and Amiskwi trails are notable for their scenery and wilderness qualities.

# 131 SHEEP MOUNTAIN
map 24

### Gentle ride to great views
**Type** out-and-back with loop on 4WD road
**Rating** moderate/novice
**Other users** hikers-1
**Distance** 11.5 km
**Time** 2-3 hours
**Map** 82 G/6 Elko
**Season** mid April through October
**Land agency** British Columbia Forest Service

### Access
On Hwy. 93, drive 3.8 km south from the junction with Hwy. 3 and turn left. Drive 100 m and park. The trail is the grassy track to the right that parallels the highway.

| | |
|---|---|
| 0.0 | trailhead |
| 1.9 | turn left on grassy old road |
| 3.7 | junction, keep right |
| 5.4 | summit |
| 7.8 | junction, keep right |
| 9.6 | keep right on doubletrack |
| 11.5 | end of ride |

This easy and beautiful ride takes you on a tour of the dry hills and meadows of the Kootenay Valley along the western edge of the Rockies. Spring is one of the most beautiful times for this ride, when the hills are alive with sunflowers and wood ticks (yech!), but autumn has its own beauty too. For summer rides try early morning or evening in order to beat the heat.

Ride south from the trailhead on an old road that becomes a classic doubletrack winding through the ponderosa pine forest and meadows. Watch for the grassy track to the left that will take you up the mountain (it's really just a big hill). At km 3.7 the route keeps to the right and makes a loop on the upper slopes before returning to this point. At km 4.7 a short detour to the right reveals an eye-popping view of the Kootenay Valley including Lake Koocanusa and the hills from Montana to Kimberley. Now the trail swings northward to wind and climb along the broad summit ridge with views eastward to the towering Rockies, the expansive bunchgrass meadowlands of Wigwam Flats, and the deep canyon of Wigwam River. The trail snakes through the open forests and grasslands of the summit, then rolls northward, descending among the hills and down some switchbacks before rejoining the up-track. Keep right and in no time at all you'll find yourself back on the valley-bottom meadows. It's a beautiful roll along the doubletrack to the finish, but this attractive ride was over all too quickly for my liking.

2    4    6    8    10   11.5

# 132  WIGWAM FLATS                           map 24

This ride is all about using bikes to enjoy the land. It's a mellow doubletrack that leads through some very beautiful country alongside two spectacular canyons. The tracks wander across a broad savanna of Douglas fir and bunchgrass above the confluence of the Elk and Wigwam rivers, both flowing in deep, colourful canyons. In summer this country is hot and dry, but spring and autumn are cooler and more colourful. The area is a wildlife sanctuary with sheep and elk commonly seen.

The ride begins on a doubletrack that rolls above the Elk River dam, then alongside the canyon. A side trip takes you across meadows and through Douglas fir forest to an overlook above the confluence of the Elk and Wigwam rivers. Enjoy the views of the canyon below and the Rocky Mountain Trench beyond. Return to the main trail and climb up a hill to the Wigwam Flats. This broad grassland studded with Douglas fir covers an extensive benchland above the river. Several doubletracks wander about the flats. The route described makes a leisurely exploration to the edge of Wigwam Canyon, then loops back across the grassland to the top of the hill. From the junction at km 14.1 a side trip can be made farther up into the valley of the Wigwam where the track eventually joins a pipeline right-of-way. When you've finished your explorations, return to the top of the hill and follow your tracks back to the trailhead.

**Classic doubletrack in an outstanding setting**

**Type** out-and-back with loop on 4WD roads

**Rating** moderate/novice

**Other users** hikers-1 motorized-1

**Distance** 22.5 km

**Time** 3-4 hours

**Map** 82 G/6 Elko

**Season** mid April through October

**Land agency** British Columbia Forest Service

**Access**
From Hwy. 3 drive south through the village of Elko for 1 km, then turn left on the gravel River Road for 0.5 km and park on the east side of the bridge. The trail continues beyond the gate.

| | |
|---|---|
| 0.0 | trailhead |
| 4.8 | junction, keep right |
| 6.7 | confluence overlook, retrace tracks |
| 8.7 | junction, turn right, up hill |
| 9.4 | keep right on grassy track |
| 10.3 | keep right on grassy track |
| 12.0 | Wigwam Canyon |
| 14.1 | junction, turn left (optional excursion is to right) |
| 17.7 | junction, keep right |
| 22.5 | end of ride |

# 133 FREEWHEELERS TRAILS map 25

These trails are a fun combination of singletrack and doubletrack that explore the hills east of Cranbrook. Although not overly difficult, the trails include a few exciting surprises and some delightful sections of singletrack as they pass through forests of Douglas fir, ponderosa pine and aspen. Several hilltop vantage points offer tremendous views over the city and the broad Kootenay Valley. The trails are mostly within the Cranbrook Community Forest, but some are on private land. Please respect the landowners' wishes. The area contains an extensive network of trails that offer endless opportunities for exploration.

Two loop rides have been developed by members of the Kootenay Freewheelers Cycle Club and are indicated by yellow or white markers fastened to trees along the route. Both rides begin at the same trailhead and both end at the College of the Rockies. A photocopied map of the trails is available from local cycle shops. Although the routes are well marked, having the map is a real asset to following the trail. I suggest you ride one or both of the loops as marked, then, if you hunger for more (you monster!), try customizing your own combination of the trails.

**Singletrack treats close to town**

**Other users** hikers-3

**Map** Kootenay Freewheelers Trails map

**Season** May through October

**Land agency** British Columbia Forest Service, private

### Access

Begin in Cranbrook at the corner of 2 Street South and 24 Avenue South. Ride east up 24 Avenue as it turns into the gravel Mount Baker Road.

# 133A YELLOW TRAIL

map 25

Photo: Stephen Wilde.

**Technical delights**

**Type** loop on 4WD road and singletrack

**Rating** moderate/intermediate

**Distance** 13.5 km

**Time** 1-2 hours

| | |
|---|---|
| 0.0 | trailhead |
| 1.8 | left through gate, then parallel fence |
| 3.1 | right on yellow |
| 5.0 | left on singletrack |
| 5.3 | right on Viewpoint trail |
| 5.4 | right |
| 6.1 | left on Viewpoint trail |
| 6.3 | right |
| 6.8 | right (easily missed) |
| 7.0 | right |
| 7.1 | left on Skid |
| 7.5 | right then left along shore |
| 7.8 | left across bridge |
| 8.1 | cross parking, right on Juniper Lane |
| 8.5 | cattle gate |
| 9.9 | right on Roller Coaster |
| 10.7 | right (may go left in future) |
| 12.4 | college |
| 13.5 | end of ride |

This loop is the shorter of the two with less climbing. It includes lots of enjoyable singletrack in a beautiful forest setting. Leave Mount Baker Road and roll along a series of singletracks and doubletracks (keep right at km 3.1) that take you up on the hillside, then drop off the powerline. This is a fun downhill and it's easy to miss the junction with Viewpoint trail. Turn right and climb up, bypassing the actual viewpoint. The trail now goes left and makes a fast, fun, descent of Viewpoint, but watch for hikers and for the obscure junction to the right at km 6.8 that takes you to Skid, then loops around Kettle Lake. Cross a gravel parking area, then climb to the right onto Juniper Lane. Keep right on the aptly named Roller Coaster, then choose from a variety of trails but generally trend left across the slope to come out at the College. Future subdivision may alter the final 2 km of trail.

# 133B  WHITE TRAIL                                    map 25

This loop is longer with more climbing. It's a beautiful ride that reaches two high vantage points. Leave Mount Baker Road and roll along a series of singletracks and doubletracks (watch for the sharp left at km 3.1) to the third Alkali Lake. Keep right on the Viewpoint trail and climb up the singletrack to Windy Bluff and a great view of Cranbrook. The trail now loops to the east, then north and climbs to the top of a high hill with views of the Rockies and Kootenay Valley as well as Cranbrook. Next comes "the plunge" down a steep doubletrack, but watch for the singletrack to the right at km 9.3. A long doubletrack descent leads to a long singletrack known as Migor. Next cross the bridge and follow a singletrack back of Kettle Lake, cross a gravel parking area, then climb to the right onto Juniper Lane. Keep right on the aptly named Roller Coaster, then choose from a variety of trails but generally trend left across the slope to come out at the college. Future subdivision may alter the final 2 km of trail.

**Aerobic and technical delight**

**Type** loop on 4WD road and singletrack

**Rating** moderate/intermediate

**Distance** 18.3 km

**Time** 1-2 hours

| | |
|---|---|
| 0.0 | trailhead |
| 1.8 | left through gate, then parallel fence |
| 3.1 | left on white |
| 5.2 | right up Viewpoint |
| 6.0 | Windy Bluff |
| 6.5 | right |
| 8.4 | summit |
| 9.3 | right on singletrack |
| 10.2 | left on Migor |
| 11.7 | left |
| 12.6 | right across bridge |
| 12.9 | cross parking, right on Juniper Lane |
| 13.4 | cattle gate |
| 14.6 | right on Roller Coaster |
| 15.5 | right (may go left in future) |
| 17.2 | college |
| 18.3 | end of ride |

# 134 KIMBERLEY NATURE PARK    map 26

**Singletrack treats close to town**
**Other users** hikers-4
**Map** Kimberley Nature Park Trail Map and Guide
**Season** May through October
**Land agency** City of Kimberley, British Columbia Forest Service

**Access**
Begin in Kimberley at the nature park trailhead at the corner of Swan and Burdet streets.

The mountainside above the mining town of Kimberley hosts a wide variety of singletrack and doubletrack trails in an area known as the Kimberley Nature Park. In addition, a network of cross-country ski trails that begin at the upper parking lot at the ski hill are integrated with the nature park trails. The area is a mid-elevation mountainside covered with fir and pine forest. Lower slopes with a southern exposure, such as Sunflower Hill, are covered by ponderosa pine and bunchgrass. Bears are very common in this area so keep alert and make noise as needed. This is a popular area; please protect your right of access by looking after the trails and being courteous to other users.

This network of trails includes everything from old roads to difficult singletrack. Many of the trail junctions are signed, but some are not so things can get confusing. You'll need the Kimberley Nature Park Map and Guide, which shows the layout of the trails and gives some natural history background. I've suggested three loop rides that combine some of the best trails and natural highlights of the area, but exploration is also fun.

# 134A SUNFLOWER HILL

map 26A

**Rugged ride with flowers and views**

**Type** loop on 4WD road and singletrack

**Rating** moderate/novice

**Distance** 12.2 km

**Time** 1-3 hours

| | |
|---|---|
| 0.0 | trailhead |
| 0.3 | left on Ponderosa |
| 1.1 | Three Corners, left on Eimer Road |
| 1.6 | right on Elbow |
| 2.1 | left |
| 4.1 | right under powerline |
| 5.8 | up switchbacks to crest of hill |
| 6.1 | Sunflower Hill |
| 7.2 | junction, keep right |
| 7.3 | go straight |
| 7.4 | left on Duck Pond |
| 9.9 | Four Corners, take Lower Army |
| 11.1 | Three Corners, left on Army |
| 11.3 | right on Ponderosa |
| 11.9 | right on road |
| 12.2 | gate, end of ride |

A relatively mellow explorer on doubletrack and singletrack, this ride takes you out to Sunflower Hill where yellow balsam root bloom in May and June. It's a stunning spot with views west up the St. Mary Valley, south over the Kootenay Valley and east to the Steeples in the Rockies.

The ride begins with the easygoing fun of Ponderosa trail, rolls past Three Corners and down Eimer's trail. Turn right onto Elbow, staying left at the junction with Apache, then turn right and follow under the powerline out to Sunflower Hill. Leave the powerline and climb up the track to the crest of the hill and continue west. Keep right at a major junction, cross Skid Road and climb uphill on the signed Duck Pond single-track. Stay on this trail as it turns to doubletrack and leads to Four Corners. Finish up on Lower Army with a detour along Ponderosa and out to the trailhead.

# 134B  DIPPER LAKE

map 26B

This ride takes you to the top of the nature park at Dipper Lake and offers side trips to a backcountry ski shelter and a spectacular high viewpoint that looks over the St. Mary Valley and east across the broad Kootenay Valley. The riding is more demanding on challenging singletrack trails and includes a fair bit of climbing.

The ride begins with the easygoing fun of Ponderosa trail, rolls through Three Corners and climbs up Lower Army to Four Corners. Continue on Army, then right up Higgins Hill. Turn left and follow Rockslide all the way up to the shores of Dipper Lake. Cross the meadows to a trail junction and make a short side trip to the ski cabin. Retrace your tracks, but keep right on Bullfrog and make a short excursion to a high viewpoint. Backtrack a bit and get ready for some technical riding action on Shannon, Rockslide and Creek. Roll down Army Road all the way to Four Corners, then enjoy the surfy fun of Duck Pond and Apache as they loop around to Three Corners. Climb back up to Four Corners, onto Upper Army, then rage along the singletrack of Romantic Ridge back to the trailhead.

**Technical delights**
**Type** loop on 4WD road and singletrack
**Rating** moderate/advanced
**Distance** 20.3 km
**Time** 2-3 hours

| | |
|---|---|
| 0.0 | trailhead |
| 0.3 | left on Ponderosa |
| 1.1 | Three Corners, right on Lower Army |
| 2.3 | Four Corners, straight on Army |
| 3.4 | right on Higgins |
| 3.9 | left on Rockslide |
| 5.9 | Dipper Lake |
| 6.2 | right to cabin |
| 6.4 | cabin, retrace tracks |
| 6.6 | right on Bullfrog |
| 7.1 | keep right |
| 7.3 | viewpoint, retrace tracks |
| 7.5 | right on Shannon |
| 7.9 | right on Rockslide |
| 8.2 | right on Creek |
| 9.0 | left on Army Road |
| 10.4 | Four Corners, right on Duck Pond |
| 12.8 | keep left |
| 12.9 | left on Apache |
| 15.3 | left on Elbow |
| 15.8 | left up Eimer Road |
| 16.3 | Three Corners, left up Lower Army |
| 17.5 | Four Corners, right on Upper Army |
| 17.6 | right on Romantic |
| 18.2 | left |
| 18.8 | right, down hill |
| 19.1 | left |
| 19.5 | left |
| 19.8 | right |
| 20.0 | road, go left |
| 20.3 | gate |

# 134C NATURE PARK                                      map 26C

This cool tour explores the central area of the nature park. It is designed to include quite a bit of singletrack and some fairly challenging riding.

Begin with a fun roll along Ponderosa, then descend Eimer's all the way down to Bench. Grope your way around the Bench, then ride south on Elbow letting Apache lead you almost to the St. Mary Valley before looping back on Duck Pond. At Four Corners go left on Army, then right up Higgins Hill. Turn left and follow Rockslide, then plunge down the action-packed singletrack of Flume and Creek. Ride Army, then back up Higgins, this time turning right onto Snowbird ski trail. Cut left on Musser's Shortcut, then drop the testy delights of Sidehill to Four Corners. Ride south on Duck Pond, then drop the Pat Morrow trail to Army Road. Climb back up to Four Corners, onto Upper Army, then rage along the singletrack of Romantic Ridge back to the trailhead.

**Technical delights**
**Type** loop on 4WD road and singletrack
**Rating** moderate/advanced
**Distance** 18 km
**Time** 2-3 hours

| | |
|---|---|
| 0.0 | trailhead |
| 0.3 | left on Ponderosa |
| 1.1 | Three Corners, left on Eimer's |
| 1.6 | left on Eimer's |
| 1.8 | right on Bench |
| 3.7 | left on Elbow |
| 3.9 | right on Apache |
| 6.3 | right on Duck Pond |
| 8.8 | Four Corners, left on Army |
| 9.9 | right on Higgins |
| 10.4 | left on Rockslide |
| 11.0 | left on Flume |
| 11.3 | left on Creek |
| 11.7 | left on Army |
| 12.0 | left on Higgins |
| 12.5 | right on Snowbird |
| 12.6 | left on Mussers |
| 13.0 | cross Snowbird, down Sidehill |
| 13.6 | Four Corners, take Duck Pond |
| 13.6 | left on Pat Morrow |
| 14.5 | left up Army |
| 15.2 | Four Corners, right on Upper Army |
| 15.3 | right on Romantic |
| 15.9 | left |
| 16.6 | right, down hill |
| 16.9 | left |
| 17.3 | left |
| 17.5 | right |
| 17.7 | road, go left |
| 18.0 | gate |

# 135  WASA TO PREMIER LAKE                    map 27

This is a mellow cruiser-style ride that loops around Premier Ridge, just off the western edge of the Rockies. It features grassy meadows and forests of ponderosa pine and Douglas fir and some of the prettiest blue lakes on the planet. Although open to motor vehicles, these two doubletracks see only light traffic.

From the south trailhead ride up the classic doubletrack of Wasa-Sheep Creek Road as it winds through the open forest and climbs into the hills. The trail follows above Speculation Lake, then rolls onward to meet the Premier Lake Park Road. Hang a right and ride up this sometimes dusty road to the park entrance. I suggest a water and swim break, you'll need a suit as there are no private beaches here. Premier Lake is one beautiful shade of blue as it reflects the towering peaks of the Rocky Mountain front. When you've had enough, retrace your tracks, turn left at the park entrance and immediately keep right on the doubletrack of Premier Lake forest service road as it climbs to a high point on the ridge above Quartz Lake. Just past the high point is a cliff-edge viewpoint with the clear deep waters of the lake below and the towering peaks of the Rockies above. The road takes a long, gentle downhill route that has lots of loose rocks and bumps to keep you on your toes. Enjoy the breeze as you race through this fragrant pine and fir forest. All too soon you roll out of the woods onto the grassy flats beside Wolf Creek Road. Turn right and ride back to the start.

**Classic doubletrack in ponderosa forest**

**Type** loop on 2WD roads and 4WD roads

**Rating** moderate/intermediate

**Other users** motorized-4

**Distance** 33.2 km

**Time** 2-4 hours

**Map** 82 G/13 Skookumchuck

**Season** May through October

**Land agency** British Columbia Forest Service, British Columbia Parks

**Access**
**south** At Wasa Lake, drive east from Hwy. 93/95 on Wasa Lake Park Drive for 1.4 km. Turn left on Wolf Creek Road for 6.2 km to the signed Wasa-Sheep Creek Road on the left. Park and ride up the Wasa-Sheep Creek Road.

**north** Begin this ride at the Premier Lake Provincial Park day-use parking lot.

| | |
|---|---|
| 0.0 | south trailhead |
| 7.5 | Speculation Lake to left |
| 13.6 | turn right on Premier Lake Park Road |
| 17.2 | junction, turn left to north trailhead and Premier Lake |
| 18.2 | Premier Lake, retrace tracks |
| 19.2 | junction, turn left keeping right on Premier Lake forest service road |
| 22.2 | view of Quartz Lake |
| 27.9 | right |
| 28.2 | keep right on Wolf Creek Road |
| 33.2 | end of ride |

# 136 TOP OF THE WORLD

map 27

This superb ride takes you up a deluxe trail to Fish Lake in Top of the World Provincial Park where a number of day hiking options await. The trail is often crowded with hikers, which means that good timing and courtesy are important to ensure future access. One important safety note—the trail is constructed to a high standard but it is crossed by numerous deep drainage ditches that are real wheel grabbers and can dump you on the ground in an instant.

Ride away from the trailhead and drop gently through a cool subalpine forest to the banks of the Lussier River. The horse trail is an option but it is rough and rooty throughout, I suggest you keep right on the hiking trail. For the remainder of the trip this quality trail climbs gently alongside the river. Giant Engelmann spruce and subalpine fir give the forest its high mountain character while mosses and rhododendrons cover the shady forest floor. Soon you'll arrive at Fish Lake surrounded by cliffs, waterfalls and towering peaks. A floating dock, log cabin open to the public, ranger cabin and campground all nestle on the shore. The trails beyond this point are not suitable for cycling so park your bike and take a hike!

Post-hike relax on the shore, then roll out to the trailhead. Remember, courtesy pays big time and don't forget the drainage ditches, they come up fast on the descent.

## Hiking Options

Lakeshore loop trail is a short hike. Wildhorse Ridge and Alpine View are steep, rugged, rewarding hikes that take about three hours each.

**Bike 'n' hike to alpine vistas**

**Type** out-and-back on singletrack

**Rating** moderate/intermediate

**Other users** hikers-6 equestrian-1

**Distance** 13 km

**Time** 3-4 hours

**Map** 82 G/14 Queen Creek

**Season** July through October

**Land agency** British Columbia Parks

**Access**

Turn east off Hwy. 93/95, 4.5 km south of Canal Flats, and at km 21.3 take the signed road to the right. Stay on this main road to the signed trailhead at km 52.

| | |
|---|---|
| 0.0 | trailhead |
| 6.5 | Fish Lake |

2    4    6    8    10    12  13

*Premier Ridge (#135).*

*Fish Lake (#136).*

*Trail of Two Rivers (#137).*

# 137 TRAIL OF TWO RIVERS                                    map 28

Ride in spring or ride in autumn on this low elevation excursion, or ride in hot weather and enjoy a dip in the lake. This trip begins and ends on paved roads with doubletrack and singletrack trails in between.

In Fairmont ride south on Columbia River Road as it turns from pavement to gravel and winds alongside the Columbia River. You'll enter a game preserve, then as the road begins to descend toward the lake, watch for a doubletrack branching off to the left across the grassy slope. Take the doubletrack, which soon turns to sweet sidehill singletrack winding and climbing through the forest above the lake. It's never very difficult riding but all too soon the singletrack turns to doubletrack and climbs well above the lake. Join a view-filled gravel road and descend into the village of Canal Flats. Real troopers will want to ride south through town to the Kootenay River and dip a tire in the water, thus completing the Two Rivers ride.

**Scenic cruise alongside Columbia Lake**

**Type** point-to-point on 2WD roads, 4WD roads and singletrack

**Rating** moderate/intermediate

**Other users** hikers-3

**Distance** 21.3 km one way

**Time** 2-3 hours

**Map** 82 J/4 Canal Flats
82 J/5 Fairmont Hot Springs

**Season** May through October

**Land agency** private, British Columbia Forest Service

**Access**
**north** In the village of Fairmont, drive south on Columbia River Road to the end of pavement. Park here and ride south on the gravel road.

**south** Park in the village of Canal Flats. Ride begins at Kootenay River and heads north on Grainger Road.

| | |
|---|---|
| 0.0 | trailhead, ride south on Columbia River Road |
| 4.6 | gate, enter Fairmont Game Preserve |
| 5.7 | take doubletrack that forks to left (right leads to lake) |
| 6.3 | creek, singletrack begins |
| 8.3 | cairn, doubletrack begins |
| 13.7 | junction with gravel road, go left (right leads to lake) |
| 15.1 | junction, go right |
| 19.5 | junction, go right |
| 19.7 | Grainger Road, Canal Flats, turn left |
| 21.3 | banks of the Kootenay River |

# 138 TOBY CREEK CANYON                    map 29

This trail is a series of sweet singletracks that roll along the southern rim of Toby Creek canyon and lead west from Invermere into the Purcell Mountains. The roaring waters of Toby Creek are always just below in the canyon as the trail snakes its way through Douglas fir along the canyon rim. The upper 3 km of trail is along a shady former mine-access wagon road carved into the canyon wall.

Ride up to the top of 14 Street where it turns into Pineridge Drive, then follow the forest road that leads up hill to the right. A cattleguard atop a hill with views over Toby Creek tells you this is the right road. Keep climbing until you come to a gravel pit. Cross the cattleguard and turn right onto a doubletrack, then take the next doubletrack to the right. Make a note of the descent route on your right at km 4.8. Soon the singletrack begins and you get a bit of a workout climbing along the canyon rim above the roaring blue-green waters. Keep your eyes on the trail! There are several trails here but the one closest to the rim is best. Keeping right at all junctions will lead you to an old bush camp, then up to a gravel road that crosses under the powerline. Keep right at the junction with the forest service road and you'll soon be riding along sweet singletrack on the old wagon road. When you reach the collapsed trestle, it's time to abandon your bike and hike the last bit to the now collapsed canyon bridge.

The return ride is a bit of a heaven—the flat wagon road, a short bit of gravel road, then the sweet snaking singletrack on the canyon's edge. Turn left at the gate at km 4.8 and ride even more singletrack, including a couple of sketchy pitches, to come out at a great viewpoint over a trash-laden hillside above the creek. Take to the road and cross the cattleguard, then drop left onto another singletrack that will have you flying down to the top of 14 Street in no time at all.

**Singletrack treats along canyon's edge**

**Type** out-and-back on 2WD roads and singletrack

**Rating** moderate/intermediate

**Other users** hikers-1

**Distance** 27.2 km

**Time** 2-4 hours

**Maps** 82 K/8 Toby Creek
82 K/9 Radium Hot Springs

**Season** May through October

**Land agency** private, British Columbia Forest Service

**Access**
Begin at the intersection of 13 Avenue and 14 Street in Invermere and ride west.

| | |
|---|---|
| 0.0 | trailhead |
| 0.6 | turn right on gravel road |
| 4.2 | cross cattleguard and turn right |
| 4.5 | turn right |
| 4.8 | note descent route to right |
| 5.0 | singletrack begins |
| 7.7 | bush camp, go left on doubletrack |
| 7.9 | junction, go right on singletrack |
| 8.2 | go right on gravel road |
| 10.5 | junction, go right onto wagon road |
| 13.6 | collapsed trestle |

# 139 PARADISE MINE                                              map 29

This is one great mountain ride featuring a beautiful climb to an abandoned mine, alpine meadows, expansive views and a killer downhill that just goes on forever.

Where to begin is the question. If you feel like riding really large, start at the Toby Creek bridge and ride 16.6 km up the Toby Creek Road toward Panorama. Otherwise do a car shuttle from the bridge and begin riding at Panorama.

Ride up the old mine access road—it's never overly steep, just steady hammering for 13 km and 1300 vertical metres to the abandoned Paradise Mine. Near the top you'll find a waterfall and mine relics to check out. The view is great and the antics of the occasional vehicle drivers will entertain. "You rode that bike all the way up here? You must be crazy!" Past the mine the road downgrades to doubletrack and snakes through alpine meadows with views to die for—Invermere, Panorama, the Rockies, the prominent peak of Mount Assiniboine. Drink your fill of this terrific setting.

Helmet tight, check brakes, GO! The next 30 km are varying degrees of downhill; drifted corners, a few airs, maybe a 4x4 or two (yikes!). Descend into the valley of Bruce Creek and roll down to the village of Wilmer. From Wilmer it is 3 km of pavement back to the Toby Creek bridge and you'll be smiling the whole way.

**Classic high mountain ride**

**Type** loop on 2WD and 4WD roads

**Rating** difficult/novice

**Other users** motorized-3

**Distance** 47.3 km

**Time** 4-5 hours

**Maps** 82 K/8 Toby Creek
82 K/9 Radium Hot Springs

**Season** July through October

**Land agency** British Columbia Forest Service

**Access**
Begin on a gravel road that departs to the right at km 18.5 of the Toby Creek Road near the Panorama Resort. Finish this ride at the Toby Creek bridge at km 2 of the Toby Creek Road.

| 0.0 | trailhead, find and follow old gravel road uphill |
| 12.2 | mine relics and artifacts |
| 13.0 | mine shaft |
| 14.7 | crest of ridge, alpine meadows begin descent |
| 34.4 | junction, keep left |
| 44.4 | Wilmer |
| 47.3 | end of ride |

10        20        30        40      47.3

# 140 THUNDERBIRD MINE                    map 29

This ride is steeped in history from bottom to top. The trail takes you up an old pack trail to the abandoned Thunderbird Mine where a handful of tumbledown buildings cling to the steep mountainside. It's a reminder of golden times when men extracted lead-zinc ore from these cliffs and pack trains of mules brought supplies up to the mine and hauled the ore down to the valley below.

Ride away from the trailhead and work your way past several washed-out sections of the old Delphine road. Watch carefully for the overgrown cat track that will take you up the precipitous mountainside. The singletrack on the grade is all rideable as you climb up four switchbacks. At km 3.3, just as the cat track turns to the right, take the singletrack that continues straight passing under a dead tree. Ride this high quality trail up six switchbacks, then follow it around the mountainside into the upper basin of Sultana Creek. You'll have to negotiate a couple of tricky washed-out avalanche gullies (km 6.6 and 7.4) before you get to the mine.

Thunderbird Mine is a magical place—three ancient, weather-beaten frame buildings including a sauna-house cling to the mountainside, almost overgrown by pine and fir. Two more buildings are pasted on the cliffs far above. High peaks and glaciers surround you while below, the valley is a canyon-like defile far removed. Enjoy this perfect setting and its special ambience, as once you depart the ride is over in a flash. The descent can be a bit of a brake burner, but there is nothing very technical—just furiously fast and fun.

**Classic high mountain ride**

**Type** out-and-back on 4WD road and singletrack

**Rating** difficult/intermediate

**Other users** hikers-2 equestrian-1

**Distance** 15.8 km

**Time** 4-5 hours

**Map** 82 K/8 Toby Creek

**Season** July through October

**Land agency** British Columbia Forest Service

**Access**
From Invermere drive up the Toby Creek Road continuing for 8.2 km past Panorama Resort. Turn right just before Delphine Creek and climb up beside a spectacular canyon for 1.8 km to a small parking area.

| | |
|---|---|
| 0.0 | trailhead |
| 1.2 | turn right onto overgrown cat track |
| 3.3 | keep left on singletrack |
| 7.9 | old buildings |

# 141 DELPHINE CREEK                                map 29

**Gentle trail in narrow mountain valley**

**Type** out-and-back on 4WD road

**Rating** moderate/novice

**Other users** hikers-2

**Distance** 13.6 km

**Time** 1-3 hours

**Map** 82 K/8 Toby Creek

**Season** July through October

**Land agency** British Columbia Forest Service

### Access
From Invermere drive up the Toby Creek Road continuing for 8.2 km past Panorama. The trail is the old road beyond the wooden gate.

| | |
|---|---|
| 0.0 | trailhead |
| 1.8 | washout, end of driveable road |
| 3.0 | Thunderbird trail departs to right |
| 4.6 | cross gravel outwash plain |
| 6.7 | junction, keep left |
| 6.8 | creek crossing, turn back |

This is a short ride into a spectacular valley in the Purcell Mountains. Glacier clad peaks tower high above the canyon-like defile of the valley while rushing Delphine Creek fills your ears with water music. The first 1.8 km of the route is driveable, but some of the magic of this valley is lost if you drive this first section with its not-to-be-missed canyon.

Begin at the quaint log gate and start climbing right away. Around the first corner the trail clings to a steep slope and you get to peer into the inner workings of a rather spectacular canyon. The road climbs onto a bench, then skirts a few washed-out sections. Pass the trail to Mount Nelson and the Thunderbird Mine trail and soon you'll come to the Sultana Creek fan where the boulder-moving power of nature is exhibited on a grand scale. The trail continues its gentle climb to a junction at km 6.7. To continue to the left requires a ford of Delphine Creek, the track to the right climbs up into the valley above and ends.

For most folks this is a good spot for a picnic before beginning the roll back to the trailhead.

2      4      6      8      10      12   13.6

# 142 BREWER CREEK TO PANORAMA                    map 29

This atomic dog style singletrack crosses a pass high above Brewer Creek, then descends along Hopeful Creek to Panorama Resort. It's a tough push on the way up, but once in the alpine the trail is mostly rideable as it passes several small lakes, rolls along an exciting alpine ridge and some clingy sidehills before dropping wildly to the valley at Panorama. This is remote backcountry at its finest and most demanding, a place where strong backcountry travel skills are essential. You must be self-sufficient and able to take care of yourself and your equipment should things go wrong.

The ride and push up the trail to the first lake is hard work, but it's also the major climb of the trip. The lakes are at treeline with lots of meadows and ridges to explore and the water is warm enough for a hot-day swim. The trail follows the timberline eastward and it's rock-and-roll riding with lots of exciting sidehills and some fun screes to descend. Look down to the parking lot far below. The trail drops into a side valley, then climbs steeply before turning toward the pass and two rustic log cabins. It's a short ride along the creekside to the pass and the first view out over the valley of Toby Creek. At this point a beautiful ride turns into a wild ride! In the next few kilometres the trail will drop more than 1000 m on a pristine singletrack. That means it's narrow and lacks shortcuts, let's keep it that way. The riding is action packed and exciting, about half way down the trail crosses a cutblock, then continues across some radical sidehills with major exposure as it plunges to the valley. Low down you will cross a cat track after which the trail is a bit overgrown as it crosses a creek and ends at the top of the golf links. Finish up on the gravel track as it winds through the greens, then angles right to the Panorama Resort.

**Remote high mountain ride**
**Type** point-to-point on singletrack
**Rating** difficult/advanced
**Other users** hikers-3 equestrian-1
**Distance** 25 km one way
**Time** 4-6 hours
**Map** 82 K/8 Toby Creek
**Season** July through October
**Land agency** British Columbia Forest Service

**Access**
From the intersection of 13 Street and 13 Avenue in Invermere, drive south on Westside Road for 18.3 km, turn right on Hawke Road and drive 24.8 km to a bridge across Brewer Creek. This is the start of the distance log although some vehicles may be able to drive another 2.5 km.

| | |
|---|---|
| 0.0 | trailhead |
| 2.5 | doubletrack ends, cross creek |
| 7.3 | junction, keep right |
| 8.1 | lake |
| 8.9 | lake |
| 10.0 | ridge top viewpoint |
| 13.0 | trail junction, keep right |
| 15.0 | cabins, trail follows creek |
| 15.3 | summit |
| 19.1 | junction in cutblock, keep right |
| 21.0 | cross cat track |
| 22.4 | golf course |
| 25.0 | Panorama |

# 143 LAKE ENID
map 30

**Family fun on gentle trails**

**Type** loop on 2WD roads, 4WD roads and singletrack

**Rating** moderate/novice

**Other users** hikers-2 motorized-3

**Distance** 15 km

**Time** 1-3 hours

**Map** 82 K/9 Radium Hot Springs

**Season** May through October

**Land agency** British Columbia Forest Service

This easy roll on doubletrack, singletrack and gravel roads explores the Columbia Valley north of Invermere. The riding is pleasant on tracks that roll past lakes and wind among grassy hills and through Douglas fir forests, then finish up on the dry hillsides above the Columbia River marshes.

Ride up Park Avenue in Wilmer as it turns into the gravel Bruce Creek forest service road and leads to the shores of pretty Lake Enid. A singletrack loops through the forests and meadows surrounding the lake, offering a bit of extra riding. Swim anyone? On the far side of the lake take the doubletrack to the northeast and begin a long descent through a recently burned forest of black snags into a dry, grassy valley. As a bright green irrigated field comes in sight, climb up a steep track to the left, then blast along a series of doubletracks through the Douglas fir forest to Westside Road. Follow this road back to Wilmer.

## Options

The dry hillsides and extensive marshes below Westside Road are protected as a national wildlife refuge. Take time to explore the area and enjoy the bird life of the marshes before returning to Wilmer.

## Access

Take Panorama Road west from Invermere, turn right just after the Toby Creek bridge and follow this road for 3.5 km to the village of Wilmer. Begin at the corner of Park and Main.

| | |
|---|---|
| 0.0 | trailhead, ride up Park |
| 5.7 | turn right |
| 6.3 | Lake Enid, take singletrack to left |
| 7.5 | junction, go left on doubletrack |
| 7.8 | junction, turn right |
| 8.2 | turn left on doubletrack |
| 8.4 | go left |
| 8.9 | go right |
| 10.7 | steep climb |
| 10.8 | junction, keep right |
| 13.0 | Westside Road, turn right |
| 15.0 | end of ride |

2    4    6    8    10    12    14 15

# 144 BAPTISTE LAKE                                    map 30

A network of mellow singletrack and doubletrack trails snake about the benchland east of Highway 95 between Sinclair Creek and Edgewater. Most of the land is part of the Kirksland Restoration Project and is open to responsible cycling, but some of the land is held by other private owners. Please respect the landowners' wishes. Exploration is the keyword here with the reflective waters of Baptiste Lake as an attractive destination.

The singletrack climbs away from the powerhouse, traverses north across a sidehill, then joins a doubletrack with lots of trails branching off to the right. Take time to explore these trails as they wind through the Douglas fir forest above Sinclair Creek, but watch for horses; these trails are used for short rides by clients of the local horse outfitter and many of the riders are inexperienced. Work your way north and climb up to a gate (or descend to it if you've been exploring the singletracks). Past the gate the singletrack splits. I prefer to keep right, then follow along a doubletrack. At the T-junction you can follow a singletrack up the hillside, then join a better road near a gravel pit. Follow it up as it turns to singletrack and rolls through a big pasture with views galore. After the pasture keep right on singletrack that soon rocks and rolls above the marshy shores of Baptiste Lake. You can return the way you came or try a variation on other trails.

**Rugged valley bottom tour**

**Type** out-and-back on 4WD roads and singletrack

**Rating** moderate/intermediate

**Other users** equestrian-4 livestock

**Distance** 17.6 km

**Time** 2-4 hours

**Map** 82 K/9 Radium Hot Springs

**Season** May through October

**Land agency** private

**Access**
Begin at the power station on the east side of Hwy. 95, 0.8 km north of the four-way stop at Radium.

| | |
|---|---|
| 0.0 | trailhead |
| 1.2 | gate |
| 3.5 | T-junction, go straight on singletrack |
| 6.0 | sand pit to left |
| 6.4 | enter pasture |
| 7.3 | leave pasture |
| 8.4 | Baptiste Lake |
| 8.8 | north end of lake |

# 145 HEART OF THE BRISCO RANGE

map 32

The road leading to the Diana Lake trailhead provides a pleasant mountain bike trip. It is a lower-quality logging road but in reasonably good condition throughout. Loose gravel lies on some of the corners and the roadbed is rough in places, but the grades are moderate and the riding is easy and fun.

The ride begins in the canyon of Kindersley Creek where a small dam supplies water to an elevated irrigation flume. Beyond the canyon the road passes the turn-off to upper Kindersley Creek and climbs over a low pass before descending into the valley of Luxor Creek. After crossing Luxor Creek the road continues to climb gently up the Pinnacle Creek valley until it becomes impassable to vehicles at the signed Diana Lake trailhead. You can cross the creek on a footbridge and ride for another 0.8 km to the singletrack that leads to the lake.

The return trip is fast, easy and fun. Watch out for vehicles and the stutter bumps on the corners above Kindersley Creek. These can be upsetting for the unwary speedster.

**Options**

The trail to Diana Lake offers a good hike if you have sufficient time and energy. See #146 for a truly hard-core, expert level cycling trip on this trail.

**Scenic cruiser**

**Type** out-and-back on 2WD roads

**Rating** moderate/novice

**Other users** motorized-3

**Distance** 38.6 km

**Time** 3-5 hours

**Maps** 82 K/9 Radium Hot Springs 82 K/16 Spillimacheen

**Season** June to mid-October

**Land agency** British Columbia Forest Service

**Access**
Kindersley forest service road is on the east side of Hwy. 95, 18 km north of Radium. The ride begins at the irrigation headworks 6 km up the road.

| | |
|---|---|
| 0.0 | trailhead |
| 1.9 | junction, keep left (right is Kindersley trail) |
| 5.8 | summit |
| 9.5 | Luxor Creek bridge |
| 18.3 | trailhead sign |
| 18.5 | footbridge across creek |
| 19.3 | singletrack trail continues to Diana Lake |

*Thunderbird Mine (#140).*

*Brewer Creek to Panorama (#142).*

*Mount Seven (#147).*

# 146 DIANA LAKE

map 32

Diana Lake and Whitetail Pass is a killer ride for the hard-core expert rider. The uphill trail is about half rideable and quickly lets you gauge your chances of riding the downhill. I found it about 90 per cent rideable downhill and some of you might be able to clean it. The combination of beautiful alpine meadows, big vertical and very intense riding makes this a hard-core delight.

Ride away from the trailhead, cross the bridge and begin the uphill on an old roadbed. Soon the singletrack begins and the going gets tough—on the bike, off the bike, it's like this most of the way to the lake. If you don't think you can ride down this stuff, then it's time to hide your bike and hike, the trail doesn't get any easier. After about 1.5 hours you will be climbing through the meadows and reach the cobalt blue waters of Diana Lake, irresistible for a swim on a hot day. A private lodge is located nearby and the trail continues on through the meadows to Whitetail Pass.

The descent of this trail is strictly for experts—you'll be riding down everything you came up. The alpine section is scenic and big fun, down to the lake then down through the meadows, but very quickly the skill level required ramps up to expert as you negotiate rocks, roots, steeps, drop-offs, very narrow trail and sometimes limited visibility. It's an exciting adrenaline pumper that left us raving. The fact that it takes almost as long to ride down the trail as it did to climb up is a good indicator of the challenges involved.

**Hard-core technical delights**

**Type** out-and-back on singletrack

**Rating** difficult/expert

**Other users** hikers-4 equestrian-1

**Distance** 14.2 km

**Time** 3-5 hours

**Map** 82 K/16 Spillimacheen

**Season** July through October

**Land agency** British Columbia Forest Service

**Access**
Drive 18 km north of Radium on Hwy. 95, turn right and follow Kindersley forest service road for 24 km to the signed trailhead.

| | |
|---|---|
| 0.0 | trailhead |
| 0.1 | aluminum bridge |
| 0.2 | keep right |
| 1.0 | follow singletrack to right |
| 6.2 | Diana Lake |
| 6.4 | cabin |
| 7.1 | Whitetail Pass |

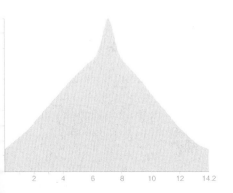

2    4    6    8    10    12    14.2

# 147 MOUNT SEVEN                                          map 37

Golden's premier ride, Mount Seven features one incredible climb, stunning views and descent options that will blow your sox off! This ride puts the mountain into mountain biking.

The Mount Seven forest service road takes you up a beautiful climb to a fabulous valley view. Turn off onto the Mount Seven Lookout road and the climb gets a whole lot steeper. Ride and push upward, it's worth it! The first summit gives big views of the Rockies and Selkirks, of Golden and the Rocky Mountain Trench. I highly recommend the ridge ride option if you have the energy.

Enjoy the views, check your brakes and launch yourself. The descent is a real brake burner and the speeds are a thrill in themselves. The descent follows the road but there are some options. First, you can take the old lookout road that forks to the left and continues steeply down the ridge to rejoin the new road. Then, if you have advanced level riding skills you can plunge to the valley on singletrack. If you plan to do this, noting where the trails leave the main road on the up-trip will make them a lot easier to find on the descent. These trails are super-satisfying with some exciting sections to entertain you. Some of the trails are on private land, please respect the owners' wishes. Kudos to local Golden riders who participated in their construction. T3 is the highest trail, T2 descends and joins T1, which rollicks down through a bermed chute to the rodeo grounds. Roll home with a big grin on your face.

## Options

1. The road to the left below the first summit leads along the ridge for 2 km toward the main peak. More pushing is rewarded by more great views. The trail ends at the third summit at an elevation of 2205 m. From here the truly ambitious can hike and scramble to the main peak of Mount Seven. The ride back along the top of the ridge is one of the best.

2. Make a short 9 km loop by riding up the road and down the singletrack of T2 and T1 to the rodeo grounds.

**Major vertical with great views and technical delights**

**Type** out-and-back on 2WD and 4WD roads and singletrack

**Rating** difficult/advanced

**Other users** motorized-2

**Distance** 25.4 km

**Time** 4-6 hours

**Map** 82 N/7 Golden

**Season** June through October

**Land agency** British Columbia Forest Service

## Access

In Golden, begin at the intersection of 9 Street South and 14 Avenue (Spruce Drive). Trip distances begin here.

| | |
|---|---|
| 0.0 | trailhead, cycle up Spruce Drive |
| 1.4 | turn left onto the Mount Seven forest service road |
| 4.2 | T1 to right |
| 6.4 | T2 to right |
| 7.1 | singletrack to left |
| 9.0 | junction, turn right on lookout road |
| 9.9 | old Mount Seven road to right |
| 12.5 | junction, turn right (left continues toward main peak) |
| 12.7 | first summit |

# 148  WEST BENCH WANDERER                     maps 37, 37A

An extensive upland, known locally as the west bench, lies to the west of the Columbia River near Golden. It is a rolling landscape that was logged extensively by the Columbia River Lumber Company at the turn of the century, when a train was used to haul the logs from the bench down to the main valley at Nicholson. The forest has regrown in a mixture of Douglas fir, cedar, aspen and birch, making the area particularly colourful in the autumn. The trails are mostly gravel backroads and the abandoned railway grade. It is a fun place to play and a great place to take the family. The riding is not technical, although there are a few fast downhills, and all the routes feature excellent views of the Rockies. The Columbia River is bridged by the Dogtooth forest service road at Golden and by Canyon Creek Road at Nicholson. This, along with the wide variety of trails, makes several loop rides possible.

The West Bench Wanderer climbs up Gorman Lake Road onto the bench, then chugs along the bed of the logging railway that was in use until 1928. The remains of a wooden trestle can be seen just downstream from the Holt Creek bridge. This smooth section of trail is a delight to ride as it passes viewpoints across the Rocky Mountain Trench to the Kicking Horse and Blaeberry valleys. Cedar Lake is reached by taking the southernmost (second) of two side roads that branch to the right at km 26.5 and 26.55 respectively. After returning from the lake, continue your ramble along Cedar Lake Road to the junction at the base of the switchbacks where you have a choice of routes. By keeping right you can ride into Nicholson and return to Golden on the pavement of Highway 95 for a loop ride of 43.2

**Scenic cruise in the Columbia Valley**

**Type** loop on 2WD and 4WD roads

**Rating** moderate/novice

**Other users** hikers-1  equestrian-2  motorized-2

**Distance** 43.4 km

**Time** 3-4 hours

**Maps** 82 N/2 McMurdo
82 N/6 Blaeberry
82 N/7 Golden

**Season** May through October

**Land agency** private,  British Columbia Forest Service

**Access**
In Golden, begin at the intersection of Hwy. 95 and 7 Street North, trip distances begin here. Ride west, 7 Street soon turns right onto Dyke Road.

| | |
|---|---|
| 0.0 | trailhead |
| 2.9 | junction with Dogtooth forest service road, keep right |
| 5.6 | golf course |
| 14.9 | four-way junction, turn left |
| 20.9 | Powerline Plunge to left |
| 23.6 | join ski hill access road |

km. Alternatively, by turning left you can use the route log to return to Golden on a four-wheel-drive road that parallels the west side of the Columbia River. Both routes cross private land, please respect the wishes of the landowners.

**Options**

1. Adventurous cyclists can take a 3.6 km-long cutoff trail that branches to the left at km 26.2 of the route log and descends to the lower 4WD road. After 0.8 km, turn right and follow a seldom-used trail that descends at a moderate grade, passing a swampy beaver dam along the way.

2. Many custom cycling routes can be put together using these roads and trails . Use map 37 to assist you in planning a ride that suits your desires and abilities.

| | |
|---|---|
| 24.7 | junction with Dogtooth road, go straight |
| 26.2 | cutoff to lower trail departs to left |
| 26.5 | junction, keep left (right is Canyon Creek) |
| 26.55 | junction, keep left (right leads 0.5 km to Cedar Lake) |
| 32.0 | junction at base of switchbacks, keep left |
| 36.4 | junction with cutoff trail, go straight |
| 40.4 | junction, turn right |
| 40.5 | junction, turn right |
| 43.4 | end of ride |

# 149 CANYON CREEK CANYON

maps 37, 37A

This exciting loop leads you high onto the west side of the Rocky Mountain Trench on logging roads, and brings you back down on a challenging and spectacular singletrack trail along the canyon rim. The view of the Rockies across the trench is superlative, but the narrow trail along the canyon's edge is definitely not for those with a fear of heights. The most challenging section is 2.3 km long; don't hesitate to get off and push if it exceeds your ability.

Begin by taking McBeath Road to the right from Nicholson and follow it to the right along the base of a steep slope. At km 2.5 take the left fork and climb five switchbacks up a steep hill. This is a private road on private property so please respect the owners' wishes. After 1 km the road levels out as you roll along the abandoned roadbed of an old logging railway. At km 8 two roads fork to the left. Take the second one, a logging road that climbs up rideable grades to a series of cutblocks. Keep left at the first fork, right at the second, which takes you past a trapper's cabin, and left at the third. From here it is 2.7 km on a rapidly deteriorating road to the canyon trail.

Turn left onto this singletrack and climb uphill to a superb overlook of Canyon Creek flowing in a deep canyon cut into soft shale. Here the trail runs along a very dry hillside covered with Douglas fir and juniper forest. After the viewpoint comes 2.3 km of narrow, often exposed, singletrack descending along the edge of the canyon. The riding is exhilarating and definitely for advanced riders only. A couple of singletracks of the Moonraker trail network join from the left and shortly after you will see a singletrack dropping to the right. Finish up on this gnarly little trail and keep to the right on old Cedar Lake road, which soon joins the paved Canyon Creek Road and leads to the end of the ride.

**Singletrack treats alongside spectacular canyon**

**Type** loop on 2WD and 4WD roads and singletrack

**Rating** moderate/advanced

**Other users** hikers-3 equestrian-2 motorized-2

**Distance** 19.5 km

**Time** 2-3 hours

**Maps** 82 N/2 McMurdo
82 N/7 Golden

**Season** May through October

**Land agency** private, British Columbia Forest Service

**Access**
Nicholson is located 7 km south of Golden on Hwy. 95. Turn right into Nicholson and turn right again onto Canyon Creek Road. Trip distances begin at the junction of Canyon Creek Road and McBeath Road.

| | |
|---|---|
| 0.0 | trailhead |
| 2.5 | junction, keep left and climb five switchbacks |
| 8.0 | junction, keep right (left leads to Cedar Lake) |
| 8.05 | junction, turn left |
| 10.1 | junction, turn left |
| 11.9 | junction, turn left |
| 14.6 | junction with Canyon Creek trail, turn left and climb hill |
| 17.8 | keep right on singletrack |
| 18.3 | keep right on gravel road |
| 18.5 | pavement |
| 19.5 | end of ride |

# 150 POWERLINE PLUNGE

map 37

A short ride, this loop climbs a gravel road onto the west bench, wanders north along the bed of an old logging railway, then brings you down on a combination of singletrack and doubletrack under the ski hill powerline.

Follow the ski hill access road for 10.1 km, then turn right onto a doubletrack along the bed of an abandoned railway. Ride on crossing three creeks and eventually coming to the powerline. The riding gets a lot more challenging as you drop and climb along the line. It's a combination of doubletrack and steep, sketchy singletrack that will keep you on your toes. When you come to the swamp make a detour to the left. Eventually you come out on the road only to plunge once again onto the steepest part of the ride. Finish up on the road.

**Downhill delights**

**Type** loop on 2WD roads, 4WD roads and singletrack

**Rating** moderate/advanced

**Other users** hikers motorized-2

**Distance** 19.8 km

**Time** 2 hours

**Map** 82 N/7 Golden

**Season** May through October

**Land agency** British Columbia Forest Service

**Access**

Begin in Golden at the intersection of Hwy. 95 and 7 Street North. Ride west, 7 Street soon turns onto Dyke Road.

| | |
|---|---|
| 0.0 | trailhead |
| 2.9 | junction with Dogtooth forest service road, turn left |
| 9.0 | junction, turn right (left goes to Cedar) |
| 10.1 | leave road and take doubletrack to right |
| 12.9 | powerline, turn right |
| 16.8 | join road |
| 19.8 | end of ride |

*Canyon Creek canyon (#149).*
Photo: Cécile Lafleur.

# 151 MOONRAKER TRAILS

maps 37, 37A

**Network of trails**

**Type** loops on 2WD roads and singletrack

**Rating** moderate/intermediate

**Other users** hikers-1 equestrian-1

**Distance** up to 20 km

**Time** 2-4 hours

**Map** 82 N/7 Golden

**Season** May through October

**Land agency** private, British Columbia Forest Service

### Access

From West Bench Wanderer (#148) at km 26.5.

From Canyon Creek canyon (#149) at km 4.3 and 16.5.

Moonraker is a network of intermediate level trails that confuse and enlighten the dedicated cyclist. The trails have some sweet singletrack sections as they snake their way over rocky ribs and uplands, but much of the time is spent winding around in the bush. It's an interesting area of cedar and fir forest with some surprisingly good views of the valley, as well as meadows, beaver ponds and streams. Some sections are confusing and the trails don't go anywhere unless you link them up. To do this you will need a trail map (available from the Forest Service in Golden or at Summit Cycle). Remember that the area is bounded by Canyon Creek trail to the west and south and by Cedar Lake and roads to the north and east. The radio tower provides a bit of a landmark as well as being central to some of the most interesting trails. Some of the trails are better than others, my favourites are Moonraker, Devil's Slide, Bear Claw and Cedar Snag.

These trails combine nicely with a ride of the Canyon Creek trail, in which case you can climb up the Moonraker trails to the upper road leading to the canyon. They also work well with West Bench Wanderer allowing you to follow singletrack south and finish up on the Canyon Creek trail.

# 152 REDBURN CREEK                    map 36

The Redburn trail, an old abandoned logging road, provides a refreshing respite from the seemingly endless gravel roads of the BC Rockies. The first section is a good gravel doubletrack. Beyond this, the trail is a singletrack that is alternatively smooth and easy, rough and tough, and occasionally overgrown. The trail climbs steadily, a fact more apparent on the return trip. The two creek crossings at km 3.5 could be troublesome at high water levels and avoiding them would require a difficult sidehill thrash.

The trail climbs out of the Blaeberry Valley passing some hoodoos standing sentinel. Near the beginning, it skirts a cutblock that was freshly burned and desolate in 1991. The trail ends in a large old cutblock where a new forest of pine and fir is about 30 years old. Extensive willow growth in the upper cutblock limits visibility, making this ride both safer and more pleasant in the autumn when the leaves have fallen.

The return ride is fast and resplendent with the many challenges that make mountain biking so much fun. The view is excellent—that is if you can take time out from the fast riding to enjoy them.

**Rugged and scenic ride**

**Type** out-and-back on 4WD road and singletrack

**Rating** moderate/intermediate

**Other users** equestrian-2 motorized-1

**Distance** 21 km

**Time** 3-4 hours

**Map** 82 N/7 Golden

**Season** mid-June through October, best after leaf-fall

**Land agency** British Columbia Forest Service

**Access**

From the junction of Hwys. 1 and 95 at Golden, drive 11 km west on the Trans-Canada Hwy. to Moberly Branch Road. Follow this road for 2.2 km to Golden-Donald Upper Road and turn left. After 0.9 km turn right onto Oberg-Johnson Road and drive 1.7 km. Turn left onto Moberly School Road, which after 0.6 km will become Blaeberry Road. It is 8.9 km on a two-wheel-drive gravel road from the Oberg-Johnson junction to Redburn Creek Road.

0.0   trailhead
3.1   rough doubletrack begins
3.5   road washed out, two fords required
10.5  end of trail

# 153 BLAEBERRY RIVER                              map 35

Blaeberry Road snakes its way through a wild and remote valley that exhibits the power of nature on a grand scale. The upper valley is a deep, narrow defile typical of the west slope of the Rockies, and is surrounded by the Freshfield and Wapta icefields and the peaks of the Continental Divide.

The riding is easy on a gravel road that sees relatively little vehicular traffic. The scenic values of this valley offset the fact that you will be riding on a road that you could drive on with your car. The road follows alongside the river for almost 10 km before crossing and climbing into the lower part of Wildcat Creek valley.

The ride begins at Mummery Creek where a huge glacier tumbles down from the peaks above. A short distance up-valley winter snowslides have cleared avalanche paths for several kilometres across the slopes of Fisher Peak. A combination of cutblocks, burns and gravel flats create a variety of vegetation types and, in spite of the fact that much of the valley has been logged, some beautiful stands of cedar and Engelmann spruce remain. The towers of Mount Termier, a peak in the Conway Group, can be seen near Doubt Hill, but the Freshfield Icefield lies out of sight to the west. Before the bridge by Doubt Hill, a sign indicates the start of a 14 km trail to Howse Pass. To the north stands Howse Peak, a prominent tooth-shaped mountain. Beyond the bridge the road climbs up into the valley of Wildcat Creek and leads to the trail to Mistaya Chalet.

It is an easy ride back to Mummery Creek.

## Options

Blaeberry Road, a good gravel logging road, can be cycled in its entirety. The best ride is either from a drop off at the upper end or in combination with the route up the Amiskwi River. The downside of this ride is the potential for dust, logging trucks and, dare I say it, boredom. It is a good idea to check with the Forest Service in Golden regarding logging activity in the area before embarking on any extended rides.

**Scenic cruise below glacier-clad peaks**

**Type** out-and-back on 2WD roads
**Rating** easy/novice
**Other users** motorized-2
**Distance** 22.6 km
**Time** 2-3 hours
**Map** 82 N/10 Blaeberry River
**Season** mid-June to mid-October
**Land agency** British Columbia Forest Service

**Access**
From the junction of Hwys 1 and 95 at Golden, drive 11 km west on the Trans-Canada Hwy. to Moberly Branch Road. Follow this road for 2.2 km to Golden-Donald Upper Road and turn left. After 0.9 km turn right onto Oberg-Johnson Road and drive 1.7 km. Turn left onto Moberly School Road, which after 0.6 km will become Blaeberry Road. It is 39 km on a two-wheel-drive gravel road from the Oberg-Johnson junction to Mummery Creek recreation site.

| | |
|---|---|
| 0.0 | Mummery Creek |
| 2.5 | junction, keep left (right is Ensign Creek trail) |
| 9.4 | Howse Pass trail to left |
| 9.8 | Blaeberry River bridge |
| 11.3 | end of ride, trail to Mistaya Chalet |

Mummery Glacier (#154).

# 154 AMISKWI PASS

map 35

The logging road up Ensign Creek provides access to Amiskwi Pass on the boundary of Yoho National Park. This is a gravel road that can be driven by most cars so be on the lookout for traffic. The grades are moderately steep and sustained as the road climbs through cutblocks and forests of Engelmann spruce. The views are superlative and they get better the higher you climb until the valley below finally resembles a deep canyon. Mummery Glacier and Freshfield Icefield lie to the northwest while to the northeast, on the Continental Divide, Howse Pass sits among peaks such as Chephren and White Pyramid.

Cross the bridge and hammer uphill keeping right at the junction with the Collie Creek Road at km 7.6 and continue up Ensign Creek. Did I say up? The climb seems endless, finally levelling out, traversing into the upper valley and ending in a cutblock below Amiskwi Pass. A fairly challenging singletrack trail leads onward for just over a kilometre to the summit of the pass.

The descent is a vista-charged, fast-paced affair with a few sharp switchback corners to keep you honest.

## Options

1. The privately owned Amiskwi Lodge is located at timberline above the upper cutblock.

2. This ride can be linked with the Amiskwi River trail (#155) to make a 51 km point-to-point ride.

3. The Collie Creek Road leads into a valley below the peaks of Mounts Baker, Ayesha, Collie and Des Poilus with several glaciers of the Wapta Icefield visible between the peaks.

**Major vertical, views of Mummery Glacier**

**Type** out-and-back on 2WD road

**Rating** difficult/intermediate

**Other users** motorized-2

**Distance** 33 km

**Time** 4-6 hours

**Map** 82 N/10 Blaeberry River

**Season** July to mid-October

**Land agency** British Columbia Forest Service

## Access

From the junction of Hwys 1 and 95 at Golden, drive 11 km west on the Trans-Canada Hwy. to Moberly Branch Road. Follow this road for 2.2 km to Golden-Donald Upper Road and turn left. After 0.9 km turn right onto Oberg-Johnson Road and drive 1.7 km. Turn left onto Moberly School Road, which after 0.6 km will become Blaeberry Road. From the Oberg-Johnson junction it is 41.4 km on a two-wheel-drive gravel road to Ensign Creek Road.

| | |
|---|---|
| 0.0 | trailhead |
| 7.6 | junction, keep right (Collie Creek Road to left) |
| 15.3 | end of road, singletrack begins |
| 16.5 | Amiskwi Pass |

10    20    30  33

# 155  AMISKWI RIVER                                    maps 34, 35

The Amiskwi Valley has seen it all! Once a pristine wilderness, it was logged extensively in the 1960s. Perhaps it was nature's wrath that brought the firestorms of the early 1970s. The last straw was when a logging road was pushed almost to Amiskwi Pass from the north and much of the valley north of the park was logged. Today the Amiskwi is a quiet place where nature is attempting to heal itself—a slow process indeed.

In spite of the past this is still a wild and beautiful place with dramatic scenery. When I cycled it I was fortunate enough to see several moose and a grizzly bear. Few people hike into this remote valley.

**Rugged and scenic ride in remote valley**

**Type** out-and-back on 4WD roads

**Rating** difficult/intermediate

**Other users** hikers-1  equestrian-1

**Distance** 57 km

**Time** 6-9 hours

**Maps** 82 N/7 Golden
82 N/10 Blaeberry River

**Season** mid-June to mid-October

**Land agency** Parks Canada

The Amiskwi fireroad is a long trip that provides easy and enjoyable cycling. Although it is possible to make a trip to the pass and back in one long day, I suggest you reserve this trail for an overnight trip.

The ride starts on a gravel road, climbing steadily for the first 2 km. Be alert for bears, especially on the first 8 km, which is heavily hedged by alders. The valley has been logged and burned from Fire Creek at km 15 almost all the way to Amiskwi Pass, and on a hot summer day can feel like "the great Amiskwi desert." The burn area is a profusion of fireweed and other colourful wildflowers in midsummer. At km 17 take the right fork and cross Otto Creek on a bridge. The road becomes increasingly rough and vegetated and at km 23.5 you will have to ford the Amiskwi River. Cycling is permitted as far as the end of the road at km 28.5.

The return trip is a fast and enjoyable ride.

## Options

1. A trail leads from the end of the road past Amiskwi Falls and on to the park boundary at Amiskwi Pass. Privately owned Amiskwi Lodge is located north of the pass. If you decide to leave your bike and continue on foot be aware that this valley is home to a clan of rambunctious porcupines. These rampaging porkies have been known to dine on knobby tires, much to the horror of the returning cyclist.

2. The Amiskwi River trail can be combined with the Amiskwi Pass trail to make a long point-to-point ride suitable for strong and determined cyclists. Cycling is not allowed through the wilderness zone between the end of Amiskwi Road and the park boundary, so you will have to carry or push your bike over this section.

## Access

In Yoho National Park, drive 2 km west from Field on the Trans-Canada Hwy., then follow Emerald Lake Road for 2 km to the Natural Bridge turn-off. Drive past the Natural Bridge to the Amiskwi River bridge and picnic area. The trail starts beyond the parking lot on the west side of the river.

| | |
|---|---|
| 0.0 | trailhead |
| 15.0 | Fire Creek bridge |
| 17.0 | junction, turn right and cross bridge (left is Otto Creek trail) |
| 23.5 | ford Amiskwi River |
| 28.5 | road ends at river |

10    20    30    40    50    57

# 156 KICKING HORSE FIREROAD                    map 34

The Kicking Horse fireroad is a short, easy doubletrack that parallels the Kicking Horse River downstream for some distance. Although a rough singletrack continues through to Porcupine Creek, it is overgrown and not suitable for cycling. If you desire a longer trip a better option is to explore the Otterhead fireroad.

The trail begins as a remarkably level and smooth dirt road covered with pine needles. Keep left at the fork at the Otterhead River and cross a log bridge (the option turns right here). Beyond this point the quality of the road deteriorates until it finally dead-ends at an avalanche path and stream. Continuing farther means dragging your bike through devil's club, a nasty little shrub covered in poisoned prickles that create intense itching. Welcome to BC bushwhacking!

**Options**

Otterhead fireroad leads you into a steep-walled side valley and climbs steadily for the first 3 km before levelling out. Rougher than Kicking Horse Road, it still provides easy cycling as it climbs from the mixed spruce and pine forests of the main valley to a beautiful old Engelmann spruce forest. From the road there are only occasional glimpses of the spectacular mountain scenery that dominates the valley—you'll have to gain further elevation if you want to enjoy the view. The best way to gain elevation in this valley is to take the old road to Tocher Ridge Lookout. This trail branches to the right at km 6.4 and climbs steeply through Engelmann spruce and subalpine fir forest to alpine meadows on the rocky crest of Tocher Ridge. This trip is best done as a hike unless you are comfortable riding down long, steep hills. Much of the uphill trip will involve pushing your bike. The seldom-staffed lookout is situated on a rocky point above an alpine meadow at 2270 m elevation. It commands an excellent view of the area including Mounts Goodsir, Assiniboine, Stephen, Hungabee and Victoria, as well as the Amiskwi and Kicking Horse valleys.

**Family fun on gentle backcountry trail**

**Type** out-and-back on 4WD roads

**Rating** easy/novice

**Other users** hikers-1  equestrian-1

**Distance** 15.6 km

**Time** 2 hours

**Map** 82 N/7 Golden

**Season** mid-May through October

**Land agency** Parks Canada

**Access**

In Yoho National Park, drive 2 km west from Field on the Trans-Canada Hwy., then follow Emerald Lake Road for 2 km to the Natural Bridge turn-off. Drive past the Natural Bridge to the Amiskwi River bridge and picnic area. The trail starts beyond the parking lot on the west side of the river.

| | |
|---|---|
| 0.0 | trailhead |
| 4.2 | junction, turn left and cross bridge (right is the Otterhead fireroad) |
| 7.8 | end of road |

# 157 OTTERTAIL ROAD                     map 34

*Wapta Falls (#158).*

The towering, glacier-clad north face of Mount Goodsir is one of the most dramatic sights in the Canadian Rockies. It's a fitting highlight to what is an already beautiful ride. The trail is an abandoned fireroad that climbs up a deep and narrow valley. The trail is alternately in the forest or crossing avalanche slopes, but the terrain gives little warning of the scenic delights ahead until the very last moment.

The old Ottertail fireroad follows the north side of the Ottertail River to the McArthur Creek warden cabin. It is a generally smooth gravel road with some steep sections and several washed-out culverts that can deceive the inattentive cyclist. A backcountry campground is hidden in the bush by McArthur Creek, but at the warden cabin the trail breaks into the open offering an inspiring view of the three towers of Mount Goodsir.

## Options

A hiking trail leads 2 km to Ottertail Falls and continues to Goodsir Pass.

**Rugged ride to views of Mount Goodsir**

**Type** out-and-back on 4WD roads

**Rating** difficult/intermediate

**Other users** hikers-3  equestrian-2

**Distance** 29 km

**Time** 3-4 hours

**Maps** 82 N/7 Golden
82 N/8 Lake Louise

**Season** mid-June to mid-October

**Land agency** Parks Canada

## Access

In Yoho National Park, drive 8.5 km west of Field on Hwy. 1 to the trailhead on the south side of the highway.

| | |
|---|---|
| 0.0 | trailhead |
| 6.0 | Float Creek |
| 14.0 | McArthur Creek trail to left |
| 14.5 | warden cabin |

2    4    6    8    10    12    14    16    18    20    22    24    26    28  29

# 158  ICE RIVER FIREROAD–BEAVERFOOT LOOP     map 33

This ride takes you south on the Ice River fireroad in Yoho National Park and brings you back on the Beaverfoot Road on provincial land adjacent to the park. The complete circuit can be cycled as a long day trip or as an overnight trip.

The old fireroad rolls alongside the Kicking Horse River and continues south beside the Beaverfoot, a much smaller stream that occupies a huge valley. The cycling is easy on a smooth, well-graded surface that is vegetated in places. Large spruce, cedar and fir trees make up the forest with an understory of devil's club and other shrubs and ferns. After a pleasant roll in the woods you arrive at the warden cabin beside the rushing Ice River. This is a good turn around point for those making an out-and-back ride.

If you wish to complete the loop, cross the river on a good footbridge and climb up onto a benchland replete with clearcuts. When you cross the bridge you are leaving the national park and entering provincial land managed for timber production. The difference serves as a "clearcut" reminder of what national parks are all about. Continue across the clearing following a rough road that leads through the cutblocks. The track steadily improves to a gravel logging road.

Beaverfoot Road is a well-maintained forest service road that leads you back to the Trans-Canada Highway. You'll pass Beaverfoot Lodge and a picnic area overlooking Wapta Falls on your somewhat dusty journey.

### Options

The ride to the Lower Ice River warden cabin makes an easy 32 km out-and-back day trip suitable for novices and families.

**Scenic cruise in Beaverfoot Valley**

**Type** loop on 2WD and 4WD roads

**Rating** moderate/novice

**Other users** hikers-1  equestrian-1 motorized-4

**Distance** 66 km

**Time** 6-8 hours

**Maps** 82 N/1 Mount Goodsir
82 N/2 McMurdo

**Season** May through October

**Land agency** Parks Canada, British Columbia Forest Service

### Access

In Yoho National Park, drive 22 km west of Field on Hwy. 1 to Hoodoo Creek Campground. Follow the right fork of the campground access road to the gated Ice River fireroad on the south side of the parking area.

| | |
|---|---|
| 0.0 | trailhead |
| 16.0 | Ice River warden cabin (Ice River trail to left) |
| 16.1 | bridge |
| 23.7 | junction, turn right |
| 26.5 | junction with Beaverfoot Road, turn right |
| 31.2 | junction with Kootenay Road, keep right |
| 42.0 | Beaverfoot Lodge |
| 56.0 | Trans-Canada Highway, turn right |
| 65.0 | turn right into Hoodoo Campground |
| 66.0 | trailhead |

# 159  MOOSE CREEK                    map 33

**Gentle ride below Mount Goodsir**
**Type** out-and-back on 2WD road
**Rating** easy/novice
**Other users** hikers-1  equestrian-3 motorized-3
**Distance** 11 km
**Time** 1-2 hours
**Map** 82 N/1 Mount Goodsir
**Season** May through October
**Land agency** British Columbia Forest Service

## Access
Beaverfoot Road begins at the Trans-Canada Hwy. just west of the west boundary of Yoho National Park. Drive south on this road passing Beaverfoot Lodge at km 14 and Kootenay Road at km 24.8. At km 29.5 turn left onto a lesser road that may be signed for Wolverine Pass. After 2.8 km, pass the road leading to the Ice River on the left. Drive a further 1.8 km to a fork in the road and park. Moose Creek trail is the fork to the left.

This is a truly easy ride on a smooth old logging road. Although officially closed to motorized traffic, you may expect to encounter the occasional renegade. The ride follows along Moose Creek into a valley surrounded by big, beautiful mountains. At the head of the valley is Mount Goodsir, elevation 3562 m. The road ends in a clearcut at km 5.5.

| | |
|---|---|
| 0.0 | trailhead |
| 4.5 | junction, keep left |
| 4.8 | junction, keep right |
| 5.5 | road ends |

There is a proposal to open a mine in this valley. If that happens, access and rideability of the trails could change.

## Options
A hiking trail continues for several kilometres up the valley.

# 160 NIPIKA TOURING CENTRE                    map 31

Nipika is a destination area with lots of mountain biking opportunities. This is a good area for novices and families to explore and have fun. Most of the trails are doubletracks that are used as ski trails in winter. A lodge and cabin on site offer service by prior arrangement. In the surrounding mountains there are a number of longer rides that, in part, utilize logging roads.

The trails loop around near the lodge and Kootenay River and lead north to the Cross River canyon. This is the highlight of the area, with trails along both sides of the canyon and two bridges so you can put loop rides together. The upper crossing of the canyon is at the Natural Bridge, a spectacularly deep and narrow chasm. Several very challenging singletracks, not suitable for novices, roll along the very edge of the canyon.

**Network of trails**

**Type** loops on 4WD roads and singletrack

**Rating** easy-moderate/novice

**Other users** hikers-1

**Distance** up to 30 km

**Time** 1-4 hours

**Map** 82 J/12 Tangle Peak

**Season** June through October

**Land agency** private, British Columbia Forest Service

**Access**
From Hwy. 93 in Kootenay National Park, drive 12 km south on Settlers Road, turn left onto Cross River Road and drive another 2 km to the signed Nipika Touring Centre.

# 161 CROSS RIVER FIREROAD
map 31

This old fire access road offers a mellow tour of the Kootenay River valley. You'll be treated to a spectacular canyon as well as some beautiful forests and vistas of this deep valley and the peaks of the Stanford Range to the west. There are no hills of any significance and the riding is easy, suitable for beginners and families.

From either the Natural Bridge trailhead or from Nipika Lodge make your way to the Natural Bridge where the Cross River surges through a deep and very narrow canyon. Past the bridge roll downhill paralleling the canyon and keep right at km 5.3. The track is a bit overgrown as it descends to the boundary of Kootenay National Park and joins the Cross River fireroad. (Travelling south, be sure to turn left here, right ends in the river.) Roll north on the old fireroad, now vegetated but easily cycled and enjoy the views of the river and the peaks above. The track variously passes through stands of Douglas fir, aspen, pine and spruce. Don't miss the giant Douglas fir with its bark rubbed smooth by grizzly bears. A nearby fir is also rubbed with lots of hair stuck in the sap.

At km 24.6 the Dog Lake trail crosses the old road—this is your exit route to the north trailhead, although the fireroad continues north for 5 km to Daer Creek where a collapsed bridge marks the end of cycling. Turn left on Dog Lake trail, roll down to the two bridges over the Kootenay River and it's all over.

## Options

A pleasant out-and-back ride can be made from the north trailhead by riding north to Daer Creek and/or south to Pitts Creek, then returning to the trailhead.

**Scenic cruiser in Kootenay Valley**

**Type** point-to-point on 4WD roads

**Rating** moderate/novice

**Other users** hikers-1

**Distance** 25.2 km one way

**Time** 2-4 hours

**Maps** 82 J/12 Tangle Peak
82 J/13 Mount Assiniboine

**Season** June through October

**Land agency** private, Parks Canada

**Access**

**south** From Hwy. 93 in Kootenay National Park, drive 12 km south on Settlers Road, turn left onto Cross River Road and drive another 4.5 km to the signed Natural Bridge trailhead.

**north** On Hwy. 93 in Kootenay National Park, begin at McLeod Meadows Campground, 15.6 km south of Kootenay Crossing Warden Station. The trail begins at the back of the campground and leads to a bridge across the river.

| | |
|---|---|
| 0.0 | south trailhead |
| 0.9 | keep right |
| 2.2 | keep right |
| 2.7 | Natural Bridge |
| 5.3 | turn right |
| 5.4 | left |
| 6.1 | park boundary |
| 6.3 | turn right |
| 20.0 | Pitts Creek |
| 21.7 | old road joins from left |
| 24.6 | four-way junction, turn left |
| 24.9 | bridge |
| 25.2 | north trailhead |

10        20      25.2

# 162  WEST KOOTENAY FIREROAD          map 32

**Family fun on gentle trail**
**Type** loop on 2WD and 4WD roads
**Rating** easy/novice
**Other users** hikers-1
**Distance** 20.1 km (8.6 on pavement)
**Time** 2 hours
**Map** 82 K/16 Spillimacheen
**Season** mid-May to mid-October
**Land agency** Parks Canada

**Access**
**north** In Kootenay National Park, begin at the Kootenay Crossing warden station on the west side of Hwy. 93, 42 km north of the Kootenay Park west gate at Radium. The trail is the gated road on the south side of the station.

**south** Begin at Crook's Meadow group campground, 9.1 km south of Kootenay Crossing on the west side of Hwy. 93. Cycle to the west side of the campground and onto the gated road.

The West Kootenay fireroad is a smooth, dirt track winding through a mixed wood forest of pine, spruce, poplar and Douglas fir. It's a pleasant but non-too-exciting ride that connects the Kootenay Crossing warden station to the Crook's Meadow group camp. The paved shoulders of Highway 93 can be used for the return trip.

All streams along the route are bridged and the only hill on the trip is the steep rocky climb at the start. Beaverfoot Bust-out (#163) branches to the right 1 km from Kootenay Crossing. Keep left at this junction, ride past the trail to Luxor Pass, and follow the road as it winds along beside Dolly Varden Creek to the south trailhead. Tangle Peak dominates the view to the south.

| | |
|---|---|
| 0.0 | north trailhead |
| 1.0 | junction, keep left (right leads to Beaverfoot Valley) |
| 3.9 | Luxor Pass trail to right |
| 11.5 | south trailhead, Hwy. 93, turn left |
| 20.1 | end of ride |

# 163 BEAVERFOOT BUST-OUT maps 32, 33

This long fat-tire trip follows the West Kootenay fireroad, some old logging roads and Beaverfoot Road as it makes its way up to the headwaters of the Kootenay River, then descends the Beaverfoot River to the Trans-Canada Highway. You can cycle it as part of a multi-day tour or arrange a car shuttle at one of the trailheads. It is 172 km by highway from Kootenay Crossing to Beaverfoot Road via Radium and Golden, a long drive for a shuttle. The northern 44.6 km of Beaverfoot Road as far as the Paul Creek forest service recreation site is open to traffic and suitable for a small car, which gives an option to shorten the ride.

Begin at Kootenay Crossing by riding up the hill and into the forest. After 1 km take the right fork and roll along the gravel and packed-dirt road as it winds through a forest of pine, spruce, fir and willow. At km 10 you'll leave the national park and enter provincial land, which is subject to resource harvesting.

Beyond the park boundary you may notice long poles leaning against trees and boxes nailed to the trees above the poles. These are "sets" used by a trapper. Bait is placed in the box at the top of the pole and a snare or trap is positioned to catch an inquisitive marten running up the pole.

The ride from here through to Paul Creek is the roughest part of the trip. Willows and alders encroach on the road, which is rutted and heavily vegetated in places, and there are several creeks to cross. The road improves after reaching a cutblock where a view opens to the Vermilion Range. After crossing a bridge over the upper Kootenay River, the road joins the wide, smooth gravel of Beaverfoot Road near the Paul Creek recreation site.

It's a long but easy and sometimes dusty ride down Beaverfoot Road from this junction to the Kicking Horse River and the Trans-Canada Highway.

**Backcountry explorer**

**Type** point-to-point on 2WD and 4WD roads

**Rating** difficult/novice

**Other users** motorized-4

**Distance** 66.5 km one way

**Time** 5-8 hours

**Maps** 82 K/16 Spillimacheen
82 N/1 Mount Goodsir
82 N/2 McMurdo

**Season** May through October

**Land agency** British Columbia Forest Service, Parks Canada

**Access**

**south** In Kootenay National Park, begin at the Kootenay Crossing warden station on the west side of Hwy. 93, 42 km north of the Kootenay Park west gate at Radium. The trail is the gated road on the south side of the station.

**north** Beaverfoot Road joins the Trans-Canada Hwy. just west of the west boundary of Yoho National Park, 30.5 km west of Field and 26 km east of Golden. The bridge over the Kicking Horse River, 1 km south on Beaverfoot Road, is a good rendezvous spot.

| | |
|---|---|
| 0.0 | south trailhead |
| 1.0 | junction, turn right (left is west Kootenay fireroad) |
| 10.0 | Kootenay National Park boundary junction, keep left |
| 21.9 | join Beaverfoot Road, turn left |
| 66.5 | north trailhead |

# FRASER VALLEY

The Fraser Valley riding area lies on the Pacific slope of the Rockies at the headwaters of the Fraser River. Farms nestle within the broad and deep Fraser Valley while the snow-covered peaks of the Rockies and Cariboos tower above. This cycling area is somewhat similar to the Kootenay and Columbia area to the south but it's more remote, wilder and less developed. Jasper lies some 100 km to the east, while the nearest cities are Prince George to the northwest and Kamloops to the south. Highways 16 and 5 form the major transportation route through the valley linking the communities of Valemount and McBride and providing access to the riding trails.

This is an area of cruiser-style mountain bike rides on old logging and lookout roads with moderate gains in elevation. All the rides tend to be very scenic and nontechnical. Canoe Mountain and Bell Mountain both offer outstanding trips to mountain summits, but both exact a toll in the work required to reach the top. Kinney Lake trail is the only singletrack described in this area.

This riding area lies on the west slope of the Continental Divide in a region of big, deep valleys and towering, glaciated peaks such as Mount Robson, the highest peak in the Canadian Rockies. The main valley is part of the Rocky Mountain Trench, a major fault system stretching for more than 1000 km and forming the western edge of the Rocky Mountains. To the west of the trench lie the Cariboo and Monashee mountains. Most of this area is in the drainage of the Fraser River, but the Canoe River, a tributary of the Columbia, drains the southern end of the valley near Valemount. The backcountry is wild—even logged areas do not have any kind of development—and nature operates here on a grand scale. The fall salmon run, from mid-August to mid-September, is a major natural spectacle. The forests range from cedar and hemlock to pine and spruce, and the rainforest along the Kinney Lake trail is one of only a very few in the Rockies.

Logging is the mainstay of the local economy and this means good access to the backcountry, but sometimes less than picture-perfect scenery. Agriculture is important in the main valley and tourism is a developing industry. This area, although big, is sparsely settled. McBride and Valemount are the only towns, each with a population of about 1,000, while Dunster and Tete Jaune Cache are rural communities. Most services are available in the valley, but there are no bike shops. Both towns offer camping with showers. The laid back local lifestyle and friendly people will make you feel right at home.

# 164 BELL MOUNTAIN BOOGIE          map 38

**Classic high mountain ride with great views**

**Type** out-and-back on 4WD roads

**Rating** difficult/intermediate

**Other users** motorized-4

**Distance** 25.4 km

**Time** 2-4 hours

**Map** 93 H/8 McBride

**Season** July to mid-October

**Land agency** British Columbia Forest Service

### Access

From the Main Street in McBride drive west on Hwy. 16 for 9.2 km to Bell Mountain Road. Turn left and drive up the road to km 4.8 and park.

| | |
|---|---|
| 0.0 | trailhead |
| 9.3 | junction, turn left |
| 12.1 | road ends at meadows, continue up track |
| 12.7 | track ends on summit |

This is an outstanding cycle trip that lets you pedal your fat tires to an alpine summit high above the Robson Valley. The summit features a 360 degree panorama of the Rockies and Cariboos and includes peaks from Mount Sir Alexander in the north to Mount Robson in the south. The trail is an old logging road unsuitable for most vehicles.

From the trailhead keep right on the signed Bell Mountain Road as it switchbacks up and contours around the mountain at an easily rideable grade. Keep left at the junction at km 9.3 and climb more steeply to the end of the road at treeline. A track continues through flower-filled meadows, passing the remains of an old ski tow, then climbing steeply to the summit. Enjoy the meadows and the view. While I was sitting on the summit I could hear wolves howling from a nearby hillside, which served as a simple reminder of the wildness of the country all around. When you've had enough of the summit splendour, it's time to point your tires down and enjoy an exciting big ring hammer back to the start—watch for vehicles.

### Options

Three more peaks to the west can be reached on foot, with even more great views.

# 165  MCBRIDE LOOKOUT                          map 38

What do most fire lookout trails have in common? If you said grinding uphills and kamikaze descents, you're right. With an elevation gain of 1300 m, the McBride Lookout is no exception. I shudder when I think of the effort to get up there, but smile when I think of the adrenaline rush accompanying the screaming descent!

The trip to the McBride Lookout provides an excellent view of the Robson Valley and the Cariboo Mountains beyond. The Robson Valley was named by locals to describe what is actually the upper part of the Fraser Valley; they wanted to help visitors distinguish this beautiful, remote valley from the lower mainland area.

Near the beginning of the road you can enjoy a short walk to Rainbow Falls. After that, get ready for some hard work, shift into a seriously low gear and grind your way uphill. Approximately half way up the mountain you reach the site of an old lookout and a pretty good view of the valley. Beyond this point the road becomes narrower, steeper and rougher. Keep cranking! The road finally emerges from the trees onto sweeping alpine meadows and ends at the abandoned lookout building.

The trip down is pure kamikaze. Good brakes are mandatory. Watch for the occasional vehicle.

## Options

Hiking beyond the lookout leads you into several alpine basins and on to the summit of Teare Mountain. The view from the summit stretches across the Rockies and includes Mount Robson to the south and the Cariboos to the west. The peaks and glaciers of the Premier Group are very dramatic. This area is part of an ecological reserve so treat it gently.

**Major vertical and great views**

**Type** out-and-back on 4WD roads

**Rating** difficult/intermediate

**Other users** hikers-2 motorized-2

**Distance** 22.8 km

**Time** 3-5 hours

**Map** 93 H/8 McBride

**Season** May to mid-October

**Land agency** British Columbia Forest Service

## Access

Turn off Hwy. 16 onto Mountainview Road at a point 0.7 km east of the Fraser River bridge at McBride. Drive for 0.6 km to Rainbow Road on your right. This is the road to the lookout. Park here and cycle from this point.

| | |
|---|---|
| 0.0 | trailhead |
| 0.5 | trail to Rainbow Falls to right |
| 5.5 | site of old lookout |
| 11.4 | end of road, abandoned lookout |

# 166 KIWA CREEK—SOUTH FORK map 40

This ride takes you away from the Rocky Mountain Trench into a steep-sided valley typical of the Cariboo Mountains. Although part of the valley has been logged, much of it is still in a natural state. The upper end is dominated by the peaks and glaciers of the Premier Group. This is wild country and good bear habitat so be on the lookout for bears.

The route follows an old gravel logging road that climbs steadily over the first 10 km, then rocks and rolls to the final cutblock at km 15. Rockslides near km 3.5 restrict motor vehicle access but are easily crossed by cyclists. The ride out is fast and fun and includes some high-speed downhill runs.

**Options**

Although there is no trail it is possible to hike and bushwhack along the edge of the valley bottom wetlands to the Kiwa Glacier. This is a worthwhile destination with dunes, moraines and a glacier to explore.

**Rugged ride in the spectacular Cariboo Mountains**

**Type** out-and-back on 4WD roads

**Rating** moderate/novice

**Other users** motorized-2

**Distance** 30.6 km

**Time** 3-4 hours

**Maps** 83 D/13 Kiwa Creek
83 E/4 Croydon

**Season** July to mid-October

**Land agency** British Columbia Forest Service

**Access**

Kiwa Creek Road leaves Tete Jaune-Croydon Road just east of the Kiwa Creek bridge. It is located 22.4 km east of Dunster Road at Dunster and 16.7 km west of Blackman Road at Tete Jaune Cache. Drive up Kiwa Creek Road for 4.2 km and park at a fork to the left. This is the trail.

| | |
|---|---|
| 0.0 | trailhead |
| 1.0 | junction, keep left |
| 2.8 | Kiwa Creek bridge |
| 3.5 | rockslides across road |
| 15.3 | end of road |

# 167 KIWA CREEK—NORTH FORK                                    map 40

This ride is an easy frolic on an old logging road. It takes you west of the Rocky Mountain Trench into the Cariboo Mountains.

The north Kiwa (often pronounced "kiwi" by the locals) is a well-compacted, smooth road that is almost a doubletrack in many places. It provides easy riding up a long, gentle gradient to the summit of the Divide between the Kiwa and Rausch drainages. The return trip can be as quick or as slow as you like it. It's great fun to zip over the roads through this luxuriant forest and alongside the rushing streams.

## Options

A rough singletrack continues beyond the end of the road and descends to the end of the Rausch River Rider allowing you to make a 48 km point-to-point ride. Be forewarned, this is a very strenuous trip through remote country.

**Gentle backcountry ride**
**Type** out-and-back on 2WD roads
**Rating** moderate/novice
**Other users** motorized-2
**Distance** 32.6 km
**Time** 2-4 hours
**Map** 83 E/4 Croydon
**Season** June to mid-October
**Land agency** British Columbia Forest Service

## Access

Park at the junction of Kiwa Creek Road and Tete Jaune-Croydon Road (see #166).

| | |
|---|---|
| 0.0 | trailhead |
| 4.2 | junction, keep right (left is Kiwa South) |
| 9.4 | junction, keep left |
| 16.3 | end of road |

# 168 RAUSCH RIVER RIDER
map 39

The Rider provides little in the way of exciting technical cycling—it's the country that's exciting. In 1998 the Rausch Valley was still one of the wildest places in the Cariboos. This may not be the case for much longer, however, as the Forest Service is proposing to build a "proper" road up here and harvest the timber. Then you will be able to cycle on a smooth road replete with logging trucks—that is, if you still want to at all.

Technically speaking, this trail isn't in the Rockies but it does provide excellent views across the valley to the Rockies. The cycling is easy on a doubletrack with little elevation gain. The trail is much easier to ride early in the season; later, as the grass grows taller, the physical exertion required increases substantially. A private road and railway crossing to the left at km 11.2 of the access route leads to this ride, but is located on private land. Please respect the landowners' wishes.

Begin the ride by cycling west, parallel to the railway tracks, for 1 km. At this point you will be on Crown land and can cross the railway and join the rough road leading into the Rausch Valley. The road passes through fields and forests as it travels west along a terrace above the Fraser River before curving into the valley. Soon you are paralleling valley-bottom wetlands and meadows with spectacular snow-covered and glaciated peaks towering above. The doubletrack ends at a range riders' camp, which makes a good turnaround point.

**Rugged ride in the spectacular Cariboo Mountains**

**Type** out-and-back on 4WD roads

**Rating** difficult/novice

**Other users** livestock

**Distance** 38.4 km

**Time** 6 hours

**Maps** 83 E/4 Croydon 94 H/1 Eddy

**Season** May to mid-October

**Land agency** private, British Columbia Forest Service

**Access**
Leave Hwy. 16 at the Dunster turn-off and drive toward Dunster. After 3.6 km turn right and follow Rausch Valley Road for 11.7 km. Park at the railway siding.

| | |
|---|---|
| 0.0 | trailhead, cycle west on north side of tracks |
| 1.0 | cross CNR and join old road on south side |
| 6.0 | flats along Rausch River |
| 11.5 | camp |
| 19.2 | end of road at camp |

# 169 HORSEY CREEK

map 40

Horsey Creek? You mean Horse Creek. No, Horsey—it was named after a person, not for one of those four-legged critters.

This adventure-packed trail follows an old compacted-dirt and gravel road into a high mountain valley. A former logging road, the route is now seldom used except by a local rancher who pastures his cows in the valley during summer. Two of the vehicle bridges that once spanned Horsey Creek have been washed away and they have since been replaced by bridges suitable for bicycle traffic. It is smooth rolling up steady but gentle grades to the head of the valley. The road forks at km 19 and both forks are rideable and provide excellent views of big rock walls and deep valleys. Although the upper valley has been logged, the rugged beauty of the towering glaciated peaks stands serene and untouched above.

**Rugged and scenic ride**

**Type** out-and-back on 4WD road

**Rating** moderate/novice

**Other users** equestrian-1 motorized-1  livestock

**Distance** 38 km

**Time** 3-4 hours

**Maps** 83 E/4 Croydon
83 E/5 Chalco Mountain

**Season** July to mid-October

**Land agency** British Columbia Forest Service

**Access**
Horsey Creek Road begins on the east side of Hwy. 16, 40 km east of McBride.

| | |
|---|---|
| 0.0 | trailhead |
| 19.0 | junction, end of ride |

# 170 SMALL RIVER
map 40

This trip offers a long, rideable, uphill approach, tremendous Rocky Mountain scenery and a fast downhill exit.

Even though the first 10 km of the road is driveable, I suggest you begin at the parking lot at Highway 16 so you can take advantage of an exhilarating downhill ride on the way back. The initial section is a long, gradual climb on an old road closely hedged by alders. Cattle are pastured here so be sure to close all gates. There is an old cabin at km 10.4 and the sound of falls below entices you to explore. The road beyond is seldom used by vehicles. Here the valley opens out and spectacular views of Mount Longstaff and its associated glaciers lure you on to the end of the road.

The downhill run back to the highway is fast and fun. If you choose to hammer, be alert for cars and cows, not to mention (scary thought) cow patties.

**Rugged and scenic ride**

**Type** out-and-back on 4WD road

**Rating** moderate/novice

**Other users** motorized-2  livestock

**Distance** 40 km

**Time** 3-4 hours

**Maps** 83 E/3 Mount Robson
83 E/4 Croydon

**Season** July to mid-October

**Land agency** British Columbia Forest Service

**Access**
Park at the Small River picnic area on the north side of Highway 16, approximately 46.7 km east of McBride and 16.2 km west of the junction of Hwys. 5 and 16.

| | |
|---|---|
| 0.0 | trailhead |
| 10.4 | cabin |
| 20.0 | end of road |

# 171 VALEMOUNT LOOKOUT

map 41

**Rugged ride with good views**

**Type** out-and-back on 4WD road

**Rating** moderate/novice

**Other users** motorized-3

**Distance** 12.4 km

**Time** 2-3 hours

**Map** 83 D/14 Valemount

**Season** May to mid-October

**Land agency** British Columbia Forest Service

## Access

Begin at the corner of Main Street and Hillside Drive in Valemount. The trail heads up Hillside Drive.

| | |
|---|---|
| 0.0 | trailhead |
| 1.1 | junction, keep right |
| 6.2 | old fire lookout, trail to meadows |

This mid-level lookout can be reached in a half-day jaunt from the village of Valemount.

The road climbs steadily, but it is all rideable on mostly-compacted gravel with the occasional washed-out section. The old lookout tower is no longer in use and you can climb the steep stairs to a 360 degree panorama. Although it's not at a particularly high elevation (I know that's hard to believe on the upward journey), the lookout provides extensive views over the Rocky Mountain Trench, the village, and the peaks of the Rockies and Cariboos.

The downhill trip is a scream. Remember, you may encounter vehicles on this road.

## Options

A hiking trail leads for 5 km to the alpine meadows above the lookout.

# 172 CANOE MOUNTAIN                                    map 41

It provides some incredibly panoramic views of the Rockies, the Cariboos and the Monashees for the strong and determined cyclist. The views begin almost immediately and continue to improve as you ascend this, the northernmost point of the Monashee Mountains.

The riding is continuously uphill on a steep gravel road but, although the road is open to vehicles, you will encounter only the occasional 4x4. You can pedal all the way to the summit if you have bionic legs and manage to always pick the best line on the loose gravel. It's a big "if." Much of the road is steep and some sections have loose rock of up to cobble size. But, even if you do have to push your bike a good part of the way it is still worthwhile, considering the excellent trip down.

The road climbs through extensive krummholz and alpine meadows and leads to four communications installations. As it climbs onto the summit ridge it provides an awe-inspiring ride along the northern end of the Monashees, with the glaciated peaks of the Premier Group in the Cariboos to the west and the massif of Mount Robson in the Rockies to the northeast. Between them lies the immense Rocky Mountain Trench occupied by the Canoe and Fraser rivers while the village of Valemount lies at your feet—physically close but spiritually a world away. The summit can be cool and windy so take some extra clothes.

Speaking of cool, the ride along the summit and the descent of the upper 7 km of the road provides some of the coolest cycling to be found anywhere. However, cool as you may feel, physically or mentally, you will soon be riding on rims of fire. I stopped three times on the descent to cool my sizzling wheels. This descent is the biggest single vertical drop (1844 m) of any cycling trail in this guide. It's an exhilarating downhill!

**Major vertical with incredible views**

**Type** out-and-back on 4WD road

**Rating** extreme/intermediate

**Other users** equestrian-1 motorized-2

**Distance** 24 km

**Time** 4-6 hours

**Map** 83 D/11 Canoe River

**Season** July to mid-October

**Land agency** British Columbia Forest Service

**Access**
The Canoe Mountain trailhead is located on the east side of Hwy. 5, 15.2 km south of Main Street at Valemount. Watch for an aluminum tractor shed beside the road.

| | |
|---|---|
| 0.0 | trailhead |
| 0.5 | junction, keep left |
| 11.7 | communications facility |
| 12.0 | summit |

2    4    6    8    10    12    14    16    18    20    22    24

# 173 KINNEY LAKE                                  map 42

Rainforests in the Rockies are about as rare as legal mountain bike trails in Mount Robson Provincial Park. Here's your chance to hammer through hemlocks, frolic past ferns and bike in the devil's club. However, being a part of the "Devil's Club" is no license to ride irresponsibly. This is a very popular trip for hikers, family groups and equestrians, so plan to encounter a high number of other users. If you choose to ride this trail, choose also to be an ambassador for the wonderful sport of mountain biking by keeping your speed slow, avoiding brake sliding, and being courteous and friendly to other users.

This trail climbs through the rainforest and leads alongside Robson River to Kinney Lake, a reflective gem set 3000 m below the summit of Mount Robson. The ride has a mystical quality about it and the feeling is ever so special as you roll back to the trailhead. The presence of big cedar and hemlock trees, soft light on the mosses and ferns, and the cool humidity of the air touch the very soul of cycling. The pervasive roaring of the Robson River is a simple reminder of the icy peaks towering overhead.

The trail is constructed of well-compacted gravel and has only a modest elevation gain, the only hill of any consequence being the rough, rocky climb at the avalanche slope 1.5 km from the trailhead. A campsite and picnic shelter nestle in the trees beside Kinney Lake. Cycling is allowed as far as the bridge at km 8 where the trail crosses the river and becomes steep and narrow. Some wonderful country lies beyond awaiting your exploration on foot.

**Scenic and gentle ride in rainforest**

**Type** out-and-back on 4WD road and singletrack

**Rating** easy/intermediate

**Other users** hikers-8 equestrian-5

**Distance** 16 km

**Time** 2-4 hours

**Map** 83 E/3 Mount Robson

**Season** May to mid-October

**Land agency** British Columbia Provincial Parks

**Access**
From Hwy. 16 at the Mount Robson junction, drive 2.5 km north to the parking area at the Berg Lake trailhead.

| | |
|---|---|
| 0.0 | trailhead |
| 4.3 | bridge, Kinney Lake |
| 6.8 | campsite |
| 8.0 | end of cycle trail |

### Options
Hide your bike and continue on foot to the Valley of a Thousand Falls (6 km) and Berg Lake (9 km).

# NORTHERN EAST SLOPES

This large cycling area includes the country along the east slope of the Rockies from the Smoky River in the north almost to the Bow River in the south. More than any other cycling area in this book, this land has a big wilderness feeling about it. Even areas with road access seem remote and northern. The main population centres are Grand Cache, Hinton, Jasper and Nordegg. The primary transportation routes are Highways 40, 93 and 11, while SR 940 provides gravel road access to many other areas.

"Adventure" is the key word for bicycle travel in this country. In keeping with the nature of the land, many of the trips are long wilderness explorations with little in the way of technical riding. Self-sufficiency and good wilderness travel skills are important on these rides that lead you into sometimes very remote country with little available in the way of assistance should you encounter problems. These long rides are all about using bikes to enjoy the country. Classic examples include the rides into the Willmore Wilderness, three long rides in Jasper National Park and one in Banff, and the rides at Ram River and at Ya-Ha-Tinda Ranch. There are also lots of shorter technical rides and some very sweet singletracks, especially at Jasper and Nordegg, and they will both delight and amaze you.

In this riding area the distances are long and the spaces wide open, with broad and gentle mountain valleys occupied by big, wide rivers. Near the Continental Divide the mountains are high, rugged and glaciated but, moving eastward, the ranges become lower with jagged ridges of limestone giving way to rounded, tree-covered foothills and finally the high boreal plains. Much of the mountain forest is spruce and pine, but to the east it becomes boreal in nature with lots of muskeg. Within the mountains and foothills the valley bottoms are frequently lined by extensive willow and shrub meadowlands giving the country an incredible esthetic appeal.

Wild though the country may seem, the northern east slopes are alive with human activity. Much of the history of this area is told in the story of the fur trade, and railway construction, coal mining and early travels by guided parties on horseback led to the region's early exploration. With the exception of tourism at Jasper, most of the local economies are primarily based on natural resources. As elsewhere in the Rockies, the search for and mining of coal was, and continues to be, an important aspect of development. Other resource extraction interests include gas and logging. For tourists, this country is off the beaten track, so don't expect to find the kinds of facilities that you would find in resort country. Popular recreations include camping, horseback trips and motorized off-roading. Quads, in particular, are travelling on almost all of the trails, which results in good maintenance but is devastating the once primo singletracks.

Jasper National Park is one of Canada's premier mountain wilderness parks. The park publishes a list of designated mountain bike trails that includes a lot of good riding opportunities. Remember that it is a privilege to ride your bike on trails in a national park and conduct yourself accordingly. The trails close to town are popular and crowded on summer weekends, making this a good time to explore some of the legendary wilderness rides for which this park is famous. The town

*Alexandra Glacier (#204).*

of Jasper is a well-known tourist destination but it remains, at heart, a small Alberta town with a bit of resort flair. Budget accommodation is available at several hostels and camping and showers are available at Whistler Campground. Showers are also available at the laundromat in town. The good folks at Freewheel Cycle will be happy to orient you to the local cycling scene and take care of all your bike needs.

Grand Cache is a relatively new town in a beautiful natural setting. Located on an upland above the confluence of the Smoky and Sulphur rivers, the town overlooks the wild peaks and valleys of Willmore Wilderness Park and offers most services, including a campground with showers. The people are friendly and mountain bikers are welcome. Inquire at Action Gear Cycle and Sport for tips on local rides. Shared use trails

circle the town and radiate out into the point of land between the Sulphur and Smoky rivers, while other trails lead to nearby mountain peaks and into the Willmore Wilderness Provincial Park. This large park allows bicycles on its trails but beware, it's a big, remote and wild place where solid backcountry travel skills and self-sufficiency are essential. The trails are either old exploration roads or horse-built singletrack, which means challenging riding. There are no bridges and some of the streams are wide and fast-flowing. This is a great place for long day rides or extended overnight trips with an orientation toward exploring wild country.

The country around Hinton, to the east of Jasper Park, offers some exceptional cycling. Located just east of the park gates on Highway 16, the Overlander Lodge makes a good base for some scenic and historic rides. Hinton is a major town with all services. Gravel pathways link Maxwell Lake and Thompson Lake on the south side of town and numerous quad trails and singletracks branch off of this pathway. Drop in to BikeSmith for the scoop on rides in the vicinity of town. The Overlander Overender is an annual cross-country and downhill race worth checking out. Highway 40 south from Hinton leads into an area known as the Coal Branch, where the village of Cadomin and the ghost town of Mountain Park are worth exploring. Coal mining is the most important industry in this area and the recently approved Cheviot Mine will alter both access and the face of the land. The Coal Branch is a popular recreation area, attracting large numbers of people for camping, horseback riding and motorized off-roading. Many of the trails provide excellent cycling, but you can expect summer weekends to be busy.

Nordegg is a small town with a big bicycle future. Almost a ghost town with lots of old buildings and the Brazeau Mine provincial historic site, Nordegg is slowly awakening to a future of recreation and tourism. Numerous trails and old roads around town offer lots of opportunities to explore this historic and scenic locale. The friendly folks at Frontier Lodge will be more than happy to introduce you to the local trails and cycling scene, including the incredible fun of heli-biking. This unique experience lets you tackle demanding descents while you are still strong and fresh as well as providing an assist for some very long backcountry trips. The Frontier Fat Tire Festival is a not-to-be-missed annual bike extravaganza with guided rides and other fun events including the Black Mountain Challenge race. Numerous singletrack and doubletrack trails radiate from Highway 11 in the vicinity of town and the lodge, as well as at the Bighorn Dam and Kootenay Plains, offering the possibility of almost endless exploration and fun.

SR 940, the Forestry Trunk Road, provides access to rides on the east slopes between Highway 11 and Highway 1. The forest service has provided a number of campgrounds and recreation areas along the route, but services are limited so it is wise to be self-sufficient when travelling here. There are many opportunities for cyclists to explore this country, I've described rides in three locations. The Ram River area features a number of wilderness trails that are popular with quads and equestrians but also offer good backcountry riding opportunities. Farther south, the Ya-Ha-Tinda Ranch area is a major equestrian destination where off-road vehicles are prohibited. This unique "prairies within the mountains" offers spectacular wilderness cycling experiences. The Waiparous Creek and Ghost River area, a short distance north of Highway 1, includes three attractive rides. The area is popular with the motorized off-road crowd and is at its best for cycling on weekdays.

# 174 GRANDE MOUNTAIN
map 43

A low peak lying just off of the mountain front, Grande Mountain is strategically placed for great views of the Grande Cache area. It also provides some pleasant mountain cycling.

The road is mostly compacted gravel and dirt with some erosion gullies and exposed bedrock. It climbs steadily with a couple of steep sections but is all rideable for most cyclists. After contouring around the upper part of the mountain the road follows along a broad, sometimes windy, ridge to the summit. There are good views along the way up but if you ride pedals-to-the-metal you probably won't notice them until you get to the top. From the summit the town of Grande Cache is at your feet, with the wild peaks of the Willmore beyond. The two prominent valleys are the Smoky River to the west and the Sulphur River to the south. To the north, Hammell Mountain and Smoky River Coal's open-pit mine lie beyond the Smoky River. This spot is accessible by motors so don't be surprised when you find garbage, graffiti and broken glass. There are three communications facilities on the summit.

The ride down is a fast and challenging affair with loose rocks, erosion gullies, bedrock and bumps to test your skill. This route has been used as the downhill part of the Bushstomper mountain bike race course. Although the racers don't have to ride up the mountain, they do have to cycle another 19 km of rock-and-roll trail after reaching the bottom.

## Options

From the summit the track along the powerline plunges to the valley below providing an optional descent route for advanced level downhill riders. It is 6.4 km from the summit to Hoppe Avenue.

**Major vertical and great views**

**Type** out-and-back on 4WD roads

**Rating** difficult/intermediate

**Other users** hikers-1 motorized-5

**Distance** 19.2 km

**Time** 2-4 hours

**Map** 83 E/14 Grande Cache

**Season** June to mid-October

**Land agency** Alberta Forest Service

**Access**
From the intersection of Hwy. 40 and Hoppe Avenue in Grande Cache, follow Hwy. 40 south for 6.6 km to a turn-off to the left. Of the two roads at the trailhead, the trail is the rougher one to the right.

| | |
|---|---|
| 0.0 | trailhead |
| 9.6 | summit |

# 175 SMOKY RIVER TRAIL                    map 43

The Smoky River trail is the main northern access into the Willmore Wilderness and leads through one of the few remaining big wilderness valleys in the Canadian Rockies. It can be cycled as a one-day trip or as part of a multi-day exploration. Located in a major valley and with little elevation gain, this trail makes a good early season ride. During the hunting season, it is popular with equestrians.

The trail follows along an abandoned forest access road and the cycling is generally straightforward on a good, wide singletrack with some technical sections. Watch for loose gravel on the short but steep hills. This trail can be muddy in wet weather.

The initial section of trail contours along the hillside above the Smoky River with views back to Hell's Gate. A short and worthwhile spur trail leads to Eaton Creek Falls. Beyond the sidehill section the valley opens out and the trail passes through aspen forests and meadows, offering beautiful valley vistas at km 9 and 10. The trail continues, in much the same fashion, to the Muddywater River ford, a convenient turnaround point for day trippers.

**Options**

The Smoky Valley contains many areas suitable for foot exploration. The main trail continues up the Smoky River as well as up the Muddywater to Sheep Creek. The ford of the Muddywater River can be difficult and dangerous so be prepared to alter your plans according to water levels. Beyond the Muddywater the trail becomes more primitive and much more challenging to cycle. This is remote wilderness country suitable only for the skilled and well-prepared wilderness traveller.

**Wilderness explorer**

**Type** out-and-back on 4WD road and singletrack

**Rating** moderate/intermediate

**Other users** hikers-2  equestrian-5

**Distance** 31.4 km

**Time** 4-6 hours

**Map** 83 E/14 Grande Cache

**Season** May to mid-October

**Land agency** Alberta Provincial Parks

**Access**

Follow Hwy. 40 north from Grande Cache. Continue for 1.3 km beyond the highway bridge across the Smoky River, turning left onto the road leading to Willmore Wilderness Park and Hell's Gate. Follow this road for 6.4 km to the staging area and signed trailhead.

| | |
|---|---|
| 0.0 | trailhead |
| 3.1 | trail to Eaton Creek falls to right |
| 15.7 | Muddywater River crossing |

# 176 HAMELL LOOKOUT

map 43

Get ready for action! This trail is perfect for the advanced rider who has energy to burn and enjoys physical and technical challenges. Most people would enjoy the upper part of the mountain with its alpine tundra and expansive views in every direction, but owing to the overall steepness and strenuous riding, it is suitable only for the very fit.

The trail consists of a series of steep, difficult sections alternating with smooth, gentle rest areas. And rest you will need; even the strongest riders are likely to do a fair bit of pushing up this trail. Rain ruts and erosion gullies combine with loose rock of varying sizes on steep, hard-packed till. If all this scares you, then choose a different trip.

Views abound and, past km 6, the trail is in the alpine zone. It contours delightfully around Hammell Mountain before making the final climb to the summit and a fire lookout tower. The summit views encompass every direction. The trail continues beyond the lookout and descends gently along a high alpine ridge to a spectacular cliff-edge viewpoint overlooking the Smoky River.

Hammell Mountain can be very windy. How strong is the wind? Well... the day I cycled it the wind was so strong I felt like I was riding in a horizontal position on the trip to the viewpoint. The wind blew so hard I had to push my bike back to the summit and, at one point on the descent, I was pushed completely off of the trail by a sudden gust.

The descent of this trail is an adrenalin junky's delight. With gravity as your questionable ally, the ride down provides a serious challenge for the skilled downhill rider.

**Major vertical and great views**

**Type** out-and-back on 4WD roads

**Rating** difficult/advanced

**Other users** motorized-3

**Distance** 18.8 km

**Time** 3-5 hours

**Map** 83 E/14 Grande Cache

**Season** June to mid-October

**Land agency** Alberta Forest Service

**Access**
Follow Hwy. 40 north from Grande Cache. Continue for 5.3 km beyond the highway bridge across the Smoky River to a turn-off to the left, near a pipeline control valve. Three tracks diverge at the trailhead, the trail is the centre one.

| | |
|---|---|
| 0.0 | trailhead |
| 0.4 | junction, turn left |
| 0.7 | junction, turn right, uphill |
| 8.6 | lookout |
| 9.4 | viewpoint |

2    4    6    8    10    12    14    16    18.8

# 177 GRANDE CACHE TRAILS
map 43

The town of Grande Cache is situated in a beautiful mountain location near the confluence of two major rivers. Surrounding the town and crisscrossing the land between the Sulphur and Smoky rivers is an extensive network of trails that provides almost endless mountain biking opportunities. "Exploration" is the key word here. Hammer on the singletrack or doubletrack, or slow down and get in step with the forest around you. Listen to the birdsongs or ride silently to the Sulphur Gate. This area is a rolling upland covered with aspen, pine and spruce. To the south and west lie the wild peaks and valleys of the Willmore while, to the east, the town of Grande Cache nestles below the slopes of Grande Mountain.

Inquire locally for an up-to-date map of the trails. The trails are not signed or numbered so you will have to be careful to keep your bearings. The trails vary from old roads to dirt doubletrack and singletrack and most are used and maintained by quad riders and equestrians. You can expect to find the occasional windfallen tree and muddy section along with many kilometres of very pleasant cycling. Keep an eye open for wildlife: deer, moose, coyotes and bears may be seen in this area.

One popular route leads from town to Fireman's park and on along the Sulphur trail to the Sulphur Gate beside the Smoky River. Return to town by following your tracks or by cycling a loop of your choice.

**Network of trails**

**Type** loop on 4WD roads and singletrack

**Rating** moderate/intermediate

**Other users** hikers-2  motorized-2  equestrians-2

**Distance** 20+ km

**Time** 2+ hours

**Map**  83 E/14 Grande Cache

**Season** May to mid-October

**Land agency** Town of Grande Cache

**Access**
Begin in the town of Grande Cache and ride west on Hoppe Avenue to the signed trailhead on the left.

# 178 BERLAND RIVER TRAIL                    map 44

The Berland River trail begins in the foothills east of the Willmore Wilderness and follows alongside the river to the Adams Creek valley in the front ranges. It is a relatively easy cycle through classic east slopes wilderness, where hills and peaks are set off by attractive valley-bottom willow meadows.

The trail is an old road that offers easy riding on a gravel and dirt surface. There are a few minor stream crossings and the occasional muddy section, although the entire trail can be muddy during wet weather.

Follow the rough and sometimes muddy access road west from where you parked your car. At the fork at km 3.2, the preferred cycling route follows the old road to the right, climbing over a low saddle before descending back to the valley. (The left fork stays in the valley, but fords the Berland twice before rejoining the old road.) Beyond the Willmore boundary the trail is restricted to non-motorized traffic such as horses, wagons and, of course, bicycles. A prominent old road to the right at km 14.1 climbs to the Adams Lookout. At km 15.1 you reach a major trail junction where the main Berland trail branches to the left. Keep right at this junction and follow the road past a trapper's cabin and on to the beaver ponds along Adams Creek.

## Options

1. Determined cyclists can continue up the Adams Creek trail. It is still a part of the old road, but its surface deteriorates considerably depending on the wetness of the year.

2. Adams Lookout provides an interesting extension to the ride for those with energy to burn. The old road climbs 650 m in 4.4 km and the grades are variously steep or gentle, but most of the route is rideable. The final 2 km of the trail ascends a long alpine ridge with excellent views over the Rockies to the west and the foothills to the east. The ride down is fast.

**Wilderness explorer**

**Type** out-and-back on 4WD roads

**Rating** moderate/novice

**Other users** equestrian-5

**Distance** 32.8 km

**Time** 4-6 hours

**Maps** 83 E/9 Moberly Creek
83 E/10 Adams Lookout

**Season** June to mid-October

**Land agency** Alberta Forest Service, Alberta Provincial Parks

**Access**
From Hwy. 40 at the Big Berland recreation area, turn west and drive 0.9 km. Turn right, follow this road past two spurs to the right, and park 4.4 km from the highway. Beyond this point the access road deteriorates rapidly.

| | |
|---|---|
| 0.0 | trailhead |
| 3.2 | junction, keep right (trail to left crosses river two times, then rejoins) |
| 5.6 | Willmore boundary |
| 14.1 | junction, keep left (Adams Lookout to right) |
| 15.1 | junction, keep right (Berland River trail to left) |
| 15.7 | trapper's cabin |
| 16.4 | beaver ponds |

10        20        30   32.8

# 179 WILDHAY RIVER                                 map 44

The Wildhay trail offers the quintessential Will-more Wilderness cycling experience. It is a land of wide valleys and long-distance trails, and the combination of true wilderness, splendid scenery and a solid trail make this one of the outstanding backcountry rides in the Canadian Rockies. This trip is a good candidate for an overnight cycling excursion. The riding is generally easy with mini-mal elevation gain and the upper end of the valley has several optional trips that will keep you more than occupied. This prime wilderness country is popular with both equestrians and hikers; protect your right of access by treating other users with respect and consideration.

The Wildhay Valley lies between the Persim-mon Range to the west and the Hoff Range to the east. Much of the valley bottom, especially be-yond km 10, is a meadowland of grasses, willows and dwarf birch, and the mountain slopes are covered by spruce, pine and aspen forest. This ride is especially delightful in early September when the leaves have turned colour and the lime-stone peaks of the Persimmon Range are dusted with new snow.

The trail follows an old exploration road to the very heart of the eastern Willmore, providing generally easy riding on a dirt roadbed. Expect the occasional mud hole and some loose cobble sections, but the entire trail can be muddy in wet weather. Owing to heavy use by horses, and the frequently wet climate, this trail is prone to sections of seemingly endless stutter bumps. Riding these can be a v.v.very f.f.fatiguing e.e.experience.

The Wildhay River must be forded at km 4.3 and this can prove difficult during periods of high water, usually from mid-June to late July. At km 15.8 a spur trail to the right leads up Thoreau Creek and just beyond the junction stands an outrageously white AFS patrol cabin. The end of

**Classic wilderness ride**

**Type** out-and-back on 4WD roads

**Rating** difficult/novice

**Other users** hikers-2  equestrian-6

**Distance** 33.6 km

**Time** 5-7 hours

**Maps** 83 E/8 Rock Lake
83 E/9 Moberley Creek
83 E/10 Adams Lookout

**Season** mid-July to mid-October

**Land agency** Alberta Provincial Parks

**Access**
Rock Lake Road begins along Hwy. 40, 40 km north of the junction of Hwys. 40 and 16. Drive west for 33.6 km continuing past the Rock Lake recreation area to the Wildhay trailhead.

| | |
|---|---|
| 0.0 | trailhead |
| 1.7 | junction, keep right (Snake Indian valley to left) |
| 4.3 | Wildhay River ford |
| 6.8 | junction, keep right (track to Rock Lake tower to left) |
| 15.8 | Thoreau Creek trail to right |
| 15.9 | white AFS cabin |
| 16.8 | junction, end of ride (Eaglesnest Pass trail to left) (Indian trail to right) |

the ride is reached at a major trail junction at km 16.8. The fork to the left leads to Eaglesnest Pass while the one to the right, the Indian trail, continues up the Wildhay Valley and eventually crosses to the South Berland River.

**Options**

1. The Thoreau Creek trail leads to an alpine pass with mining relics to view along the way.

2. Eaglesnest Pass can be added to the Wildhay ride for a very rewarding day. It is 6.6 km one way to the pass.

3. Indian Trail. The old road continues up the Wildhay Valley and gradually deteriorates until a good singletrack is all that remains. The riding is still reasonable and the scenery is splendid. For an extended trip, the hard-core biker might descend the Berland and link up with ride #178, although several fords and hike-a-bike sections must be negotiated.

*Rock Creek valley.*

*Both photos Eaglesnest Pass.*

# 180 EAGLESNEST PASS & ROCK CREEK     map 44

This is a multi-day cycling trip suited to those who have lots of energy and are well prepared. Camping-out is essential if you are to have any time to enjoy the country and, in this case, enjoying the country is what the trip is all about. The beauty of Eaglesnest Pass is beyond words and provides a fitting gateway to the remote and peaceful wilderness of the Rock Creek valley. If you venture into this remote country, be sure to make thorough preparations—you must be self sufficient, both in terms of equipment and personal safety.

Begin by cycling the Wildhay River trail to km 16.8 and take the left fork, which leads to Eaglesnest Pass. This singletrack trail follows along an old seismic road with frequent detours around washed-out and muddy sections. The trail drops off the pass and reaches Rock Creek at a location known as Mile 51 camp. This valley is notable for the broad willow and grass meadow that stretches between the Starlight and Persimmon ranges. At km 33.8 the abandoned Mile 58 forestry patrol cabin stands sentinel and marks the end of the ride. Good camping spots abound.

**Options**

Several hikes are possible from Mile 58. Hardcore backcountry bikers may wish to continue onward. The road deteriorates and becomes a seismic line as it makes its way over a low pass into the drainage of the Sulphur River, then swings west. It crosses the South Sulphur River at about km 52 and continues up the valley of the West Sulphur River for another 5 km.

**Remote wilderness explorer**

**Type** out-and-back on 4WD road and singletrack

**Rating** difficult/intermediate

**Other users** equestrians-5

**Distance** 67.6 km

**Time** 2+ days

**Maps** 83 E/7 Blue Creek
83 E/10 Adams Lookout

**Season** July to mid-October

**Land agency** Alberta Provincial Parks

**Access**

This ride begins at the Wildhay trailhead near Rock Lake. Follow the Wildhay trail (#179) for 16.8 km to the point where the Eaglesnest trail branches to the left.

| | |
|---|---|
| 0.0 | trailhead |
| 16.8 | junction, turn left (right is Indian trail) |
| 23.4 | Eaglesnest Pass |
| 25.7 | junction at Mile 51 camp, keep right |
| 33.8 | Mile 58 cabin |

# 181 OGRE CANYON
map 45

This short, easy ride leads to a spectacular limestone canyon.

Beginning at the end of pavement in the historic coal-mining community of Brule, a well-compacted gravel and dirt road leads west to Ogre Creek. You will have to share the road with a few cars and, judging by the tracks in the dust, perhaps a bear or two. Along the way the road passes through a montane forest of spruce and aspen, an area resplendent in autumn. The limestone crags of Bedson Ridge tower above the trail while to the south lie the railway and the flat, gray expanse of Brule Lake. Two short access roads lead to the railway and provide foot access to the shore of the lake. Across the lake rise the front range peaks of Roche a Perdrix and Roche Miette.

Ogre Creek marks the end of the road and from there a short singletrack leads for 0.5 km to the canyon. On a hot day it's fun to wade through the plunge pools to the base of the falls in the inner recesses of the canyon.

The roads beyond Ogre Creek have been closed and rehabilitated by the Forest Service. They provide startling evidence of the erosive power that wind and water can have on sandy soils once the vegetation has been removed.

## Options

Several old roads and trails lead to the site of the old Brule Mines on the hillside just above town.

**Gentle ride to deep canyon**

**Type** out-and-back on 4WD roads

**Rating** easy/novice

**Other users** equestrian-2 motorized-5 livestock

**Distance** 16 km

**Time** 2-3 hours

**Maps** 83 F/4 Miette 83 F/5 Entrance

**Season** May to mid-October

**Land agency** Alberta Forest Service

## Access

This trip begins at the village of Brule, located 16 km west of Hwy. 40 on Brule Road. Begin from anywhere in the village and ride west on the only road leading out of town.

| | |
|---|---|
| 0.0 | trailhead |
| 7.5 | Ogre Creek, follow singletrack to right |
| 8.0 | Ogre Canyon |

## 182 BRULE LAKE DUNES                           map 45

Photo: Jim Greenfield.

**Scenic and historic ride with sand dune treats**

**Type** out-and-back on 4WD roads and singletrack

**Rating** difficult/intermediate

**Other users** motorized-6

**Distance** 24.2 km

**Time** 3-4 hours

**Maps** 83 F/4 Miette
83 F/5 Entrance

**Season** May through October

**Land agency** Alberta Forest Service

**Access**
Begin at a side road on the north side of Hwy. 16, 0.2 km west of Overlander Lodge.

| | |
|---|---|
| 0.0 | trailhead |
| 0.3 | keep left |
| 0.4 | keep left |
| 1.1 | turn right |
| 2.3 | turn left |
| 2.6 | campsite, keep left |
| 4.2 | Brule Lake |
| 11.5 | trail climbs up to a stony bench |
| 11.9 | follow track to right into dunes |
| 12.0 | cross creek |
| 12.1 | train station |

This ride leads through a region of sand dunes along the east shore of Brule Lake. The dunes are very active and are constantly shifting in the wind. Classic dune vegetation, dramatic front range scenery and a large shallow lake complete the setting. The Grand Trunk Pacific Railway was constructed through the dunes in 1910 and abandoned some six years later. Artifacts include partially buried telegraph poles and the old Park Gate train station. The dunes attract a fun-loving group of folks, many on motorbikes, so be prepared—weekdays are quiet, weekends are not. This ride is so incredible that the minor annoyance of motors is a small price to pay for its many redeeming values.

Ride down the old roads, then along the quad track. Beyond the camp it becomes narrower and sandy with some very exciting bermed corners as it descends to the shores of Brule Lake. This shallow lake is almost completely filled with fine silt and sand. Notice the partially buried telegraph poles that mark the former track bed—it's almost always windy here and the sand is always on the move.

Time to test your sand riding technique—keep the weight back and no sudden movements, you'll find it's easier to ride on the wet sand along

Photo: Jim Greenfield.

the shore. Take time to check out the views of Boule Range to the west and Roche Miette to the south. The great dunes at km 8 are simply irresistible so take time to drop a few dunes, a little sand never hurt anyone. Also take time to check out the motorized folks, you'll find them friendly and some are amazingly talented riders.

About km 11.5 the quad track climbs up onto a gravel bench blown free of sand and leads back into the dunes. The partially collapsed Park Gate train station is a hidden surprise buried in the sand with no other evidence of the railway to be found. The trail continues up to the Wildhorse Lake road but the station makes a good point to turn back and retrace your tracks to the trailhead or, if you have two vehicles, try the option.

### Options

The old rail bed continues east to Hwy. 40. To ride the rail-trail return to the lakeshore and continue downstream to km 15 where the quad track climbs up into the dunes and onto the track bed. Ride the rails, so to speak, with a minor detour at km 24.1, turn left on a logging road at km 25, cross the railway and continue on the rough road to Hwy. 40 at km 28.

# 183 OVERLANDER LODGE TRAILS

map 45

Do you have the urge to explore? These trails are an unmapped maze with something for everyone. It's a network of trails that begin at the lodge and radiate out into the hills to the north and extend to the shores of Brule Lake (see #182) and the park boundary. The setting is grand—a south-facing slope overlooking the Athabasca Valley where the river exits the Rockies.

Parts of the area were once logged and have now revegetated. Stands of aspen tremble in the breeze and turn golden in the autumn. This entire area is a wildlife sanctuary so you won't have to dodge hunter's bullets. This is, in all, a perfect fall ride.

Novices can roll along easy doubletracks and through vista-charged meadows; hard-cores can hammer to their hearts' content on singletrack and doubletrack. These trails are used each spring for the annual Overlander Overender mountain bike race. You must be prepared to share these popular trails with equestrians and some ATVs.

The trails are doubletrack and singletrack on gravel, dirt and sand, and they can be muddy in wet weather. I suggest you ride north from the lodge, then explore the singletracks that branch off of the powerline/pipeline right-of-way. "Exploration" is the key word here, but don't forget how to get back to the lodge.

**Network of trails**

**Type** loop and out-and-back on 4WD roads and singletrack

**Rating** moderate/intermediate

**Other users** equestrian-5 motorized-5

**Distance** 20+ km

**Time** 2+ hours

**Maps** 83 F/4 Miette
83 F/5 Entrance

**Season** May to mid-October

**Land agency** private, Alberta Forest Service

**Access**
Begin at Overlander Lodge, just east of the east boundary of Jasper Park on Hwy. 16. The trails lie immediately north of the lodge.

# 184 WHITEHORSE CREEK                                          map 46

**Rugged ride below jagged limestone peaks**

**Type** out-and-back on 4WD roads

**Rating** moderate/novice

**Other users** equestrian-3 motorized-3

**Distance** 24.8 km

**Time** 3-4 hours

**Maps** 83 C/13 Medicine Lake
83 C/14 Mountain Park
83 F/3 Cadomin
83 F/4 Miette

**Season** June to mid-October

**Land agency** Alberta Forest Service

**Access**
Take the gravel road south from Cadomin for 6 km to the Whitehorse Creek Equestrian Staging Area (56 km south of Hwy. 16). The trail begins at the west end of the staging area.

| | |
|---|---|
| 0.0 | trailhead |
| 0.7 | junction, keep left |
| 1.0 | junction, keep right |
| 4.5 | junction, keep left |
| 7.7 | junction, keep left (Fiddle Pass to right) |
| 11.2 | junction, turn left |
| 12.4 | end of trail |

This is front-range riding at its finest. The trail leads to the very heart of a range of jagged limestone peaks and much of the valley bottom is an expansive willow meadow laced with a sparkling stream.

The trail is an old logging skid road kept in good condition through continual usage by horses and ATVs. There are several easy fords, some rocky stretches and a few mud holes but, in general, the riding is smooth and easy. Follow the trail to its end at the foot of a waterfall below four precipitous limestone faces. There is a camping spot here for those so inclined and a footpath climbs above the falls.

## Options

This ride can be combined with a trip to Fiddle Pass (#185).

# 185 FIDDLE PASS

map 46

**Rugged ride to high alpine pass**

**Type** out-and-back on 4WD roads and singletrack

**Rating** difficult/intermediate

**Other users** equestrians-3 motorized-3

**Distance** 26 km

**Time** 4-5 hours

**Maps** 83 F/3 Cadomin
83 F/4 Miette

**Season** July to mid-October

**Land agency** Alberta Forest Service

**Access**
Take the gravel road south from Cadomin for 6 km to the Whitehorse Creek Equestrian Staging Area (56 km south of Hwy. 16). The trail begins at the west end of the staging area.

Do you like technical riding? How about trails that lead through alpine meadows? This trip offers an unbeatable combination of doubletrack, singletrack, technical delights and scenic extras.

Take the Whitehorse Creek trail to km 7.7, then follow a prominent trail leading uphill to the right. Most of this trail is rideable as it climbs gently but steadily to a series of alpine meadows and basins, culminating at Fiddle Pass. Initially a wide singletrack, at km 10.3 the trail narrows considerably and becomes more technical and a lot more fun. You hard-core bikers who continue onward will be rewarded by some challenging technical riding in a beautiful alpine setting. Fiddle Pass marks the boundary of Jasper National Park and the end of the ride.

## Options

There are extensive alpine meadows, basins and ridges to be explored in this area. Several of the nearby peaks can be ascended by scrambling and this is a good area for viewing wildlife.

| | |
|---|---|
| 0.0 | trailhead |
| 0.7 | junction, keep left |
| 1.0 | junction, keep right |
| 4.5 | junction, keep left |
| 7.7 | junction, turn right (Whitehorse Creek to left) |
| 10.3 | narrow singletrack begins |
| 13.0 | Fiddle Pass |

2   4   6   8   10   12   14   16   18   20   22   24   26

# 186 CARDINAL DIVIDE                                    map 46

The Cardinal Divide is a windswept alpine tundra overlooking the McLeod River to the north and the Cardinal River to the south. This divide marks the watershed between the Athabasca River drainage flowing to the Arctic Ocean via the Mackenzie River and the North Saskatchewan River drainage flowing to Hudson Bay.

The travelling is wide open and exploration is the key to having fun here. Rocky doubletracks lead along the ridge to the east and west of the road at the summit.

The valley to the north of Cardinal Divide is the location of the proposed Cheviot Mine. Although the divide is a protected area, you can expect changes in access and esthetics.

**Alpine ridge explorer**

**Type** out-and-back on 4WD roads

**Rating** moderate/intermediate

**Other users** motorized-7

**Distance** 10+ km

**Time** 2+ hours

**Map** 83 C/14 Mountain Park

**Season** July to mid-October

**Land agency** Alberta Forest Service

**Access**
Take the gravel road south from Cadomin for 21 km to the summit of the Cardinal Divide (71.5 km south of Hwy. 16). The trail is the 4WD road climbing to the east and west of the summit.

Photo: Gillean Daffern.

# 187  CARDINAL RIVER                                            map 46

*Rocky Pass.*

This trail leads to the headwaters of the Cardinal River amidst spectacular front range peaks. Elevation gain is minimal as the trail passes through willow meadows and forests of pine and spruce.

A former seismic line, the trail is used extensively by ATVs. It varies from dirt to gravel with a few poorly-drained sections made considerably worse by ATV use. After 4.6 km the trail turns north and winds its way to the inner valley beneath the cliffs of Prospect Mountain in the Nikanassin Range.

**Rocky Pass Option**

Cycling to Rocky Pass is strictly for the gonzo rider. It provides the access or exit for the Rocky River Rider cycle trip (#189) through Jasper National Park. The fact that a 1 km push or carry is rewarded by only 1 km of riding in the alpine meadows at the pass makes this route more feasible as a hike.

If you choose to go anyway, follow the main horse trail that leaves the Cardinal River trail at km 1.9. The trail wanders along the valley bottom for 2.7 km, crossing the river three times. Bikes can be left near the third crossing, after which the trail is steep and unrideable for 1 km until the alpine meadows are reached. The final kilometre to the pass offers exciting riding in a spectacular setting.

**Wilderness explorer**

**Type** out-and-back on 4WD roads and singletrack

**Rating** moderate/intermediate

**Other users** equestrians-3 motorized-5

**Distance** 18 km

**Time** 3-4 hours

**Map** 83 C/14 Mountain Park

**Season** July to mid-October

**Land agency** Alberta Forest Service

**Access**
Take the gravel road south from Cadomin for 22.6 km to an obvious trailhead on the right (73.1 km south of Hwy. 16). The trail is the seismic line heading west.

| | |
|---|---|
| 0.0 | trailhead |
| 1.9 | junction, keep right (Rocky Pass trail to left) |
| 4.6 | junction, keep right (left leads to river and Rocky Pass) |
| 9.0 | end of road |

# 188 JACQUES LAKE                                    map 46

This is a fun ride in a beautiful valley dotted with pretty turquoise lakes and surrounded by rugged limestone peaks. The trail leads through a narrow pass between the crags of the Colin Range and the Queen Elizabeth Range, then descends gently to Jacques Lake.

The ride begins on a smooth, hard-packed old road that leads up the valley to Beaver Lake, a blue-green beauty tucked beneath the steep, grey limestone slabs of the Queen Elizabeth Range. The road ends at the two Summit Lakes, which straddle a drainage divide. It is difficult to tell which way they flow because there is no visible outlet. Sirdar is the imposing mountain beyond the lakes and was probably named after Field Marshall Lord Kitchener (1850-1916) who was made "sirdar," or commander, of the Egyptian Army. Lovely, peaceful surroundings and easy cycling suitable for families and tot-trailers make this the perfect destination for a lazy day.

Cyclists continuing on to Jacques Lake will, however, have anything but a lazy day. From South Summit Lake onward the trail is a basic, backcountry singletrack. This means that it is muddy, rocky and laced with roots—perfect terrain for the advanced rider looking for a skill-testing ride. The trail is about 90 per cent rideable, possibly more in a dry year, and it is just possible that some of you may be able to clean it! This is a trail where choosing the right line makes the difference between those who ride and those who push.

Jacques Lake is a delightful spot with a campground, bridge and warden cabin at the east end. Take a break, then begin the challenging return trip.

**Options**

The out-and-back trip to South Summit Lake is a 10 km easy/novice ride suitable for families.

**Family fun to Summit Lakes/ technical delights beyond**

**Type** out-and-back on 4WD roads and singletrack

**Rating** difficult/intermediate

**Other users** hikers-5 equestrian-3

**Distance** 24.6 km

**Time** 4-5 hours

**Map** 83 C/13 Medicine Lake

**Season** May to mid-October

**Land agency** Parks Canada

**Access**

In Jasper National Park, drive up Maligne Lake Road for 30 km to a picnic area at the southeast end of Medicine Lake. The trail starts at a gated road in the picnic area.

0.0   trailhead
1.6   Beaver Lake
5.0   South Summit Lake singletrack begins
6.4   North Summit Lake
11.2  junction, keep right
12.2  Jacques Lake campsite
12.3  bridge

# 189 ROCKY RIVER RIDER

map 46

This strenuous ride takes you through the Rocky River valley and some very remote wilderness country in the front ranges of Jasper National Park. It is essential that you be prepared for any situation that might arise—be it mechanical or otherwise. There are no feasible alternate exits from the trail in case of difficulties. Cycling this trail requires a very long day, but this is preferable to overnighting unless you are comfortable riding technical singletrack with a pack on your back. The trail can be cycled in either direction and, in either case, a long car shuttle or a pick up will have to be arranged.

Begin by riding the trail to Jacques Lake. If you find this trail too demanding, then forget about the Rocky River trail; once you depart Jacques Lake you must be totally committed to completing the trip. The trail descends gradually for 11 km into the valley of the Rocky River. The next 36 km is rough riding on valley bottom singletrack. This long section of trail is mostly hidden away in the forest where the occasional meadow provides a view of the surrounding peaks. There is a bridged crossing of the Rocky River at km 33. In the Rocky Forks area the forest becomes more open and a large meadow lies to the west near the warden cabin, providing a dramatic view of Mount Balcarres.

Beyond Rocky Forks the trail begins to climb as it follows the Medicine Tent River for 10 km to the junction with the trail to Rocky Pass. The ascent to the pass is as rough and rocky as it is beautiful, and some pushing will be required to reach the alpine meadows at the summit. Follow the Rocky Pass option of the Cardinal River trail (#187) to the trailhead near the Cardinal Divide.

**Remote wilderness ride**

**Type** point-to-point on singletrack

**Rating** extreme/advanced

**Other users** hikers-3  equestrian-4

**Distance** 69.3 km one way

**Time** 10-12 hours

**Maps** 83 C/13 Medicine Lake
83 C/14 Mountain Park

**Season** July to mid-October

**Land agency** Parks Canada

**Access**

**west**  Same as the Jacques Lake trail (#188).

**east**  Begin on Cardinal River trail (#187). Follow the Rocky Pass option.

| | |
|---|---|
| 0.0 | west trailhead |
| 12.3 | Jacques Lake |
| 23.3 | Rocky River valley |
| 33.3 | Rocky River bridge |
| 49.3 | junction, keep left (Rocky Forks area to right across river) |
| 59.3 | junction, turn left (South Boundary trail to right) |
| 62.6 | Rocky Pass |
| 67.4 | junction with Cardinal River trail, turn right |
| 69.3 | east trailhead |

# 190 OVERLANDER TRAIL
maps 47, 48

Here is your chance to pedal your fat tires in the footsteps of explorers, fur traders, gold seekers and homesteaders. This trail begins as an easy valley-bottom roll and ends with a challenging sidehill singletrack. It provides a very satisfying ride in either direction.

The Overlander trail is part of a historic route through the Rockies that has been in use for centuries. Used in prehistoric times by native people, this was the route followed by the fur brigades as they travelled between Jasper House and the Athabasca Pass and, in later years, the Yellowhead Pass. In 1862 a large group of people travelled this route on their way "over land" to the Cariboo gold fields and it is from them that the trail takes its name. By the late 1800s several families had settled in the valley, but they moved from the area in 1907 when the Jasper Forest Park was created. A few years later two transcontinental railways were built through the valley, but today only one railway remains, along with a major highway and a pipeline.

Start at the Sixth Bridge crossing of the Maligne River and follow the road toward the park horse facility, keeping left on singletrack just before the gate. The trail winds through a forest of Douglas fir, lodgepole pine and aspen, then crosses some beautiful grassy meadows. The wildly upthrust ridges of the Colin Range form the eastern wall of the valley while Pyramid Mountain and the valley of the Snaring River form the western skyline. The ruins of the John Moberly homestead lie beside the trail at km 7.

**Singletrack treats along historic route**

**Type** loop on 2WD roads and singletrack

**Rating** moderate/intermediate

**Other users** hikers-4 equestrian-3

**Distance** 36.2 km (20.5 km on pavement)

**Time** 3-5 hours

**Maps** 83 D/16 Jasper
83 E/1 Snaring

**Season** late April through October

**Land agency** Parks Canada

**Access**
**south** In Jasper National Park, the trail begins at the Sixth Bridge picnic area off of the Maligne Lake Road. Cycle across the bridge and follow the gravel road.

**north** The signed trailhead is just east of the Athabasca River bridge, 16.5 km east of Jasper on Hwy. 16.

| | |
|---|---|
| 0.0 | trailhead at Sixth Bridge |
| 0.8 | keep left on singletrack |
| 1.5 | junction, keep right |
| 2.5 | trail makes sharp left |
| 7.0 | Moberley buildings |
| 15.0 | junction, keep right |
| 15.7 | Hwy. 16, turn left |
| 16.2 | Athabasca River bridge |
| 32.2 | junction with Maligne Road, turn left |
| 34.5 | turn left to Sixth Bridge picnic area |
| 36.2 | end of ride |

Beyond the homestead the character of the trail changes as the river squeezes it onto the rocky side wall of the valley. The trail becomes a challenging skill-tester as it winds its way across a series of exciting sidehills and gullies. Glide through a "mossway" and on into the black forest.

Park wardens burned this forest in 1989. The legacy of Smoky the Bear had become so effective that habitat for the herd of bighorn sheep living here was rapidly disappearing. Grasses now flourish amongst the charred sentinels of the old forest. Watch for sheep on the cliffs and ridges along this section of the trail. Morro Canyon provides an opportunity, for those with time to spare, to check out the local limestone. Two trails descend to Highway 16 near the Cold Sulphur Spring, the one to the right provides the easiest riding. Return to your start point by riding on Highway 16 and Maligne Lake Road.

# 191 MALIGNE CANYON TO OLD FORT POINT   map 48

This trail offers a mellow cycling tour of the Athabasca Valley at Jasper. It's a fascinating place with forests of Douglas fir, lodgepole pine and spruce, and some expansive grassy meadows. Highlights include some very pretty lakes that are often warm enough for a swim, the muddy, roiling waters of the Athabasca River, and the rushing waters, springs and canyon of the Maligne River. The trail is marked with #7 signs throughout. Be prepared to share the trail with horses and hikers. Watch for bears and elk.

Follow the trail north along the river shore as it passes Jasper Park Lodge (or take the paved road that goes the same way). Cross Maligne Road and once again ride the shoreline singletrack to the Sixth Bridge picnic area beside the Maligne River. Ride across the bridge and follow the trail to the right beside the rushing waters of the Maligne River. The trail passes a number of springs where subterranean channels discharge water that has flowed underground for 16 km from Medicine Lake. Upstream of the Fifth Bridge lies Maligne Canyon, one of the most popular attractions in Jasper. Cycling is not allowed on the trails along the canyon rim to avoid conflicts with hikers, however, I highly recommend pushing your bike along this super-scenic section of trail.

From the top of the canyon cross the highway bridge and pick up trail #7 as it enters the trees to the left. A fast and fun descent returns you to the valley bottom where the trail briefly joins an old paved road before departing to the left. The smooth, sandy trail is swoopy-fast and well marked as it rolls through the woods back of Lake Edith and Lake Annette, then climbs around the golf course on its way back to Old Fort Point.

**Family fun on gentle trail**

**Type** loop on singletrack

**Rating** easy/intermediate

**Other users** hikers-4   equestrian-6

**Distance** 24 km

**Time** 2-4 hours

**Maps** 83 D/16 Jasper
83 C/13 Medicine Lake

**Season** late April through October

**Land agency** Parks Canada

**Access**
Begin at Old Fort Point, on the east side of the Athabasca River near Jasper townsite.

| | |
|---|---|
| 0.0 | trailhead, follow trail #7 north alongside river |
| 5.0 | cross Maligne Lake Road |
| 8.8 | Sixth Bridge picnic area, cross bridge, turn right |
| 10.5 | junction, keep left and push bike for 2.2 km alongside Maligne Canyon |
| 12.7 | Maligne Canyon parking lot |
| 13.0 | Maligne Lake Road, turn right, cross bridge, trail leads uphill to left |
| 13.9 | cross Signal Mountain Road |
| 16.3 | junction with old road, keep left and follow #7 signs |
| 17.7 | junction, keep left |
| 19.8 | junction, keep left (right goes to Jasper Park Lodge) |
| 22.3 | junction, keep left |
| 23.0 | junction, keep right (Valley of Five trail to left) |
| 24.0 | trailhead |

# 192 SIGNAL MOUNTAIN LOOKOUT                    map 48

Photo: John Gibson.

**Major vertical and great views**
**Type** out-and-back on 4WD road
**Rating** difficult/novice
**Other users** hikers-6
**Distance** 18.8 km
**Time** 3-5 hours
**Maps** 83 D/16 Jasper
83 C/13 Medicine Lake
**Season** June through October
**Land agency** Parks Canada

**Access**
The trailhead is located at km 5.3
of Maligne Lake Road.

| | |
|---|---|
| 0.0 | trailhead |
| 8.4 | campsite |
| 8.5 | Skyline trail to left |
| 9.4 | summit |

Here we go again—sweat and grunt uphill, race downhill. This now-closed access road leads to a nonexistent fire lookout and offers the key to one of Jasper's best views. You can count on meeting lots of hikers as this is the northern end of the popular Skyline trail.

Select a suitably easy gear and begin the long uphill grind. The road makes a number of big switchbacks as it climbs up the mountain at continuously rideable grades. Not soon enough, it leaves the trees behind and climbs across the alpine tundra to the site of the old fire lookout where a wonderfully panoramic vista awaits. The town of Jasper lies at your feet and the Athabasca, Miette and Maligne valleys reach to the four points of the compass.

When you have had your fill of views it is time to check your brakes and peel off the summit. Here is a chance to practise your high-speed handling skills (or learn them!). Always ride in control of your bicycle.

2     4     6     8     10     12     14     16     18.8

# 193 VALLEY OF FIVE LAKES & WABASSO LAKE   maps 48, 49

Pleasant singletrack riding on a popular trail, this trip utilizes the Icefields Parkway and the Valley of Five Lakes trail signed #9 to create a loop that can be cycled from Jasper townsite. The trail traverses a number of quartzite ridges that resemble the Canadian Shield in northern Ontario or Manitoba. When it runs parallel to the ridges it is mostly smooth and sandy, where it crosses the ridges it is rough and rocky. This trail provides delightful cycling on relatively level terrain with a few challenging technical sections. Watch for hikers and equestrians throughout.

Begin by pounding the pavement to the south trailhead and rolling into the woods. This part of the trail is a bit rough with some technical goodies to test your skills as the trail climbs over a number of rocky ridges. Soon you'll be rolling along the shores of Wabasso Lake, a peaceful but popular fishing spot. Beyond the lake the trail follows alongside marshy Wabasso Creek—a rich wildlife habitat that numbers great blue herons and beaver among its inhabitants. The name Wabasso is derived from the Cree word for "rabbit."

About half way to the Valley of Five Lakes the trail leaves the forest to cross Prairie de la Vache, or Buffalo Prairie, a dry, open river terrace with expansive views.

Turn right at the four-way trail junction and follow the trail as it crosses a ridge and drops into the Valley of the Five Lakes. These jade-green beauties are a popular destination for hikers and equestrians too; cautious cycling is in order. The trail crosses to the north side of the valley and winds through an open forest of Douglas fir beside the lakes. Beyond the lakes the trail again takes to the uplands and ridges providing some exciting technical action. Near Old Fort Point, the left branch of the trail ends with stairs while the right branch has a good, but steep, gravel track leading down to the parking lot.

**Singletrack treats**

**Type** loop on 2WD roads and singletrack

**Rating** moderate/intermediate

**Other users** hikers-6  equestrian-3

**Distance** 37.8 km (15.5 km on pavement)

**Time** 2-4 hours

**Maps** 83 D/16 Jasper
83 C/13 Medicine Lake

**Season** late April through October

**Land agency** Parks Canada

**Access**
**north** Begin at Old Fort Point, on the east side of the Athabasca River near Jasper townsite.

**south** Begin at the Wabasso Lake trailhead, 16 km south of Jasper on Hwy. 93.

| | |
|---|---|
| 0.0 | north trailhead, cycle south on Hwy. 93 |
| 10.0 | Valley of the Five trailhead, continue south on highway |
| 15.5 | south (Wabasso Lake) trailhead |
| 17.6 | junction, turn left up switchback |
| 19.2 | Wabasso Lake |
| 20.5 | junction with Shovel Pass trail, keep left |
| 26.0 | four-way junction, turn right (left leads to Hwy. 93, straight ahead avoids the Five Lakes) |
| 26.3 | junction, keep right |
| 27.0 | Valley of the Five Lakes |
| 27.5 | junction, keep left |
| 30.5 | junction, keep right |

**Options**

1. There are many ways to customize this ride: for example, a shorter trip can be made by beginning at the Valley of the Five Lakes trailhead located 10.5 km south of Jasper.

2. For those who delight in long singletrack rides, I recommend a 40 km figure-eight loop from Old Fort Point trailhead. Ride the trail south to the Valley of Five Lakes, then out to Hwy. 93. Head south, then follow the trail to Wabasso Lake and on to the four-way junction. Continue straight through and rejoin the Valley of Five Lakes trail to return to Old Fort Point.

| | |
|---|---|
| 35.5 | junction, keep right on trail #1A |
| 36.8 | junction with trail #7, keep left |
| 37.8 | end of ride |

# 194 PALISADES LOOKOUT                              maps 47, 48

Oh no! Not another fire lookout! Dude—relax, Palisades is better than most. Getting there will provide you with a good aerobic workout, the view from the top is superb and the roll back to town is swift and thrilling.

From the gate at the trailhead, follow the good gravel of the Pyramid Mountain communication facility access road. The road rocks and rolls along the shore of Pyramid Lake, then gradually climbs toward the Palisades. Turn right at the junction at km 7.7 onto the much rougher and steeper road leading to the old lookout site. It is all rideable, although a rest stop or two along the way could be justified.

The lookout was removed about 1979, but they sure didn't remove the view. This looks out over the broad Athabasca River as it flows toward the edge of the mountains. The rugged limestone peaks of the Colin Range form the dramatic eastern skyline and to the south, Mount Edith Cavell and the upper Athabasca Valley highlight the main ranges of the Rockies.

The ride back is fast paced to say the least. Watch for vehicles on the access road. The inviting waters of Pyramid Lake offer the perfect post-ride cool down.

## Options

Keep left at the junction at km 7.7 and cycle 3.3 km to the CN telecommunications installation at the base of Pyramid Mountain. From here it is possible to explore the timberline meadows or scramble to the summit of the mountain.

**Major vertical and great views**
**Type** out-and-back on 4WD roads
**Rating** difficult/intermediate
**Other users** hikers-2  motorized-1
**Distance** 22 km
**Time** 3-4 hours
**Map** 83 D/16 Jasper
**Season** mid-May to mid-October
**Land agency** Parks Canada

### Access
In the town of Jasper, follow Pyramid Lake Road for 6.7 km to its end at a locked gate beside Pyramid Lake.

| | |
|---|---|
| 0.0 | trailhead |
| 7.7 | junction, turn right (left leads to base of Pyramid Mountain) |
| 11.0 | summit |

# 195 MINA & RILEY LAKES

map 48

Although the Pyramid Bench, known locally as "The Bench," is laced with trails, only three of them are open for cycling. Most are heavily used by equestrians rendering them into a churned up mess that you wouldn't want to ride through anyway. With lots of other users on the trails, caution and courtesy are essential.

The Bench is a rolling upland situated higher than, and just to the north of, Jasper. It is a land of rocky quartzite ridges and gentle valleys, many of which contain small lakes. The vegetation consists of everything from Douglas fir to lodgepole pine, juniper, aspen and marshlands.

Begin this ride by cycling up the Cabin Lake fireroad. The Mina-Riley loop is signed as trail #8. It can be cycled in either direction, although a clockwise direction will put most of the elevation gain on the gravel road. Take the second #8 fork to the right, then ride along a wide, sometimes rooty singletrack frequented by horses. Pass a small lake on your left before coming to Mina Lake with its heavily trampled shoreline area, clearly a favourite place for horse "parties." Continue on the sometimes rooty and muddy singletrack to the Riley Lake trail junction. It is a 1 km side trip to the shore of this quiet lake. From Riley Lake, return to the loop and, turning left, climb over a low hill on a good trail that is only occasionally used by horses. A long, gently winding, fun singletrack descends back to the fireroad. Roll along the road back to town.

## Options

You can return to Jasper by following the fireroad to Cabin Lake, then turning left onto an exciting singletrack trail that descends across a steep hillside to town.

## Rugged ride to lakes

**Type** loop on 4WD roads and singletrack

**Rating** moderate/intermediate

**Other users** hikers-4  equestrian-5

**Distance** 12.5 km

**Time** 1-3 hours

**Map** 83 D/16 Jasper

**Season** May through October

**Land agency** Parks Canada

## Access

Begin in Jasper at the intersection of Pyramid Avenue and Pyramid Lake Road and cycle north toward Pyramid Lake.

| | |
|---|---|
| 0.0 | trailhead at intersection of Pyramid and Pyramid in Jasper |
| 1.8 | turn left onto the Cabin Creek fireroad |
| 2.3 | junction, keep left |
| 3.5 | junction, turn right (left continues to Cabin Lake) |
| 4.7 | Mina Lake |
| 5.2 | junction, keep right |
| 6.2 | junction, turn left |
| 7.2 | Riley Lake, retrace tracks to junction |
| 8.2 | junction, turn left |
| 10.2 | junction with fireroad, turn left |
| 10.7 | Pyramid Lake Drive, turn right |
| 12.5 | end of ride |

# 196 SATURDAY NIGHT LAKE                    map 48

Saturday Night Lake is a small lake nestled between quartzite ridges on the upper part of Pyramid Bench below Cairngorm Mountain. The trail begins as a doubletrack, then becomes one of Jasper's finest singletracks as it snakes its way up to the lake.

Begin by cycling up trail #2 from town and turn left onto Cabin Lake fireroad. Climb up the hill and roll along the townsite fireguard to Cabin Lake, formerly the town water supply. Ride west on the smooth needle-covered singletrack as it winds its way across hillsides and climbs gently but relentlessly onto the upper part of The Bench. From the trail junction at km 10 a spur trail leads 0.5 km uphill to the lake.

The return ride on this fast swoopy singletrack is one of the best, but beware—it's possible to ride very fast so give other users a brake!

## Options

You can avoid the fireroad section of the trail by beginning at the trailhead on Cabin Creek Road and riding up the singletrack to Cabin Lake. This 2.2 km trail joins the route log at km 5.3.

**Singletrack treats**

**Type** out-and-back on 4WD roads and singletrack

**Rating** moderate/intermediate

**Other users** hikers-4 equestrian-3

**Distance** 21 km

**Time** 2-3 hours

**Map** 83 D/16 Jasper

**Season** May through October

**Land agency** Parks Canada

**Access**

In Jasper townsite, begin at the intersection of Pyramid Lake Drive and Pyramid Avenue. Trail #2 leads uphill above the road.

| | |
|---|---|
| 0.0 | trailhead |
| 1.8 | turn left onto Cabin Lake fireroad |
| 5.3 | Cabin Lake, keep right on singletrack (optional start joins route here) |
| 10.0 | junction, turn right up hill |
| 10.5 | Saturday Night Lake |

# 197 MINNOW LAKE                    map 48

**Singletrack treats**
**Type** out-and-back on singletrack
**Rating** moderate/intermediate
**Other users** hikers-4 equestrian-2
**Distance** 20 km
**Time** 2-3 hours
**Map** 83 D/16 Jasper
**Season** May through October
**Land agency** Parks Canada

**Access**
In Jasper townsite, begin at the trailhead on Cabin Creek Road. Follow the trail to the left.

| | |
|---|---|
| 0.0 | trailhead |
| 2.3 | Marjorie Lake |
| 2.6 | trail to Hibernia Lake to right |
| 3.9 | junction, keep right |
| 4.3 | Caledonia Lake |
| 9.4 | junction, keep left |
| 10.0 | Minnow Lake |

Minnow Lake trail traverses the valleys and ridges of Pyramid Bench, passing several small lakes and ending at Minnow Lake. This is a smooth, swoopy, needle-covered singletrack trail that gains a fair bit of elevation en route to the lake.

The trail leads behind some residences before climbing up a hill to the town fireguard, keep right and climb into the valley that contains Marjorie and Caledonia lakes. Past the lakes it climbs steadily, but it's always rideable as it climbs onto quartzite ridges and snakes along sidehills. At km 9.4 the Minnow trail branches to the left and ends at a campsite on the lakeshore. Elysium Mountain is the pyramid-shaped peak in the distance. The return ride is very fast and exciting as the trail swoops and carves its way across ridges and sidehills and dives down the valleys. Watch for others and be courteous as you speed down this fabulous trail.

2    4    6    8    10    12    14    16    18    20

# 198 TWENTY MILE CIRCLE                                    map 48

Twenty Mile Circle consists of two fast, swoopy, fun singletracks linked by a more difficult and demanding section of trail that will challenge the skills of advanced riders. Many cyclists choose the option of out-and-back rides on Saturday Night Lake (#196) and Minnow Lake (#197) trails rather than the loop ride. This trail works equally well in either direction, the description is for a counterclockwise ride.

Follow the route of the Saturday Night Lake ride by travelling north on Cabin Creek Road, then following Pyramid Lake Road to join the fireroad to Cabin Lake. From the lake ride the smooth singletrack as it rolls past marsh-filled hollows and climbs over Douglas fir-lined ridges of quartzite. After a brief excursion to Saturday Night Lake continue up the trail.

Beyond the junction, the trail quickly loses its well-travelled appearance and, the farther you advance toward the far point of the loop near High Lakes, the more basic the trail becomes. Low bushes close in, rocks abound, roots are everywhere and what trail there is, is frequently wet. Negotiating this section is a good challenge for a skilled rider. Overall, this trail seems unable to make up its mind—excellent singletrack fades to hardly any track, then, after 7 km of "challenges," things start to improve once again. Rapidly. From Minnow Lake junction onward the riding is just plain fun. This section of singletrack trail rocks and rolls across sidehills and over hill and dale. Ride past the inviting waters of Caledonia Lake, then Marjorie Lake, either one a good spot for a refreshing dip on a hot day. Finish up by rolling down the last few hills on a very good singletrack that leads back into town.

## Options

Avoid the road and fireroad section by following the singletrack from the trailhead to Cabin Lake.

**Rugged ride with singletrack treats**

**Type** loop on 4WD roads and singletrack

**Rating** difficult/intermediate

**Other users** hikers-2 equestrian-2

**Distance** 29.4 km

**Time** 3-5 hours

**Map** 83 D/16 Jasper

**Season** mid-May to mid-October

**Land agency** Parks Canada

**Access**
In Jasper townsite, begin at the trailhead on Cabin Creek Road. Ride north on Cabin Creek Road.

| | |
|---|---|
| 0.0 | trailhead, ride north on Cabin Creek Drive |
| 1.5 | turn left onto Pyramid Lake Road |
| 3.3 | turn left onto Cabin Lake fireroad |
| 6.8 | Cabin Lake, junction, keep right (left is shortcut from Jasper) |
| 11.5 | junction, keep left (Saturday Night Lake is 0.5 km to right) |
| 16.9 | junction, keep right (High Lakes to left) |
| 20.0 | junction, keep left (Minnow Lake is 0.6 km to right) |
| 25.1 | Caledonia Lake |
| 25.5 | junction, keep left |
| 26.8 | Hibernia Lake trail to left |
| 27.1 | Marjorie Lake |
| 29.4 | trailhead |

# 199 SNAKE INDIAN FALLS

The ride up the Snake Indian Valley captures the feeling and spirit of the wilderness with its long distances, deep and wide valley and remote peaks. This ride covers the first leg of the North Boundary trail, a legendary 175 km-long backpack trip that crosses the Rockies to Mount Robson. The travelling is easy enough that the ride could be done as an overnighter, which would give you more time to enjoy the wilderness spirit of the country.

Begin by crossing the Snake Indian River bridge and enjoy the scenery as you roll along the old fireroad above the river. Next comes a long section of trail in the forest, but about halfway to the falls, the "shale banks" provide a welcome opportunity for a break. These 120 m-high black-shale cliffs are a natural mineral lick that attracts sheep and goats.

You will hear Snake Indian Falls before you see it. It is a large, thundering waterfall at the head of a steep-walled canyon. This is a great spot for lunch and a break before beginning the long cycle back to the trailhead or, if you have arranged a car shuttle, continuing on to Rock Lake.

**Options**

For those heading on to Rock Lake, the fireroad continues becoming a good quality singletrack at km 27.2. Gradually the mixed-wood forests open out to a series of meadows along the bottom of the broad Snake Indian Valley. Distant peaks with names such as Bosche, De Smet, Simla, Daybreak and The Ancient Wall can only hint at the magic of this north boundary country.

At the junction at km 37.7 the cycling trail turns to the right and leads to the Willow Creek warden station. This station was formerly occupied year-round, as attested to by the big barn and fenced pasture. Just imagine living in such a place. It is still a major base for park warden patrols.

**Classic wilderness ride to big waterfall**

**Type** out-and-back on 4WD roads

**Rating** difficult/novice

**Other users** hikers-3 equestrian-3

**Distance** 51.4 km

**Time** 5-7 hours

**Maps** 83 E/1 Snaring
83 E/8 Rock Lake

**Season** May to late October

**Land agency** Parks Canada

**Access**

In Jasper National Park, Snaring Road branches off Hwy. 16, 10 km east of Jasper. Beyond the end of the pavement it is known as Celestine Lake Road. The first 14 km is a two-way road that becomes one way for the last 14.8 km as it winds along a narrow, cliff-hanging section and around some blind corners. The permitted direction of travel changes according to a time schedule. Check with the park information office in Jasper to find out the times before heading out.

| | |
|---|---|
| 0.0 | trailhead |
| 0.2 | bridge over Snake Indian River |
| 4.7 | junction, keep left on North Boundary trail |
| 16.7 | shale banks |
| 25.7 | Snake Indian Falls |

10    20    30    40    50 51.4

Beyond the warden station the trail is a good dirt singletrack. You will probably have to share this section of the trail with horses as many equestrians enter the park via this route. The Rock Creek crossing at km 44.7 is usually bridged but may require a ford. Soon the park boundary marker is passed and at km 49.5 the trail joins Wildhay Road (#179) for the homestretch to the Rock Lake trailhead at km 51.2.

# 200 CELESTINE LAKE ROAD map 47

For reliable off-season cycling, this trip can't be beat. Located in the dry Athabasca Valley, the ride follows along a road often clear of snow both early and late in the season. This is a good place for the true aficionado to get a fat-tire fix.

Celestine Lake Road begins east of the Snaring Campground and ends at the trailhead for the North Boundary trail. It's a rough, narrow, winding gravel road that climbs and descends several terraces above the Athabasca River and leads to the bridge over the Snake Indian River. During the summer it is open to motorized travel, but on a controlled basis owing to a narrow, cliff-hanging section and some blind corners, and the permitted direction of travel changes according to a time schedule. Even so, this is not a busy road.

Most of the route is along dry sidehills above the Athabasca River and Jasper Lake. Stands of Douglas fir and spruce alternate with grasslands and limestone cliffs. Bighorn sheep and whitetail deer are frequently seen along the rocky sidehills, especially near Windy Point.

I don't advocate this ride in summer, it's too dry and dusty. Spring and autumn are the time to go when there are no cars and the weather is cooler. The bridge on the Snake Indian River makes a good day-trip destination.

**Scenic cruise in Athabasca Valley**

**Type** out-and-back on 2WD roads

**Rating** moderate/novice

**Other users** motorized-6 (summer only)

**Distance** 30 km

**Time** 3-6 hours

**Map** 83 E/1 Snaring

**Season** mid-April through November

**Land agency** Parks Canada

**Access**
In Jasper National Park, Snaring Road branches off Hwy. 16, 10 km east of Jasper. Beyond the end of the pavement it is known as Celestine Lake Road. The first 14 km of the road is open for two-way traffic. Park at the control gate.

| | |
|---|---|
| 0.0 | control gate |
| 3.7 | Windy Point |
| 11.5 | junction, keep left |
| 14.8 | end of public road |
| 15.0 | Snake Indian River bridge |

# 201 WHIRLPOOL RIVER                                        map 50

Athabasca Pass was the scene of one of the great dramas of Canadian history. Fur trade legends tell how, for more than half of the nineteenth century, the voyageurs laboured over this pass and along the Whirlpool trail carrying superhuman loads of furs and supplies. This route was the main east-west link in the fur trading empire of the Hudson's Bay Company.

Although cycling to the pass is not permitted, you can still ride along a fireroad that follows part of the route and provides an opportunity to get caught up in the romance associated with this historic valley.

Past the gate the first 0.5 km of the old Whirlpool fireroad has been downgraded but, overall, it is a smooth gravel road that is partly vegetated.

Mount Edith Cavell rises to the north while Whirlpool Peak towers to the south of the fast and powerful Whirlpool River. At km 6.6 the quiet waters of the pond at the Whirlpool Campground reflect the surrounding mountains and provide a strong contrast to the roiling river. The road ends at a spot known as the Tie Camp Meadow. At one time, trees were cut here and floated down the Whirlpool and Athabasca rivers to Jasper to be cut into railway ties.

Beyond this point, the trail is a rough singletrack closed to cycling.

**Family fun on gentle historic trail**
**Type** out-and-back on 4WD roads
**Rating** easy/novice
**Other users** hikers-2 equestrian-1
**Distance** 18.4 km
**Time** 2-3 hours
**Maps** 83 C/12 Athabasca Falls
83 D/9 Amethyst Lakes
**Season** May through October
**Land agency** Parks Canada

**Access**
In Jasper National Park, drive 15.5 km south on Hwy. 93A from its junction with Hwy. 93 (or 9 km north from Athabasca Falls), then proceed south on the Whirlpool fireroad for 7 km. The gated road to the left is the trail.

| | |
|---|---|
| 0.0 | trailhead |
| 6.6 | campsite |
| 9.2 | end of road at Tie Camp |

## Options

1. This historic trail continues for another 40 km to the Committee Punch Bowl on Athabasca Pass. David Thompson, one of Canada's greatest fur trade explorers, made the first recorded crossing of this pass in 1811. The pass became the main fur trading route through the Rockies.

2. The entire road can be cycled beginning at Highway 93A for a total distance of 32.4 km. This is more enjoyable during the off season when the road is closed to vehicles.

# 202 FRYATT CREEK                           map 50

**Family fun on gentle valley bottom ride**

**Type** out-and-back on 4WD roads
**Rating** easy/intermediate
**Other users** hikers-3
**Distance** 19.6 km
**Time** 3-4 hours
**Map** 83 C/12 Athabasca Falls
**Season** June to mid-October
**Land agency** Parks Canada

### Access
In Jasper National Park, drive 1 km north of Athabasca Falls on Hwy. 93A. Turn left and follow the gravel road for 2 km to the Fryatt trailhead.

0.0   trailhead
9.8   lower Fryatt campsite

Fryatt Lake mirrors the peaks surrounding a beautiful alpine valley. This popular hiking and climbing destination can be reached by means of an enjoyable bike 'n' hike—by cycling the lower part of the trail you can visit the upper Fryatt Valley on a long day trip. It's a pleasant cycling trip, even if you venture no farther than the end of the designated cycling trail at lower Fryatt Campground.

You can expect to find easy cycling on a smooth old road for most of the way to the campsite. At km 6 the trail passes close to the Athabasca River and the sound of cars on the highway across the river reminds you that you have not strayed far from the pavement. Farther along, the trail overlooks Fryatt Creek where erosion of the bank has formed rudimentary hoodoos. Mount Christie and Brussels Peak are the dominant mountains to the west. The cycling trail ends at lower Fryatt Campground, nestled on the banks of Fryatt Creek in the shadow of Fryatt Peak.

### Options
The trail to Fryatt Lake climbs steeply up the valley beyond the campsite. Leave your bike and continue on foot for the 7.2 km and 440 m of elevation gain to Fryatt Lake.

2      4      6      8      10      12      14      16      18    19.6

# 203 ATHABASCA RIVER TO FORTRESS LAKE    map 50

This ride takes you through exciting and spectacular country where big valleys and towering, glaciated mountains form the very headwaters of the Athabasca River. The Columbia and Chaba icefields feed two fast-flowing rivers, the Athabasca, which can be crossed on a suspension bridge, and the Chaba, which must be forded to get to the lake. Fortress Lake is a large mountain lake lying just west of the Continental Divide in Hamber Provincial Park, British Columbia.

Cross the bridge over the canyon and roll south on the old road up the Athabasca Valley. Lightly vegetated and covered in pine needles, it offers easy travelling as it loses elevation for the first 7 km to the Big Bend campsite. Here the trail breaks out of the pine forest to dramatic views of Dragon Peak, Fortress Mountain and Quincy Peak. The fork to the right at km 13 leads to the Chaba warden cabin overlooking a pond, which is the richest shade of blue you'll find anywhere in the Rockies. The old road ends at the Athabasca River.

Cross the suspension bridge and continue up the Chaba Valley on a somewhat rough and rooty singletrack trail. Before you get to Fortress Lake the Chaba River will have to be crossed. This ford is difficult and dangerous during periods of high water. Continue up the valley and cross the nearly flat Great Divide to the lakeshore.

We first cycled this road in 1972. It was Thanksgiving weekend as we rode our skinny-tired 10-speeds as far as the Athabasca crossing. As there was no bridge at that time, we waded the river and hiked on to Fortress Lake. Two days later, our return trip became a bit of an epic as an early winter blizzard dumped 20 cm of snow on us. From the icy river crossing to coaxing our bikes through the snow for 8 km, we had lots of opportunity to reflect on the role untamed nature plays in mountain bicycling adventure.

**Classic wilderness ride below glacier-clad peaks**

**Type** out-and-back on 4WD roads and singletrack

**Rating** difficult/intermediate

**Other users** hikers-3  equestrian-2

**Distance** 48 km

**Time** 7-8 hours

**Maps** 83 C/12 Athabasca Falls
83 C/5 Fortress Lake

**Season** June to mid-October

**Land agency** Parks Canada

**Access**
In Jasper National Park, begin at Sunwapta Falls viewpoint, 55 km south of Jasper on Hwy. 93. Cross the bridge to the trail.

| | |
|---|---|
| 0.0 | trailhead |
| 7.0 | Big Bend campsite |
| 13.0 | junction, keep left |
| 16.5 | Athabasca River bridge |
| 20.0 | Chaba River ford |
| 24.0 | Fortress Lake |

# 204 ALEXANDRA RIVER map 51

This former fireroad provides access into a spectacular region of glacier-clad mountains just east of the Continental Divide. The lack of major hills and minimal elevation gain make this ride suitable for an overnight venture.

In 1972 this fireroad offered easy 10-speeding, but it has had little in the way of maintenance since then. Some parts of the old road are overgrown by spruce trees and shrubs, which makes the riding awkward and limits visibility. Bridges over two tributary streams have collapsed resulting in difficult fords and making this trip unsuitable during periods of high water. Several sections of road are washed-out and you will have to either bushwhack around them or ford the stream. All this sounds much worse than the reality, and this valley is just too beautiful to resist.

Roll across the bridge over the glacier-fed North Saskatchewan River and ride the old road. It parallels the river for 6 km before it turns west into the big U-shaped valley of the Alexandra River. The road is in the forest and a bit overgrown but then, with an eyeful of views, it breaks onto the valley bottom flats. Mount Alexandra and other peaks of the Continental Divide form a dramatic backdrop to the west. Enjoy the scenery as the road crosses a series of gravel flats and braided stream channels with views eastward to Sunset Pass and south to Mount Amery towering above the flats. Terrace Creek is crossed at km 14, just below an outstanding limestone canyon.

Beyond, the riding is easy and it's a good thing too, because the scenery in this country demands all of your attention. This part of the valley is about as close to biker's scenic heaven as I ever expect to get (Himalaya excepted, of course). The towering glaciated peaks of Mount Lyell and Mount Alexandra dominate the view while big glaciers descend into the valley. This is wild country!

The end of the road is indicated by an important marker. Here, on an obvious tree, one of the most prominent residents of the valley has rubbed his back for years. The bark is smooth and covered with long grizzled hairs.

**Classic wilderness ride below glacier-clad peaks**

**Type** out-and-back on 4WD road

**Rating** difficult/intermediate

**Other users** hikers-1 equestrians-1

**Distance** 41.6 km

**Time** 5-7 hours

**Maps** 83 C/2 Cline River
83 C/3 Columbia Icefield

**Season** mid-May to mid-October

**Land agency** Parks Canada

**Access**
In Banff National Park, the trail begins on the west side of Hwy. 93, 24.3 km north of the junction with Hwy. 11 at Saskatchewan Crossing.

| | |
|---|---|
| 0.0 | trailhead |
| 0.2 | Saskatchewan River bridge |
| 6.0 | trail turns west |
| 12.3 | bypass trail to right |
| 14.0 | Terrace Creek |
| 20.8 | end of road |

This valley was visited in 1900 by C. S. Thompson and, two years later, by Sir James Outram. Outram, in a fit of first ascents, climbed Mounts Alexandra and Lyell, then went on up the Castleguard Valley to ascend Mounts Bryce and Columbia.

**Options**

A footpath continues up the Castleguard Valley to spectacular alpine country at Thompson Pass and the Castleguard Meadows.

# 205 KOOTENAY PLAINS map 52

In the good old days the Stoney Indians rode the Kootenay Plains on horses; now you, too, can ride the plains. The Kootenay Plains are, or should I say were, a very extensive valley-bottom grassland within the mountains. A large part of the grasslands were flooded following construction of the Bighorn Dam. This route follows a disused logging road from the blue suspension bridge east to the grasslands on the south side of Abraham Lake.

Ride across the suspension bridge and roll east on an old logging road keeping left at the trail junction for Siffleur Falls. Hanging a right onto a shortcut trail at km 3.7 will save you 1.9 km. The road rocks and rolls across a forested upland, then slowly descends to the grasslands of the Kootenay Plains and ends on the shores of Abraham Lake. Some parts of the road have been scarified, but the riding is generally easy although you will have to jump or climb over the occasional windfallen tree.

Before the lake was created and flooded this area, the road crossed the North Saskatchewan on a wooden bridge and passed by the homestead cabins of Tom Wilson and Jim Simpson. During the early years of this century Wilson and Simpson trapped in this country in the winter. Although you can see the highway across the lake, you are still relatively isolated from it. Here is a chance to wander about the grasslands and enjoy the mountain scenes extending in every direction. Unless you have arranged for a boat to come across the river and pick you up, you will have to content yourself with the pleasant task of retracing your tracks to the trailhead.

**Scenic cruise on mountain grasslands**

**Type** out-and-back on 4WD roads

**Rating** moderate/novice

**Other users** equestrian-2

**Distance** 27 km

**Time** 2-3 hours

**Map** 83 C/1 Whiterabbit Creek

**Season** May through October

**Land agency** Alberta Forest Service

**Access**
Begin at the Siffleur Falls trailhead on Hwy. 11, 27 km east of the junction of Hwys. 93 and 11.

| | |
|---|---|
| 0.0 | trailhead |
| 0.7 | suspension bridge |
| 1.2 | junction, keep left (Glacier trail to right) |
| 1.9 | Siffleur River bridge |
| 2.0 | junction, keep left (Siffleur Falls to right) |
| 3.7 | take shortcut trail to right |
| 4.1 | shortcut rejoins road |
| 8.4 | junction, keep left (Whiterabbit trail to right) |
| 13.5 | Kootenay Plains |

## Options

The Whiterabbit Creek trail branches to the right at km 8.4. This singletrack provides access to the upper Whiterabbit Creek valley and eventually to the Ram River valley at Tin Roof cabin. I have not ridden the Whiterabbit, so you are on your own here. An extended-trip possibility would be to ride up the Whiterabbit and down the Ram.

2    4    6    8    10    12    14    16    18    20    22    24    26  27

# 206 SIFFLEUR FALLS                      map 52

Photo: Gillean Daffern

This short ride leads to an interesting waterfall and limestone canyon. It makes a good evening ride from the nearby campground, or it can be combined with a ride to the Kootenay Plains (#205). Watch for hikers on this popular trail.

From the trailhead it is a short view-filled spin to the blue suspension bridge. Riding across this bridge will be but the first test of your concentration in riding high above roiling waters. Beyond the bridge keep left on the good gravel of an old logging road, cross the Siffleur River bridge, then keep right at the trail junction. (The left fork leads to the Kootenay Plains.) Soon the road ends and the trail narrows to a good singletrack, take the upper trail as it parallels above the edge of the canyon. A few rocks, roots and windfallen trees add challenge to your ride. At the falls the river makes a modest drop into an impressive canyon cut along the bedding planes of layers of limestone.

The ride back is short. Those of you who are searching for adrenaline will, no doubt, want to take the lower trail, which descends along the very rim of the canyon. This route is only for the well-balanced (or should I say the totally unbalanced?) rider as a mistake here could send you tumbling into some heavy-duty water in the canyon.

**Rugged ride to waterfall**

**Type** out-and-back on 4WD roads and singletrack

**Rating** easy/intermediate

**Other users** hikers-7

**Distance** 9.4 km

**Time** 1-2 hours

**Map** 83 C/1 Whiterabbit Creek

**Season** mid-May through October

**Land agency** Alberta Forest Service

**Access**
Begin at the Siffleur Falls trailhead on Hwy. 11, 27 km east of the junction of Hwys. 93 and 11.

| | |
|---|---|
| 0.0 | trailhead |
| 0.7 | suspension bridge |
| 1.2 | junction, keep left (Glacier trail to right) |
| 1.9 | Siffleur River bridge |
| 2.0 | junction, turn right (left leads to Kootenay Plains) |
| 4.7 | Siffleur Falls |

14

13

2    4    6    8   9.4

# 207 GLACIER TRAIL                    map 52

This ride features a variety of challenges, but will likely be best remembered for its tremendous scenery and generally mellow nature. As of 1998 two major creek crossings have been bridged and signage has been improved making travel a whole lot easier.

From the trailhead it is a short spin to the blue suspension bridge across the North Saskatchewan River. The ride across the bridge is an exercise in concentration, especially if the river is at high water levels. Beyond the bridge turn right onto an old logging road and roll westward through grassy meadows and open forests of aspen and spruce. Mountain vistas are everywhere.

Not far past Spreading Creek bridge the trail becomes faint where it crosses an old sawmill site, then continues westward but deteriorates, making the cycling all the more enjoyable. The loggers removed just the right amount of timber to enable appreciation of the delightful vistas in this broad mountain valley. Mount Wilson is the glacier-clad mountain to the west, while Mount Cline lies across the valley to the north. A wildfire in this area in 1998 may alter the quality of parts of the trail. At km 24 the logging road ends and it is time to retrace your tracks unless you have arranged a car shuttle.

To continue to Highway 93 near the Saskatchewan Crossing warden station you must first choose among the skid roads, one turns into a singletrack that leads west. Expect windfallen trees and, at high water some fording of side channels will be required. Parks expects you will push your bike for the last 5 km to the highway as this isn't a designated bike trail. The last section of trail, from Warden Lake to the warden station, is a good doubletrack. You can either arrange a car shuttle or cycle a loop of 61 km by following Highways 93 and 11 back to your starting point.

**Gentle wilderness explorer**

**Type** point-to-point on 4WD roads and singletrack

**Rating** difficult/intermediate

**Other users** equestrian-1

**Distance** 31.3 km

**Time** 3-4 hours

**Maps** 82 N/15 Mistaya Lake
82 N/16 Siffleur River
83 C/1 Whiterabbit Creek
83 C/2 Cline River

**Season** mid-May to mid-October

**Land agency** Alberta Forest Service, Parks Canada

**Access**
Begin at the Siffleur Falls trailhead on Hwy. 11, 27 km east of the junction of Hwys. 93 and 11.

| | |
|---|---|
| 0.0 | trailhead |
| 0.7 | suspension bridge |
| 1.2 | junction, turn right (left to Siffleur Falls and Kootenay Plains) |
| 12.2 | Spreading Creek |
| 14.6 | sawmill site |
| 24.0 | end of road, singletrack begins |
| 25.8 | Banff Park boundary |
| 31.3 | Hwy. 93 |

# 208 LANDSLIDE LAKE                    map 52

This classic endurance ride involves a steep hike-a-bike over a high mountain pass followed by 23 km of challenging singletrack riding.

Begin at the Landslide trailhead by riding, pushing and carrying your bike for 5 km to the pass above Landslide Lake. Dramatic vistas and an inspiring but bleak alpine environment enhance the excitement of the ride ahead. Descend to the lake on a nebulous trail across and down thumbnail scree; woo hoo, skiing on a bike! The stretch along the lake can be trying as neither the trail nor the lakeshore offers easy travelling. Once on the trail north of the lake you will make good use of your advanced riding skills to negotiate boulders, logs and steep descents. The riding is fun but also serious business as help is far away. The riding gradually gets easier as you progress down the trail and by km 18 you'll be racing along an excellent backcountry singletrack. From here to the trailhead the ride is pure pleasure on a trail that winds, dips and curls through the forest with lots of entertaining stunts including roots, logs, bridges, creeks and airtime.

## Options

1. As a heli-bike this trail rules. Get lifted to the pass to the south of Landslide Lake where you have the choice of following the route as described or descending to the west trailhead.

2. Begin at the east trailhead and ride an out-and-back on the good singletrack in the Cline River valley.

**Wilderness explorer with technical challenges**

**Type** point-to-point on singletrack

**Rating** extreme/advanced

**Other users** hikers-4 equestrian-3

**Distance** 28.2 km one way

**Time** 6-9 hours

**Maps** 83 C/2 Cline River
83 C/1 Whiterabbit Creek

**Season** July through October

**Land agency** Alberta Forest Service

**Access**
**west** Landslide Lake trailhead on Hwy. 11, 69 km west of SR 940.

**east** Pinto Lake trailhead on Hwy. 11, 46.3 km west of SR 940.

| | |
|---|---|
| 0.0 | west trailhead |
| 5.0 | summit of pass |
| 9.2 | Landslide Lake |
| 11.3 | north end of lake |
| 14.7 | Lake of the Falls junction, go right |
| 20.0 | camp by Cline River |
| 28.2 | end of ride |

# 209 BIGHORN EXPLORER                    map 53

This ride explores the hills to the east of the Bighorn Dam. A sandy beach lapped by the turquoise waters of the lake is a highlight, not to be outdone by a sweet doubletrack rolling past several attractive beaver ponds and through some fabulous mixed wood forest and flower-filled meadows.

Ride across the Bighorn Dam and turn right on a gravel road. After negotiating a gravel pit you'll find yourself rolling along doubletrack all the way to a beach known locally as "California Dreaming." Turquoise waters lap against white sand and the walls of the Rockies tower beyond. After a sun and swim break retrace your tracks for a short distance and follow the doubletrack as it passes a succession of beaver ponds with views of the hills to the south. Now the trail winds through a beautiful forest of pine, spruce and aspen with lots of grassy, flower-filled meadows as it makes its way back to the dam.

## Options

If you want more (and who wouldn't), follow the Aylmer trail to the right at km 14.9 for 5 km and return on the gravel exploration road. This bonus ride features more beautiful meadows and an abandoned homestead with a well-preserved log house. This option rejoins the route log at km 16.8 and adds a total of 7 km to the ride.

**Family fun on gentle backcountry trails**

**Type** loop on 4WD roads
**Rating** moderate/intermediate
**Other users** motorized-5
**Distance** 17.9 km
**Time** 2-3 hours
**Map** 83 C/8 Nordegg
**Season** May through October
**Land agency** Alberta Forest Service

**Access**
From Hwy. 11, 21 km west of SR 940, drive south for 4.4 km, then turn right and drive another 0.7 km to the gated trailhead atop the Bighorn Dam.

| | |
|---|---|
| 0.0 | trailhead |
| 0.5 | junction, turn right |
| 3.3 | join cutline, go left |
| 3.4 | four-way junction, go straight |
| 4.6 | four-way junction, go straight |
| 7.3 | junction at lake, go right |
| 8.2 | Bighorn Reservoir, retrace tracks |
| 9.0 | (= 7.3) turn right |
| 9.6 | junction, go left |
| 10.6 | lake and views |
| 12.3 | cross cutline |
| 14.9 | junction with Aylmer trail, go left |
| 16.8 | junction with road, go left through dip |
| 17.9 | end of ride |

Aylmer trail (#210).

# 210 AYLMER TRAIL                     map 53

This trail leads along the south side of the North Saskatchewan River from Bighorn Dam to SR 940. The first 16 km is a rollicking, fun-filled doubletrack used by quads. The next 13 km is a singletrack that will challenge the skills and endurance of advanced riders.

Ride across the Bighorn Dam keeping left on the exploration road until you pass through a deep dip. On the far side of the dip the signed doubletrack trail departs to the right. This trail will have you smiling ear to ear as you climb and drop and soar around bermed corners. The trail passes through aspen and spruce forest and crosses expansive, view-filled meadows. Take time to enjoy the scenery and explore several abandoned log cabins.

Beyond km 16 the nature of the ride changes as the trail becomes a rugged singletrack and climbs onto the valley side above the river. Roots and logs, steep climbs and descents, switchbacks and drop-offs will occupy your attention and require all your skills and strength. It's great fun, but the farther you go the harder the trail seems to get and you're getting more and more tired. Back on the river flats the trail becomes faint, but just keep riding east until the trail once again takes to the hillside and bumps along to the finish. This section is tough going but it has ample views and lots of technical excitement for rewards. Still, it's a relief to tumble out of the woods at the Saskatchewan River bridge.

**Rugged backcountry ride in classic foothills setting**

**Type** point-to-point on 4WD road and singletrack

**Rating** difficult/advanced

**Other users** equestrian-1 motorized-4

**Distance** 29.3 km one way

**Time** 4-6 hours

**Map** 83 C/8 Nordegg

**Season** May through October

**Land agency** Alberta Forest Service

**Access**

**west** From Hwy. 11, 21 km west of SR 940, drive south for 4.4 km, then turn right and drive another 0.7 km to the gated trailhead atop the Bighorn Dam.

**east** The ride finishes at the Saskatchewan River bridge on SR 940, 11.2 km south of Hwy. 11.

| | |
|---|---|
| 0.0 | west trailhead |
| 0.5 | junction, keep left |
| 1.1 | signed trail to right |
| 3.1 | junction, go left |
| 5.5 | trail crosses road |
| 6.3 | log cabins |
| 7.7 | cabin |
| 8.1 | go left on road |
| 9.5 | trail leaves road to left |
| 11.7 | go left |
| 13.1 | go left |
| 15.5 | go left to cabin |
| 15.7 | cabin |
| 15.9 | (= 15.5) go left |
| 16.0 | singletrack begins |
| 25.0 | cross channel on log |
| 29.1 | go left on old road |
| 29.3 | bridge, end of ride |

10          20          29.3

# 211 BLACK MOUNTAIN CHALLENGE                    map 53

Black Mountain offers relentless fun on doubletrack and singletrack trails that have been used for the Black Mountain Challenge race course. The climbs are often steep with some unrideable sections, the upper levels feature cool high mountain forests and great views, and the descents are inspirational. Airtime Alley needs no explanation and the double diamond single-track (really not that hard) will rock your sox off!

This is a network of trails so you can customize your ride. The distance log describes a looping route that captures all of the trails and gives you two descents of the singletrack.

Begin by riding up the valley keeping left at the bottom of Airtime and climbing high onto the valley side on trail A. A quick descent brings you to the top of Airtime where a steep climb (push) takes you to the ridge above and some stupendous views. A fast descent leads to the reflecting pond and yet another climb leads to the final ridge. Watch on the right for the double diamond sign and ride this classic singletrack down rocky drop-offs and through beautiful mixed wood forest to the access road. Turn left and follow trail C as it loops back up to the top of the singletrack; down we go again. Now keep right and climb up trail B to the reflecting pond, up to the top of the ridge, then down a brake-burning hill to the top of Airtime Alley. The rest of the ride is pure pleasure as you wildly ride and fly back to the trailhead.

## Rugged ride on race course

**Type** loop on 4WD road and singletrack

**Rating** difficult/advanced

**Other users** equestrian-1 motorized-4

**Distance** 32 km

**Time** 3-5 hours

**Map** 83 C/8 Nordegg

**Season** June through October

**Land agency** Alberta Forest Service

## Access

Follow Hwy. 11 for 10 km west of SR 940, turn right and follow the Snow Creek Group Camp access road for 2 km to the signed trailhead.

| | |
|---|---|
| 0.0 | trailhead |
| 0.8 | junction, go left on A |
| 5.7 | junction, keep right |
| 6.6 | junction, go left (Airtime Alley to right) |
| 7.2 | junction, keep right |
| 7.6 | junction, keep right |
| 9.0 | reflecting pond |
| 9.5 | junction, go left (trail B to right) |
| 11.0 | double diamond singletrack, turn right |
| 13.6 | access road, go left |
| 14.0 | turn left on trail C |
| 17.9 | junction, go left |
| 20.0 | double diamond, turn left |
| 22.6 | access road, go right |
| 23.1 | four-way junction, turn right on trail B |
| 26.0 | junction, go left |
| 28.9 | junction, go left on Airtime |
| 31.2 | junction, go left |
| 32.0 | end of ride |

## 212 BLACK CANYON CREEK                    map 53

This wooded singletrack leads alongside Black Canyon Creek from Frontier Lodge to the Saskatchewan River valley. The ride then follows the rolling powerline doubletrack to Hwy. 940 and finishes up on roads.

Begin at Frontier Lodge on the singletrack between the two lower cabins, then keep left at two junctions and you are on your way. Watch for a tricky spot on a cutline at km 3.2 where the trail jogs left for about 15 m. The trail is a narrow singletrack with lots of roots and sidehills as it follows alongside the creek and passes through some pretty meadows and by some beaver ponds. You'll need to do a bit of routefinding at km 6.2. Don't cross the creek, instead find and follow a singletrack climbing left up the bank. This section of trail is poorly defined, but just keep heading down valley toward the river staying above the creek on a variety of game trails. An open hillside offers a superb panorama of the Rockies and the North Saskatchewan River valley. Soon you'll see the powerline and reach the good doubletrack. Roll east along the trail enjoying the great views and taking some air on the bumps.

To complete the loop climb up the dusty and somewhat tiresome gravel of SR 940, then follow Hwy. 11 west and finish up on the singletrack that parallels the road to the lodge.

**Options**

Wagon Road (#213) branches off SR 940 at km 18.9 and can be followed back to Frontier Lodge. This option avoids most of the roads and results in a 30 km difficult/intermediate loop.

**Rugged valley tour**
**Type** loop on 2WD and 4WD roads and singletrack
**Rating** moderate/intermediate
**Other users** hikers-1 motorized-3
**Distance** 28.3 km
**Time** 3-4 hours
**Map** 83 C/8 Nordegg
**Season** May through October
**Land agency** Alberta Forest Service

**Access**
This ride begins at Frontier Lodge. On Hwy. 11, drive 1.9 km west of SR 940, then turn left for a further 2.7 km.

0.0   trailhead, ride south through lodge property
1.1   junction, go left
1.4   junction, go left
3.2   cutline, jog left for 15 m
5.9   keep right
6.1   junction, keep right
6.2   take faint singletrack up bank to left
7.8   powerline doubletrack, turn left
13.3  SR 940, turn left
18.9  Wagon Road (option) to left
23.7  Hwy. 11, turn left
25.6  turn left
28.3  Frontier Lodge

# 213 WAGON ROAD                              map 53

Ride this trail of the pioneers as part of a forested loop from Frontier Lodge.

Follow the singletrack as it parallels the road from the lodge to Hwy. 11, turning east, then south on SR 940. Watch for the Wagon Road trail branching to the right at km 9.4 near the top of the big hill. The trail winds and rolls through spruce forest crossing a couple of boggy areas and passing a small cemetery on its way west to the valley of Black Canyon Creek. Open hillsides offer good views west to the Rockies with the valley of the North Saskatchewan River below. When the Wagon Road meets some cutlines and turns left at a four-way junction you want to go straight through and follow the cutline. Ride the singletrack on the cutline as it detours right to avoid a muskeg, then left to descend a steep hill. Below the hill watch carefully for a singletrack to the right that will take you back to the lodge. Keep right at two more trail junctions, cross the fireguard and it's all over.

**Rugged valley tour**

**Type** loop on 2WD and 4WD roads and singletrack

**Rating** moderate/intermediate

**Other users** hikers-1 motorized-3

**Distance** 19.8 km

**Time** 2-4 hours

**Map** 83 C/8 Nordegg

**Season** May through October

**Land agency** Alberta Forest Service

**Access**
This ride begins at Frontier Lodge. On Hwy. 11, drive 1.9 km west of SR 940, then turn left for a further 2.7 km.

| | |
|---|---|
| 0.0 | trailhead |
| 2.7 | Hwy. 11, turn right |
| 4.6 | SR 940, turn right |
| 9.4 | turn right on doubletrack |
| 14.6 | four-way junction, go straight |
| 16.6 | turn right on singletrack |
| 18.4 | junction, keep right |
| 18.7 | junction, keep right |
| 19.8 | Frontier Lodge |

# 214 TWELVE LEVEL MINE map 53

This classic doubletrack ride explores some old mine workings in the Brazeau Range as it climbs over the summit of the range and drops to the North Saskatchewan River. After a stretch on the gravel of SR 940 the trail leads through the Brazeau Mine, a provincial historic site, and returns to Nordegg.

Begin by riding past the church and follow the Twelve Level Mine road up the mountain past several old mine workings. Ride by the Telus junction and roll along the ridge top to the summit. Several spectacular vantage points look north over Nordegg and Coliseum Mountain and west over the Saskatchewan River to the front ranges.

The trail down is steep and challenging as well as fast and exciting. Loose rocks and erosion gullies will test your skills, but much of the riding is just plain fast with lots of airtime. Once in the valley follow along the powerline doubletrack to SR 940. The ride up the gravel road is a bit tiresome and dusty, but soon you'll be turning right into the Brazeau Mine site. The mine closed in 1955 but most of the structures are still intact and in reasonable repair. Guided tours are available. When you are mined out, roll back to Nordegg, passing more historic structures and the old church on your way to the finish.

**Options**

A shorter 12.8 km out-and-back ride is possible on the Twelve Level Mine road. Descending the Black Mountain Challenge downhill race course adds considerable pizazz to this ride. To do this, watch for the singletrack entrances as you climb up the road: on the right at km 3.7, on the left at km 4.5, and on the left at km 5.4. The course starts at the Telus tower, turn right at km 5.9 and reach the tower at km 6.4.

**Backcountry explorer with historic mine relics**

**Type** loop on 2WD and 4WD roads

**Rating** difficult/advanced

**Other users** motorized-4

**Distance** 28.4 km

**Time** 3-4 hours

**Map** 83 C/8 Nordegg

**Season** June through October

**Land agency** Alberta Forest Service

**Access**
Begin in Nordegg at the golf course clubhouse on Main Street.

| | |
|---|---|
| 0.0 | trailhead, ride south |
| 0.9 | keep left past church |
| 1.2 | go right |
| 1.6 | junction, go left |
| 1.9 | gate |
| 2.0 | junction, go left |
| 5.9 | junction, keep left (Telus tower to right) |
| 6.9 | junction, keep right |
| 7.1 | go left |
| 7.9 | summit |
| 9.3 | junction, keep left |
| 12.3 | powerline doubletrack, turn right |
| 16.2 | SR 940, turn right |
| 25.1 | turn right through black gate |
| 25.8 | junction at Brazeau Mine, go straight |
| 26.5 | gate, junction, keep right |
| 26.8 | junction, go left |
| 28.4 | end of ride |

# 215 COLISEUM MOUNTAIN                    map 53

**Classic heli-bike trip**
**Type** out-and-back on singletrack
**Rating** difficult/advanced
**Other users** hikers-4 equestrian-2
**Distance** 15 km
**Time** 4-5 hours
**Maps** 83 C/8 Nordegg
83 C/9 Wapiabi Creek
**Season** June through October
**Land agency** Alberta Forest Service

**Access**
From Hwy. 11 at Nordegg, follow
Upper Shunda Road for 1.2 km
and turn right for 0.6 km to the
signed trailhead.

| | |
|---|---|
| 0.0 | trailhead |
| 0.5 | four-way junction, turn left |
| 7.5 | summit |
| 14.5 | four-way junction, right to trailhead (left to heli-base) |
| 15.0 | end of ride |

Nordegg's premier riding experience, this adventure is not to be missed if you have the skill level to handle it. The trip is at its best with a helicopter shuttle to the summit followed by a wild-assed ride back to the valley. I did the heli-bike and have to say it was one of my most exciting trips ever. The strong but impecunious may prefer to ride and push to the summit, but it's a tough slog with lots of roots and loose rocks to challenge your ascent.

The summit vista is a full circle panorama of foothills and mountains with the foundation of the old lookout a reminder of why the trail exists. Blast off the alpine summit and almost immediately deal with the delights of the first technical section—a few drops and some loose scree. Next the trail rolls through little trees along the ridge above the "coliseum." A short climb leads to a wide open traverse of a scree slope below the cliffs—exciting and challenging to ride. Another short climb leads to a tricky bedrock chute followed by a series of rough and rocky switchbacks. Some hikers and riders have cut the switches but hey, it shortens your ride and rips up the mountainside, so give nature a break! The trail down the mountain is pretty rough, full suspension earns its keep here. At the four-way junction go left to the heli-base or right to the trailhead parking.

# 216 COLISEUM CIRCLE                    map 53

This ride takes you all the way around Coliseum Mountain on gravel roads and doubletrack. It's a scenic lower elevation cruiser that can be wet and muddy depending on the weather. The trail passes through cutblocks and meadows with lots of views and provides a full day of entertainment. Frequent ditches built to prevent erosion provide puddles for you to play in and the opportunity for lots of air time. Families tend to like this ride because it lacks any monster climbs or killer downhills and the riding is mostly on smooth doubletrack.

Begin by shuttling or riding up the Shunda Lookout road to km 6.5. Follow the doubletrack away from this trailhead as it climbs gently, then rolls and descends through the hills north of Coliseum Mountain. The route circles the mountain and your choices at trail junctions should reflect this fact. Watch carefully for the somewhat nebulous junction at km 22.4 where you leave the gravel road to follow a grassy reclaimed road on your right. After a short distance you will cross a small creek, then climb over a hill to a four-way junction that includes a creek crossing. Cross the creek and take the doubletrack to the right. A short climb leads to a long descent with lots of jumps and finally dumps you out on Hwy. 11.

**Options**

Many riders use a car shuttle and begin the ride at km 6.5 of the route log.

**Scenic cruiser**

**Type** loop on 2WD and 4WD roads

**Rating** difficult/intermediate

**Other users** motorized-3

**Distance** 34.3 km

**Time** 2-4 hours

**Maps** 83 C/8 Nordegg
83 C/9 Wapiabi Creek

**Season** May through October

**Land agency** Alberta Forest Service

**Access**

Begin at the junction of Hwy. 11 and Upper Shunda Road, 0.3 km west of Nordegg.

| | |
|---|---|
| 0.0 | trailhead |
| 2.2 | turn right on lookout road |
| 2.5 | keep left |
| 6.5 | turn right on doubletrack (shuttle drop-off point) |
| 8.0 | junction, go left |
| 10.8 | junction, keep right |
| 19.0 | junction, keep right |
| 22.4 | turn right onto grassy reclaimed roadbed |
| 23.1 | four-way junction |
| 29.8 | Hwy. 11 |
| 34.0 | Nordegg junction |
| 34.3 | end of ride |

5    10    15    20    25    30  34.3

# 217 RAM RIVER
map 54

The Ram River trail is a wilderness cycling trip par excellence. You may have to share it with a few horses and ATVs; then again, if you go on a weekday, you may have it all to yourself.

The trailhead is at a major equestrian staging area. It's a crowded place, but don't let the presence of cowboys, horses, horse trailers, a major horse-outfitting operation and a few ATVs deter you. Within a few kilometres of the trailhead everything sorts itself out. Very few travellers continue up the Ram.

Three major fords mark the initial stages of this trip—Hummingbird Creek at the trailhead and the Ram River at km 5 and again at km 6.5. These fords are difficult and dangerous at high water levels. The trail is in good condition, gravelly and rocky in places, and with a few stretches of mega-dust. Incidentally, as I found out by experience, mega-dust turns to mega-mud after a rainfall. Beyond the second ford of the Ram the trail stays on the north side of the river and wanders through a long string of meadows. Continuing on, the trail makes a number of easy fords of the Ram as it winds its way through forest and meadows to the AFS patrol cabin and on to historic Tin Roof (Headwaters) Cabin. This wild and scenic country can be reached as part of a long day trip, but if you wish to explore the area it may be preferable to camp overnight. Camping spots abound in the valley. ATVs go all the way to the cabin.

## Options

1. Explore the Ranger Creek valley.

2. Although I have not cycled it, it appears the trail down Whiterabbit Creek could be ridden as part of a long and adventurous point-to-point backcountry cycling trip. See Kootenay Plains (#205) for the north access.

3. Cycle a loop to Canary Creek (#219).

**Rugged wilderness explorer**

**Type** out-and-back on 4WD road and singletrack

**Rating** difficult/intermediate

**Other users** equestrian-5 motorized-3

**Distance** 68 km

**Time** 8-9 hours

**Maps** 82 N/16 Siffleur River 83 B/4 Elk Creek 83 C/1 Whiterabbit Creek

**Season** mid-July to mid-October

**Land agency** Alberta Forest Service

**Access**
From SR 940, 2.7 km north of the Ram Falls recreation area, drive west for 5.3 km on the road to Hummingbird Creek equestrian staging area.

| | |
|---|---|
| 0.0 | trailhead |
| | ford Hummingbird Creek |
| 0.7 | trail joins old road, keep left |
| 5.0 | Ram River ford |
| 6.5 | junction, keep right and ford river (Ranger Creek trail to left) |
| 9.0 | outfitter campsite |
| 18.0 | junction, keep left (right leads to Canary Creek) |
| 19.0 | ford |
| 27.0 | AFS patrol cabin |
| 34.0 | Headwaters cabin |

# 218 ONION LAKE                                map 54

This valley is a popular place, especially on summer weekends. Campers, horseback riders, fishermen, off-roaders, motorists—expect to meet them all. Timing can make or break your trip so get an early start and beat the competition or, better yet, try a weekday. In any case be prepared to share the country with other users.

Onion Lake is a beautiful subalpine lake nestled within a major front ranges basin. The route follows alongside a very expansive and attractive valley-bottom shrub meadow and the scenery along the way more than makes up for the presence of motorists.

Although the 2 km after the starting point are rough, dusty and in the trees, the better part of the remaining 14 km of road follows a beautiful valley-bottom willow meadow. Vistas include Ram Ridge to the east and distant mountains to the west. It's easy riding on a clay and gravel road to Onion Lake, a beautiful spot nestled among grassy hills but showing a few signs of abuse by off-road vehicles.

To add a little variety to your return trip, continue west from the lake and follow a dirt singletrack to the left through the meadows until it rejoins Onion Creek Road.

## Options

1. A 4WD road leaves the route at km 14.8, climbs over a low pass and descends to the North Ram River, eventually reaching SR 940.

2. There are a number of singletrack trails in the block of country lying north of the Ram River and west of Onion Creek. I didn't check these out, but they will no doubt prove challenging to hard-core bike explorers. Access is from the Ram River trail, Canary Creek trail, Hummingbird Creek trail and from Onion Lake. You can expect to share these trails with horses.

**Scenic cruiser**

**Type** out-and-back on 4WD roads

**Rating** moderate/novice

**Other users** equestrian-2 motorized-5

**Distance** 33.3 km

**Time** 3-4 hours

**Maps** 83 B/4 Elk Creek 83 C/1 Whiterabbit Creek

**Season** mid-June to mid-October

**Land agency** Alberta Forest Service

**Access**
From SR 940, 2.7 km north of the Ram Falls recreation area, drive west for 5.3 km on the road to Hummingbird Creek equestrian staging area. Continue on for another 3.2 km to Canary Creek.

| | |
|---|---|
| 0.0 | trailhead |
| 3.5 | junction, keep right (Hummingbird Creek trail to left) |
| 14.8 | junction, keep left (right leads to North Ram River) |
| 16.4 | Onion Lake; junction, keep left (or return the way you came) |
| 17.8 | follow singletrack to left |
| 20.5 | Onion Lake Road, turn right |
| 33.3 | end of ride |

10          20          30   33.3

# 219 CANARY CREEK                                    map 54

This is a very popular area, especially on summer weekends. Begin the ride by fording Onion Creek and heading west on a dusty old road that can be muddy in wet weather. There are lots of creek crossings on this trip so you might as well opt to get your feet wet right at the start. The road fords Canary Creek twice and winds its way through valley-bottom willow meadows as it climbs into the heart of the Ram Range. At km 6.4 a major washout portends the end of the road. A singletrack trail continues onward for approximately 4 km into some beautiful sub-alpine country. Although used by quads and easy to follow, this trail is rough and difficult to cycle. It ends at a three-way junction with one trail leading south to the Ram River and the other north to Hummingbird Creek.

## Options

A loop with the Ram River trail is possible. If you choose to do this I suggest riding up the Ram and down Canary Creek. This way you get to check out the two difficult fords on the Ram River before you are committed. In addition, the upper part of the Canary Creek trail is all rideable in the downhill mode.

**Wilderness explorer**

**Type** out-and-back on 4WD road and singletrack

**Rating** moderate/intermediate

**Other users** hikers-1  equestrian-4  motorized-4

**Distance** 20 km

**Time** 3-4 hours

**Maps** 83 B/4 Elk Creek
83 C/1 Whiterabbit Creek

**Season** mid-June to mid-October

**Land agency** Alberta Forest Service

## Access

From SR 940, 2.7 km north of the Ram Falls recreation area, drive west for 5.3 km on the road to the Hummingbird Creek equestrian staging area. Continue on for a further 3.2 km to Canary Creek.

| | |
|---|---|
| 0.0 | trailhead<br>ford Hummingbird Creek |
| 6.4 | road washed-out,<br>singletrack continues |
| 10.0 | junction and end of ride (left to Ram River, right to Hummingbird Creek) |

20
19
18
17

2    4    6    8    10    12    14    16    18    20

# 220 CLEARWATER VALLEY                    map 55

This is a long valley-bottom ride that offers relatively easy but unexciting access into the remote and beautiful Clearwater Valley east of Banff National Park. The first 15 km of the ride is a routine bush slog, but the next 15 km from the vicinity of the Fortymile Cabin almost to the Banff boundary are challenging riding in a wild and beautiful setting. Overnight camping would help to temper the long distances involved in reaching the upper part of the valley, and provide an opportunity to explore some of the country. Hard-core bikers can make the entire trip in one very long day.

Ride away from the trailhead on a major equestrian trail that is a combination of doubletrack and singletrack and is occasionally wet, rocky and rooty. Beyond km 8 the trail is within a Forest Land Use Zone where neither motors nor cattle are permitted. Watch for a tricky right-hand turn and creek crossing at km 12.7 where going straight will dead-end you in a beaver pond. The Fortymile forestry patrol cabin and the trail leading south to the Ya-Ha-Tinda Ranch are reached at km 16 and here the forest opens into a beautiful valley bottom meadow surrounded by limestone peaks. The trail continues west to a major ford of the Clearwater River, which can usually be crossed on foot by mid-July. The ride to the ford and back to the trailhead makes a relatively easy day trip.

Beyond the ford a combination of doubletrack and singletrack continues through meadows and mixed wood forest becoming somewhat more rugged near the boundary of Banff National Park. This area of the park is zoned as wilderness and cycling is not permitted.

## Options

Combine this ride with the Ya-Ha-Tinda Ranch to Clearwater River trail (#224). It is 25.5 km from Fortymile Cabin over the summit to the Ya-Ha-Tinda Ranch on the Red Deer River and a lengthy car shuttle is required.

**Classic wilderness ride**

**Type** out-and-back on 4WD roads and singletrack

**Rating** difficult/intermediate

**Other users** hikers-1  equestrian-6  motorized-1  livestock

**Distance** 72 km

**Time** 8-12 hours

**Map** 82 O/13 Forbidden Creek

**Season** mid-June to mid-October

**Land agency** Alberta Forest Service

## Access

From SR 940, at a point 1.7 km north of the Seven Mile Flats recreation area, turn west onto the Cutoff Creek access road. Follow this road for 19 km to the equestrian staging area.

| | |
|---|---|
| 0.0 | trailhead |
| 7.0 | keep left on singletrack |
| 7.7 | junction, turn left |
| 12.7 | make sharp turn to right and ford creek |
| 16.0 | junction, keep right (left is trail to Ya-Ha-Tinda Ranch) |
| 16.3 | Fortymile Cabin |
| 20.4 | Clearwater River ford |
| 36.0 | Banff boundary |

10    20    30    40    50    60    70  72

# 221 LIMESTONE LOOKOUT                              map 56

The Limestone Fire Lookout provides excitement for fun-loving riders and speed freaks. The route is a combination of a gravel road in the forest, and doubletrack and singletrack through alpine meadows and along a rocky ridge to the summit. If you came here for reasons other than cycling, the ride can be shortened by driving to the top of the ridge.

Begin by grinding your gears up the hill to the ridge top. Beyond the Shell repeater the trail has some rough sections, but the ride across the alpine meadows makes up for it with a great view of the Bighorn Range to the west. Finally, a rough and rocky singletrack provides challenging riding as it leads around a minor summit and up to the fire lookout. Even if you do not score a cup of coffee at the lookout, the views of the Clearwater Valley and of the Bighorn Range to the west are ample reward for your efforts.

Gravity is your ally as you negotiate the tricky singletrack, then fly down the gravel road on the return trip. Watch for motor vehicles as you speed toward the valley bottom.

**Major vertical, great views**

**Type** out-and-back on 2WD and 4WD roads and singletrack

**Rating** difficult/intermediate

**Other users** hikers-2  motorized-3

**Distance** 20.8 km

**Time** 3-5 hours

**Map** 82 O/14 Limestone Mountain

**Season** mid-June to mid-October

**Land agency** Alberta Forest Service

**Access**
From SR 940, 10 km south of the James-Willson recreation area, turn north and follow a gas well access road for 14.1 km to a signed junction for LM6. The road to the right, leading uphill, is the cycle route.

| | |
|---|---|
| 0.0 | trailhead |
| 2.1 | junction, keep right |
| 3.2 | junction, keep right |
| 6.4 | junction, keep right |
| 8.0 | Shell repeater |
| 10.4 | fire lookout |

# 222 JAMES PASS & EAGLE LAKE
map 57

James Pass is a short, relatively easy ride that leads through the Bighorn Range, from the foothills on the east to the "prairies within the mountains" on the west.

From the east trailhead, cross the good-news gate (no motors!) and ride westward on a grassy doubletrack through valley-bottom willow meadows. The limestone cliffs of the Bighorn Range tower above the trail as you cross the infant James River at km 5. Continue on the rocky doubletrack past James Lake and on to the summit of the pass and Eagle Lake, known for its fishing but also offering a refreshing swim on a hot day. Pass the lake along the south shore on a doubletrack that is sometimes under water, or on a rough singletrack along the north shore. The trail leads west from the lake through more meadows, then descends a doubletrack along Eagle Creek, passing a nouveau-gauche western village shortly before it reaches Ya-Ha-Tinda Ranch Road.

## Options

Ride this trail as an out-and-back trip from the east trailhead. Combining it with some of the rides on the Ya-Ha-Tinda Ranch makes a very special day trip.

**Gentle ride from foothills to mountains**

**Type** point-to-point on 4WD roads and singletrack

**Rating** moderate/intermediate

**Other users** equestrian-3 motorized-1 livestock

**Distance** 10.6 km one way

**Time** 2-3 hours

**Map** 82 O/11 Burnt Timber Creek

**Season** mid-June to mid-October

**Land agency** Alberta Forest Service

## Access

**east** The trailhead is located on SR 940, 16.9 km north of the Red Deer River bridge.

**west** The trailhead is on Ya-Ha-Tinda Road, 18.5 km west of SR 940.

| | |
|---|---|
| 0.0 | east trailhead |
| 5.0 | James River ford |
| 6.0 | James Lake |
| 6.9 | James Pass |
| 7-8.0 | Eagle Lake |
| 10.6 | west trailhead |

# 223 YA-HA-TINDA RANGE RIDERS            map 57

Think of the prairie grasslands. Now imagine them surrounded by beautiful mountains. Voila—Ya-Ha-Tinda. This beautiful mountain grassland is largely owned by Parks Canada. The Ya-Ha-Tinda Ranch is used to raise and winter the park warden's horses, and is also home to a large herd of elk and, not uncommonly, bears and wolves. The area is drier than the surrounding mountains and this accounts for the sweeping fescue plains. The public is welcome to use the roads and trails on the ranch, but please remember that it is private property—respect signs and close gates.

Although you can drive across part of the ranch I suggest you park either at the ranch gate or at the Bighorn Campground and cycle from there. The area is beautiful and much of the experience is missed by driving. The ranch is crisscrossed by a variety of rough gravel roads and singletrack, and some of the shorter trails can be combined to provide an enjoyable day of riding. Elevation gain is minimal. This area is popular with equestrians, so please respect the rights of others and do your part to enhance the image of our sport.

The route log describes the ride across the ranch to the east boundary of Banff National Park. This trail leads west from Ya-Ha-Tinda Road and fords Scalp Creek, an easy task except during high runoff. The route is on a gravel, and sometimes very rocky road that goes west to the park boundary. This part of the park is zoned wilderness and bicycles are not permitted. For a much more interesting return trip follow the singletrack horse trails that wind between the river and the road and cut across the Scalp Creek fan.

**Ride the prairies within the mountains**

**Type** loop and out-and-back on 4WD roads and singletrack

**Rating** moderate/intermediate

**Other users** equestrian-6

**Distance** up to 60 km

**Time** 2-6 hours

**Maps** 82 O/11 Burnt Timber Creek
82 O/12 Barrier
82 O/13 Forbidden Creek

**Season** mid-may to mid-October

**Land agency** Parks Canada, Alberta Forest Service

**Access**
From SR 940, on the north side of the Red Deer River bridge, follow Ya-Ha-Tinda Ranch Road west for 19.2 km to the east gate of the ranch.

## Options

1. Old Wellsite. Turn right at km 5.7 of the route log and follow an old gravel exploration road as it climbs gradually for 6.3 km to a vantage point high above the valley. Those with hiking aspirations can easily reach the alpine ridge tops from here. Return the same way or follow the cutline west, then south to rejoin the main route.

2. Bighorn Pastures. This dirt doubletrack begins by climbing uphill on the east side of the Bighorn bridge. At km 2 the trail forks. The right branch leads to the northeast corner of the ranch and, for the hiker, high onto the shoulder of the Bighorn Range. The left branch leads to some cutblocks along the north boundary of the ranch.

3. Eagle Lake (#222). The ride from the ranch to Eagle Lake is short and pleasant on a good doubletrack.

4. Scalp Creek (#224). As part of a ride at the ranch, this trail should not be missed. Start just west of the Bighorn bridge on a singletrack leading uphill. Follow this dirt trail past Bighorn Falls and gradually climb to an incredible vantage point on the upper range. From here the view sweeps to the south and west across the grasslands and Red Deer River to the mountains. To the east James Pass and the Bighorn Range provide an impressive backdrop to the rangelands.

| | |
|---|---|
| 0.0 | east gate of Ya-Ha-Tinda Ranch |
| 2.3 | trail to Bighorn pastures leads uphill to right |
| 2.3 | Bighorn Creek bridge |
| 2.4 | junction, keep left (trail to upper Scalp Creek and Clearwater River to right) |
| 5.1 | junction, turn left (ranch headquarters to right) |
| 5.3 | ford Scalp Creek |
| 5.7 | junction, keep left (old wellsite to right) |
| 15.3 | west boundary of ranch |
| 17.4 | Banff Park boundary |

# 224 YA-HA-TINDA TO CLEARWATER RIVER     maps 57, 55

Do you like wild, remote country that has a real backcountry charm? This route reminds me of what it was like cycling the (now-closed) Cascade fireroad. The ride is on an old exploration road that leads north from the Ya-Ha-Tinda Ranch on the Red Deer River almost to the Fortymile patrol cabin on the Clearwater River. The road was constructed in the late 1950s in an unsuccessful search for oil and gas and, today, makes an excellent mountain bike route. The area is a Forest Land Use Zone so there are no motor vehicles allowed on these trails (Yahoo!).

Ride north on the singletrack as it climbs to the west of Bighorn Creek and passes Bighorn Falls. The trail climbs onto the upper range and provides you with some sweeping views of this incredible mountain grassland. Beyond km 3 the old gravel road is again rideable as it cuts above the ranch and climbs steadily along Scalp Creek.

Upper Scalp Creek flows in a very attractive valley—a worthy destination on its own. At km 13 the road rolls through extensive subalpine meadows covering the summit of the pass between Scalp and Skeleton creeks, then descends gradually through meadows and forest to Forbidden Creek. Here, where the road turns west, ford Forbidden Creek and ride downstream on a rocky doubletrack that leads to the Clearwater Valley trail. Fortymile Cabin is located 0.5 km west in a large and beautiful meadow surrounded by high limestone peaks. This is one of those idyllic spots where a person is sometimes possessed of a desire to stay forever.

## Options

1. Upper Scalp Creek valley can be accessed by a singletrack trail branching to the left at km 14.5.

2. The exploration road continues up Forbidden Creek for more than 5 km permitting easy exploration of the upper part of this valley.

3. See Clearwater Valley (#220) for additional options.

**Classic east slopes wilderness ride**
**Type** out-and-back on 4WD roads
**Rating** difficult/intermediate
**Other users** equestrian-4
**Distance** 51.6 km
**Time** 6-8 hours
**Maps** 82 O/12 Barrier
82 O/13 Forbidden Creek
**Season** July to mid-October
**Land agency** Alberta Forest Service, Parks Canada

**Access**
Begin at the Bighorn Creek bridge on the Ya-Ha-Tinda Ranch. Take the singletrack trail leading uphill on the west side of the bridge.

| | |
|---|---|
| 0.0 | Bighorn Creek bridge, ride west |
| 0.1 | keep right on singletrack leading uphill |
| 1.5 | Bighorn Falls |
| 3.0 | trail turns to left, old road begins |
| 5.0 | four-way junction, go straight |
| 9.8 | cross rough creek gully |
| 13.0 | summit |
| 14.5 | junction, keep right (left is upper Scalp Creek trail) |
| 22.4 | Forbidden Creek (road swings west), ford creek and follow doubletrack downstream |
| 25.5 | four-way junction, turn left |
| 25.8 | Fortymile patrol cabin |

21
20
18
16
15

10        20        30        40     51.6

# 225 BLUE HILL LOOKOUT
map 57

The Blue Hill Lookout is reached by one of the most pleasant lookout-road rides to be found. Instead of the usual straight up and down access road, this one is all rideable and the mountain and foothills panorama is second to none.

The trail is a good doubletrack, mostly gravel with a few clay sections. For the first 4 km it climbs, winds and dips along a forested ridge beside Logan Creek, but after crossing the creek on a bridge the climbing becomes more serious. By km 5 the forest begins to open out with views to the southwest and as you climb higher the views just keep getting better. Although below treeline, the summit has been cleared, providing an excellent overlook of the mountains, foothills and plains.

The lookout consists of a tower and house. When I was there the towerperson had set up a number of greenhouse beds in an attempt to bring some semblance of a normal life to this extraordinary occupation and location.

The trip down is fast paced and exciting. Once past the creek the riding is just plain rock and roll fun back to the trailhead.

**Gentle climb to great views**

**Type** out-and-back on 4WD roads

**Rating** moderate/intermediate

**Other users** hikers-2  motorized-2

**Distance** 16 km

**Time** 2-4 hours

**Map** 82 O/11 Burnt Timber Creek

**Season** mid-June to mid-October

**Land agency** Alberta Forest Service

**Access**
The trail begins at a locked gate on the north side of Hwy. 27, 2.9 km east of its junction with SR 940.

| | |
|---|---|
| 0.0 | trailhead |
| 4.0 | bridge |
| 8.0 | lookout |

# 226 WAIPAROUS CREEK                              map 4

Waiparous is a relatively easy ride into a low-elevation mountain valley. The trail leads from the foothills to a finale beneath the big rock walls of the front ranges. Here the edge of the mountains is very clearly defined by towering cliffs of Cambrian and Devonian limestone. The landscape is typical of the east slopes with pine and spruce forests and avens-covered river flats.

I suggest you begin riding at the Y-junction, although high-clearance and four-wheel-drive vehicles can drive for quite a distance up the road. You came here to cycle, right? Bump your way along the hard-packed and well-drained cobble road. Even in wet weather this route is rideable—with a couple of muddy sections and full potholes of course! At km 10.7 you pass the turn-off for Margaret Lake and encounter the first of six fords, which can prove quite difficult during periods of high runoff. The mountains seem to beckon you onward and soon you find yourself riding beneath the big walls of the Waiparous. It is a remarkable place.

This is a favourite area for the motorized recreation crowd, particularly on summer weekends, so time your visit accordingly. Especially at the beginning of the route, you will see lots of evidence of the behaviour that has given dirt biking a bad name with the environmental community. It is a clear statement of how a few renegades and thoughtless individuals can fashion the public image of an entire group (sound familiar?). As you proceed up the valley, the evidence of other users becomes somewhat less obtrusive. The return trip is quick and bumpy.

**Scenic cruise to front range ramparts**

**Type** out-and-back on 4WD roads

**Rating** moderate/novice

**Other users** equestrian-2 motorized-7

**Distance** 36 km

**Time** 5-6 hours

**Map** 82 O/6 Lake Minnewanka

**Season** mid-July to mid-October

**Land agency** Alberta Forest Service

**Access**
On SR 940, drive 13.3 km north of the Forest Reserve boundary. Turn west and follow Waiparous Valley Road for 2.8 km to a Y-junction. Park here. The trail is the left fork.

| | |
|---|---|
| 0.0 | trailhead |
| 10.7 | junction, Margaret Lake is 1.7 km to right |
| 10.8 | first ford |
| 18.0 | end of trail |

## Options

Margaret Lake. From the junction just before the first ford, follow a good trail to the right and up a hill. After 1 km follow the second cutline leading to the left for 0.7 km to the lake.

# 227 MOCKINGBIRD LOOKOUT                    map 4

Photo: Gillean Daffern.

This is a short ride to a lookout perched atop a high foothill. Mockingbird overlooks the spectacular cliff-edge formed by the front ranges to the west as well as providing a view over a sea of foothills. Ride this trail early in the day to get the hills silhouetted against the morning haze. The view includes an extensive panorama from Moose Mountain, south of the Trans-Canada Highway, to the Bighorn Range, north of the Red Deer River.

The ride up the access road passes a gate shortly after the trailhead and another shortly before the lookout. The uphill ride is a bit of a grind, but it never gets excessively steep. The road is constructed on well-drained materials and provides good riding in any weather. The return trip is a 10-minute scream. Because this ride is so short it is well suited to an evening jaunt.

**Gentle climb to great views**

**Type** out-and-back on 4WD roads

**Rating** moderate/novice

**Other users** hikers-3 motorized-3

**Distance** 6.2 km

**Time** 1-2 hours

**Map** 82 O/6 Lake Minnewanka

**Season** June to mid-October

**Land agency** Alberta Forest Service

**Access**
On SR 940, drive 13.3 km north of the Forest Reserve boundary. Turn left and follow Waiparous Valley Road for 3.8 km. The lookout road is on the right.

0.0    trailhead
3.1    lookout

# 228 DEVIL'S GAP                                      map 4

Photo: Gillean Daffern.

**Rugged ride below towering crags**

**Type** out-and-back on 4WD roads and singletrack

**Rating** moderate/intermediate

**Other users** hikers-1 equestrian-2

**Distance** 22 km

**Time** 2-3 hours

**Maps** 82 O/6 Lake Minnewanka 82 O/3 Canmore

**Season** May through October

**Land agency** Alberta Forest Service, Parks Canada

**Access**
From Cochrane, drive 13 km west on Hwy. 1A to SR 940, then north for 26 km to Ghost River Road, an unsigned, gated gravel road (200 m north of Richards Road). Drive 16 km west on this rough road and park at the top of a steep hill overlooking the Ghost River and Devil's Gap.

| | |
|---|---|
| 0.0 | trailhead, ride down hill and across river channel |
| 3.5 | park boundary sign |
| 8.0 | junction, keep left (right is ford to Lake Minnewanka trail) |
| 11.0 | Lake Minnewanka |

Although the access is a bit on the rough side, this is the perfect way to spend a day riding singletrack trails through the awe-inspiring Devil's Gap. Towering limestone cliffs line both sides of this narrow defile that leads from the foothills through the first range of mountains to Lake Minnewanka.

Begin by riding the road down the hill, then across the Ghost River diversion works to the park boundary sign. Past the sign the trail is a bit confusing, generally keep to the left until you find yourself on a good singletrack. The trail descends gently westward beneath the towering crags, passes the Ghost Lakes and comes to a signed trail junction and ford. Cross here if you are riding through to Banff. Otherwise follow the singletrack to the left passing the last of the Ghost Lakes and continuing on to the shores of Lake Minnewanka. This is a good spot to end your ride, although the trail continues for another 5 km along the lakeshore.

## Routes described in text

| | |
|---|---|
| paved | ———————————— |
| 2WD dirt | — — — — — — — |
| 4WD dirt | —··—··—··—··— |
| singletrack | - - - - - - - - - |

## Other routes

| | |
|---|---|
| paved | ———————————— |
| 2WD dirt | — — — — — — — |
| 4WD dirt | —··—··—··—··— |
| singletrack | - - - - - - - - - |

| | |
|---|---|
| pass | ⌣ |
| peak | ▲ |
| campground | △ |
| building | ■ |
| viewpoint | ✳ |
| distance between points | ●—3.5—● |
| trail number | **71** |
| land above 1800 m | ⬭ |
| urban area | ▬ |
| lake | ⬬ |

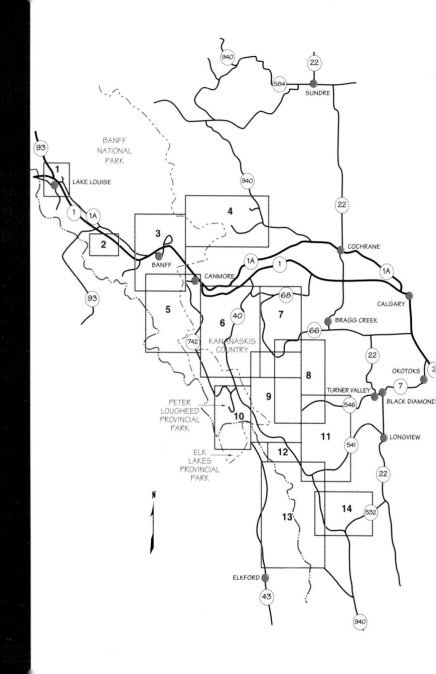

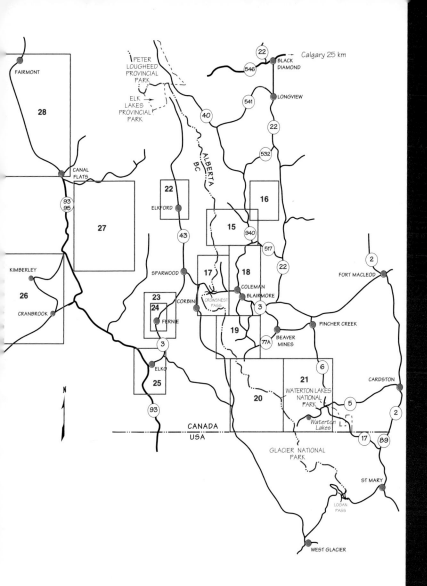

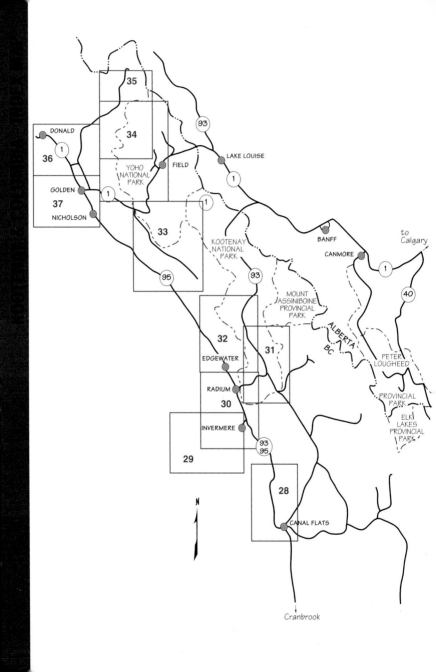

35

DONALD

36

1

34

YOHO
NATIONAL
PARK

FIELD

93

LAKE LOUISE

1

GOLDEN

1

37

NICHOLSON

33

KOOTENAY
NATIONAL
PARK

95

93

BANFF

to
Calgary

CANMORE

1

MOUNT
ASSINIBOINE
PROVINCIAL
PARK

40

32

31

ALBERTA
BC

PETER
LOUGHEED

EDGEWATER

RADIUM

PROVINCIAL
PARK

30

INVERMERE

ELK
LAKES
PROVINCIAL
PARK

29

93
95

28

N

CANAL FLATS

Cranbrook

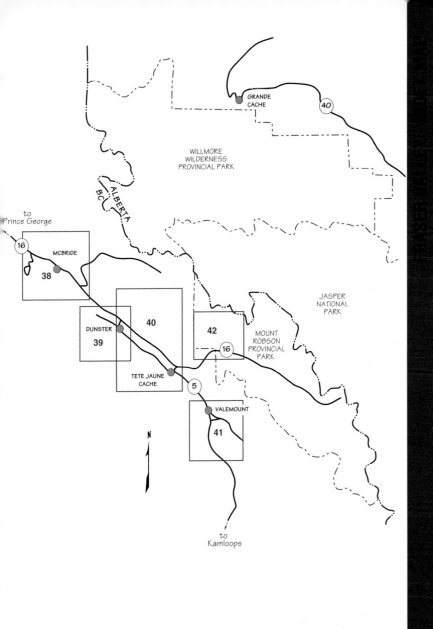

to Prince George

16

MCBRIDE

38

WILLMORE
WILDERNESS
PROVINCIAL PARK

GRANDE
CACHE

40

ALBERTA
BC

JASPER
NATIONAL
PARK

DUNSTER

39

40

42

MOUNT
ROBSON
PROVINCIAL
PARK

16

TETE JAUNE
CACHE

5

VALEMOUNT

41

N

to
Kamloops

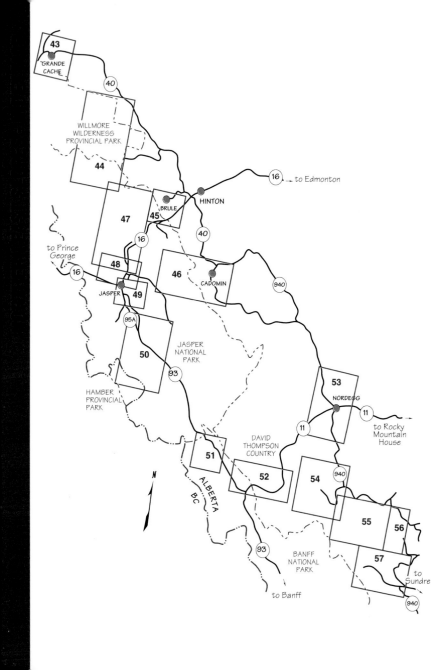

**43**
GRANDE CACHE

(40)

WILLMORE WILDERNESS PROVINCIAL PARK

**44**

**47**

BRULE
HINTON

**45**

(16) → to Edmonton

(16)

(40)

to Prince George

(16)

**48**

**46**
CADOMIN

(940)

JASPER

**49**

(95A)

**50**

JASPER NATIONAL PARK

(93)

HAMBER PROVINCIAL PARK

**53**
NORDEGG

(11) → to Rocky Mountain House

**51**

DAVID THOMPSON COUNTRY

(11)

**52**

**54**

(940)

N

ALBERTA
BC

**55**

**56**

(93)

BANFF NATIONAL PARK

**57**

to Sundre

to Banff

(940)

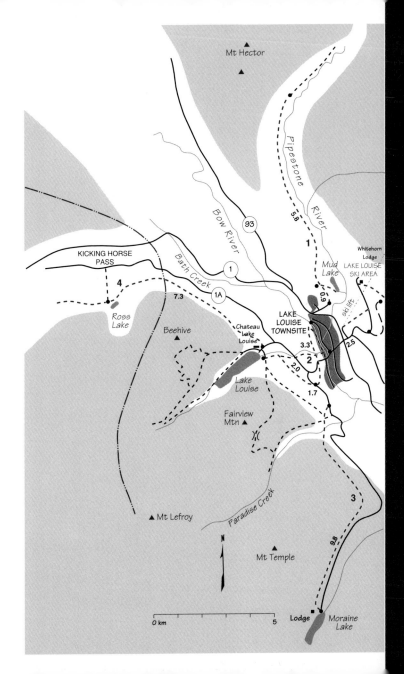

Mt Hector

Pipestone River

Bow River

93

5.8

1

Bath Creek

1

KICKING HORSE PASS

1A

Whitehorn Lodge

Mud Lake

LAKE LOUISE SKI AREA

4

7.3

0.9

ski lift

Ross Lake

Beehive

Chateau Lake Louise

LAKE LOUISE TOWNSITE

3.3

2.5

2

2.0

Lake Louise

1.7

Fairview Mtn

Mt Lefroy

Paradise Creek

3

N

Mt Temple

9.8

Lodge

Moraine Lake

0 km          5

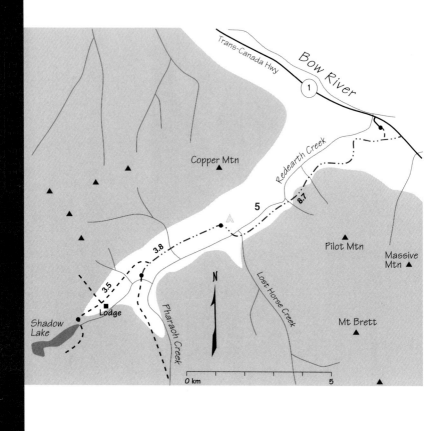

Trans-Canada Hwy

Bow River

1

Copper Mtn

Redearth Creek

5

8.7

3.8

Pilot Mtn

Massive Mtn

3.5

Lost Horse Creek

Shadow Lake

Lodge

Pharaoh Creek

Mt Brett

N

0 km          5

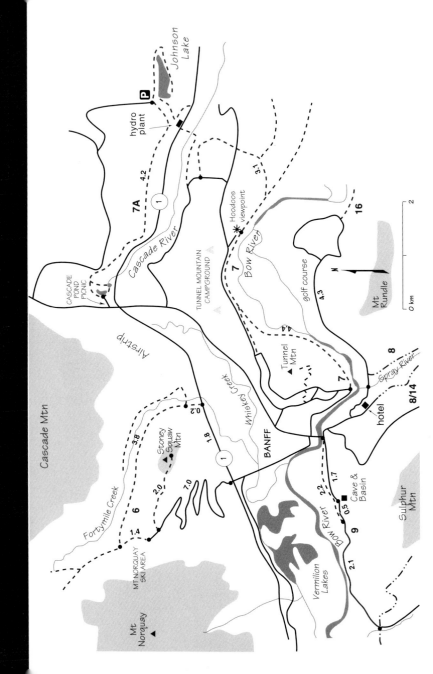

Johnson Lake

P

hydro plant

7A

4.2

1

Cascade River

CASCADE POND PICNIC

Airstrip

Cascade Mtn

Mt Norquay

MT NORQUAY SKI AREA

1.4

6

2.0

7.0

Stoney Squaw Mtn

3.8

0.2

1.8

1

Whiskey Creek

Fortymile Creek

BANFF

Vermilion Lakes

Bow River

2.1

9

0.5

Cave & Basin

1.7

2.2

TUNNEL MOUNTAIN CAMPGROUND

Tunnel Mtn

Hoodoos viewpoint

3.1

7

Bow River

1.1

16

golf course

4.3

N

0 km        2

Mt Rundle

7

hotel

8

Spray River

8/14

Sulphur Mtn

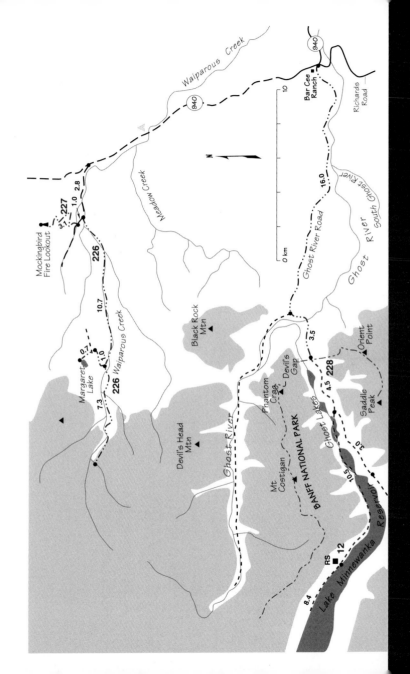

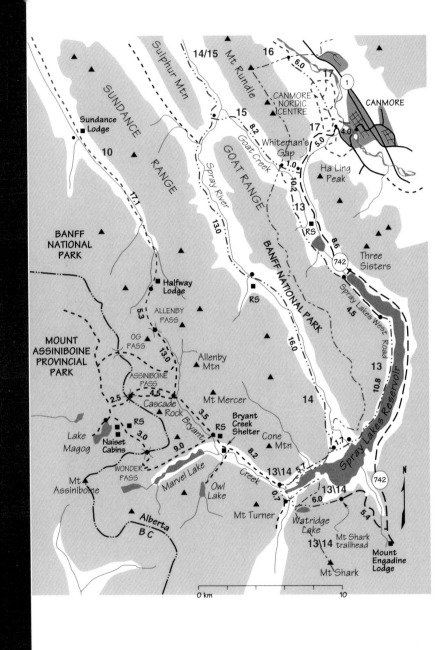

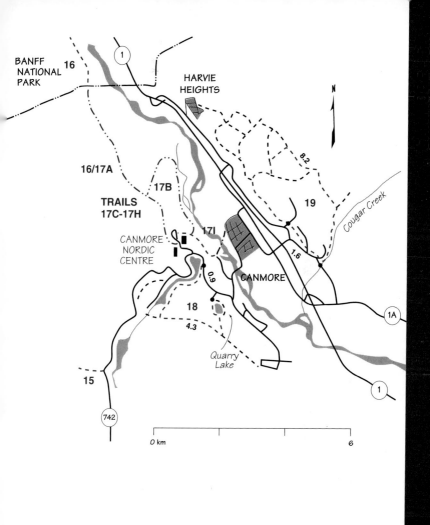

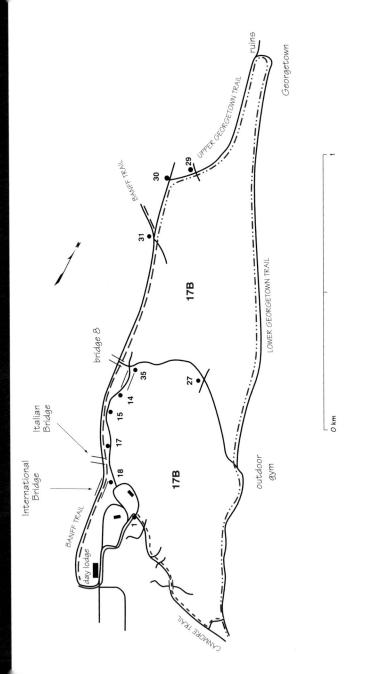

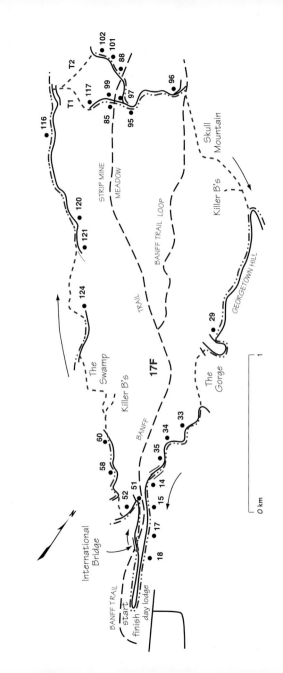

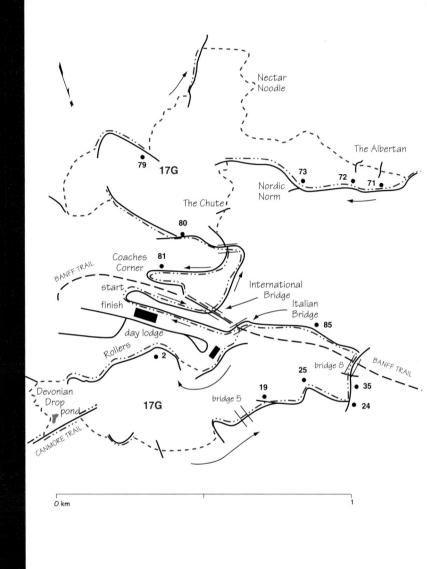

Nectar
Noodle

The Albertan

79   **17G**

73      72    71

Nordic
Norm

The Chute

80

Coaches   **81**
Corner

International
Bridge

Italian
Bridge

*BANFF TRAIL*

start

finish

85

day lodge

Rollers

• 2

25    bridge 8

*BANFF TRAIL*

19

35

Devonian
Drop
pond

**17G**

bridge 5

24

*CANMORE TRAIL*

0 km                                                                1

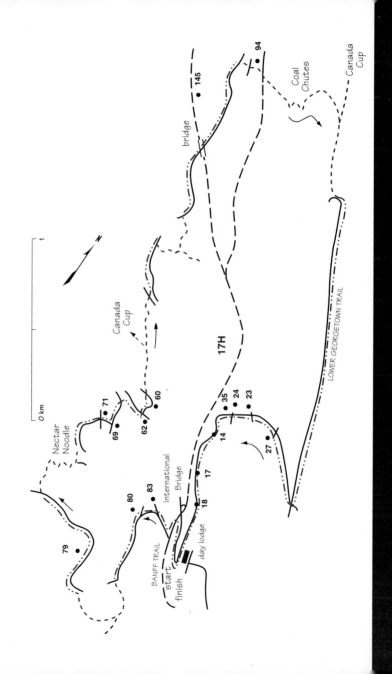

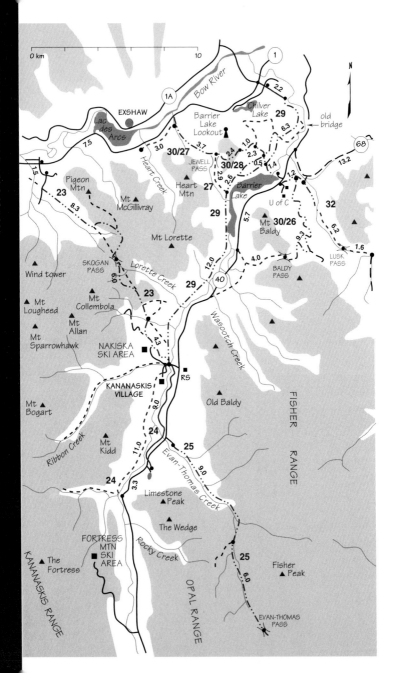

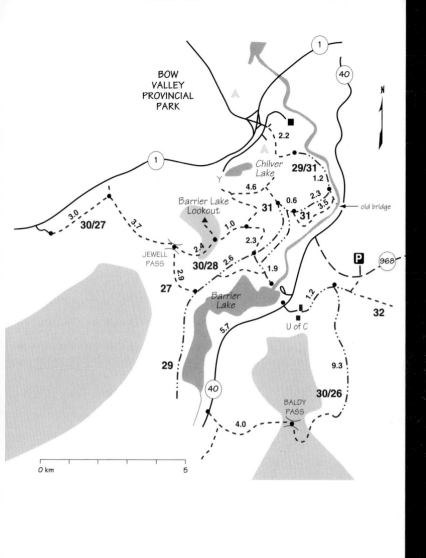

BOW
VALLEY
PROVINCIAL
PARK

Chilver
Lake

29/31

Barrier Lake
Lookout

31

31

old bridge

30/27

JEWELL
PASS

30/28

27

Barrier
Lake

U of C

32

29

BALDY
PASS

30/26

0 km                    5

Y

1
40
1
968
40

2.2
1.2
4.6
0.6
2.3
3.5
3.0
3.7
1.0
2.4
2.3
2.6
2.9
1.9
5.7
1.2
9.3
4.0

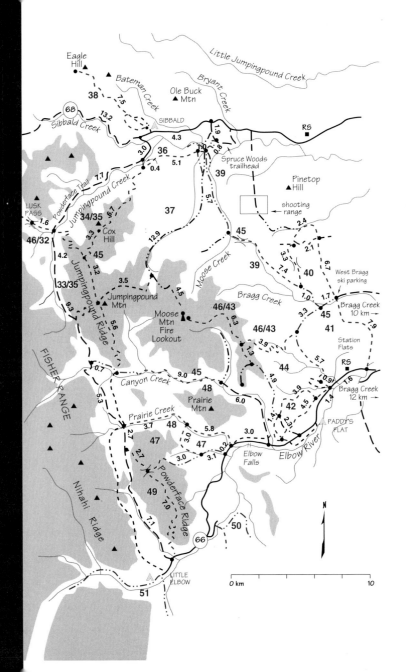

Little Jumpingpound Creek

Eagle Hill ▲

Bateman Creek

Bryant Creek

Ole Buck ▲ Mtn

38

7.5

68

13.2

Sibbald Creek

SIBBALD

4.3

1.9

RS ■

0.8

Spruce Woods trailhead

3.0

36

0.4

5.1

39

Pinetop ▲ Hill

Powderface Trail

1.7

Jumpingpound Creek

37

5.7

shooting range

LUSK PASS ▲

1.6

34/35

6.7

45

2.4

46/32

3.3

Cox Hill ▲

12.9

39

2.1

3.3

40

West Bragg ski parking

4.2

45

3.2

3.5

Moose Creek

7.4

1.0

1.7

33/35

9.3

Jumpingpound Mtn

4.5

Bragg Creek

3.3

45

Bragg Creek 10 km →

5.6

46/43

41

7.9

Jumpingpound Ridge

Moose Mtn Fire Lookout

6.3

46/43

5.7

Station Flats

FISHER RANGE

1.1

1.3

44

RS ■

0.9

0.7

9.0

45

3.9

4.9

3.9

Bragg Creek 12 km →

5.3

Canyon Creek

48

4.9

42

4.5

1.4

Prairie Mtn ▲

6.0

1.4

2.3

PADDY'S FLAT

Prairie Creek

3.7

48

5.8

3.0

Elbow River

2.7

47

3.0

0.2

Elbow Falls

2.7

47

3.0

3.1

Nihahi Ridge

Powderface Ridge

49

7.0

N

7.1

66

50

0 km        10

LITTLE ELBOW

51

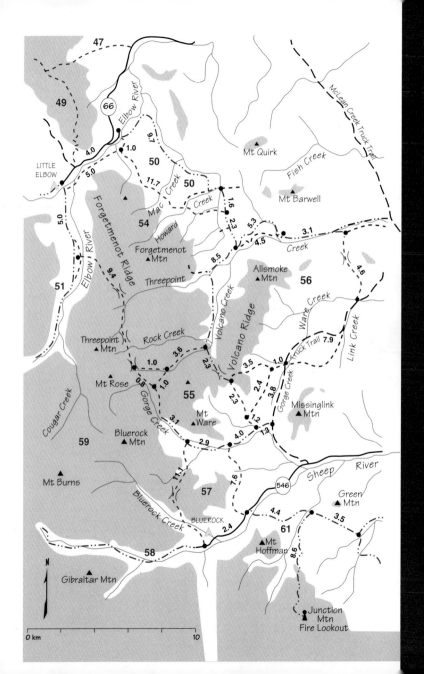

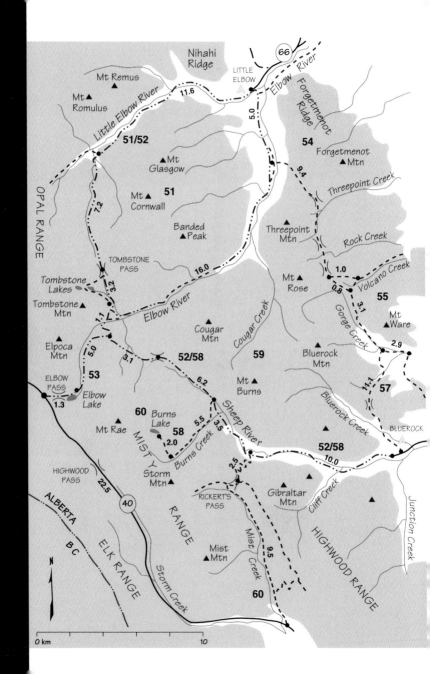

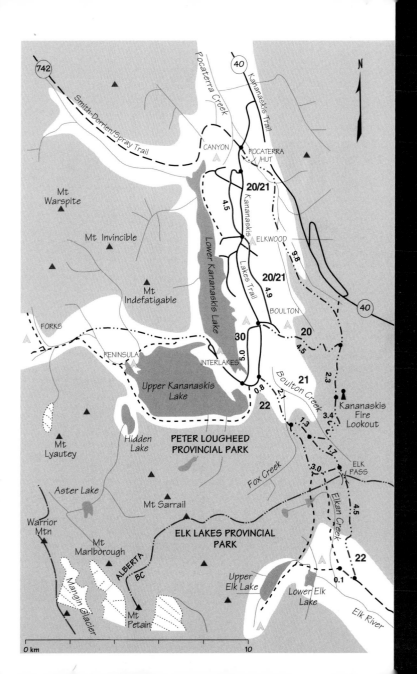

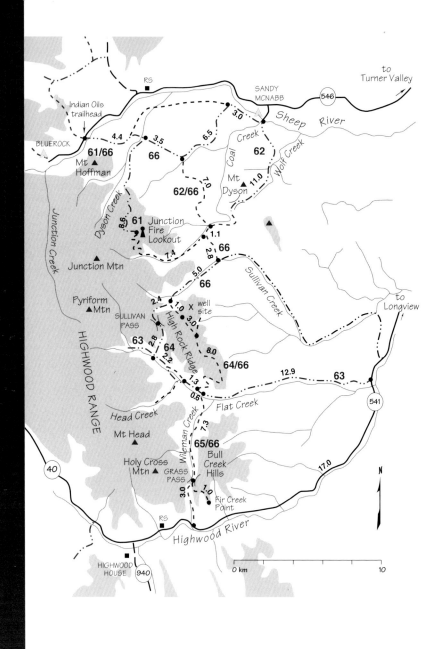

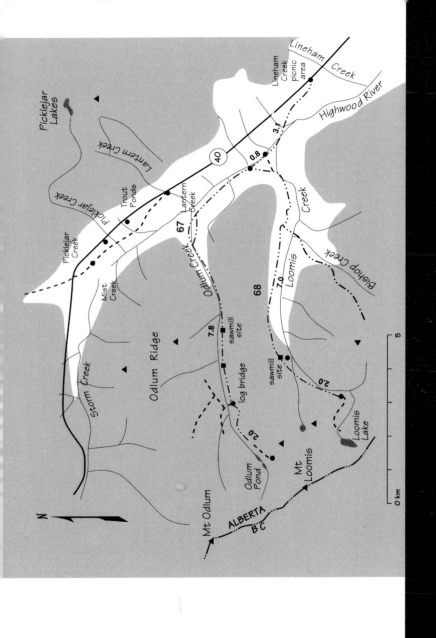

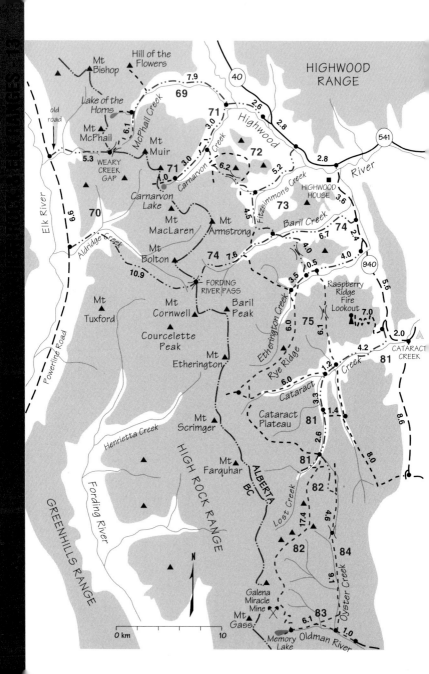

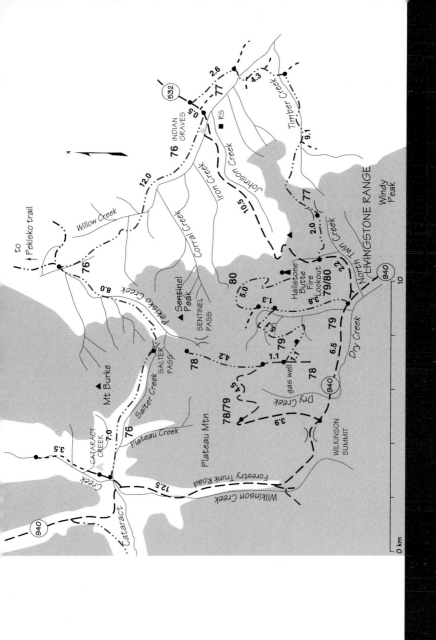

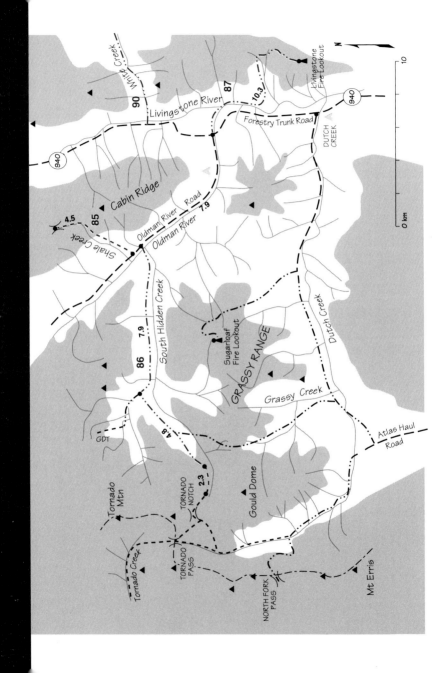

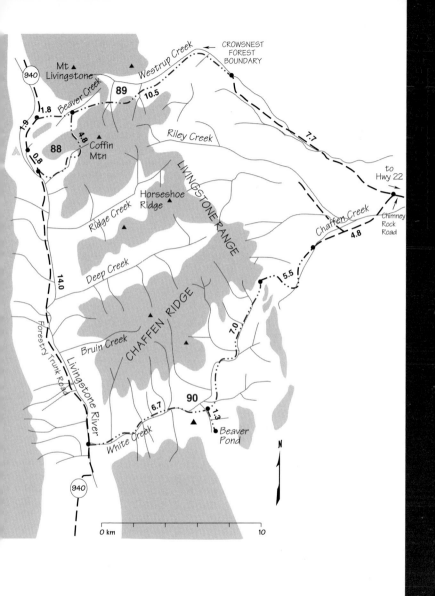

940

Mt Livingstone ▲

Westrup Creek

CROWSNEST FOREST BOUNDARY

Beaver Creek

89

10.5

1.9

1.8

4.8

88

0.8

Coffin Mtn ▲

Riley Creek

7.7

to Hwy 22

LIVINGSTONE RANGE

Horseshoe Ridge ▲

Chaffen Creek

Chimney Rock Road

Ridge Creek ▲

4.8

5.5

Deep Creek

CHAFFEN RIDGE

14.0

▲

Bruin Creek

7.0

▲

Forestry Trunk Road

Livingstone River

6.7

90

1.3

▲

White Creek

Beaver Pond

N

940

0 km          10

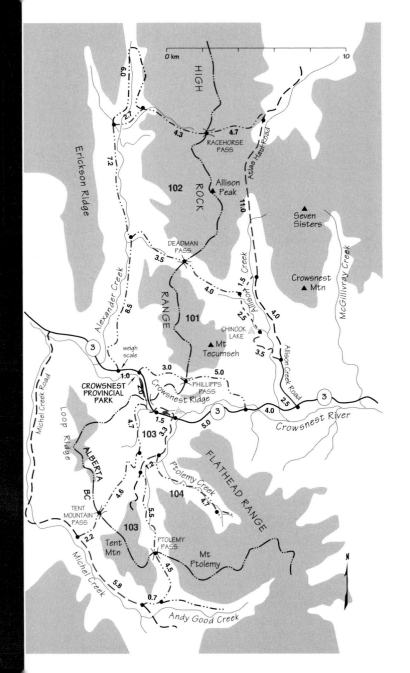

HIGH

6.0

2.1

7.2

Erickson Ridge

4.3    4.7
RACEHORSE PASS

102

ROCK

Allison
Peak

0.11

DEADMAN
PASS

3.5

RANGE

8.5

4.0

101

Alexander Creek

weigh
scale

3.0

1.0

CROWSNEST
PROVINCIAL
PARK

Crowsnest Ridge

Michel Creek Road

Loop Ridge

4.7

1.5

ALBERTA

BC

103  3.3

4.6

TENT
MOUNTAIN
PASS

2.2

103

Tent
Mtn

5.8

Michel Creek

0.7

0 km                                    10

Atlas Haul Road

Seven
Sisters

1.5 Creek

Allison Creek

2.5

Crowsnest
Mtn

4.0

CHINOOK
LAKE

3.5

▲ Mt
Tecumseh

PHILLIPPS
PASS

5.0

3

5.0

4.0

Crowsnest River

Allison Creek Road

2.5

3

McGillivray Creek

FLATHEAD
RANGE

Ptolemy Creek

104

4.7

5.5

PTOLEMY
PASS

4.5

Mt
Ptolemy

Andy Good Creek

N

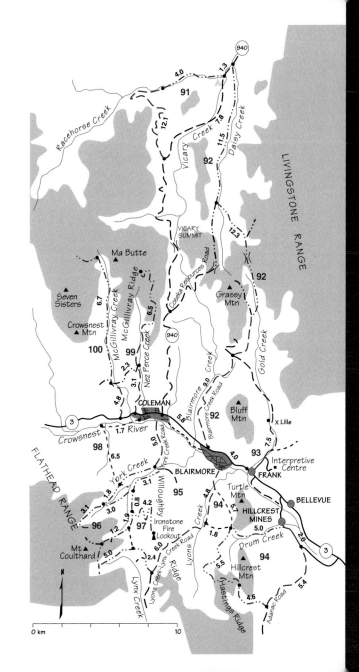

940

4.0

91

1.3

12.1

Racehorse Creek

7.8

Vicary Creek

11.5

92

Daisy Creek

LIVINGSTONE RANGE

VICARY
SUMMIT

12.3

Ma Butte

92

McGillivray Ridge

Grassy
Mtn

Seven
Sisters

6.7

McGillivray Creek

6.5

Crosska Resources Road

Crowsnest
Mtn

100

99

2.3

3.1

940

Gold Creek

Nez Perce Creek

Blairmore Creek Road

9.0

Bluff
Mtn

4.8

COLEMAN

5.8

92

X Lille

3

1.7  River

Crowsnest

98

6.5

5.0

York Creek Road

York Creek

4.0

7.5

93

Interpretive
Centre

FLATHEAD RANGE

3.1

Willoughby

3.1

95

FRANK

BELLEVUE

3.1

1.8

0.8

4.2

BLAIRMORE

4.8

Turtle
Mtn

94

5.1

HILLCREST
MINES

3.0

1.9

97

Ironstone
Fire
Lookout

Lyons Creek

1.8

5.0

2.0

3

96

1.2

Lyons Creek-Lynx Creek Road

Lyons Creek Road

Drum Creek

94

Mt
Coulthard

5.0

2.4

5.5

Hillcrest
Mtn

Lynx Creek

Hastings Ridge

4.6

Adanac Road

5.4

N

0 km                    10

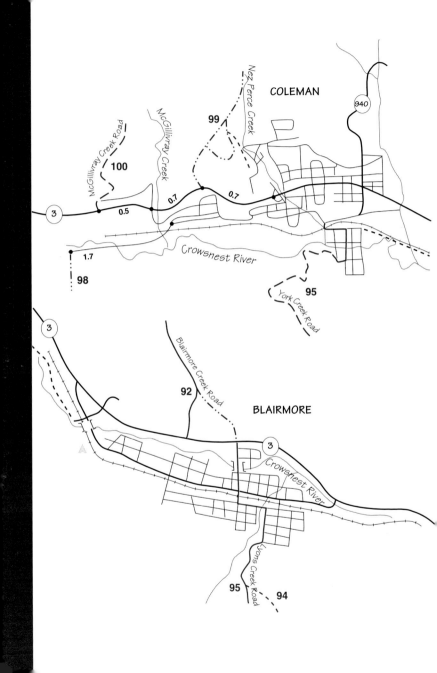

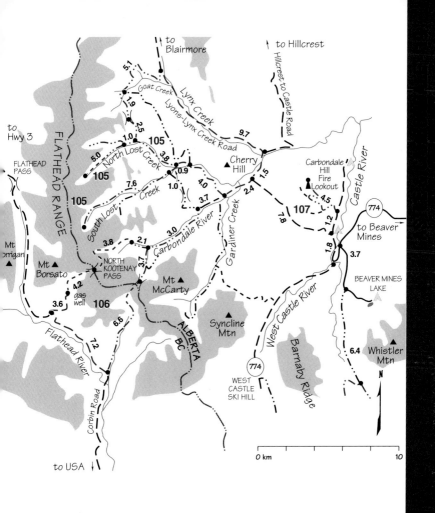

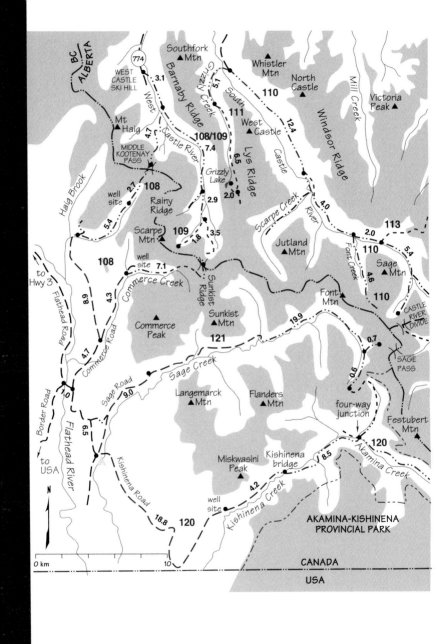

BC / ALBERTA

774

WEST CASTLE SKI HILL

Southfork Mtn

▲ Whistler Mtn

▲ North Castle

Mill Creek

Victoria Peak ▲

West Castle River

Barnaby Ridge

Grizzly Creek

South Castle

3.1

5.1

110

111

108/109

7.4

6.5

West Castle ▲

Windsor Ridge

12.4

Mt Haig ▲

4.7

MIDDLE KOOTENAY PASS

Lys Ridge

Grizzly Lake

2.0

2.7

108

well site

Rainy Ridge

2.9

Scarpe Creek

4.0

113

2.0

Haig Brook

5.4

Scarpe Mtn ▲

109

1.8

3.5

Jutland Mtn ▲

Font Creek

110

5.4

Sage Mtn ▲

well site

7.1

108

Commerce Creek

Sunkist Ridge

4.6

110

CASTLE RIVER DIVIDE

to Hwy 3

Flathead Road

8.9

4.3

Commerce Road

Commerce Peak ▲

Sunkist Mtn ▲

121

19.9

Font Mtn ▲

0.7

SAGE PASS

4.7

Sage Creek

Langemarck Mtn ▲

Flanders Mtn ▲

0.6

Border Road

1.0

Sage Road

9.0

four-way junction

Festubert Mtn ▲

to USA

Flathead River

6.5

Kishinena Road

Miskwasini Peak ▲

Kishinena bridge

8.5

120

Akamina Creek

N

well site

4.2

18.8

120

Kishinena Creek

AKAMINA-KISHINENA PROVINCIAL PARK

0 km                    10

CANADA

USA

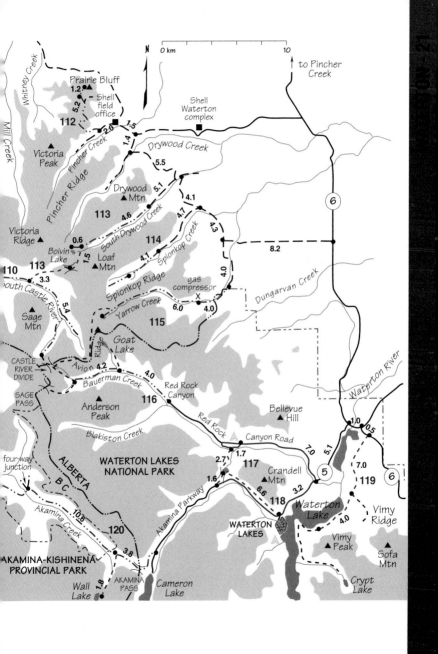

to Pincher Creek

N

0 km          10

Whitney Creek

Mill Creek

Prairie Bluff
1.2 ▲
5.2
Shell field office
112
2.0    1.5
1.4
Drywood Creek
5.5

Victoria Peak
Pincher Creek
Pincher Ridge

Shell Waterton complex

Drywood ▲ Mtn
5.1
4.1
113    4.6
4.7
South Drywood Creek
114    4.3
Victoria Ridge ▲
0.6
Boivin Lake
1.5    Loaf Mtn
4.1    Spionkop Creek
8.2
110    113
3.3
South Castle River
5.4
Spionkop Ridge
gas compressor
X
4.0
Dungarvan Creek

Sage ▲ Mtn
Yarrow Creek
6.0    4.0
115

CASTLE RIVER DIVIDE
Avion Ridge    4.2
Goat Lake
Bauerman Creek    4.0
Red Rock Canyon
SAGE PASS
Anderson ▲ Peak
116

Bellevue ▲ Hill

Waterton River

Blakiston Creek

four-way junction
ALBERTA
B C
WATERTON LAKES NATIONAL PARK
Red Rock Canyon Road
▲
1.7
2.7
117
Crandell ▲ Mtn
7.0
5.1
1.0    0.5
5
119    7.0
6

Akamina Creek    10.6
1.6
Akamina Parkway
6.6
118    3.2
Waterton Lake
4.0

AKAMINA-KISHINENA PROVINCIAL PARK
120
3.8
WATERTON LAKES

Vimy ▲ Peak
Vimy Ridge
Sofa ▲ Mtn

Wall Lake    1.8
AKAMINA PASS
Cameron Lake
Crypt Lake

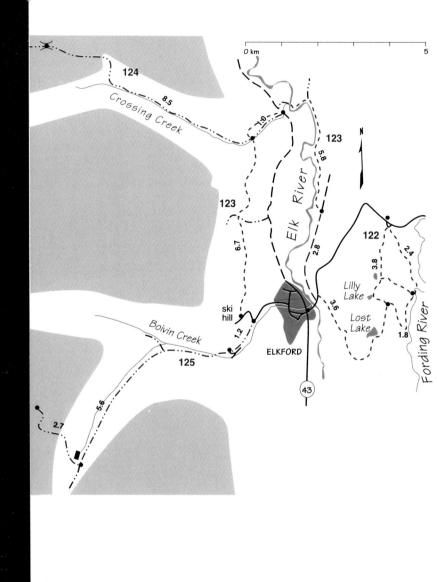

O km 5

124

Crossing Creek

8.5

7.0

123

5.8

123

6.7

N

Elk River

2.8

122

2.4

3.8

Lilly Lake

ski hill

1.2

3.6

Lost Lake

1.8

Boivin Creek

125

ELKFORD

Fording River

43

5.6

2.7

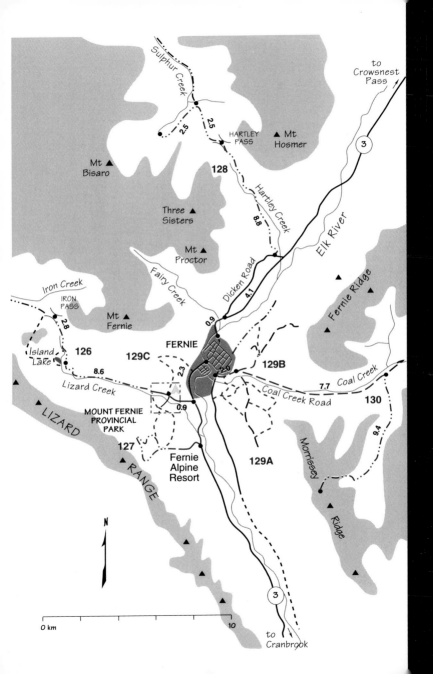

Sulphur Creek
to Crowsnest Pass
3
2.5
2.5
HARTLEY PASS
Mt Hosmer ▲
128
Mt Bisaro ▲
Hartley Creek
8.8
Three Sisters ▲
Elk River
Mt Proctor ▲
Fairy Creek
Dicken Road
4.1
Iron Creek
0.9
Fernie Ridge
IRON PASS
2.8
Mt Fernie ▲
FERNIE
Island Lake
126
129C
129B
8.6
2.3
2.0
7.7
Coal Creek
Lizard Creek
0.9
130
MOUNT FERNIE PROVINCIAL PARK
Coal Creek Road
9.4
127
Fernie Alpine Resort
129A
Morrissey Ridge
LIZARD RANGE
N
3
0 km                    10
to Cranbrook

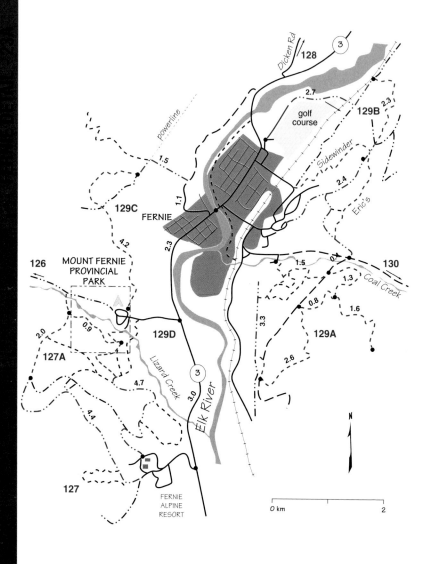

Dicken Rd

128

3

2.7

golf
course

129B

2.3

powerline

Sidewinder

1.5

2.4

Eric's

1.1

129C

FERNIE

2.3

130

1.5

0.4

Coal Creek

126

MOUNT FERNIE
PROVINCIAL
PARK

4.2

1.3

0.8

1.6

2.0

0.9

129D

3.3

129A

127A

2.6

Lizard Creek

4.7

3

3.0

Elk River

4.4

127

FERNIE
ALPINE
RESORT

N

0 km                    2

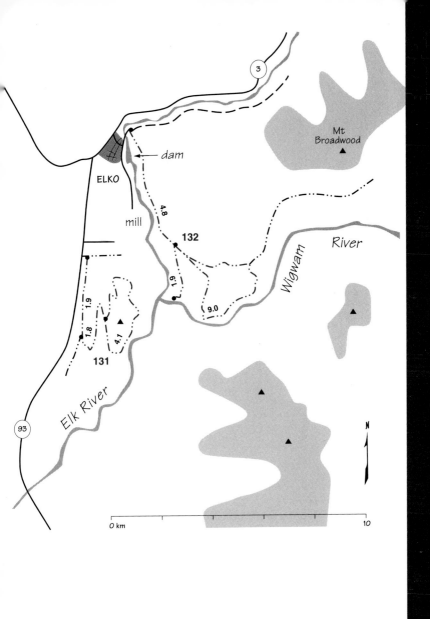

3

Mt
Broadwood
▲

dam

ELKO

4.8

mill

**132**

River

Wigwam

6.1

9.0

1.9

1.8

4.1

**131**

▲

Elk River

93

▲

▲

▲

N

0 km                                    10

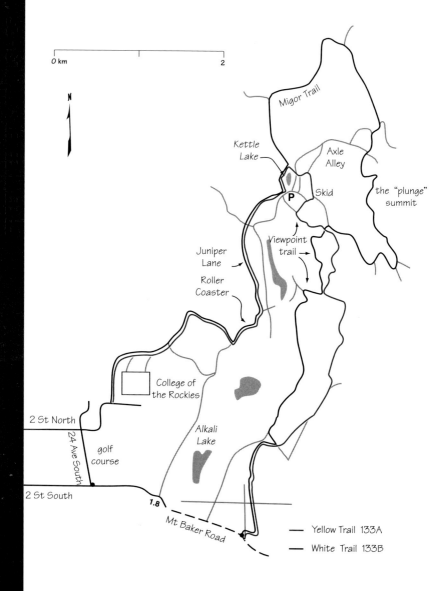

0 km                    2

N

Migor Trail

Kettle
Lake

Axle
Alley

P

Skid

the "plunge"
summit

Viewpoint
trail

Juniper
Lane

Roller
Coaster

College of
the Rockies

2 St North

24 Ave South

golf
course

Alkali
Lake

2 St South

1.8

Mt Baker Road

—— Yellow Trail 133A

—— White Trail 133B

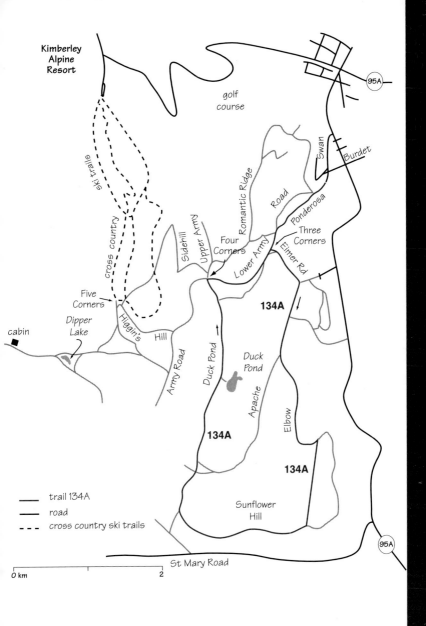

Kimberley
Alpine
Resort

golf
course

95A

Swan

Burdet

ski trails

cross country

Romantic Ridge

Road

Ponderosa

Three
Corners

Sidehill

Upper Army

Four
Corners

Lower Army

Elmer Rd

Five
Corners

134A

Higgin's
Hill

Dipper
Lake

cabin

Army Road

Duck Pond

Duck
Pond

Apache

Elbow

134A

134A

Sunflower
Hill

95A

St Mary Road

_____ trail 134A

_____ road

- - - cross country ski trails

0 km                    2

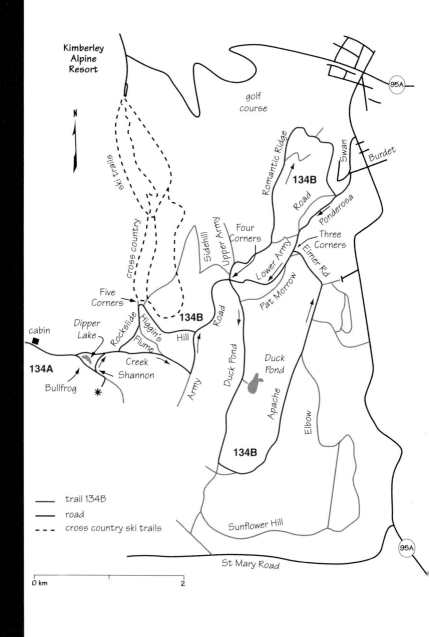

Kimberley Alpine Resort

N

golf course

ski trails

cross country

Romantic Ridge

134B

Swan

Burdet

Ponderosa

Sidehill

Upper Army

Four Corners

Road

Three Corners

Lower Army

Elmer Rd

Five Corners

Higgin's

134B

Pat Morrow

cabin

Dipper Lake

Rockslide

Flume

Hill

Road

Duck Pond

Duck Pond

134A

Creek

Shannon

Army

Apache

Elbow

Bullfrog

☀

134B

Sunflower Hill

95A

St Mary Road

95A

trail 134B
road
cross country ski trails

0 km                    2

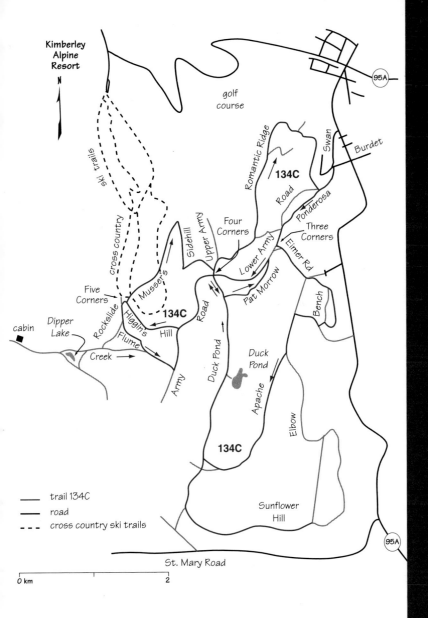

Kimberley
Alpine
Resort

N

95A

golf
course

ski trails

cross country

Romantic Ridge

Swan

Burdet

134C

Road

Ponderosa

Sidehill

Four
Corners

Three
Corners

Upper Army

Lower Army

Elmer Rd

Mussel's

Five
Corners

134C

Pat Morrow

Rockside

Higgins

Hill

Road

Bench

cabin

Dipper
Lake

Flume

Duck Pond

Duck
Pond

Creek

Army

Apache

Elbow

134C

Sunflower
Hill

95A

trail 134C
road
cross country ski trails

0 km                    2

St. Mary Road

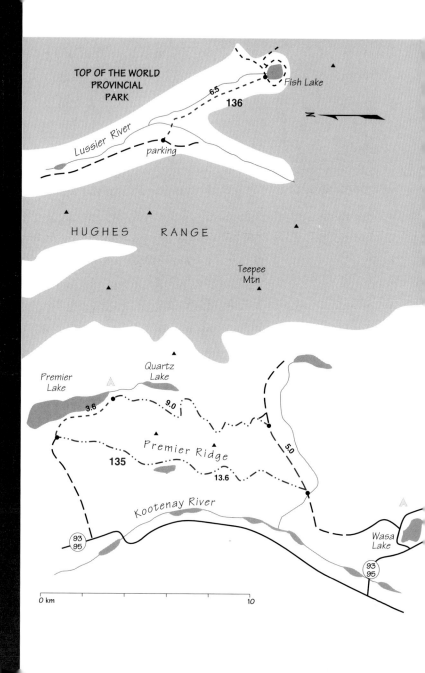

TOP OF THE WORLD
PROVINCIAL
PARK

Fish Lake

6.5

**136**

Lussier River

parking

N

HUGHES RANGE

Teepee
Mtn

Quartz
Lake

Premier
Lake

3.6

9.0

Premier Ridge

**135**

13.6

5.0

Kootenay River

Wasa
Lake

93
95

93
95

0 km                                    10

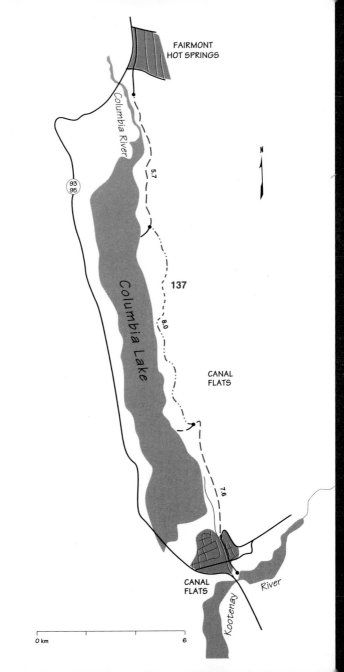

FAIRMONT
HOT SPRINGS

Columbia River

93
95

5.7

Columbia Lake

**137**

8.0

CANAL
FLATS

N

7.6

CANAL
FLATS

Kootenay River

0 km                                    6

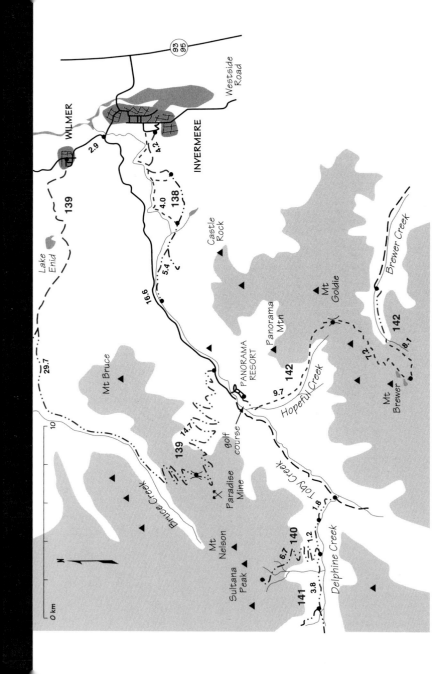

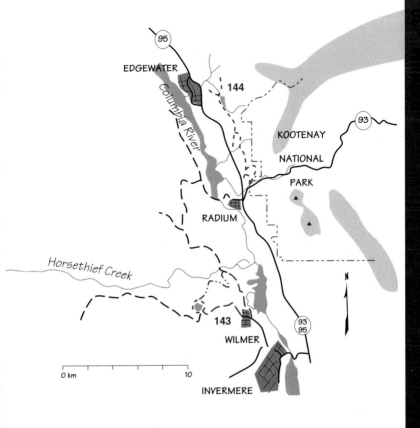

95

EDGEWATER

144

Columbia River

KOOTENAY

NATIONAL

PARK

RADIUM

93

Horsethief Creek

N

143

93
95

WILMER

0 km                    10

INVERMERE

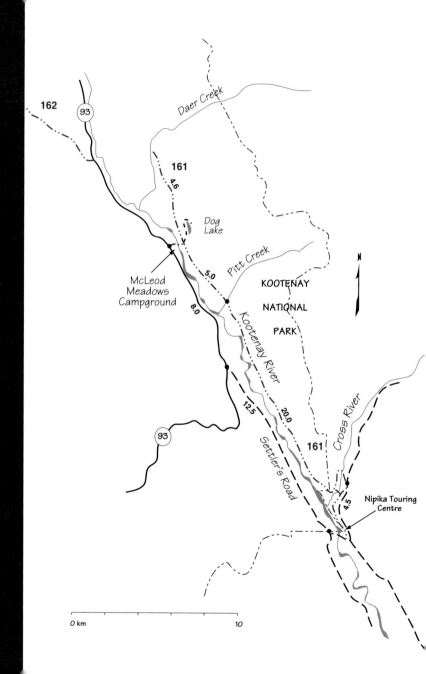

162

93

Daer Creek

161

4.6

Dog
Lake

5.0

Pitt Creek

McLeod
Meadows
Campground

8.0

KOOTENAY

NATIONAL

PARK

Kootenay River

N

93

12.5

20.0

161

Settler's Road

Cross River

4.5

Nipika Touring
Centre

0 km                    10

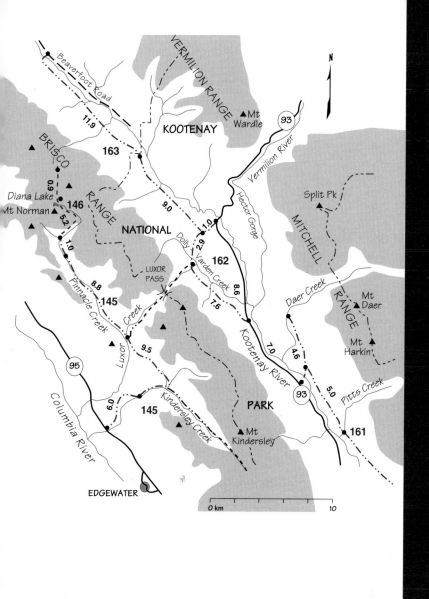

Beaverfoot Road

VERMILION RANGE

KOOTENAY

▲Mt Wardle

93

11.9

BRISCO

163

Vermilion River

Split Pk
▲

0.90

▲

Diana Lake

146

Hector Gorge

MITCHELL

Mt Norman ▲

5.2

▲

NATIONAL

9.0

1.0

RANGE

1.0

Dolly

2.9

162

Varden Creek

Mt Daer ▲

8.8

LUXOR PASS

8.6

Daer Creek

145

Pinnacle Creek

7.6

Mt Harkin ▲

Creek

Kootenay River

Luxor

9.5

7.0

4.6

95

6.0

145

Kindersley Creek

5.0

Pitts Creek

Columbia River

PARK

93

▲Mt Kindersley

161

EDGEWATER

0 km                    10

N

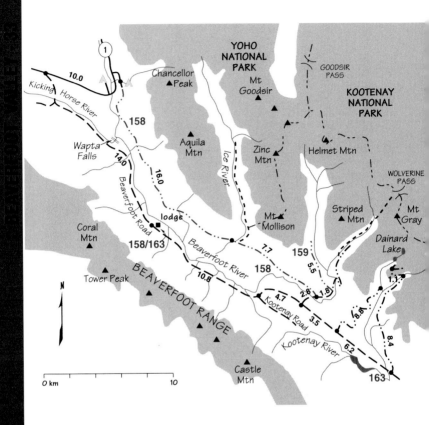

YOHO
NATIONAL
PARK

GOODSIR
PASS

KOOTENAY
NATIONAL
PARK

Kicking Horse River

10.0

Chancellor
▲ Peak

Mt
Goodsir
▲

▲

Wapta
Falls

158

14.0

16.0

Aquila
Mtn
▲

Ice River

Zinc
Mtn
▲

Helmet Mtn

WOLVERINE
PASS

Coral
Mtn
▲

Beaverfoot Road

lodge

Beaverfoot River

Mt
Mollison
▲

Striped
▲ Mtn

Mt
▲ Gray

Dainard
Lake

158/163

7.7

159

5.5

1.1

Tower Peak
▲

158

10.8

4.7

2.6

1.8

8.4

N

BEAVERFOOT RANGE

Kootenay Road

3.5

8.4

▲

▲

Kootenay River

6.2

163

0 km                    10

Castle
Mtn
▲

1

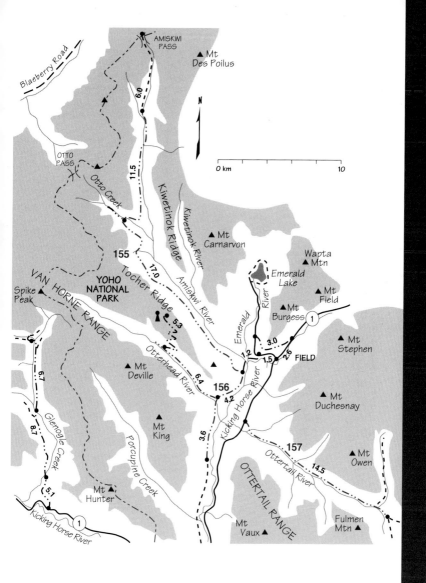

AMISKWI PASS

▲ Mt Des Poilus

Blaeberry Road

6.0

OTTO PASS

Otto Creek

11.5

N

0 km — 10

Kiwetinok Ridge

Kiwetinok River

▲ Mt Carnarvon

Wapta Mtn ▲

Emerald Lake

155

Tocher Ridge

17.0

VAN HORNE RANGE

YOHO NATIONAL PARK

Spike Peak ▲

5.3

Emerald River

▲ Mt Field

▲ Mt Burgess

1

3.0

2.6 FIELD

1.2

1.5

▲ Mt Stephen

Amiskwi River

Otterhead River

6.4

▲

156

4.2

6.7

▲ Mt Deville

▲ Mt King

8.7

Glenogle Creek

Porcupine Creek

5.1

Kicking Horse River

3.6

Kicking Horse River

▲ Mt Hunter ▲

1

▲ Mt Duchesnay

157

14.5

Ottertail River

OTTERTAIL RANGE

▲ Mt Owen

Mt Vaux ▲

Fulmen Mtn ▲

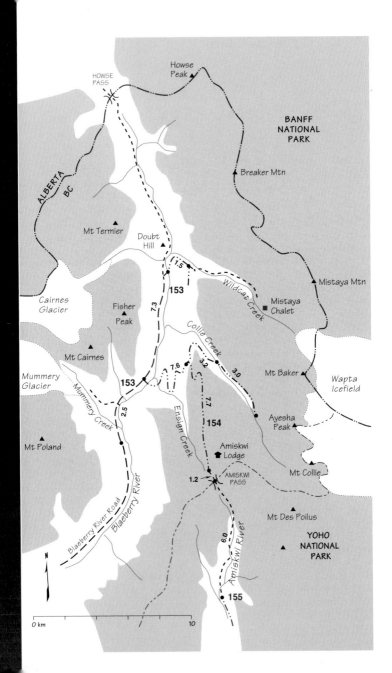

HOWSE PASS

Howse
Peak ▲

BANFF
NATIONAL
PARK

ALBERTA

BC

▲ Breaker Mtn

Mt Termier ▲

Doubt
Hill ▲

1.5

153

Wildcat Creek

▲ Mistaya Mtn

Mistaya
Chalet ■

Cairnes
Glacier

Fisher
Peak ▲

7.3

Collie Creek

Mt Cairnes ▲

3.2

7.6

3.0

Mummery
Glacier

153

Mt Baker ▲

Wapta
Icefield

Mummery Creek

2.5

Ensign Creek

7.7

154

Ayesha
Peak ▲

Mt Poland ▲

Amiskwi
Lodge ⌂

Mt Collie ▲

Blaeberry River Road

Blaeberry River

1.2

AMISKWI
PASS

Mt Des Poilus ▲

N

6.0

Amiskwi River

YOHO
NATIONAL
PARK

155

0 km                    10

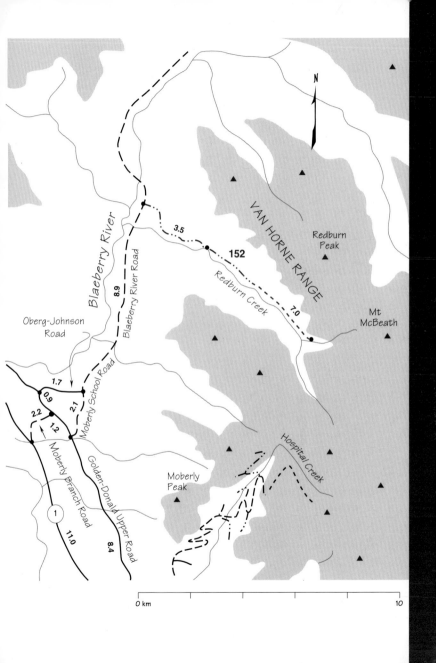

N

Blaeberry River

VAN HORNE RANGE

Redburn Peak

3.5

152

7.0

Redburn Creek

Mt McBeath

Oberg-Johnson Road

Blaeberry River Road

Moberly School Road

1.7

0.9

2.1

2.2

1.2

Golden-Donald Upper Road

Moberly Branch Road

1

11.0

8.4

Moberly Peak

Hospital Creek

0 km                                                                                    10

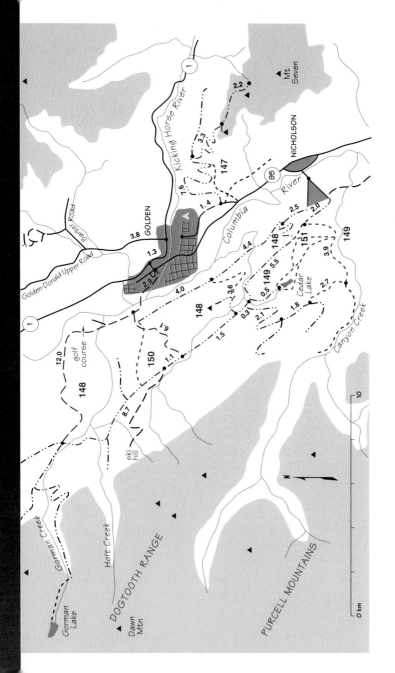

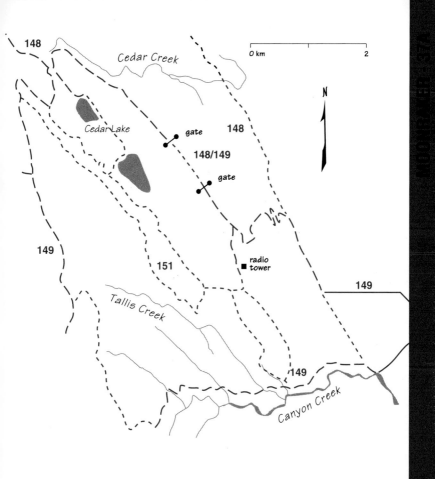

148

Cedar Creek

*0 km*           2

N

Cedar Lake

gate

148

148/149

gate

149

151

radio
tower

149

Tallis Creek

149

Canyon Creek

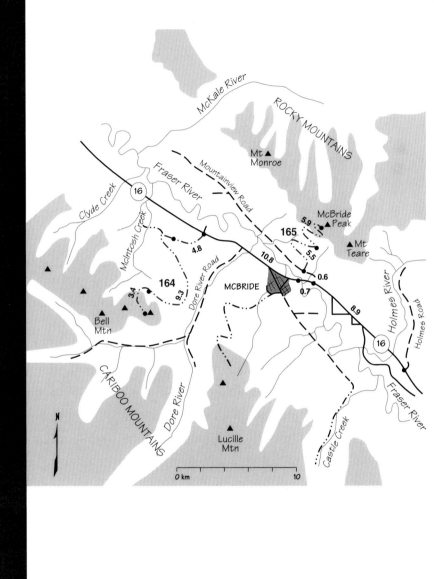

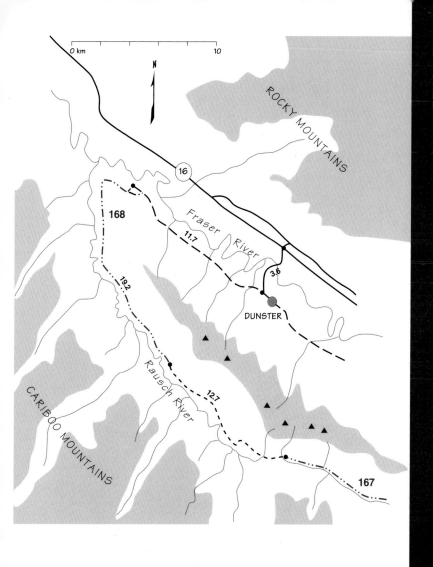

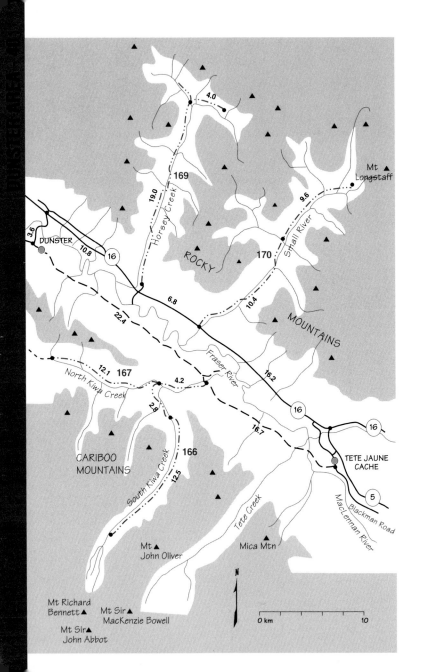

4.0

169

19.0

Horsey Creek

Mt ▲
Longstaff

9.6

Small River

3.6

DUNSTER

10.8

16

ROCKY

170

6.8

10.4

MOUNTAINS

22.4

Fraser River

16.2

North Kiwa Creek

12.1 167

4.2

2.9

16

16

CARIBOO
MOUNTAINS

South Kiwa Creek

166

12.5

16.7

TETE JAUNE
CACHE

5

Tete Creek

Mica Mtn

MacLennan River

Blackman Road

N

Mt ▲
John Oliver

Mt Richard
Bennett ▲

Mt Sir ▲
MacKenzie Bowell

Mt Sir ▲
John Abbot

0 km                    10

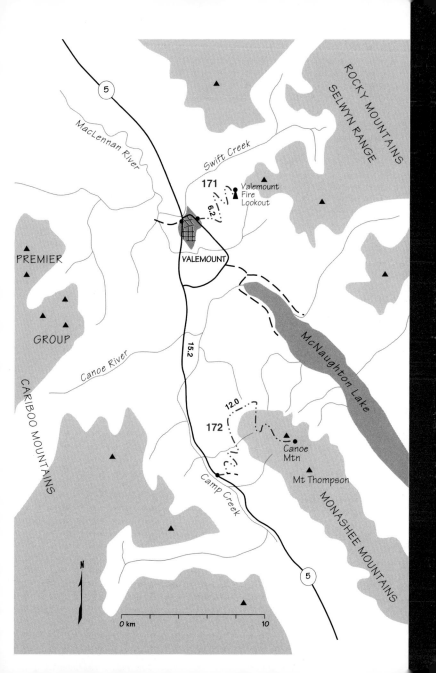

ROCKY MOUNTAINS
SELWYN RANGE

MacLennan River

Swift Creek

**171**

6.2

Valemount
Fire
Lookout

**VALEMOUNT**

PREMIER

GROUP

Canoe River

CARIBOO MOUNTAINS

McNaughton Lake

15.2

12.0

**172**

Canoe
Mtn

Mt Thompson

Camp Creek

MONASHEE MOUNTAINS

N

0 km                    10

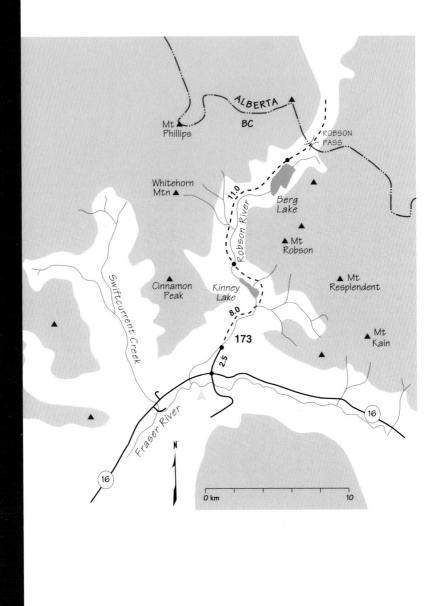

ALBERTA
BC

Mt
Phillips

ROBSON
PASS

Whitehorn
Mtn ▲

11.0

Robson River

Berg
Lake

▲ Mt
Robson

Cinnamon
Peak ▲

Kinney
Lake

▲ Mt
Resplendent

Swiftcurrent Creek

8.0

173

2.5

▲ Mt
Kain

16

Fraser River

N

16

0 km                                    10

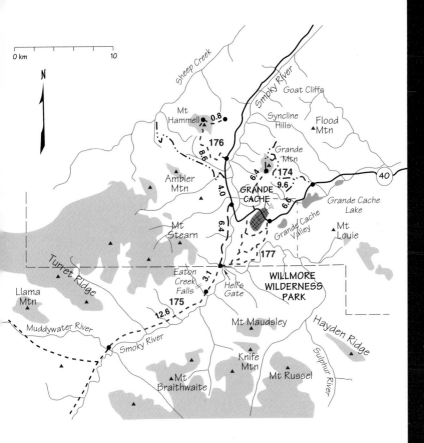

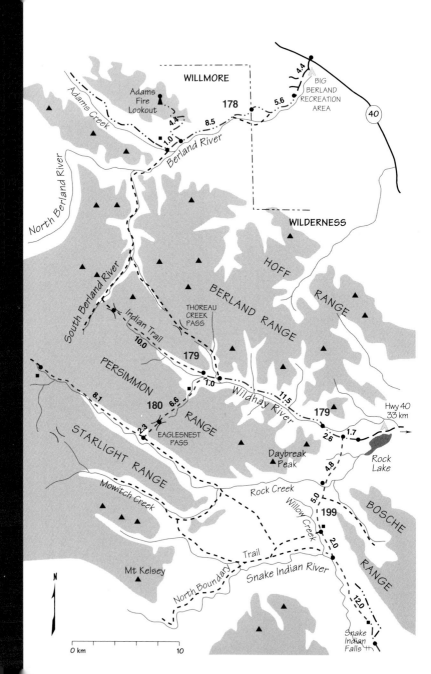

WILLMORE

Adams Fire Lookout

Adams Creek

44

5.6

BIG BERLAND RECREATION AREA

40

178

8.5

4.4

1.0

Berland River

North Berland River

WILDERNESS

HOFF

RANGE

South Berland River

BERLAND RANGE

Indian Trail

THOREAU CREEK PASS

10.0

179

PERSIMMON

1.0

Wildhay River

11.5

179

Hwy 40 33 km

8.1

180

6.6

RANGE

2.3

EAGLESNEST PASS

2.6

1.7

STARLIGHT RANGE

Daybreak Peak

4.8

Rock Lake

BOSCHE

Mowitch Creek

Rock Creek

Willow Creek

5.0

199

2.0

RANGE

Mt Kelsey

North Boundary

Trail

Snake Indian River

12.0

N

0 km                                     10

Snake Indian Falls

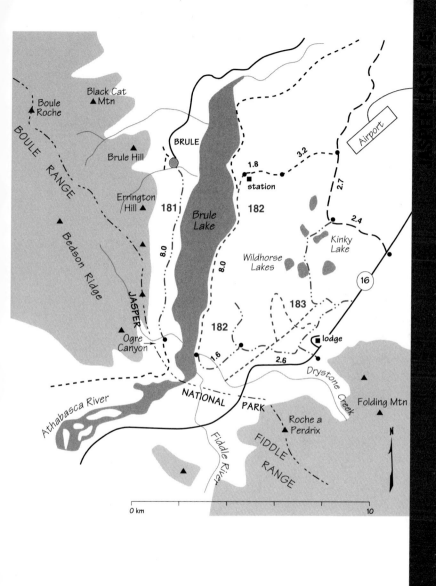

Boule
Roche

Black Cat
▲ Mtn

BOULE RANGE

Brule Hill ▲

BRULE

Airport

3.2

1.8

station

2.7

Errington
Hill ▲

181

Brule
Lake

182

2.4

▲

Kinky
Lake

16

Bedson Ridge

▲

Wildhorse
Lakes

▲

JASPER

183

▲

Ogre
Canyon

182

lodge

▲

8.0

8.0

1.6

2.6

Drystone Creek

Folding Mtn
▲

Athabasca River

NATIONAL    PARK

Roche a
Perdrix ▲

Fiddle River

FIDDLE
RANGE

▲

N

0 km                                          10

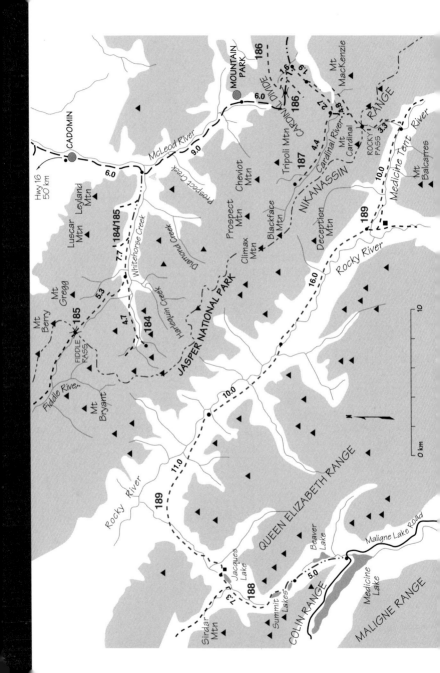

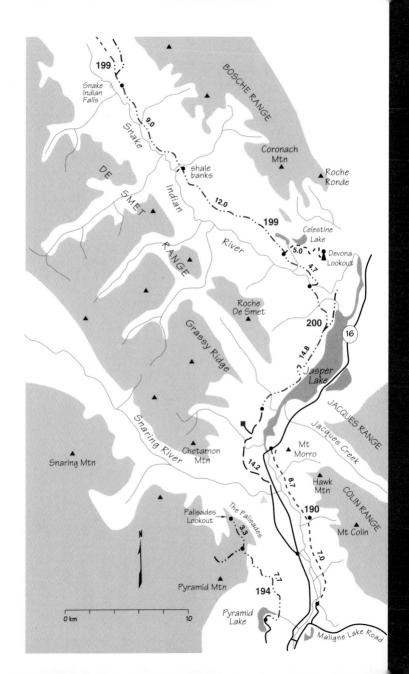

**199**

Snake Indian Falls

9.0

Snake

DE

Indian

shale banks

SMET

BOSCHE RANGE

Coronach Mtn

Roche Ronde

RANGE

12.0

River

**199**

Celestine Lake

5.0

Devona Lookout

4.7

Roche De Smet

**200**

14.8

16

Grassy Ridge

Jasper Lake

JACQUES RANGE

Jacques Creek

Snaring River

Chetamon Mtn

Snaring Mtn

14.2

Mt Morro

8.7

Hawk Mtn

COLIN RANGE

**190**

Mt Colin

7.0

Palisades Lookout

The Palisades

3.3

N

Pyramid Mtn

7.7

**194**

Pyramid Lake

Maligne Lake Road

0 km          10

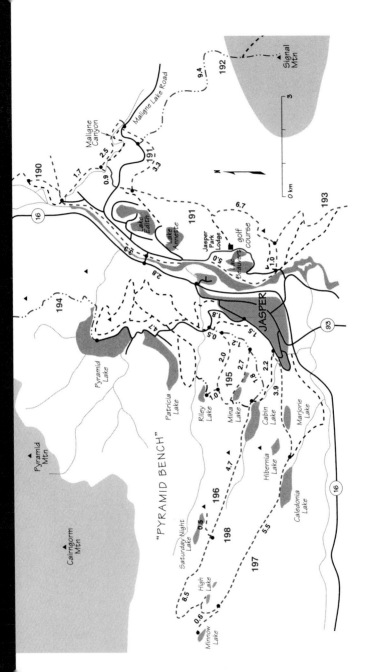

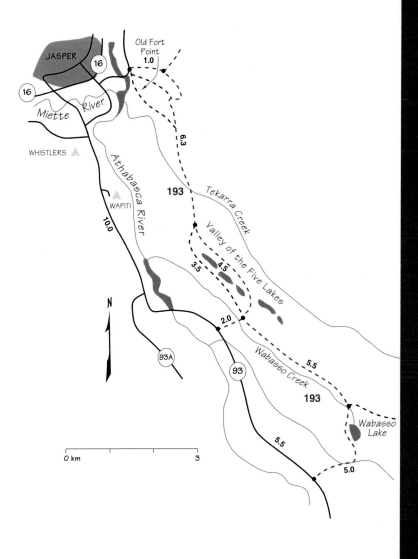

JASPER

16

16

Old Fort
Point
1.0

Miette River

WHISTLERS

Athabasca River

WAPITI

10.0

6.3

193

Tekarra Creek

Valley of the Five Lakes

3.5

4.5

2.0

93A

93

Wabasso Creek

5.5

193

Wabasso Lake

5.5

5.0

N

0 km                3

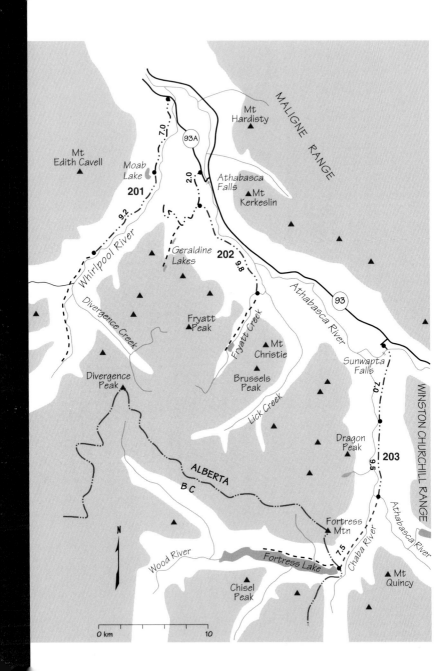

Mt Edith Cavell ▲

Mt Hardisty ▲

MALIGNE RANGE

93A

7.0

Moab Lake

**201**

2.0

Athabasca Falls

▲Mt Kerkeslin

9.2

Whirlpool River

Geraldine Lakes

**202**

9.8

Divergence Creek

Fryatt ▲ Peak

Fryatt Creek

▲Mt Christie

Athabasca River

93

Divergence Peak ▲

Brussels Peak ▲

Lick Creek

Sunwapta Falls

7.0

WINSTON CHURCHILL RANGE

ALBERTA

B C

Dragon Peak ▲

9.5

**203**

Wood River

Fortress Mtn

7.5

Chaba River

Athabasca River

Fortress Lake

Chisel Peak ▲

▲ Mt Quincy

N

0 km                    10

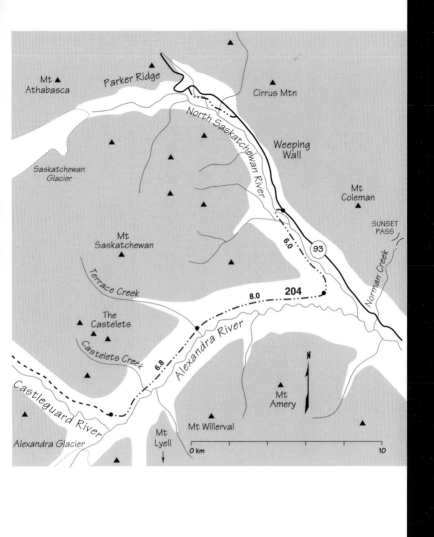

Mt Athabasca

Parker Ridge

North Saskatchewan River

Cirrus Mtn

Weeping Wall

Saskatchewan Glacier

Mt Coleman

SUNSET PASS

6.0

93

Mt Saskatchewan

Terrace Creek

8.0    204

The Castelets

Castelets Creek

6.8

Alexandra River

Norman Creek

Castleguard River

N

Mt Amery

Alexandra Glacier

Mt Lyell

Mt Willerval

0 km          10

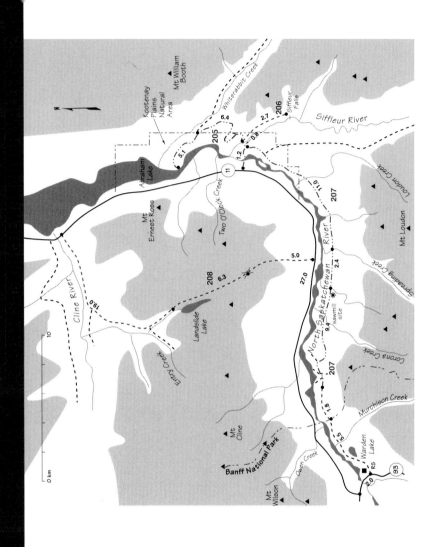

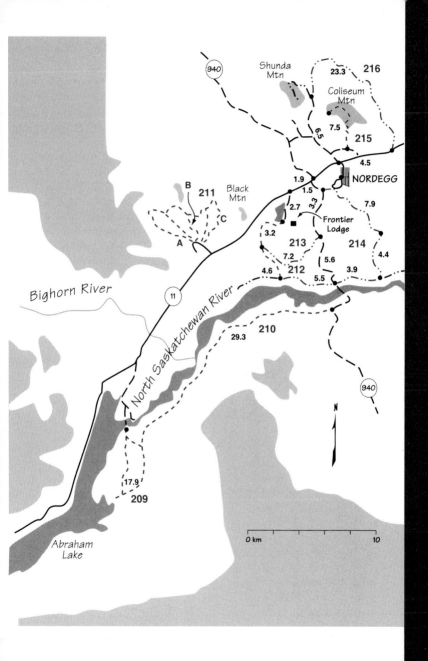

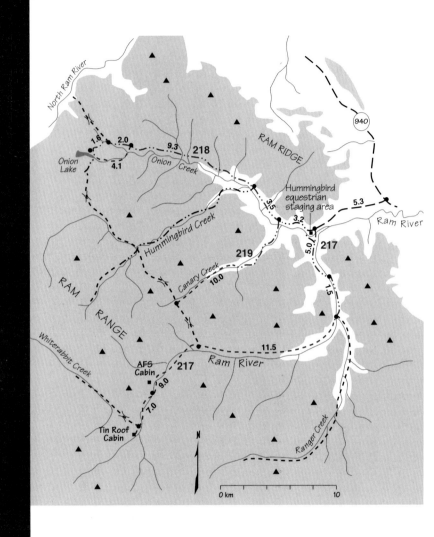

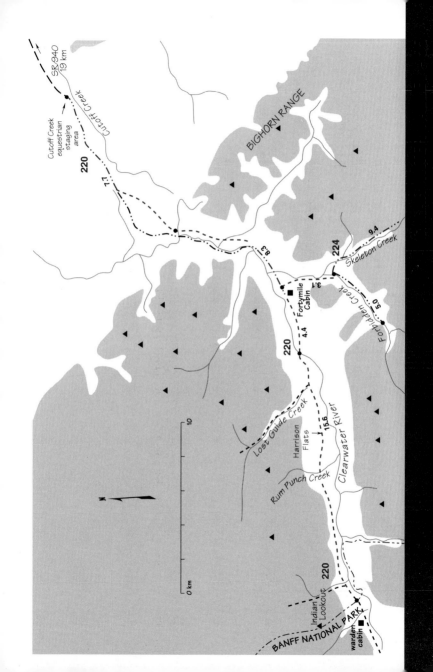

SR 940
19 km

Cutoff Creek equestrian staging area

Cutoff Creek

220

7.7

BIGHORN RANGE

8.3

9.4

224

Skeleton Creek

Fortymile Cabin

3.1

4.4

220

5.0

Forbidden Creek

Lost Guide Creek

15.6

Harrison Flats

Rum Punch Creek

Clearwater River

N

10

0 km

Indian Lookout

220

BANFF NATIONAL PARK

warden cabin

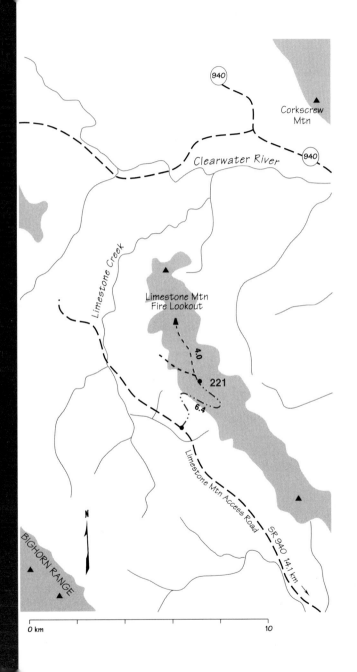

940

Corkscrew
Mtn

940

Clearwater River

Limestone Creek

Limestone Mtn
Fire Lookout

4.0

221

6.4

Limestone Mtn Access Road

SR 940   14.1 km

N

BIGHORN RANGE

0 km                                                    10

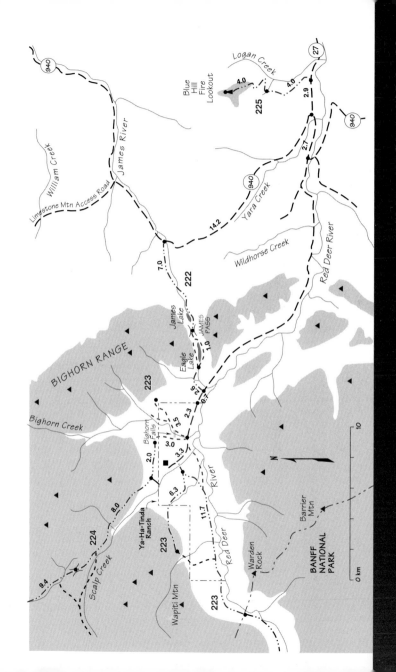

# Useful Phone Numbers

| | |
|---|---|
| Weather, Calgary | 403-299-7878 |
| Weather, Banff | 403-762-2088 |
| Weather, Revelstoke | 250-837-4164 |
| Weather, Jasper | 780-852-3185 |
| | |
| Fernie Information Centre | 250-423-6868 |
| Lake Louise Information Centre | 403-522-3833 |
| Banff Information Centre | 403-762-1550 |
| Canmore Information Centre | 403-678-5277 |
| Barrier Lake Information Centre | 403-673-3985 |
| Gooseberry Information Centre | 403-949-4261 |
| Invermere Information Centre | 250-342-6316 |
| Hinton Information Centre | 780-865-2777 |
| Kananaskis Country | 403-678-5508 |
| | |
| BC Provincial Parks, Wasa | 250-422-4200 |
| | |
| Mount Robson Provincial Park | 250-566-4325 |
| Jasper National Park | 780-852-6162 |
| Banff National Park | 403-762-1500 |
| Yoho National Park | 250-343-6783 |
| Kootenay National Park | 250-347-9615 |
| Waterton Lakes National Park | 403-859-5133 |
| | |
| Alberta Forest Service, Blairmore | 403-562-3210 |
| Alberta Forest Service, Rocky Mountain House | 403-845-8272 |

# Index of Rides

## In an Emergency

In an emergency, contact
the Royal Canadian Mounted Police (RCMP) or
the nearest Ranger or Warden Office

RCMP Emergency                    24 Hour 1-800-642-3800

**Park Ranger or Warden Offices**
Kananaskis Country Emergency              403-591-7767
Banff, Yoho, Kootenay Warden Service      403-762-4506
Jasper Warden Service                     780-852-6156
Waterton Lakes Warden Service             403-859-2224

## Your Feedback is Appreciated

Let us know what you liked, didn't
like and what you would like to see
in future editions.
Send comments to the author care of
Rocky Mountain Books.

## Visit us at www.rmbooks.com